WOMEN'S POSITION AND DEMOGRAPHIC CHANGE

The International Union for the Scientific Study of Population Problems was founded in 1928, with Dr Raymond Pearl as President. At that time the Union's main purpose was to promote international scientific co-operation to study various aspects of population problems, through national committees and by its members themselves. In 1947 the International Union for the Scientific Study of Population (IUSSP) was reconstituted into its present form. It expanded its activities to:

- stimulate research on population
- develop interest in demographic matters among governments, national and international organizations, scientific bodies, and the general public
- foster relations between people involved in population studies
- disseminate scientific knowledge on population.

The principal ways through which the IUSSP currently achieves its aims are:

- organization of worldwide or regional conferences
- operations of Scientific Committees under the auspices of the Council
- organization of training courses
- publication of conference proceedings and committee reports.

Demography can be defined by its field of study and its analytical methods. Accordingly, it can be regarded as the scientific study of human populations primarily with respect to their size, their structure, and their development. For reasons which are related to the history of the discipline, the demographic method is essentially inductive: progress in knowledge results from the improvement of observation, the sophistication of measurement methods, and the search for regularities and stable factors leading to the formulation of explanatory models. In conclusion, the three objectives of demographic analysis are to describe, measure, and analyse.

International Studies in Demography is the outcome of an agreement concluded by the IUSSP and the Oxford University Press. The joint series is expected to reflect the broad range of the Union's activities and, in the first instance, will be based on the seminars organized by the Union. The Editorial Board of the series is comprised of:

Women's Position and Demographic Change

Edited by

NORA FEDERICI
KAREN OPPENHEIM MASON
SØLVI SOGNER

CLARENDON PRESS · OXFORD
1993

Oxford University Press, Walton Street, Oxford OX2 6DP

Oxford New York Toronto
Delhi Bombay Calcutta Madras Karachi
Kuala Lumpur Singapore Hong Kong Tokyo
Nairobi Dar es Salaam Cape Town
Melbourne Auckland Madrid
and associated companies in
Berlin Ibadan

Oxford is a trade mark of Oxford University Press

Published in the United States
by Oxford University Press Inc., New York

© IUSSP 1993

British Library Cataloguing in Publication Data
Data available

Library of Congress Cataloging in Publication Data
Women's position and demographic change / edited by Nora Federici,
Karen Oppenheim Mason, Sølvi Sogner.
p.   cm. — (International studies in demography)
Includes bibliographical references.
1. Demographic transition. 2. Women—Social conditions.
3. Fertility, Human. I. Federici, Nora. II. Oppenheim Mason,
Karen. III. Sogner, Sølvi, 1932– . IV. Series.
HB887.W66 1993 304.6—dc20 93–21753

ISBN 0–19–828792–5

1 3 5 7 9 10 8 6 4 2

Typeset by Best-set Typesetter Ltd., Hong Kong

Printed in Great Britain
on acid-free paper by
Bookcraft (Bath) Ltd,
Midsomer Norton, Avon

Preface

THIS volume is based on a conference on 'Women's Position and Demographic Change in the Course of Development', held in Asker, near Oslo, Norway, 15–18 June 1988. The Conference was jointly sponsored by the International Union for the Scientific Study of Population (IUSSP), the Norwegian Demographic Society, the Nordic Demographic Society, and the International Commission for Historical Demography.

The Organizing Committee, selected by the IUSSP, was chaired by Nora Federici (Italy), with Sølvi Sogner (Norway) serving as deputy. The members were Ester Boserup (Denmark), William Brass (United Kingdom), Shireen Jejeebhoy (India), Karen Oppenheim Mason (United States), Nafis Sadik (Pakistan), Georges Tapinos (France), and Catalina Wainerman (Argentina). Bruno Remiche from IUSSP headquarters served as secretary, assisted by Irène Grignac. The Local Organizing Committee that finalized the Conference programme and oversaw the arrangements in Asker was chaired by An-Magritt Jensen, and included as members Sølvi Sogner, Anne Lise Ellingsæter, and Grete Brochmann.

The Conference was financed through the generosity of the Norwegian Ministry of Co-operation, the United Nations Fund for Population Activities, the Ford Foundation, the Rockefeller Foundation, and the Norwegian Research Council, whose support is gratefully acknowledged.

Also acknowledged are the Istituto de Ricerche sulla Popolazione of the Consiglio Nazionale delle Ricerche of Italy, as well as the Dipartimento di Scienze Demografiche and the Dipartimento di Scienze Politiche of the Università degli Studi di Roma 'La Sapienza', who kindly sponsored meetings of the Organizing Committee and the Editorial Committee. Assistance was also provided by the Population Institute of the East–West Center, the Population Studies Center of the University of Michigan, the Department of History of the University of Oslo, the Norwegian Central Bureau of Statistics, and the Norwegian Demographic Society. All of these institutions are to be commended for their generosity in aiding the organization of the Conference and the preparation of this volume.

The Conference was attended by 145 people, fifty-one from developing countries and the remainder from developed countries. A total of thirty-six countries were represented. Representation by region was sixty-seven participants from Europe, twenty-one from Asia, twenty-one from North America, twelve from Africa, twelve from Latin America, nine from the Middle East, and three from Oceania. Of the participants 102 were women, and forty-three were men. The Conference's scientific programme consisted of six formal sessions incorporating a total of sixteen solicited papers, and nine parallel discussion sessions based on a total of sixty-two contributed papers. As the large number of contributed papers and representation of both women and men from all parts of the globe suggest, the Conference was highly successful in attracting participants. Those of us who believe that the situation of women and demographic change constitute two of the most vital issues of the late twentieth century are gratified indeed that the Conference was held and that it attracted so many scholars from around the world. We very much hope that this volume will further the work begun at the Conference.

N. F.
K. O. M.
S. S.

Oslo, Honolulu, and Rome
December 1990

Contents

Contributors

SHAPAN ADNAN — Winrock International, Dhaka

EVA M. BERNHARDT — Department of Demography, University of Stockholm

MEAD T. CAIN — The Population Council, New York

JOHN CALDWELL — Department of Epidemiology and Population Health, Australian National University, Canberra

PAT CALDWELL — Department of Epidemiology and Population Health, Australian National University, Canberra

VIVIANA EGIDI — Universita' di Roma, 'La Sapienza', Rome

GHISLAINE JULÉMONT — Ministry of Social Affairs, Brussels

LIN LEAN LIM — Labour and Population Team for Asia and the Pacific, International Labour Office, Bangkok

PAULINA MAKINWA-ADEBUSOYE — Nigerian Institute of Social and Economic Research, Ibadan

KAREN OPPENHEIM MASON — East West Population Institute, Honolulu

CHRISTINE OPPONG — Employment Planning and Population Branch, Employment and Development Department, ILO, Geneva

ANTONELLA PINNELLI — Department of Demographic Sciences, Universita' di Roma, 'La Sapienza', Rome

JOSEPH E. POTTER — Harvard School of Public Health, Boston

SØLVI SOGNER — Department of History, University of Oslo

JACQUES VALLIN — Institut National d'Études Démographique, Paris

ÉTIENNE VAN DE WALLE — Population Studies Center University of Pennsylvania

FRANCINE VAN DE WALLE — Population Studies Center University of Pennsylvania

ARDUINO VERDECCHIA — Instituto Suepriore di Sanità, Rome

LETITIA P. VOLPP — Harvard School of Public Health, Boston

HELEN WARE — Australian International Development Assistance Bureau, Canberra

Abbreviations

BBS   Bangladesh Bureau of Statistics
FFW   Food for Works
GDP   gross domestic product
GNP   gross national product
ILO   International Labour Office/Organization
INED   Institut National d'Études Démographiques
ISTAT   Istituto Centrale di Statistica
IUSSP   International Union for the Scientific Study of Population
IVF   *in vitro* fertilization
NGO   non-governmental organization
NIMS   National Infant Mortality Surveillance
OECD   Organization for Economic Co-operation and Development
SMAM   singulate mean age at marriage
TF   total fertility
UN   United Nations
UNFPA   United Nations Fund for Population Activities
Unicef   United Nations (International) Children's (Emergency) Fund
UP   Union *Parishad*
WFS   World Fertility Survey
WHO   World Health Organization

Introduction

NORA FEDERICI, KAREN OPPENHEIM MASON, AND SØLVI SOGNER

In this volume a series of problems that arise from two of the most dramatic revolutions of our time is discussed. The first of these is the demographic transition, that is the shift from death and birth rates that are high but closely balanced, to rates that are low but again closely balanced. Most demographers agree that this demographic transition has involved a re-volution in people's sexual and reproductive values and a change in behaviour. Pregnancy and childbirth, which used to be the unquestioned and unavoidable outcome of sexual activity, have gradually entered the 'calculus of conscious choice', as have methods to prevent or avoid births, when the individual's calculations suggest that this would be in her or his best interests.[1] Although populations in which birth planning and the use of contraception are rare still exist, especially in sub-Saharan Africa, the vast majority of the world's population have experienced the mortality transition and, even though they may not be living under modern fertility conditions, can at least be said to be living in the midst of a transition to such conditions. Thus, while the demographic transition is far from complete and could be reversed, it, none the less, constitutes one of the most widespread and rapid forms of social change in recent human history.

The other dramatic revolution that inspires this volume is the trans-formation of consciousness that occurred during the nineteenth and twentieth centuries concerning authority and equality, especially between the sexes.[2] Although the extent of women's powerlessness and impoverishment has varied in different historical and cultural settings, it has been relatively extreme in the agrarian civilizations and states that have dominated recorded

---

[1] The phrase 'calculus of conscious choice' is taken from A. J. Coale, 'The Demographic Transition Reconsidered', in IUSSP, *Proceedings of the Population Conference, Liège 1973* (Liège, 1973), i. 52–73. In this paper Coale suggested that three preconditions are necessary for fertility to decline to modern levels: it must enter into the calculus of conscious choice, there must be awareness that the means to control or limit fertility exist, and there is a perception that the limitation of fertility is beneficial.

[2] In much of this introduction we use the term 'gender' in preference to 'sex' to describe the socially constructed roles, rights, and privileges that are granted to individuals by virtue of their being identified as female or male. Although we sometimes refer to 'the sexes', we reserve the term 'sex' to refer to the sexual act, or to the biological and reproductive differentiation between females and males.

history.[3] Only during the aftermath of the American and French revolutions, and the movement towards democracy to which they gave rise, has a new ideology of equality between the sexes developed as a counter to the traditional precepts of women's inferiority and submission. Although the feminist movement is neither as widespread nor as manifest in individual behaviour as is the demographic revolution, it is, none the less, one of the most dramatic transformations of modern society during this century.[4]

During recent years, increased awareness of these two revolutions has generated renewed interest in the question of how the situation of women relative to that of men both affects, and is affected by, demographic change. Although in earlier research specific questions related to this theme were explored—for example, the question whether women's paid employment outside the home leads them to reduce the number of children they bear—until recently there has been little attempt to explore systematically the conceptual and empirical links that exist between women's status and more broadly defined demographic phenomena. It was these links that the IUSSP Conference on 'Women's Position and Demographic Change in the Course of Development', held in June 1988, was intended to investigate. As far back as 1983 the idea of analysing the interaction between the status of women, demographic behaviour, and socio-economic development was first voiced within the IUSSP in a conversation between Georges Tapinos and Nora Federici.[5] The subject was raised with increasing frequency at demographic seminars and congresses, and in 1984 the IUSSP Council decided that a more profound study would be of value. They consequently asked Nora Federici to prepare a brief synthetic document that would outline the topic, indicate the 'state of the art', and identify areas in which further research was needed.

Assisted by Monica Fong, Nora Federici asked several colleagues, who were experts in particular aspects of demography, to work on this document, which was published by the Union in 1986.[6] Collaborators for sections that dealt with the developed countries included Chantal Blayo on fertility, Graziella Caselli and Viviana Egidi on morbidity and mortality, Henriette

---

[3] R. L. Blumberg, *Stratification: Socioeconomic and Sexual Inequality* (Dubuque, Ia., 1978); R. Collins, *Sociology of Marriage and the Family: Gender, Love, and Property* (Chicago, 1985), ch. 13.

[4] In a number of studies of gender roles in the family it has been noted that actual roles usually lag behind the ideology of these roles; see, e.g., P. Blumstein and P. Schwartz, *American Couples* (New York, 1983), pp. 144–46. Typically, women employed full-time outside the home continue to do most of the housework and child care, even when they and their husbands pay lip service to the ideal of gender equality.

[5] It had been raised independently in other settings as well. For example, in 1983, the Rockefeller Foundation assembled a group of experts to discuss the desirability of setting up a research programme on the status of women and fertility, a programme that has sponsored open-grant competitions since 1984.

[6] N. Federici and M. Fong, 'The Status of Women, Population and Development', *IUSSP Newsletter*, 23–24 (1985).

Damas on migration, and Nora Federici on the family cycle. As regards less developed countries, contributors were Monica Das Gupta on the family cycle, Sarah Loza on fertility, Maria Helena Henriques on mortality, Monica Fong on infant mortality, and Paulina Kofoworola Makinwa and Landing Savane on migration. The document was distributed during the IUSSP General Conference in Florence in 1985, and led to an exchange of views between those who had collaborated on the paper on how to further the work of the IUSSP on this topic. These discussions resulted in an agreement to organize a conference devoted solely to the issue of the interrelations between women's status and demographic change. The Council of the Union accepted this proposal and set up an Organizing Committee. At a meeting in January 1987 in Rome, this Committee drew up the scientific programme for the Conference and agreed on a meeting site in Asker, near Oslo. Supervision of the Conference's detailed organization was entrusted to Sølvi Sogner, who also acted as a member of the Local Organizing Committee which was appointed by the Norwegian Demographic Society.

Because the gender perspective is relevant for the whole of demography, and not just for such obviously gender-related issues as whether women's non-familial employment influences their reproductive behaviour, the Organizing Committee decided to cover a wide range of topics at the Conference, rather than focus on only a few, relatively narrow issues. This was decided despite the recognition that, in many areas of demographic study, research related to gender roles was lacking, and that authors who wished to provide an overview would consequently be forced to deal with conceptual and theoretical issues, rather than with well-established empirical findings. Because historical and cross-cultural similarities and differences in the interrelations between women's status and demographic behaviour might provide important insights into the dynamics of gender and demographic change, the Organizing Committee also decided to include studies of historical and contemporary situations in both developed and less developed countries in the programme.

The result was a Conference that provided a first overview of a wide range of specific topics, with many of the solicited papers being frankly speculative. Because the present volume consists largely of these papers, supplemented by a few of the more than sixty contributed papers presented at the Conference, it, too, is characterized by a wide-ranging view, and a tone which is often speculative. It is thus best viewed as a provocative introduction to a rapidly growing field of scientific enquiry, rather than as a traditional 'state of the art' assessment. It is hoped that the chapters will stimulate further thought and research; most make no pretence of offering the final word on the topics that they discuss.

The book is organized according to whether the position of women is treated primarily as the determinant of demographic change, or as its outcome. Within each of these broad sections are chapters on fertility, mortality, and migration, some of which contain material on both less developed and developed countries; others are focused on only one type of setting. In a final chapter, a series of crisis issues related to women's position and demographic change is identified. All sections of the book deal with the unequal power and differentiated roles of women and men; in particular with the question of women's situation relative to that of men, and how this influences, or is influenced by, changes in demographic variables, such as fertility, mortality, or migration. Does the position that women hold in the family, community, and society affect patterns of marriage, reproduction, mortality, or geographical mobility? Conversely, do these demographic patterns affect the position of women in the family, community, or society? Although many other questions are discussed in specific chapters, these are the fundamental problems that underlie all the essays that appear in this volume.

One of the major themes is that the ways in which particular aspects of women's domestic and societal position can affect demographic trends are numerous and complex. Although demographers have often discussed women's status as if it could be measured along a single dimension for all women in all cultures, there are, in fact, many dimensions along which women and men can be unequally ranked, or have differentiated roles and responsibilities.[7] Moreover, the way in which any particular aspect of gender inequality affects some aspects of demographic behaviour, or is affected by it, typically depends on the cultural and historical context. What in some settings may enhance women's status, or lead to a decline in fertility, may, in others, have the opposite effect.

The complexity of women's position and its interaction with demographic changes make generalization difficult. When women's position is regarded as the determinant of demographic change, however, at least two major types of possible influence can be identified. The first consists of a differentiated set of attitudes, interests, or strategies that arises from the distinctive positions and socialization of the sexes; attitudes, interests, or strategies that may, in turn, affect the proximate determinants of fertility, mortality, or migration. For example, it has sometimes been argued that, because women suffer the physical risks associated with pregnancy, childbirth, and lactation, they are inherently more inclined to accept the idea of fertility control than men, and thus, when the means for control of reproduction become available, they are quicker to adopt them than men are.[8] If this is correct, it would suggest that, in populations in which women enjoy relative autonomy from control by men, fertility would also be relatively low, at least once birth

---

[7] See Ware, Chapter 13 in this volume.

[8] K. Oppenheim Mason and A. M. Taj, 'Differences between Women's and Men's Reproductive Goals in Developing Countries', *Population and Development Review*, 13 (1987), pp. 611–38.

control has become readily available.[9] A similar example is the claim that, because of their responsibilities for child-rearing, women are typically more concerned about children's nutrition and health than men, so that, when women have control over their own incomes, improvements in child survival will be greater than would appear after a rise in incomes controlled by men.[10]

The other major influence of women's position on demographic behaviour involves discrimination against females caused by their inferior status, or restricted social and economic roles. This type of causal linkage differs from the first, because the mechanism which connects women's position and demographic behaviour is not a distinctive set of interests and actions taken by women and men, but rather consists of various forms of discrimination that women (as well as men) employ against members of their own sex. In the case of fertility, it is assumed that discrimination will give rise to highly skewed preferences for sons, a preference that can result in the maintenance of relatively high fertility under certain demographic conditions.[11] In the case of morbidity and mortality, discrimination against females in nutrition and medical care can raise women's (and thus also total) rates of morbidity and mortality.[12] As regards migration, discrimination against females can either block migration opportunities for women, and this, coupled with labour migration of men, often results in a high prevalence of households headed by women,[13] or it may force women to migrate when they marry, search for work, or are forced by their employers to move.[14]

Recognition that there exist at least two major ways in which the unequal power and differentiated social roles of the sexes can influence demographic trends has important implications for those aspects of demographic analysis that take account of social and economic variables. One implication is that behavioural models in which the household is treated as a unified decision-making body must be approached with great caution, if not outright suspicion. As the gender-sensitive view represented in this volume should make clear, the interests of different members of the household—female and male, young and old—do not necessarily coincide.[15] Moreover, although these conflicts of interest do not necessarily determine all demographic trends, they can affect the behaviour that ultimately determines fertility, mortality, and migration.

Another implication of recognizing that there are dual mechanisms by

[9] It should be noted that there is actually little evidence to suggest that this line of argument is correct. See Mason and Taj, op. cit. in n. 8.

[10] J. C. Caldwell, 'Routes to Low Mortality in Poor Countries', *Population and Development Review*, 12 (1986), pp. 171–220.

[11] See Cain, Chapter 2 in this volume.

[12] See Potter and Volpp, Chapter 7 in this volume.

[13] See Makinwa-Adebusoye, Chapter 15 in this volume.

[14] See Lim, Chapter 11 in this volume.

[15] This is illustrated in van de Walle and van de Walle, Chapter 3 in this volume.

which the position of women can influence demographic trends is to accept that the position of women can be regarded as deprived, or their status as low, even when women themselves help to perpetuate the low status of members of their own sex. Usually, women do this because of the dependency and vulnerability that is a result of their low status, not because they are necessarily happy with the position in which they find themselves. For instance, poor women may have to choose whether to feed all their children equally and thereby increase the risk that much-needed sons will die, or they can, instead, choose to feed their sons in preference to their daughters in order to increase the formers' chances of survival. In a society in which women's own chance of survival depends on their having sons, it may seem to be in women's best interest to give preference to sons, even though it is clear to an outsider that this perpetuates a system that harms females.

A second general theme common to the chapters in this volume is the recognition that the status of women can be conceptualized at either an aggregate or an individual level, and that it is, therefore, necessary to identify the level of conceptualization that is used when hypotheses relating to demographic change are formulated. Women's prestige, for instance, may be thought of as something that varies for each individual woman depending on her characteristics and behaviour (including her demographic behaviour), or as a gender-wide characteristic that varies in different social groups and will depend on their gender-role ideologies and practices. Both conceptualizations are represented in this volume, often in the same chapter. For example, Helen Ware speculates about the effects of fertility both on the prestige of the individual woman, and on the prestige of women as a class. Clearly, unless the level on which women's position is being conceptualized is specified, sensible hypotheses about its interrelations with demographic change will not be forthcoming.

In addition to these general points, a number of specific problems are considered in different chapters. In her 'state of the art' assessment of the impact of women's position on fertility and mortality in less developed countries, Karen Oppenheim Mason suggests that there are a variety of mechanisms through which women's autonomy or control over resources could influence fertility or mortality. In almost all cases, the hypothesis is that these mechanisms operate in conjunction with other changes that are occurring in society, such as rising incomes, the spread of mass education, or the introduction of family-planning programmes. Thus, the typical hypothesis that relates women's status to fertility or mortality posits the existence of an interaction between women's status and socio-economic conditions in affecting demographic outcomes. Women's status does not necessarily influence demographic change directly. Rather, it may enhance or reduce the effects of other socio-economic changes.

This assumed interaction between women's status and other forms of change is elaborated by Mead Cain for the case of fertility in less developed countries. Using a 'safety-first' model, in which it is posited that people worry about securing the minimum needed for survival before worrying about maximization of the quality of life, Cain argues that in poor countries fertility is likely to remain higher when women are economically dependent on men than when they have some degree of independence, even in the face of modernizing changes that encourage fertility reduction. The reason is that, in patriarchal systems, females are unable to make economic contributions to their parents. Thus, members of both sexes will desire sons, because it is only sons who can provide insurance against risk, and social security in old age, both of which are important for survival in poor countries. Moreover, because of their special vulnerability to risk, women will have especially strong desires for sons. Cain thus suggests that trends which are normally anti-natalist—such as declining infant mortality, increases in women's age at marriage, rising average incomes, and increased school enrolment of girls—will be associated with a sustained decline in fertility only in systems in which patriarchy is relatively weak, a supposition that is partially supported by a cross-sectional analysis of fertility in twenty-eight less developed countries. Thus, the position of women in society may be primarily important for the fertility transition because it conditions the impact of other forms of social and economic change.

Implicit in the chapter on the Sahel region of west Africa by Francine and Étienne van de Walle is the question whether an improvement in women's status in a population with natural fertility will necessarily lead to a decline in fertility. Mali and Burkina-Faso, the sites of the van de Walles' research, are characterized by polygyny, young ages at marriage for women, but high ages of marriage for men, marriages arranged by the girls' fathers, extensive breast-feeding, a moderately long period of post-partum sexual abstinence, and little use of contraception. The authors argue that this structure of kinship and gender relations serves the dual function of maintaining men's control over women's sexual and reproductive lives, and maximizing the population's reproductive rate. It is not clear, however, that the development of a more egalitarian couple-oriented system of gender and family relationships will necessarily result in lower fertility. The van de Walles observe that in companionate marriages, unlike in traditional ones, husbands tend to pressure wives to resume sexual relations shortly after childbirth. Although some of the companionate couples use contraception, the shortening of the period of post-partum abstinence, nevertheless, suggests that greater equality in gender relations may result in increased fertility, at least until contraception has become widespread. It is, therefore, a mistake to think that the emancipation of women will invariably reduce fertility.

As Eva M. Bernhardt makes clear in the opening of her chapter on 'Changing Family Ties, Women's Position, and Low Fertility', the ·critical issue in contemporary developed countries—in all of which fertility is now insufficient for long-term replacement—is not whether improvements in women's status are likely to precipitate the fertility transition, but rather whether women's emancipation invariably results in extremely low fertility. It is difficult to give a definitive answer to this question from the evidence available. Bernhardt suggests that it is the conflict between work and rearing children that ultimately causes low fertility, and that this conflict arises from the particular type of the 'emancipation' of women that has occurred in the West during the period after the Second World War, more specifically, from a system in which women have adopted men's career patterns, but men have failed to adopt women's domestic roles. Bernhardt speculates that, if a different model of gender equality were adopted, in which members of both sexes shared equally in both family roles and paid employment, the costs to women of bearing children would be lower, and the birth rate might rise, as it has done in Sweden, where the government has instituted programmes to reduce some of the opportunity costs incurred by parents in rearing children. This alternative model of gender equality could also help women to achieve greater equality with men, a goal that Bernhardt argues has remained elusive up to now, despite rising rates of labour-force participation by women in the West.

In one of the most speculative chapters in this volume, Ghislaine Julémont discusses the causes of fertility decline and changes in the status of women since the beginning of industrialization in the West. Following an argument first put forward by Philippe Ariès, Julémont suggests that fertility declined in the West during industrialization, not because women's status improved—it actually deteriorated, she argues—but, rather, because the position of children changed. Children ceased to be regarded as sources of labour for the family economy; instead, they were considered to represent the family's future. This led parents to restrict the number of their children, in order to be able to invest more heavily in each child. Women's status, Julémont suggests, only began to improve when women started to protest against their domestication. Moreover, the potential to achieve equality with men could be realized only after contraceptives had been developed that gave women the opportunity to control their reproductive lives. Julémont agrees with Bernhardt that the full potential of this development has yet to be realized, because women have adopted men's career patterns, rather than more flexible ones. She ends by suggesting that, in contemporary developed societies, the education of women is important in initiating the process that may eventually result in raising their status, but that education by itself does not guarantee either equality or fertility decline.

Turning from reproduction to mortality and morbidity, the chapter by John and Pat Caldwell on child mortality and morbidity in less developed countries illustrates a problem that is common to much of social demography. A moderate to strong correlation between mother's education and child survival has been found in many studies, but the causal mechanisms that underlie this correlation are poorly understood. In some settings, the Caldwells note, the autonomy of women associated with their having achieved relatively high levels of schooling appears to play an important part in child survival, but in other settings differences between household incomes associated with education, or differences between treatment provided by the health services for better and less well-educated clients, appear to be more important. It is also not made clear in existing studies, they argue, whether women's autonomy or education affects child survival in the absence of modern medical facilities. Some authors have suggested that only the availability of modern medical knowledge and care leads to an advantage in the survival of the children of better educated mothers; others have suggested that the advantages of a better education of the mother are universal. It is, therefore, important to investigate whether the position of women affects child survival only in interaction with other factors, especially the health-care environment.

The chapter by Joseph Potter and Letitia Volpp which deals with differences between the mortality of the two sexes in childhood and adolescence in less developed countries is focused on discrimination against female children as a cause of the excess mortality of females. There is fairly good evidence for the existence of such discrimination in those parts of Asia in which excess mortality of females is found (primarily in south and west Asia). Discrimination is, in turn, thought to arise from a gender division of labour that deprives women of significant economic roles. Potter and Volpp note that there are only a few studies in which it was asked whether discrimination against females also explains other forms of excess mortality of females found in less developed countries, in particular maternal mortality, but they suggest that this is a possibility. Where women have little control over their lives or access to material resources, their ability to limit their fertility is likely to be weak (pregnancy and childbirth are, by definition, the fundamental cause of maternal mortality). Lack of resources, or restrictions on their freedom of movement, also reduce the chance of women receiving the antenatal or postnatal medical care that they need, and may result in increased vulnerability to complications of pregnancy and childbirth by reason of poor nutrition or stunted growth. Potter and Volpp note, however, that the research needed to confirm these hypotheses is as yet largely not available.

As in the case of fertility, issues relating to the relation between women's position and mortality are different in developed and less developed societies, a point that Antonella Pinnelli makes in opening her chapter on infant and child mortality and health in developed countries. In these countries, the risk of dying during the first five years of life is very low, and mortality differences between the sexes either do not exist or favour females, probably for biological, rather than social, reasons. However, a variety of new problems related to the ill-health of infants and children can be found in developed countries, including those associated with the excessive medicalization of pregnancy and childbirth, and the emotional problems associated with changing family patterns. As fully satisfactory data on children's health and welfare are not available, Pinnelli speculates that changes in women's roles, especially improvements in their education and increasing entry into the labour force, have had both negative and positive effects on children's welfare in developed countries. Positive effects come from improved schooling and better information about antenatal care and the postnatal care of mothers and children; negative effects from the greater fragility of family relationships and the reduction of the parents' presence in the family home. Pinnelli concludes that the changes which have increased women's economic independence in the West have not necessarily resulted in an improvement in their children's welfare.

Jacques Vallin, in his chapter, takes up a continuing controversy in the study of mortality in developed countries: whether the increasing difference between the life expectancies of men and women is due to biological or to social causes. Although there is plausible evidence for a model in which a biological advantage in favour of women as regards frailty is included, Vallin argues that the increasing difference between the life expectancies of women and men which has been found in France and other developed countries reflects behavioural rather than biological differences between the sexes. In particular, Vallin suggests that women not only take fewer risks than men, but that they are generally more concerned about maintaining their health and youthfulness, and that this leads them to make fuller use of modern medical care. Thus, although women in developed countries have, indeed, regained an older biological advantage in survival, Vallin suggests that they have increased this advantage by taking better care of their health and well-being during an era when medical knowledge improved.

The theme of differences in health-related behaviour between women and men as an explanation for differences in the morbidity and mortality of the sexes in developed countries is continued in the chapter by Viviana Egidi and Arduino Verdecchia, which is focused on morbidity and mortality from cancer in Italy. Although Italian women have begun to adopt 'masculine' forms of behaviour that increase the risk of cancer morbidity, as have women in other developed countries (e.g. smoking, and the consumption of alcohol), women's chances of surviving the disease once they have contracted it exceed those of men. The authors use age and sex-specific statistics on cancer sites, and the duration of illness, to suggest that behavioural differences between the sexes account for a large proportion of women's advantage in survival. Particularly important may be women's greater tendency to care for their bodies and to seek early diagnosis and treatment. Thus, although biological differences between the sexes in frailty and susceptibility to disease may exist, Egidi and Verdecchia, like Vallin, suggest that modern women's advantage in survival reflects the greater attention they devote to their personal health.

Although migration is just as much part of demography as is mortality or fertility, Lin Lean Lim begins her chapter on migration by noting that in discussions of women's status much less attention has been paid to migration than to either mortality or fertility. She notes that this makes the task of describing possible or actual linkages between women's status and migration difficult, as does the complexity of migration. To facilitate her task, Lim looks at existing frameworks for the study of migration in order to analyse whether they contain any material about women's status as a determinant of migration, and then proceeds to offer a general framework for the study of women's position in relation to the migration of females. In her review of possible linkages, Lim makes it clear that the situation of women may have contradictory effects on their propensity to move, and that these may simultaneously encourage and discourage mobility. The situation of women may have a greater impact on the distribution of female migrants by age or marital status than on their numbers—i.e. it may influence the kinds of women who move, or their reasons for moving, more than their average propensity to move. She also makes it clear that the effects of women's situation on the propensity to move is likely to vary in different family, social, and economic contexts. Thus, in migration, too, a major effect of women's status may be to condition how other variables influence migration.

The remaining chapters in this volume are concerned primarily with understanding the position of women, rather than with understanding demographic change. To provide a historical context for studying changes in women's status, Sølvi Sogner traces the history of women's family and economic roles in the West. She argues that the practice of women participating in production alongside their husbands which was characteristic of pre-industrial societies was abandoned during the process of industrialization, with the rise of the doctrine of separate spheres and of the 'professional' housewife, only to be regained during the post-industrial period when housewives who had become increasingly lonely left their homes to seek gainful employment in the labour force. Thus, although the nature of the work they do differs from that of three centuries ago, women's participation in production has come full circle during this period. An overarching theme in Sogner's survey is that women's history is often distinct from that of men, and that, by studying women's history, we may achieve not only a new understanding of their contemporary situation, but also new explanations for demographic change. For example, Sogner speculates that mortality may have declined in the West, not only because of the introduction of new public health measures, improvements in nutrition, or advances in medical science, but also because of the new and improved care that married women provided for their families, once they had become full-time, professional housewives.

Continuing the focus on the determinants of women's position, Helen Ware discusses the impact of several variables, including fertility. At the individual level she notes that, in less developed countries, to have children and in some cases to have relatively many, often enhances the individual woman's prestige, but that, at the aggregate level, high fertility is often associated with a relatively low status for women, partly because women's lives often tend to be fully occupied with child-bearing and child-rearing in societies in which fertility is high, and partly because high rates of population growth (to which high fertility is an important contributor) may result in scarcities that, in turn, deprive women of opportunities and resources. Ware repeatedly stresses, however, that any such effects are heavily conditioned by other factors. The same applies to other determinants of women's position that Ware examines, namely, family organization, the sex structure of the labour market, and technology, especially contraceptive technology. Whilst it seems likely that each of these factors influences the position of women, especially the degree of their autonomy and control over material resources, the relationships are complex. Thus, interaction effects are likely to exist among the determinants of women's status, just as they exist among the determinants of demographic change.

Shapan Adnan provides a detailed case study of how demographic, economic, and political change can affect the situation of women. Focusing on Bangladesh, where women's independence and autonomy have been severely restricted by the norms of *parda* (seclusion), Adnan argues that the fragmentation of landholdings and the growth of the landless class in Bangladesh have forced many women out of the isolation of the household and into the workforce, thereby increasing their value on the marriage market, and, potentially, their power in the political arena. Because both landlessness and fragmentation of holdings result, in part, from a rapid rate of natural increase, Adnan's case study illustrates how high fertility, even though it may restrict women's opportunities in the short run, could ultimately break down the social institutions that support their social and economic oppression.

In her chapter, Pauline Makinwa-Adebusoye considers the impact of one type of population movement, the labour migration of men, on the situation of women who are left behind, especially in sub-Saharan Africa where female-headed households caused by such migration have become increasingly common. Her basic point is that heading a household is very much a mixed blessing for women. Though it may give them greater autonomy in decision-making, in sub-Saharan Africa, where women are rarely able to own land on their own, the absence of a male household head typically results in extreme economic hardship for the women. As Makinwa-Adebusoye puts it, few or no resources are placed at the disposal of women to back up their newly acquired powers of decision-making. The overall effect of labour migration on the situation of women in sub-Saharan Africa has, therefore, been more negative than positive.

The poverty and hardship that result when men are physically or economically absent from the family household is also a major theme in the chapter by Christine Oppong, the final chapter of this volume. Oppong's purpose is to alert us to three major crises which are faced by society today: the crisis of 'motherhood', i.e. the insufficiency of resources available to women to maintain and bring up their children; the crisis of 'conjugal relations', which involves the breakdown of a supportive environment for complementary heterosexual relationships; and the crisis of 'social and economic security in old age'. Although these crises are especially acute for poor women, Oppong makes the point that they are world-wide and exist among the poor in the world's richest countries, as well as in poor countries, such as those located in sub-Saharan Africa. Each of these crises, Oppong argues, is due to some combination of institutional breakdown, economic crisis, and the persistence of traditional forms of gender discrimination and inequality. The crises women face, which Oppong argues put 'the capacity of societies to reproduce both physically and socially . . . at risk', are thus an outcome as well as a cause of persistent gender bias. If Oppong is right, the survival of orderly social life may depend on the eradication of this bias. Thus, all human beings, male and female alike, have a stake in seeing the subordinate position of women improved.

In sum, as the different chapters in this volume make clear, there are many reasons for believing that the situation of women both affects and is affected by demographic patterns. Although we do not fully understand the nature of these interrelationships and do not know whether they exist in all settings, the plausibility of the existence of certain ties between demographic change and the position of women seems overwhelmingly likely. That the subject with which the papers in this volume deal is important, both from a scientific and a practical point of view, is, therefore, beyond question. For those interested in understanding demographic change, or the change in the situation of women, possible links between women's position and demographic change cannot be ignored.

Unfortunately, factual evidence relating to the mechanisms that connect women's situation to demographic change is weak. Although the authors of the different chapters in this volume have ably summarized a vast body of empirical analysis and deftly outlined a number of conceptual frameworks and hypotheses, definitive evidence that gender relations influence the onset, timing, or rapidity of change in mortality, fertility, migration, or their proximate determinants has yet to be obtained in most cases. Nor is the evidence about the impact of demographic change on the position of women much firmer.

There are several reasons for this, especially in studies in which attempts have been made to explain demographic change. The first is the tendency to use data collected for general demographic purposes, rather than those specifically designed for the study of the relations between women's position and demographic change. The main shortcomings of multi-purpose data sets, such as the World Fertility Survey or the Demographic and Health

Surveys, is the absence of direct high-quality measures of women's situation relative to that of men, especially their position within the household. Thus, although women's educational levels or labour-force participation rates may provide partial clues about their status or roles in relation to men, such measures, although available in most demographic surveys, fail to describe the situation of women directly or in detail. The use of multi-purpose data thus at best provides indirect evidence about possible linkages between gender relations and demographic change.

Another reason for the paucity of evidence is the tendency to limit comparisons to those between individuals or households, or, alternatively, between aggregates, such as entire countries. The former individual comparisons are particularly problematic from the point of view of understanding how the culturally influenced situation of women is related to demographic change. Because social values and norms vary in different communities and cultural groups, rather than between households in a given group, a study in which individuals or households in the same socio-cultural group are compared cannot provide information about gender relations as a culturally controlled system. Comparisons made strictly between groups suffer from a different shortcoming, the inability to document how aggregate variations in women's situation can be translated into the individual choices that, in turn, determine demographic trends. For example, an aggregate correlation between the average level of girls' schooling and the level of child survival, though consistent with the hypothesis that well-educated mothers provide better care for their children than less well-educated ones, does not reveal whether it is the maternal behaviour of well and poorly educated women respectively that accounts for this correlation, or, instead, some other process, such as a stronger demand for facilities for maternity and child health and welfare services in societies in which women are relatively well educated.

Herbert Smith and others have suggested that multi-level comparative studies in which both aggregate and individual level variations are incorporated offer the best hope of understanding the precise linkages between women's situation and demographic change.[16] By comparing groups with different gender-role regimes, and using data that also provide information about the behaviour of individual women, it is possible to obtain detailed evidence about the interrelation between women's situation and demographic change. However, multi-level comparative studies are expensive and complex, and few, therefore, have been undertaken. Fortunately, such studies are now being carried out in several regions of the world. Some of these studies compare socially differentiated communities within a particular country, and others, communities in different countries. It is hoped that, as the results of

[16] H. L. H. Smith, 'Integrating Theory and Research on the Institutional Determinants of Fertility', *Demography*, 26 (1989), pp. 171–84.

these studies become available, our understanding of how women's position is linked to demographic change will improve. Certainly, the subject is important enough for the future well-being of the earth's human population to warrant more careful attention than it has so far received.

Part I

Women's Position as a Cause of Demographic Change

1 The Impact of Women's Position on Demographic Change during the Course of Development

KAREN OPPENHEIM MASON

The purpose of this chapter is to summarize what we know about the impact of women's social position on demographic change during the course of development. Because this task is well beyond the scope of a single chapter, I have limited myself in three ways. First, 'women's position' is here taken to mean women's control over resources, compared to that of men; the degree of their autonomy from men's control; or other aspects of their privilege or oppression that arise from the society's institutions. The focus is thus on women in comparison to men (usually men in their own culture, caste, or class), rather than on socio-economic variation among women. The focus is also on how the social institutions of gender affect demographic regimes, rather than on how the vagaries of class, caste, ethnicity, or individual life histories affect these regimes.[1]

Secondly, only two forms of demographic change are considered: the mortality and fertility transitions. Migration is ignored, as are short-term changes in fertility and mortality. The main reason for this is the complexity of the relationship between migration and women's status, and the paucity of research on this topic.[2]

Finally, the phrase 'in the course of development' is interpreted to refer to studies conducted in countries that are still undergoing development: those that are commonly referred to as the 'developing', 'less developed', 'under-developed', 'poor', or 'Third World' countries. Studies focused on the relationship between women's position and demographic change in the developed nations of the world are largely ignored.

---

[1] The *position* of women is also distinct from the *value* of women. The latter term refers to the value of women to others in the family (husbands or parents) for economic, social, or reproductive purposes. As the example of slavery suggests, women can be highly valuable to others, but have virtually no autonomy or control over resources. Indeed, Rubin has argued that the fundamental historical reason for women's oppression is their unique value to men as reproducers (G. Rubin, 'The Traffic in Women: Notes on the "Political Economy" of Sex', in R. Reiter (ed.), *Towards an Anthropology of Women* (New York, 1975), pp. 157–210).

[2] See Lim, Chapter 11 in this volume.

Before turning to what we know about the impact of women's position on the fertility and mortality transitions, it is worth noting the roles that women's position might *in principle* play in determining the course of demographic change. Here are five possible relationships between women's position and the demographic tradition, depicted in the form of equations that use the conventions for describing structural-equation models.[3]

1. Change in women's position (ΔP) directly contributes to the mortality or fertility transition (ΔT).

$$\Delta T = \beta_0 + \beta_1 \Delta P + \sum_{i=2}^{m} \beta_i X_i + \varepsilon,$$

$$\beta_1 \neq 0. \tag{1}$$

2. Change in women's position is an intervening variable that explains why other variables (X_i) lead to the mortality or fertility transition.

$$\Delta T = \beta_0 + \sum_{i=1}^{m} \beta_i X_i + \varepsilon,$$

$$\Delta T = \beta'_0 + \sum_{i=1}^{m} \beta'_i X_i + \gamma \Delta P + \varepsilon', \tag{2}$$

$$\beta_i \neq 0 \text{ and}$$

$$|\beta'_i| < |\beta_i|.$$

3. The pre-existing nature of women's position (P) conditions the impact of other factors on the mortality or fertility transition.

$$\Delta T = \beta_0 + \beta_1 P + \sum_{i=2}^{m} \beta_i X_i + \sum_{i=2}^{m} \gamma_i (P X_i) + \varepsilon, \tag{3}$$

$$\gamma_i \neq 0.$$

4. Women's position, or change therein has no relationship to the mortality or fertility transition.

$$\Delta T = \beta_0 + \beta_1 \Delta P + \varepsilon,$$
$$\text{or } \Delta T = \beta_0 + \beta_1 P + \varepsilon, \tag{4}$$
$$\beta_1 = 0.$$

5. Change in women's position is determined by the mortality or fertility transition, *not vice-versa*.

$$\Delta P = \beta_0 + \beta_1 \Delta T + \sum_{i=2}^{m} \beta_i X_i. \tag{5}$$

---

[3] The models shown are of a simple, recursive form. There are, of course, more complex models in which women's power or autonomy are both a cause and a consequence of demographic change.

The first possibility shown is perhaps the most straightforward, namely that a change in women's position directly and independently contributes to a change in fertility or mortality. In other words, regardless of other conditions, an increase in women's autonomy, independence, or control of resources leads to a lowering (or a rise) in fertility or mortality. It is this model that many people seem to have in mind when they argue that improving the 'status' of women will lower fertility, or infant and child mortality rates.

The second possible relationship between women's position and demographic change is that change in women's autonomy or dependency helps to explain why other social or economic changes lead to a decline in fertility or mortality. Women's autonomy may, in other words, be an intervening variable—one that is determined by other social or economic factors, and which explains why these other factors precipitate the fertility or mortality transitions. Thus, in this model, although there is a significant zero-order relationship between the other factors and changes in mortality or fertility (which is why $\gamma_i \neq 0$), these relationships weaken or disappear once the position of women, or change in their position, is held constant. The possibility that women's power plays the role depicted in this second model is important because, if true, it would suggest that fertility or mortality could be lowered, and women's status raised, by changing the exogenous variables.[4] Thus, for example, if men resist giving women new legal rights, but do not oppose increased (though possibly segregated) schooling for their daughters; and if women's education increases their autonomy and thereby lowers fertility or mortality, then a policy designed to improve girls' schooling might simultaneously affect the desired demographic change and improve the position of women.

The third possible relationship involves a statistical interaction between women's position, other variables, and demographic change. In this model, the pre-existing nature of women's position *conditions* the impact of other factors on the change in fertility or mortality; for example, it determines whether the introduction of a family-planning programme has relatively little or great impact on contraceptive acceptance and fertility rates. In this model it is not posited that an improvement or deterioration in women's position in turn triggers a change in fertility or mortality. Rather, the extent to which other changes (represented by the X_i) influence fertility and/or mortality depends on the pre-existing nature of women's position. This model is especially important because it suggests that it is not necessary for the situation of women to change in order that their position should play an

---

[4] Certainly, whether the position of women in the sense in which we are using this term here is normally affected by other social and economic variables amenable to rapid change is at least open to question. The institutions of gender are often treated as part of a 'cultural' system that also incorporates religion and the norms that govern the family system, and this is viewed as separate from, and only loosely linked to, the structure of the economy, or the social relationships of production.

important role in the decline of fertility or mortality. As I suggest later, this is, in fact, the form that major substantive hypotheses about women's position and demographic change take.[5]

The fourth possible relationship between women's position and demographic change is that there is no relationship. Although there is considerable resistance to this idea among feminists,[6] it is worth keeping in mind.[7] What is plausible does not always turn out to be true.

The final possible relationship is also worth keeping in mind. This is, that it may be the decline in fertility or mortality that typically changes women's power or autonomy, rather than that their autonomy or power plays a role in initiating or accelerating the fertility or mortality transition. The idea that fertility decline is especially important for improving the position of women is, in fact, popular among non-demographically oriented feminist scholars and activists. Thus, even if women's 'status' and demographic change were correlated, this final model alerts us to the possibility that the correlation may have little to do with the effects of women's position on demographic change.

In the next section of this chapter I give an overview of problems in the empirical literature. These reflect both the conceptual disarray in the field, and problems of research design and operationalization. In subsequent sections I consider the mortality and fertility transitions. In each of these sections I review first major hypotheses, and then the empirical evidence itself. In a closing section I suggest directions for future research.

Problems in the Empirical Literature

Although good and bad studies exist in any body of empirical work, the literature on women's position and demographic change is characterized by five general problems. The first is a tendency to vagueness about the particular aspects of women's position that are important for demographic change, a vagueness that makes it difficult to judge the quality of any given

---

[5] Cain has also noted the importance of this model (M. Cain, *Women's Status and Fertility in Developing Countries: Son-Preference and Economic Security* (Washington, 1984)).

[6] B. Hartman, *Reproductive Rights and Wrongs: The Global Politics of Population Control and Contraceptive Choice* (New York, 1987), pp. 36–54.

[7] It is not just self-defined feminists who believe that women's position is important for fertility or mortality decline. Many traditional demographers are also convinced that women's 'status' is a key variable in explaining fertility or mortality decline; see, e.g., J. C. Caldwell, 'Routes to Low Mortality in Poor Countries', *Population and Development Review*, 12 (1986), pp. 171–220; N. Eberstadt, 'Introduction', in N. Eberstadt (ed.), *Fertility Decline in the Less Developed Countries* (New York, 1981), pp. 1–28; ESCAP, 'Female Autonomy and Fertility: An Overview of the Situation in South Asia', *Asia-Pacific Population Journal*, 2 (1987), pp. 43–52.

study. As others have noted,[8] there is a plethora of terms in the demographic literature used to describe women's position, and many of these terms have alternative meanings when used by different authors.[9] That so many terms are used is not surprising in view of the evidence that women's position in relation to men is multi-dimensional.[10] Unfortunately, though some authors have been careful to identify the specific aspects of women's position that are thought to influence demographic change,[11] many are vague, or define women's position so broadly that the term becomes meaningless. In these latter studies, it is difficult to judge whether, or how well, women's position has been measured.

A second problem in the literature also involves measurement. This is the ambiguous relationship between many commonly available statistical indicators of women's position and the dimensions thought to be important in effecting demographic change. Measures of women's economic activity and of their education are two key examples here. As I discuss below, in the theoretical literature on women's position and demographic change it is argued that such dimensions as the extent to which women are free to take action on their own, or must, instead, obtain their husbands' or their mothers'-in-law permission, or the extent to which help, loyalty, and money flow from children to their mothers and aunts, rather than to their fathers and uncles, are important for demographic change. Whether women's participation in paid work, or the number of years of schooling they receive, are reliable and accurate indices of these theoretically important dimensions is unclear, and often a matter of controversy. For example, while many authors seem to assume that working for money automatically gives women some degree of decision-making autonomy from their husbands or mothers-in-law,[12] others have suggested that a variety of social institutions may keep money-earning women powerless and unable to make decisions of their own.[13] Because information on intra-familial economic exchanges, or on the

---

[8] See R. Dixon, 'Women's Rights and Fertility', *Reports on Population/Family Planning* (New York, 1975); *Rural Women at Work: Strategies for Development in South Asia* (Baltimore, 1978); K. Mason, *The Status of Women: A Review of its Relationship to Fertility and Mortality* (The Rockefeller Foundation, New York, 1984); K. Oppenheim Mason, 'The Status of Women: Conceptual and Methodological Issues in Demographic Studies', *Sociological Forum I* (1986), pp. 284–300.

[9] The most notorious of these is the term 'status', which is sometimes used to refer to the prestige of women, or the esteem in which they are held by virtue of their sex, and at other times to their overall socio-economic position, or the extent of their subjugation to men.

[10] M. K. Whyte, *The Status of Women in Preindustrial Societies* (Princeton, NJ, 1978).

[11] Cain, op. cit. in n. 5.

[12] R. H. Chaudhury, *Social Aspects of Fertility with Special Reference to Developing Countries* (New Delhi, 1982), pp. 71–106; Dixon (1978), op. cit. in n. 8; N. H. Youssef, 'The Inter-relationship between the Division of Labour in the Household: Women's Roles, and their Impact on Fertility', in R. Anker, M. Buvinic, and N. H. Youssef (eds.), *Women's Roles and Population Trends in the Third World* (London, 1982), pp. 173–201.

[13] S. Greenhalgh, 'Sexual Stratification: The Other Side of "Growth with Equity" in East Asia', *Population and Development Review*, 11 (1985), pp. 265–314; C. Safilios-Rothschild, 'Female

24   Karen Oppenheim Mason

decision-making autonomy of women of reproductive age, or even on the total workload shouldered by individuals of different ages and sexes is seldom collected in official statistics, studies on women's position and demographic change rarely contain direct measures of these dimensions.

A third problem in the empirical literature on women's position and demographic change involves the level of aggregation at which the analysis is performed, and/or the units that are compared with one another. In a substantial proportion of studies, the individuals studied come from a single country or population. Although some countries contain sub-regions or sub-populations in which the social institutions of gender vary in important ways (e.g. Malaysia), others are culturally homogeneous. In these latter settings an individual-level analysis cannot reveal anything about the impact on demographic change of women's position *as it is determined by the social institutions of gender*, unless the analysis covers a period during which these institutions have changed significantly. Cross-national or cross-cultural analyses conducted wholly at the aggregate level (for example, those in which countries are used as the units of analysis) avoid this problem, but often suffer from other shortcomings, for example, the problem of making inferences about individual behaviour from correlations computed at the aggregate level.

A fourth problem in the literature involves the cross-sectional focus of most studies. Although understanding the point-in-time relationship between women's position and mortality or fertility (or their proximate determinants) can provide clues about the dynamic relationship between these factors, it is well known that cross-sectional estimates do not necessarily give an unbiased picture of the time-series relationship.[14] Many empirical studies concerned with women's position and demographic change do not consider change directly at all.

The final problem in the literature on women's position and demographic change is an unusually high level of technical sloppiness in what might otherwise be some of the theoretically most relevant and important studies. I suspect that this reflects the unusually strong representation of non-demographers in this literature. A substantial proportion of the research in this area has been produced by individuals whose theoretical sophistication exceeds their technical training. While there is much to be applauded in what these authors offer, a high level of technical rigour is often absent. This, too, makes it difficult to reach firm conclusions about the specific hypotheses to which I now turn.

Power, Autonomy, and Demographic Change in the Third World', in Anker, Buvinic, and Youssef, op. cit. in n. 12, pp. 117–32; J. W. Salaff, *Working Daughters of Hong Kong: Filial Piety or Power in the Family?* (Cambridge, 1981), pp. 257–76.

[14] For an empirical example, see P. N. Hess, 'Static and Dynamic Cross-Sections: Inferences for the Contemporary Fertility Transition', paper presented at the Annual Meeting of the Population Association of America, New Orleans, 1987.

Mortality: Hypotheses and Evidence

There are two major hypotheses in the literature that relate women's position to the mortality transition.[15]

1. Women's autonomy and economic independence contribute to child survival by increasing the mother's ability to provide her children with adequate nutrition and medical care.
2. Women's economic independence contributes to child survival by increasing the value of daughters and thereby encouraging greater nutritional and medical investments in daughters as well as sons.

The first hypothesis suggests that two aspects of women's position relative to that of men—their decision-making autonomy, and their economic independence—help to improve infant and child survival by increasing women's ability to ensure that their children receive adequate nutrition and medical care.[16] The basic premiss that underlies this hypothesis is that, because women give birth to and are responsible for the day-to-day care of young children in all human cultures,[17] they are normally highly motivated to ensure child survival,[18] and are more sensitive to and concerned about the early symptoms of illness than are men.[19] Consequently, when they have the ability to improve child nutrition (e.g. because they earn money and can buy food for their children), or have the ability to take advantage of medical services (e.g. because they have the freedom to make decisions on their own without having to consult their husbands or mothers-in-law), they will act on this ability, and child survival will improve.

Note that this hypothesis, in part, takes the form of the third model discussed above; it posits that women's autonomy will condition the impact of other changes on the mortality decline. For example, where women's autonomy is high, the introduction of modern medical services, or new programmes to improve child survival, are likely to have a much greater demographic impact than where women's autonomy, and hence their ability to make use of medical services, is low. This hypothesis also implies, however, that women's economic independence can have a direct impact on child

[15] A third hypothesis relates women's position to the decline of maternal mortality, but is ignored here both for want of space and because of the evidence that it is less significant for the mortality transition in many Third World populations than are reductions in infant and child mortality.

[16] J. C. Caldwell, 'Education as a Factor in Mortality Decline: An Examination of Nigerian Data', *Population Studies*, 33 (1979), pp. 395–413; see also Caldwell, op. cit. in n. 7.

[17] N. Chodorow, 'Family Structure and Female Personality', in M. Z. Rosaldo and L. Lamphere (eds.), *Women, Culture and Society* (Stanford, Calif., 1974), pp. 43–66.

[18] H. Ware, *Women, Demography and Development* (Canberra, 1981), pp. 67–77.

[19] J. C. Caldwell, P. H. Reddy, and P. Caldwell, 'The Social Component of Mortality Decline: An Investigation in South India Employing Alternative Methodologies', *Population Studies*, 37 (1983), pp. 185–205.

survival. If women's opportunities to earn money improve, this may translate directly into improved child nutrition and survival.

The second hypothesis that relates women's position to mortality decline concerns the inflated levels of infant and child mortality that may result when there is systematic nutritional or medical-care discrimination against female children. In so far as this discrimination results from a high degree of women's economic dependency on male family members, and hence a low economic value of daughters, as Cain, Khanam, and Nahar have argued,[20] it suggests that an improvement in women's opportunities to support themselves or contribute to family income will lessen nutritional and medical discrimination against daughters, and will thus improve overall levels of child survival. This hypothesis thus takes the form of the first or second model discussed above—that is, it treats change in women's economic dependency as the immediate cause of a decline of mortality among female children.

What is the evidence for and against these hypotheses? As regards the first, there is considerable, although mostly indirect, evidence that is consistent with the idea that women's autonomy and economic independence help to promote child survival. There are few studies in which women's autonomy or economic independence have been measured directly, or in which systematic comparisons have been made between settings in which the level of autonomy or dependency varies. Among the few such, however, the results usually suggest that the autonomy of women of reproductive age helps to promote child survival. For example, Caldwell has analysed data for ninety-nine developing countries in order to understand why in some countries mortality declined much faster than would have been predicted on the basis of their economic development, whilst in others it fell much more slowly. These differences in the rate of decline are highly correlated with the proportion of the population who are Muslims; mortality fell faster in non-Muslim than in Muslim populations. Caldwell has argued that the significance of this religious difference lies in the seclusion of women that is a feature of most Muslim populations.[21] In another part of his analysis, Caldwell also found that the single strongest correlate of the absolute level of infant mortality in all ninety-nine countries was the primary-school enrolment rate of girls, a result that also suggests the potential importance of women's autonomy for child survival.[22]

Another systematic comparative study which contains evidence that favours the first hypothesis is Dyson's and Moore's analysis of data from the

---

[20] M. Cain, S. R. Khanam, and S. Nahar, 'Class, Patriarchy and Women's Work in Bangladesh', *Population and Development Review*, 5 (1979), pp. 405–38.

[21] Caldwell, op. cit. in n. 7. There are exceptions, such as Indonesia, where women are not heavily secluded, but they do not appear in Caldwell's lists of underachievers.

[22] One potentially important variable that Caldwell failed to consider, however, is income distribution within countries. The inclusion of this variable in the analysis might alter the importance of girls' school enrolment rates.

states of India.[23] On average, infant and child mortality rates are considerably higher in the north of India than in the east or south. It is also in the north that kinship structure tends to isolate younger married women from their natal kin, thus making them relatively powerless, and where the practice of purdah, the extent of women's illiteracy, the absence of women's employment, and the strength of son-preference are all especially marked. (Dyson and Moore have presented statistical data to document the latter four regional differences.) Thus, although no individual-level data were presented which showed that infant or child deaths occur more frequently among secluded women, Dyson's and Moore's state-level data suggest that women's autonomy and economic independence contribute to child survival.[24]

In addition to these few comparative studies, there are numerous studies at an individual level and within countries which show that levels of girls' schooling are strongly correlated with child nutrition, the use made of medical services, and/or child survival.[25] Although there are several reasons why education might influence child survival, only some of which involve women's autonomy or economic independence, Caldwell, Reddy, and Caldwell have made a persuasive case for the importance of women's autonomy as the key factor that explains the relationship between women's education and child survival in south Asia.[26] In addition to studies of girls' schooling and child survival, there are a few studies in which the authors have examined the role played by women's economic activity in child survival. According to one recent review of these studies,[27] women's engagement in income-earning activities appears to be correlated with relatively low levels of infant and child mortality, even in rural areas.

Although these findings are consistent with the idea that women's autonomy and socio-economic independence contribute to child survival

---

[23] T. Dyson and M. Moore, 'On Kinship Structure, Female Autonomy, and Demographic Behavior in India', *Population and Development Review*, 9 (1983), pp. 35–60.

[24] In a more limited comparative study which was focused solely on Kerala and west Bengal it has also been suggested that women's unusually high levels of literacy and employment may help to account for the unusually low levels of infant and child mortality in Kerala; see M. Nag, 'The Impact of Social and Economic Development on Mortality: Comparative Study of Kerala and West Bengal', in S. B. Halsted, J. A. Walsh, and K. S. Warren (eds.), *Good Health at Low Cost: Proceedings of a Conference Held at the Bellagio Conference Centre, Bellagio, April 29–May 2 1985* (New York, 1985), pp. 57–77.

[25] See Caldwell, op. cit. in n. 7, 16; S. H. Cochrane, J. Leslie, and D. J. O'Hara, 'Parental Education and Child Health: Intracountry Evidence', in S. H. Cochrane, D. J. O'Hara, and J. Leslie, *The Effects of Education on Health* (Washington, 1980)—in this paper the authors review 16 different studies and find that almost all the relationships between education and child mortality are 'boringly inverse'; also R. A. LeVine, S. E. LeVine, A. Richman, and C. S. Correa, '*Schooling and Maternal Behavior in a Mexican City: The Effects on Fertility and Child Survival*' (New York, 1987); K. Streatfield, M. Singarimbun, and I. Singarimbun, *The Impact of Maternal Education on the Use of Child Immunization and Other Health Services* (Canberra, 1986).

[26] See Caldwell, Reddy, and Caldwell, op. cit. in n. 19.

[27] A. S. Carloni, *Women in Development: A.I.Ds Experience, 1973–1985*, i. *Synthesis Paper* (Washington, 1987).

because women are motivated to see their children survive, and hence will act in the interests of achieving this goal when they have the autonomy or resources to do so, some possible exceptions to this hypothesis should be noted. One is the apparent lack of interest of women in parts of south Asia in enhancing the chances of survival of their daughters,[28] and the regular practice of the infanticide of girls in some foraging societies, whose members live under harsh economic conditions.[29] Obviously, mothers do not inevitably value child survival, especially the survival of daughters. Although the extent to which they value the survival of daughters may reflect their own situation (especially their economic dependency, as is suggested by the second hypothesis), there is some evidence that the infanticide of girl babies is influenced by factors other than women's economic independence.[30] The best-documented cases of widespread infanticide or neglect of girls, however, are, indeed, found in settings where women tend to be economically dependent on men.

Another possible exception to the hypothesis that women's autonomy and economic independence lead to improved child survival involves the evidence from a study in south India that rising incomes resulted in the purchase of more prestigious foods (e.g. polished instead of brown rice), but not in any measurable improvement of nutrition.[31] If this pattern were to hold generally, increases in women's economic independence could result in changed feeding patterns of children, but not in improvements in child survival. This suggests that, in some cultural settings, modern education, or an understanding or acceptance of a scientific approach to nutrition, may have to accompany an increase in women's economic independence before there will be a significant impact on child survival. This does not really negate the hypothesis that women's position is related to child survival, but merely modifies it for certain cultural settings.

As regards the second hypothesis, systematic comparative studies in which women's position is related to sex differentials in childhood mortality are quite numerous, but do not always yield results consistent with the hypothesis. It is well established that girls' survival rates during childhood are unusually low in much of south and west Asia, unlike the situation in other regions, where the survival rates of females usually exceed those of males at all ages.[32] Although there is evidence that excess mortality of girls in south

[28] See, e.g., B. D. Miller, *The Endangered Sex: Neglect of Female Children in Rural North India* (New York, 1981).

[29] A. Balikci, *The Netsilik Eskimo* (Garden City, NY, 1970), pp. 147–62.

[30] S. C. M. Scrimshaw, 'Infanticide as Deliberate Family Regulation', in R. Bulatao and R. D. Lee (eds.), *Determinants of Fertility in Developing Countries* (New York, 1983), pp. 720–37.

[31] J. R. Behrman and A. B. Deolalikar, *Will Increased Income Improve Developing Country Nutrition? A Case Study for Rural South India* (New York, 1986).

[32] R. Bairagi, 'Food Crisis, Nutrition, and Female Children in Rural Bangladesh', *Population and Development Review*, 12 (1986), pp. 307–15; S. D'Souza and L. C. Chen, 'Sex Differentials in Mortality in Rural Bangladesh', *Population and Development Review*, 6 (1980), pp. 257–70; L. Heligman, 'Patterns of Sex Differentials in Mortality in Less Developed Countries', in A. D.

Asia reflects discrimination against daughters in respect of nutrition and medical care,[33] and is especially likely to occur when the girl has an older sister,[34] it is less clear that this discrimination reflects women's economic dependency. Consistent with the idea that it does is the finding that the ratio of boys' to girls' childhood mortality varies between countries according to the strength of son-preference, as expressed in fertility surveys,[35] and the additional evidence that son-preference varies according to the overall extent of gender differentiation in the society.[36] Also consistent with this idea is Dyson's and Moore's finding that excess mortality of girls varies in the states of India inversely with the level of women's employment and literacy, and directly with the prevalence of women's seclusion.[37] Econometric analyses of India at the individual, district and state levels which have shown that excess mortality of girls is inversely related to women's labour-force participation[38] are also consistent with the second mortality hypothesis.

There are exceptions, however. For example, in a recent study of World Fertility Survey (WFS) data from ten countries (six of them in south and west Asia) no within-country differences in excess mortality of females were found according to parental education, mother's labour-force participation, father's occupation, or urban–rural residence.[39] This result contradicts the

Lopez and L. T. Ruzicka (eds.), *Sex Differentials in Mortality: Trends, Determinants and Consequences* (Canberra, 1983), pp. 7–32; M. A. Koenig and S. D'Souza, 'Sex Differences in Childhood Mortality in Rural Bangladesh', *Social Science and Medicine*, 22 (1) (1986), pp. 15–22; United Nations Population Division, 'Are Sex Differences in Life Expectancy on the Increase?', *Population Newsletter*, 44 (1987), pp. 1–11; M. B. Weinberger and L. Heligman, 'Do Social and Economic Variables Differentially Affect Male and Female Child Mortality?', paper presented at the Annual Meeting of the Population Association of America, Chicago, 1987.

[33] K. H. Brown, R. E. Black, S. Becker, and A. Hoque, 'Patterns of Physical Growth in a Longitudinal Study of Young Children in Rural Bangladesh', *American Journal of Clinical Nutrition*, 36 (1982), pp. 294–302; K. H. Brown, R. E. Black, S. Becker, S. Nahar, and J. Sawyer, 'Consumption of Foods and Nutrients by Weanlings in Rural Bangladesh', *American Journal of Clinical Nutrition*, 36 (1982), pp. 878–89; L. C. Chen, E. Huq, and S. D'Souza, 'Sex Bias in the Family Allocation of Food and Health Care in Rural Bangladesh', *Population and Development Review*, 7 (1981), pp. 55–70; Miller, op. cit. in n. 28. But see S. L. Huffman, A. K. M. A. Chowdhury, J. Chakraborty, and N. K. Simpson, 'Breastfeeding Patterns in Rural Bangladesh', *American Journal of Clinical Nutrition*, 33 (1980), pp. 144–54, for evidence that there is no discrimination against daughters in breastfeeding.

[34] M. A. Koenig, S. D'Souza, and R. Karim, 'The Determinants of Infant and Child Mortality in Rural Bangladesh', paper presented at the Annual Meeting of the Population Association of America, Minneapolis, 1984.

[35] Weinberger and Heligman, op. cit. in n. 32.

[36] F. Arnold and E. C. Y. Kuo, 'The Value of Daughters and Sons: A Comparative Study of the Gender Preferences of Parents', *Journal of Comparative Family Studies*, 15 (1984), pp. 299–318.

[37] Dyson and Moore, op. cit. in n. 23.

[38] M. R. Rosenzweig and T. P. Schultz, 'Market Opportunities, Genetic Endowments and Intrafamily Resource Distribution: Child Survival in India', *American Economic Review*, 72 (1982), pp. 803–15; T. P. Schultz, 'Women's Work and their Status: Rural Indian Evidence of Labor Market and Environment Effects on Sex Differences in Childhood Mortality', in Anker, Buvinic, and Youssef, op. cit. in n. 12, pp. 202–32.

[39] Weinberger and Heligman, op. cit. in n. 32.

idea that women's economic dependency is an important determinant of nutritional or medical discrimination against daughters.[40] Also inconsistent with the second hypothesis is the finding in the same study that sex composition of the family predicts the ratio of males' to females' mortality, not because of variation between households in daughters' risks of dying, but rather because of variation in sons' risks of dying. Weinberger and Heligman have suggested that this may reflect parents' efforts to enhance the chances of their sons' survival, rather than to reduce those of their daughters. However, this pattern of variation in sons', but not daughters' survival probabilities is inconsistent with the direct evidence from Bangladesh and elsewhere that parents do, indeed, tend to discriminate against their daughters nutritionally, and in the provision of medical care.

Overall, however, the evidence in support of the idea that women's position plays either a direct or a conditioning role in the mortality transition is quite suggestive. Certainly, there is need for additional studies that provide a better measure of women's position across settings in which the institutions of gender differ, that systematically relate these measures to the timing and rapidity of the mortality transition, and that explore whether women's position appears to have played a direct or conditioning role in that transition. Compared to studies of the fertility transition, however, the empirical evidence which links women's position to the mortality transition seems relatively strong.

Fertility: Hypotheses and Evidence

There are seven major ideas in the literature about the impact of women's position on the fertility transition, or the proximate determinants thereof.

Effects by Way of Women's Age at Marriage

1. An increase in women's autonomy will facilitate the postponement of marriage and hence the decline of fertility by reducing the need to control unmarried women's sexuality through early marriage.
2. In family systems that give all rights of women's labour to the husband's family, women's economic independence will facilitate the postponement of marriage and hence the decline of fertility; in other family systems, the effects of women's economic independence on marriage are indeterminate.

---

[40] The evidence that purdah is often more closely observed in affluent families than in poor rural ones, where women's labour is critical to family survival (see Youssef, op. cit. in n. 12) may explain the failure to observe within-country differences by parental education, father's occupation, and urban–rural residence, but seems unlikely to explain the absence of a difference by the mother's labour-force participation.

Effects by Way of Motivation to Limit Fertility within Marriage

3. Because it channels the rewards of children disproportionately to men and the costs of rearing them disproportionately to women, patriarchal family structure encourages high fertility; egalitarian family structure facilitates fertility decline.
4. Women's economic dependency on men produces strong son-preferences among both women and men and hence relatively high fertility desires for purposes of risk insurance and old age security; in a conjugally oriented family system, women's economic independence facilitates fertility decline.
5. The extent of women's autonomy and economic dependency determine women's dependency on the maternal role for legitimacy, security, and satisfaction, and hence the opportunity costs of having children and the motivation to limit fertility.

Effects by Way of Costs of Fertility Regulation

6. Women's autonomy influences their access to modern knowledge and modes of action and hence their propensity to engage in innovative behaviour, including fertility limitation within marriage.
7. Social equality and emotional intimacy between husbands and wives tend to influence fertility by affecting the role that the wife's health and well-being plays in fertility decision-making, and by influencing the likelihood or effectiveness of contraceptive use.

The first two hypotheses concern the impact of women's autonomy and economic independence on their age at marriage, itself a proximate determinant of the fertility transition in contemporary developing countries. The first idea is that women's age at marriage is directly linked to their autonomy, because early marriage is a strategy used by family elders to control the sexuality of unmarried females.[41] Thus, an increase in women's autonomy is likely to mean that the pressures for early marriage of women have weakened. For the same reason, in societies in which women's autonomy has traditionally been relatively high, women's marriages may also have been postponed during the course of development, at least when they previously occurred at relatively young ages. Note that this hypothesis treats women's autonomy as a conditioning factor, rather than as a direct cause of the fertility transition. There may be forces that keep women's age at marriage low, even when their autonomy is relatively great. When changes occur that favour a rise in women's age at marriage, then, the greater the

---

[41] Cain, op. cit. in n. 5; P. Caldwell and J. C. Caldwell, 'Kinship Forms, Female Autonomy, and Fertility: What Are the Connections?', paper prepared for the Rockefeller Foundation Workshop on the Status of Women in Relation to Fertility and Mortality, Bellagio, Italy, 6–10 June 1988.

traditional autonomy of women, the longer should marriage be postponed in response to these changes.

The other major hypothesis that relates women's position to their age at marriage concerns their economic value, which is partly determined by their autonomy (heavily secluded women are usually prevented from making independent economic contributions to the family). Specifically, where the family system gives most or all rights to a married woman's labour to her husband's family, rather than to the wife's family or the conjugal unit, parents will be motivated to postpone their daughters' marriage, if it is socially acceptable for post-pubescent women to leave the home to earn money.[42] Thus, in this type of family system, women's autonomy may again facilitate the postponement of marriage, when other conditions, such as employment opportunities for unmarried women, change. Where the family system does not grant all rights to the wife's labour to her husband's family, the effect of women's autonomy on postponement of marriage is indeterminate, because a strategy in which women marry early but earn income after marriage may be possible. In this situation, an improvement in employment opportunities for women may actually reduce women's age at marriage, rather than raise it.[43]

The third, fourth, and fifth hypotheses concern the impact of women's position on the motivation to limit fertility within marriage. The first argues that a 'patriarchal' family system tends to impede the fertility transition, while a relatively egalitarian one facilitates it, because men in patriarchal family systems receive a disproportionate share of the benefits of children, whilst shouldering relatively little of the burden of caring for them.[44] In societies with a patriarchal family structure, men are more positively

---

[42] J. W. Salaff and A. K. Wong, 'Chinese Women at Work: Work Commitment and Fertility in an Asian Setting', in S. Kupinsky (ed.), *The Fertility of Working Women* (New York, 1977), pp. 81–145.

[43] Cain, op. cit. in n. 5.

[44] E. Boserup, 'Economic and Demographic Interrelationships in Sub-Saharan Africa', *Population and Development Review*, 3 (1985), pp. 383–97; J. C. Caldwell, *Theory of Fertility Decline* (London, 1982); N. Folbre, 'Of Patriarchy Born: The Political Economy of Fertility Decisions', *Feminist Studies*, 9 (1983), pp. 261–84. But see M. Cain, 'Perspectives on Family and Fertility in Developing Countries', *Population Studies*, 36 (1982), pp. 159–75, for a critique. A closely related idea is that women will be motivated to maintain high fertility whenever their workload is heavy, and assistance from husbands or other family members minimal; see N. Birdsall and W. P. McGreevey, 'Women, Poverty and Development', in M. Buvinic, M. A. Lycette, and W. P. McGreevey (eds.), *Women and Poverty in the Third World* (Baltimore, 1983), pp. 3, 13; Boserup, op. cit. above; X. Bunster, 'Market Sellers in Lima, Peru: Talking About Work', in Buvinic, Lycette, and McGreevey, op. cit. above, pp. 92–103; Cain, op. cit. in n. 5; J. C. Caldwell and P. Caldwell, 'The Cultural Context of High Fertility in Sub-Saharan Africa', *Population and Development Review*, 13 (1987), pp. 409–37; T. W. Merrick and M. Schmink, 'Households Headed by Women and Urban Poverty in Brazil', in Buvinic, Lycette, and McGreevey, op. cit. above, pp. 244–71; C. Safilios-Rothschild, 'A Class and Sex Stratification Theoretical Model and its Relevance for Fertility Trends in the Developing World', in C. Höhn and R. Mackensen (eds.), *Determinants of Fertility Trends: Theories Re-examined* (Liège, 1980), pp. 189–202; Youssef, op. cit. in n. 12.

oriented to high or uncontrolled fertility than women, who would supposedly like to practise fertility control, but are relatively powerless to do
so. In contrast, where families are less hierarchically structured, the division
of labour between the sexes and the benefits of children to women and men
are likely to be more balanced; the voices of women in determining whether
family limitation is practised should also be more influential. Both of these
will encourage the limitation of fertility provided other macro-social and
cultural conditions are favourable. Thus, the hypothesis posits that relatively
egalitarian family structures may hasten the fertility decline, given a set of
exogenous changes conducive to family-planning programmes, the rise
of mass education, and its increased importance for economic success, or a
shift from labour-intensive familial models of production to wage-earning or
mechanized agriculture. As in the earlier hypotheses, this hypothesis, too,
treats women's power within the family as a facilitating condition for the
fertility transition.

The second hypothesis concerned with the motivation to limit fertility
within marriage (Number 4) argues that, the greater women's economic
dependency on male family members, the more both women and men will
value sons as security assets—that is, as potential sources of economic
support.[45] This is because daughters will be unable to provide economic
support for their parents in emergencies, or in old age. Thus, in settings
where economic risks are high and non-familial (or non-child) sources
of security or risk insurance are minimal, both women and men will be
motivated towards at least moderately high fertility, because of a desire to
ensure an adequate supply of surviving sons. Because of their extreme
economic vulnerability, women in these settings should have specially strong
desires for sons. On the other hand, in a conjugally-oriented family system,
the economic independence of women should facilitate the fertility transition
by reducing dependency on sons.[46] Thus, in this hypothesis, too, the
position of women is posited to play a conditioning role in the fertility
transition. Where women have traditionally enjoyed a high level of economic
independence, the introduction of anti-natalist ideas should influence the
actual course of fertility far more rapidly than in societies in which women
have had little or no economic independence.

The final hypothesis concerned with the motivation to limit fertility
within marriage (Number 5) posits that the greater women's seclusion and
dependency, the greater will be their need to maintain high fertility in order

---

[45] See Cain, op. cit. in n. 5; Cain, Khanam, and Nahar, op. cit. in n. 20; Safilios-Rothschild,
op. cit. in n. 44; M. Wolf, *Women and the Family in Rural Taiwan* (Stanford, Calif., 1972),
pp. 32–41.
[46] Where the family system is lineage-oriented (as in sub-Saharan Africa), or matrifocal (as
in much of the Caribbean), women's economic independence may fail to facilitate fertility
decline because of the heavy workload that women have to bear, and their dependency on
children to help with this work. See Boserup, op. cit. in n. 44; Cain, op. cit. in n. 5.

to gain power within the family, to gain a claim to familial resources, or to gain prestige and respect within the family or broader community.[47] The greater women's seclusion and dependency, the lower, too, will be the opportunity cost of having children.[48] According to this hypothesis, then, the extent of women's seclusion or dependency is not only likely to play a direct role in the fertility transition, but is also likely to condition the impact of social and economic development on fertility decline. Specifically, the creation of modern wage-earning opportunities is less likely to encourage family limitation where norms of seclusion prevent women from responding to these opportunities than in settings where women are free to leave the home in pursuit of a wage.

The last two hypotheses relate the position of women to the costs of fertility regulation within marriage. The first of these (Number 6) posits that women's autonomy is important for the fertility transition, because it helps to determine whether women engage in innovative behaviour, specifically the parity-specific use of contraception within marriage.[49] In much of recent literature on the fertility transition it has been argued that the idea of fertility limitation within marriage, its social legitimacy, or the methods by which it can be achieved have rarely been known or accepted in traditional settings.[50] The adoption of fertility limitation within marriage that becomes increasingly widespread during the fertility transition is thus a behavioural innovation. To the extent that this is true, women's traditional autonomy, their access to modern information, or their exposure to Western forms of thought and action may determine their propensity to adopt family limitation, especially in advance of its widespread adoption in the community. Thus,

---

[47] J. Blake, 'Demographic Science and the Redirection of Population Policy', *Journal of Chronic Diseases*, 18 (1965), pp. 1181–200; K. Davis, 'Institutional Patterns Favouring High Fertility in Underdeveloped Areas', *Eugenics Quarterly*, 2 (1955), pp. 33–39; Dixon (1975), op. cit. in n. 8, p. 15; C. L. Kamuzora, 'Survival Strategy: The Historical and Economic Roots of an African High Fertility Culture', in E. van de Walle (ed.), *The Cultural Roots of African Fertility Regimes: Proceedings of the Ife Conference, February 25–March 1, 1987* (Ile-Ife and Philadelphia, 1987), pp. 307–29; N. Keyfitz, 'The Family That Does Not Reproduce Itself', in K. Davis, M. S. Bernstam, and R. Ricardo-Campbell (eds.), *Below Replacement Fertility in Industrial Societies: Causes, Consequences, Policies*, Supplement to *Population and Development Review*, 12 (1986), pp. 139–54; C. Oppong, 'Women's Roles, Opportunity Costs, and Fertility', in R. A. Bulatao and R. D. Lee, op. cit. in n. 30, pp. 439–73; F. van de Walle and N. Ouaidou, 'Status and Fertility among Urban Women in Burkina-Faso', *International Family Planning Perspectives*, 11 (1985), pp. 60–64; K. B. Ward, *Women in the World System: Its Impact on Status and Fertility* (New York, 1984); Youssef, op. cit. in n. 12.

[48] G. Standing, 'Women's Work Activity and Fertility', in Bulatao and Lee, op. cit. in n. 30, pp. 416–38.

[49] Dyson and Moore, op. cit. in n. 23; J. Knodel, N. Debavalya, and P. Kamnuansilpa, 'Thailand's Continuing Reproductive Revolution', *International Family Planning Perspectives*, 6 (1980), pp. 85–97; E. Mueller, 'Measuring Women's Poverty in Developing Countries', in Buvinic, Lycette, and McGreevey, op. cit. in n. 44, pp. 272–85.

[50] J. Cleland and C. Wilson, 'Demand Theories of the Fertility Transition: An Iconoclastic View', *Population Studies*, 41 (1987), pp. 5–30; A. Coale and S. C. Watkins (eds.), *The Decline of Fertility in Europe* (Princeton, NJ, 1986); R. D. Retherford, 'A Theory of Marital Fertility Transition', *Population Studies*, 39 (1985), pp. 249–68.

where high-parity children are already viewed by parents as relatively costly, or as bringing few benefits, the extent of women's autonomy may help to determine the rapidity with which fertility limitation is adopted, and fertility declines. This hypothesis thus implies that such macro-level changes as the rise of mass education, or the shift from familial production to wage-earning, will be more likely to precipitate a fertility decline where women's autonomy is relatively great than where it is limited.

The final hypothesis posits that social equality and emotional intimacy between husbands and wives may lower the costs of fertility regulation for two reasons: either because there is greater agreement between spouses about the factors that should enter into fertility decisions, or because there is greater ability to discuss sex, reproduction, and contraception.[51] Specifically, some degree of equality and intimacy between spouses may be necessary before husbands will become concerned with the implications of repeated pregnancies for their wives' health and physical well-being. Intimacy may also facilitate discussion of sexual and reproductive matters, including the use of birth control. There are some obvious qualifications that should be applied to this hypothesis. For example, whether communication between spouses is necessary for effective use of contraception is likely to depend on the types of contraceptive techniques available, and the social rules that surround their use (for instance, whether wives need their husbands' permission or co-operation before they can acquire, or effectively use, the methods available). Nevertheless, this hypothesis suggests that responsiveness to anti-natalist ideas in the society or economy may depend, in part, on the characteristic relationship between spouses. Where intimate communication between spouses is socially proscribed, fertility may be less responsive to the introduction of a strong family-planning programme, or to the rise of mass education than where spouses can communicate more intimately.

The evidence for most of these hypotheses is indirect, and not always consistent with what is being argued. An exception, however, is evidence concerning women's age at marriage, most of which is consistent with the first two hypotheses. There have been few studies in which the question of how women's autonomy or economic independence influences their age at marriage is considered explicitly, but when this is done it is generally found that measures of women's 'status' are positively related to the ages at which they marry. For example, Safilios-Rothschild, in an aggregate analysis of data from seventy-seven developing countries,[52] has shown that the singulate

---

[51] L. J. Beckman, 'Communication, Power and the Influence of Social Networks on Couple Decisions on Fertility', in Bulatao and Lee, op. cit. in n. 30, pp. 856–78; Dixon (1975), op. cit. in n. 8, p. 15; P. E. Hollerbach, 'Fertility Decision-Making Processes: A Critical Essay', in Bulatao and Lee, op. cit. in n. 30, pp. 797–828; van de Walle and Ouaidou, op. cit. in n. 47.
[52] C. Safilios-Rothschild, *The Status of Women and Fertility in the Third World in the 1970–1980 Decade* (New York, 1985).

mean age at marriage (SMAM) of women is significantly correlated with several measures of women's 'access to resources', based on their economic activity, their schooling, or their mortality risks.[53] SMAM tends to be higher in countries in which women are economically active, well schooled, and at low risk of dying, than in countries in which women are inactive, illiterate, or at high risk of dying. Unfortunately, Safilios-Rothschild's analysis does not control for development level, or for other confounding factors. Because her measures of women's economic activity refer to activity among all women, not just among the unmarried, it is not clear whether her results reflect the impact of women's autonomy on the postponement of marriage, or on a country's level of modernization.

Although in another study of women's position and fertility, in which country-level data from twenty-one WFS countries were used,[54] women's mean age at marriage was not analysed as a dependent variable, a re-analysis of the data used in that study shows that there is a strong inverse relationship between the measure of women's economic dependency used by the author (the average age difference between spouses) and women's age at marriage, even when gross national product per head is held constant.[55] If the age difference between spouses were, indeed, a valid measure of women's autonomy, as several authors have argued,[56] then this result is consistent with the hypotheses reviewed earlier.

In addition to the analyses that are explicitly focused on the impact of women's position on age at marriage, there have been many other individual-level and aggregate studies in which women's educational levels or pre-marital economic activities are related to age at marriage.[57] In almost all these studies it has been shown that education and pre-marital economic activity are strongly related to women's age at marriage in a manner consistent with the hypothesis that women's autonomy or economic independence leads to postponement of marriage. Indeed, Cochrane concluded that the most important impact of women's education on fertility probably operated through age at marriage, while Standing reached the same conclusion with regard to women's economic activity before marriage. Although several authors have noted the complexities that underlie these relationships and the sometimes ambiguous causal ordering between women's education, or pre-marital economic activity, and the ages at which women marry, taken

---

[53] The correlations are generally in the range between 0.5 and 0.6.

[54] Cain, op. cit. in n. 5.

[55] The metric slope of the regression which relates the average age difference between spouses to age at marriage was −0.56 (standard error 0.19).

[56] Cain, op. cit. in n. 5; H. B. Presser, 'Age Differences between Spouses: Trends, Patterns and Social Implications' *American Behavioral Scientist*, 19 (1975), pp. 190–205; Ware, op. cit. in n. 18, pp. 92–93.

[57] S. H. Cochrane, 'Effects of Education and Urbanization on Fertility', in Bulatao and Lee, op. cit. in n. 30, pp. 992–1026; P. C. Smith, 'Age at Marriage and Proportions Marrying: Levels and Trends, Fertility Impact, and Determinants', in ibid., pp. 902–47; Standing, op. cit. in n. 48.

together these results, none the less, suggest that an increase in women's autonomy or economic independence may encourage the postponement of marriage.

The evidence with regard to the motivation to limit fertility within marriage and the costs of fertility regulation is less clear-cut, partly because in most studies fertility, or the use of contraception, is analysed *per se*, rather than direct measures of motivation to limit fertility, or the perceived costs of fertility regulation. Direct measures of such factors as the extent to which family structure is 'patriarchal', the extent to which women are economically dependent on men, or the extent to which they are secluded, are almost never used. In several studies, country- or state-level data have been used to analyse the impact of women's 'status' on fertility, but most of these studies are seriously flawed. For example, in a study by Ward in which a world-systems framework was used,[58] it was found that employment of women in the modern sector was inversely related to total fertility, but this was based on an analysis in which less developed and developed countries were lumped together, a strategy that is bound to produce strong correlations between variables that tend to be high in one type of country and low in the other (as is the case with fertility and women's employment in the modern economic sector). Similarly, in one of the studies by Safilios-Rothschild alluded to earlier,[59] although it was focused on less developed countries only, no multivariate analyses were used. This makes it difficult to interpret the finding that such factors as women's share of paid employment, women's school enrolment or completion rates, and women's life expectancy are inversely related to total fertility. In another difficult-to-interpret study, the states, territories, and the Federal District of Mexico were analysed.[60] In this study composite measures of women's situation and fertility were used, which may explain why, once the level of socio-economic development was controlled, one scale that measured the position of women was *positively* related to fertility, and the other was unrelated.

The most useful aggregate-level comparative studies of women's situation and fertility are those by Cain, and by Dyson and Moore.[61] Cain, in his multivariate analysis of twenty-one WFS countries, not only found (net of development indicators) that the gap between the ages of husband and wife was positively related to total fertility, but also showed that it interacted with several development indicators in predicting total fertility, much as the hypotheses that treat women's autonomy as a conditioning variable predict. For example, in countries in which the mean difference between the ages of

[58] Ward, op. cit. in n. 47.

[59] Safilios-Rothschild, op. cit. in n. 52.

[60] C. J. Ireson, *Development, Women's Situation and Fertility: The Mexican Case* (East Lansing, Michigan State University, Office of Women in International Development Working Papers, No. 95; 1985).

[61] Cain, op. cit. in n. 5; Dyson and Moore, op. cit. in n. 23.

the husband and wife is large (five years or more), the logarithm of gross national product per head was not correlated with total fertility, whilst in countries where this difference was smaller, the relationship was negative. Although this particular interaction effect was not significant statistically (others were), its form is, none the less, consistent with the idea that greater women's autonomy or economic independence, will result in a larger demographic response to socio-economic development. Although he did not use multivariate techniques in this part of the analysis, Cain showed that the age difference between spouses was positively, though weakly, related to the strength of son-preference, which in turn was positively related to total fertility. These results are also consistent with the idea presented in the fourth hypothesis that women's economic dependency on men produces strong preferences for sons, that in turn help keep fertility high.

Dyson and Moore, in their analysis of the states of India, did not use multivariate techniques, but their work is of interest because they presented direct information on women's seclusion. In the south and east of India, where kinship structure is said to give women relatively great autonomy, the percentages of women who practised purdah were, indeed, far lower than in the north of the country, where women are isolated from their natal kin (women's labour-force participation rates are also far higher in the southern and eastern states). It is also in the south and the east that total fertility is generally lowest, and the percentage of couples 'protected by family planning' highest (although there are some important exceptions to the latter generalization). Dyson and Moore also showed that son-preference was generally stronger in the north of India than in the south or east. Their results are consistent with the idea that women's autonomy encourages fertility decline and does so, in part, because it produces relatively weak son-preference.

Although the results of the best aggregate studies are thus consistent with the hypotheses reviewed earlier, they provide indirect evidence only. Individual-level studies are therefore of interest, especially those in which more direct measures of women's autonomy, dependency, or domestic power are used. Unfortunately, results of the few studies that contain direct survey measures of these variables are rather inconsistent. Two analyses of cross-sectional survey data collected by Goldberg during the early 1970s in Mexico City and in Ankara showed moderate-to-strong relationships between fertility or contraceptive use and scales based on the wife's report of her freedom of movement and say in family decisions.[62] Similar measures used in an analysis of 1980 survey data from Tamil Nadu, India, however, failed to predict any of the proximate determinants of fertility, other than the

---

[62] R. P. Bagozzi and M. F. van Loo, 'Toward a General Theory of Fertility: A Causal Modelling Approach', *Demography*, 15 (1978), pp. 301–20; D. Goldberg, *Modernism* (Voorburg, 1974).

wife's freedom from secondary sterility,[63] a rather curious result. Hogan, Chamratrithirong, and Xenos also failed to detect significant impacts on fertility of women's self-reports on family decision-making and freedom of movement.[64] Thus, even if the cross-sectional nature of these analyses and their focus on inter-household rather than cross-cultural variation is ignored, their inconsistent results leave it unclear whether women's reported autonomy or freedom has implications for their fertility.

Most numerous, of course, are individual-level studies in which women's education or their economic activity are related to their fertility or contraceptive use. It has been known for some time that the wife's education tends to be negatively related to fertility, especially in more urbanized countries.[65] The wife's education also tends to be more strongly related to fertility than does that of the husband, a result consistent with the idea that it is women's knowledge or attitudes, rather than their socio-economic status, that influences their reproductive behaviour most strongly. A multivariate analysis reported in 1987 of data from thirty-eight WFS countries has confirmed these results.[66] In this analysis, not only was the wife's education more strongly related to recent fertility than the husband's; neither husband's education nor wife's economic activity could explain the relationship between her schooling and her recent record of child-bearing. Certainly, this does not demonstrate that the reason why the wife's level of schooling influences her fertility is the degree of autonomy or economic independence that her schooling gives her. The results of an intensive study of three hundred urban women in Mexico have suggested that the fertility of better-educated women is lower for reasons that include their greater say in household decisions, their lower expectations of help from their children, their improved information about the outside world, and the greater amount of time they spend interacting with their infants.[67] Taken together, then, these results seem quite consistent with the hypotheses reviewed earlier.

The results of studies in which women's economic activity is related to fertility are far less often consistent with these hypotheses. It has been noted in several reviews that employment in the modern sector of the economy is the only type of women's employment that is consistently related to lower fertility.[68] Analysis of data from the WFS has helped to confirm the absence

[63] S. J. Jejeebhoy, 'Women's Status and Fertility: A Time-Series Analysis of Tamil Nadu, India, 1970–1980', paper presented at the Rockefeller Foundation Workshop on Women's Status and Fertility, Mount Kisco, New York.

[64] D. P. Hogan, A. Chamratrithirong, and P. Xenos, *Cultural and Economic Factors in the Fertility of Thai Women* (Honolulu, 1987).

[65] S. H. Cochrane, *Fertility and Education: What do we really know?* (Baltimore, 1979); see also Cochrane, op. cit. in n. 57.

[66] J. Cleland and G. Rodriguez, *The Effect of Parental Education on Marital Fertility in Developing Countries* (New York, 1987).

[67] Le Vine *et al.*, op. cit. in n. 25.

[68] Standing, op. cit. in n. 48; Ware, op. cit. in n. 18, p. 103.

of any consistent relationship between women's general employment after marriage and their fertility.[69] There are a few intensive micro-studies, in which it has been suggested that women's employment may be an important motivation for family limitation within marriage,[70] but there are also others which suggest the opposite, and where it is argued that an increase in women's dependency caused by the loss of their traditional form of economic activity actually *increased* their desire for family limitation—for example, Mernissi's analysis of Moroccan slum dwellers.[71] It should be noted that the lack of any consistent relationship between women's economic activity and their fertility potentially contradicts the idea that the opportunity cost of children influences fertility. Indeed, whether women work for pay is an indirect indicator of the opportunity cost of children (it is generally argued that their potential wage level is a more direct indicator). One would, nevertheless, expect an inverse relationship between labour-force participation of females and fertility, if the opportunity-cost idea were correct.

In addition to studies in which the question of the effect of women's position on their fertility or use of contraception is directly considered, there are others in which the secondary implications of the hypotheses reviewed earlier are touched upon. For example, the third hypothesis implies that women will desire fewer children, or will be more favourably disposed to practise family limitation, than men, at least in settings with patriarchal family structures.[72] In a review of published statistics on women's reproductive goals compared to those of men, however, no consistent difference between the sexes was found.[73] Indeed, although such differences were found more often in settings where fertility was high than in those where the fertility transition had already begun, or had been completed, it was often women who were more pro-natalist than men, rather than the converse. This failure to find the expected difference between the reproductive goals of the two sexes calls into question the idea that a patriarchal family structure will act as a support for high fertility.

[69] J. Cleland, 'Marital Fertility Decline in Developing Countries: Theories and the Evidence', in J. Cleland and J. N. Hobcraft (eds.), *Reproductive Change in Developing Countries: Insights from the World Fertility Survey* (Oxford, 1985), pp. 223–52.

[70] See, e.g., J. H. Caldwell, P. H. Reddy, and P. Caldwell, 'The Causes of Demographic Change in Rural South India: A Micro-Approach', *Population and Development Review*, 8 (1982), pp. 689–727.

[71] F. Mernissi, 'Obstacles to Family Planning Practice in Urban Morocco', *Studies in Family Planning*, 6 (1975), pp. 418–25.

[72] R. Anker, 'Demographic Change and the Role of Women: A Research Programme in Developing Countries', in Anker, Buvinic, and Youssef, op. cit. in n. 12, pp. 29–51; J. C. Caldwell, 'Direct Economic Costs and Benefits of Children', in Bulatao and Lee, op. cit. in n. 30, pp. 370–97; ESCAP, op. cit. in n. 7, J. Knodel and E. van de Walle, 'Lessons from the Past: Policy Implications of Historical Fertility Studies', *Population and Development Review*, 5 (1979), pp. 217–45; R. D. Lee and A. Bulatao, 'The Demand for Children: A Critical Essay', in Bulatao and Lee, op. cit. in n. 30, pp. 233–87.

[73] K. Oppenheim Mason and A. M. Taj, 'Differences between Women's and Men's Reproductive Goals in Developing Countries', *Population and Development Review*, 13 (1987), pp. 611–38.

An implication of the fourth hypothesis is that the strength of women's or of men's son-preferences will influence fertility positively. Although there exist studies at the individual level in which this conclusion was found to hold,[74] there are also others in which it did not.[75] As Williamson has noted,[76] son-preference should, in principle, influence fertility only under certain conditions; for example, where fertility limitation is practised by those who have already achieved their desired number of sons (in other words, in populations with natural fertility son-preference is unlikely to affect fertility). This suggests that the fourth hypothesis may hold only in special circumstances—for example, where contraceptives are widely available and their use is approved, even though they are not as yet generally used.

Finally, the last hypothesis implies that equality between spouses, or communication between them about sexual matters, should be correlated with the (effective) use of contraception, or with lower fertility. According to past reviews of studies focused on couples' relationships, however, the evidence for these ideas is mixed, and the quality of studies generally poor.[77]

All in all, then, the empirical literature provides less consistent evidence for the idea that women's position influences the fertility transition (other than through age at marriage) than it does for the idea that their position influences the mortality transition. There are, indeed, suggestive findings in the literature, but they provide indirect evidence at best. Certainly, we cannot conclude at this time that we fully understand the implications of variations in the roles and status of women for demographic change in the Third World.

Conclusion

I think it is clear that we are unlikely to make much progress in understanding the impact of women's position on the fertility transition without abandoning the use of standard fertility surveys and the statistics that governments normally collect. These sources suffer from two signal shortcomings. First, and most important, they do not measure the aspects of women's position

---

[74] L. C. Coombs, 'Prospective Fertility and Underlying Preferences: A Longitudinal Study in Taiwan', *Population Studies*, 33 (1979), pp. 447–55; M. Khan and I. Sirageldin, 'Son Preference and the Demand for Additional Children in Pakistan', *Demography*, 14 (1977), pp. 481–95; T. W. Pullum, 'Correlates of Family-Size Desires', in Bulatao and Lee, op. cit. in n. 30, pp. 278–98.

[75] R. Bairagi and R. L. Langsten, 'Sex Preference for Children and its Implications for Fertility in Rural Bangladesh', *Studies in Family Planning*, 17 (1986), pp. 302–07; Y. Ben-Porath and F. Welch, *Chance, Child Traits and Choice of Family Size* (Santa Monica, Calif., 1972).

[76] N. E. Williamson, 'Parental Sex Preferences and Sex Selection', in N. G. Bennett (ed.), *Sex Selection of Children* (New York, 1983), pp. 223–39.

[77] Beckman, op. cit. in n. 51; Hollerbach, op. cit. in n. 51.

that are theoretically relevant to the fertility or mortality transition, and, secondly, they are normally collected from widely dispersed probability samples of national populations, and thus do not permit systematic comparisons of women situated in settings governed by different gender transitions. We also need to strike a reasonable compromise between studies that are conducted wholly at the individual level and provide a detailed picture of the forces that affect individual fertility decision-makers but little understanding of the broader institutional context in which those decision-makers operate, and studies conducted wholly at the aggregate level that provide a comparison between units whose institutional conditions vary, but keep hidden from view how these institutions impinge upon individuals. Finally, we also need to make *change* in fertility the focus of investigation.

I suggest, then, that we need multi-level, comparative studies of women's position and fertility change. These studies should seek to compare the dynamics of fertility change across villages, states, regions, or countries that vary in their institutions of gender. Comparisons should be made between the experiences of different cohorts in order to understand how the forces that affect fertility have altered. Information should be collected both from family members and from community informants on the typical flow of authority and resources within family units, the freedoms granted to, and restrictions placed on, women, the nature of the interpersonal relationship between spouses, and the extent to which women and men view relatively large numbers of children or sons as critical to their short- or long-term survival and well-being. Information should also be collected on changes in the economic, educational, political, communications, health, and family-planning spheres in order to understand the objective forces of change that impinge on local residents. Finally, these changes need to be related to traditions of gender relations, and the situations of different households to their reproductive behaviour. Such studies are obviously complex and expensive, but I suggest that without them we are unlikely to develop a good understanding of how women's position affects demographic change.

2 Patriarchal Structure and Demographic Change

MEAD T. CAIN

The effect of women's status (variously defined) on fertility is typically described as operating either through the opportunity costs of children or through women's autonomy in decisions relating to reproduction. In both cases, improvements in women's status are thought to have a negative influence on fertility. I will argue that these hypotheses largely misstate the effects of women's status on fertility in contemporary Third World societies; that, while these channels of influence may, indeed, operate in such settings, they are overshadowed by less direct, but more profound, effects. I argue that the principal means by which women's status—defined in terms of the extent of women's economic dependence on men—affects fertility is through preference for the sex of children. I take as given that children are highly valued as sources of economic security by parents in the great majority of contemporary less developed countries and that reproductive goals are strongly influenced by perceived security needs. In societies in which women are highly dependent on men (i.e. where women's status is low), security goals will, of necessity, be defined in terms of surviving sons. Where women are relatively independent economically, it is more likely that children of either sex can serve security needs. Given similar security needs, and other things being equal, fertility will be considerably higher in settings where there is a strong preference for sons than in settings where son-preference is weak.

A Safety-First Model of Fertility

My interpretation of the relationship between women's status and fertility is based on a more general understanding of the determinants of fertility. I have proposed a 'safety-first' (LSF) model of fertility elsewhere.[1] The model posits a lexicographic decision process based on the criterion of safety-first.

---

[1] M. Cain, 'Fertility as an Adjustment to Risk', *Population and Development Review*, 9 (1983), pp. 688–702.

Originally developed to study innovation-adoption behaviour of farmers, the assumption in the LSF model is that farmers, in making production decisions, are motivated not only by a desire to maximize net returns, but also by the condition that net returns should not fall beneath some specified 'disaster level'.[2] In the case of agricultural production, disaster is crop failure, and the choice variable is crop variety (or some other input decision). In our case, the disaster is income insufficiency in old age (and/or other contingencies), and the choice variable is fertility. It is assumed that parents wish to maximize utility subject to the chance constraint that the probability of inadequate support and quality of life in old age is less than or equal to some target probability. Here, the first priority is to make adequate provision for the future with reasonable certainty. Only after this constraint is fulfilled do parents concern themselves with the fertility implications of the more familiar time and commodity costs and benefits of children.

This model suggests that parents define minimum requirements for old-age security in terms of a certain number of surviving children. Suppose, for example, that this minimum is one healthy and loyal surviving child. The fertility level that is consistent with this goal will depend primarily on the probability of child survival and the probability of child default. The higher the level of child mortality, the greater the fertility necessary to achieve the goal. Similarly, concern over child default should induce higher fertility than if there were no such concern. Mortality and default risks may cause the operational 'rule of thumb' to be revised upward, so that the survival of two children through infancy becomes the goal. In particular less developed societies, the way in which targets are defined, and thus their implications for fertility strategies, will depend on several factors. These include the harshness of the risk environment, and the availability and adequacy of alternative sources of insurance.

The Role of Women's Status

Women's status is relevant to the safety-first model in two ways. The first relates to whether or not the sex of offspring is a factor in framing security targets. In societies in which women are relatively independent economically, and where they share relative equality with men with respect to economic opportunity and control of property, parents will be relatively indifferent about the sex of offspring as regards insurance and security. In societies in which women are more dependent on men, and where they are excluded from mainstream economic activities, parents will place a greater premium on sons. Other things being equal, the fertility level associated with a

---

[2] J. A. Roumasset, J. Boussard, and I. Singh (eds.), *Risk, Uncertainty and Agricultural Development* (New York, 1979).

need for sons will be considerably higher than that implied by a security target that can be satisfied by children of either sex.

The second way in which women's status enters the model is as a distinct source of risk for which additional insurance may be needed. Economic dependence on men can entail special risks for women—risks that are independent of other sources, such as natural disasters or the process of ageing, to which both men and women are exposed. Widowhood, divorce, separation, or incapacitating illness of the husband are threatening events in societies in which women are excluded from mainstream sources of income, and are thus prevented from providing for themselves through their own labour and enterprise. An important source of insurance against the risk of losing the economic support of a husband is sons. The greater the economic dependence of women on men, the greater the salience of this source of risk.

Both son-preference and 'patriarchal risk' stem from the same cause: the economic dependence of women. They do not, however, have the same consequences for fertility. Of the two, son-preference may be viewed as the more significant, because it affects security target-setting irrespective of source of risk. If there is a need to have sons in order to achieve security goals, this requirement will hold for old-age security and other contingencies, as much as for insurance against patriarchal risk. With respect to the risks that dependent women face, it could well be that the fertility level consistent with the target set for old-age security is sufficiently high to satisfy the demand for insurance created by such risks, in which case the presence of patriarchal risk may only serve to reinforce reproductive goals and make them more resistant to change.

Family Structure: Boundaries of the Corporate Group

Too often, analyses that focus on women's status abstract from the corporate context of the family, and therefore overlook the fact that, regardless of tangible indications of inequality between men and women, women's welfare and interests are often closely aligned with the corporate interests of the family as a whole.[3] It is also important to note, however, that the boundary of the corporate family group is not the same in all developing societies. In Asia, this boundary typically encompasses the nuclear family unit—husband, wife, and children. Although the system of family formation that characterizes this region is aptly labelled 'joint',[4] and while most nuclear family units experience periods of extension in their developmental cycles, the majority

[3] M. Cain, 'Perspectives on Family and Fertility in Developing Countries' *Population Studies*, 36 (1982), pp. 159–76.
[4] J. Hajnal, 'Two Kinds of Preindustrial Household Formation Systems', *Population and Development Review*, 8 (1982), pp. 449–94.

of households at any given time will, nevertheless, be nuclear in structure. The relatively high degree of corporateness that is typical of the conjugal unit in Asia is, however, not characteristic of sub-Saharan African or Caribbean (and some Latin American) societies.

In the 'Caribbean' family system the conjugal bond is relatively weak: formal marriage is the exception rather than the norm, a substantial part of reproduction occurs outside marriage or stable unions, women often experience a series of unions with different men during the course of their reproductive lives, and the biological father often bears little or no financial responsibility for his children.[5] In much of sub-Saharan Africa, the conjugal bond also tends to be weak. There, however, the locus of reproductive decisions, and the appropriate referent when considering the costs and benefits of children, is the larger kin-group, rather than one or another parent, as in the case of the Caribbean family system, or the conjugal unit, as in Asian family systems.[6]

In both sub-Saharan Africa and the Caribbean, women possess considerable economic autonomy. However, while these regions would tend to be relatively free of the fertility incentives associated with a high degree of women's dependence, aspects of their family systems may introduce other pro-natalist forces. In the case of the Caribbean, the fact that a father may share in the benefits of reproduction while avoiding the costs creates the possibility of a 'free-rider' situation. In sub-Saharan Africa, it is the dominance of lineage over the conjugal pair and the associated diffusion of the costs (and benefits) of particular children that is of most significance.

A Structural Perspective on Women's Economic Status

Obviously, it is important to locate the analysis of women's status and fertility at the appropriate level of aggregation. It makes little sense to propose or conduct household- or individual-level analyses of a variable that is properly measured at a higher level of aggregation. One can think of many individual-level measures of women's economic dependence on men; however, the factors that condition an individual's experience—the sexual division of labour, labour-market segmentation, inheritance rules, religious norms of behaviour, rules of marriage and family formation—are located in a society's institutional structure. While there may exist substantial variation in the individual experience of women in a particular society, the distribution of such experience will be constrained by institutionally determined bounds. In important respects, therefore, women's status—the extent to which they

---

[5] G. W. Roberts, 'Family Unions in the West Indies and Some of their Implications', in L. T. Ruzicka (ed.), *Nuptiality and Fertility* (Liège, 1982), pp. 243–69.

[6] C. Oppong (ed.), *Female and Male in West Africa* (London, 1983).

are economically dependent on men—should be viewed as a structural phenomenon.

Situations in which women are highly dependent on men involve structured inequality: systems of stratification that give advantage to men over women. Corporate households notwithstanding, men benefit from their dominant positions in such systems and, just as with élites more generally, they have a vested interest in protecting their rank and the system that elevates them to positions of power and control. These interests represent a potentially powerful source of resistance to change, over and above the 'dead hand of tradition'.

Patriarchal structure, by which I mean the sum of institutional mechanisms that serve to limit women's economic autonomy relative to men's,[7] may thus possess considerable inertia. When considering the prospects for change in any one element of patriarchal structure—women's age at marriage, for example—one must reckon with the weight of the entire structure. For our purposes, knowing why different institutional arrangements have evolved in different regions of the developing world is less important than recognition that particular patriarchal structures have deep historical roots, and that the pattern of variation in patriarchal structure which can be observed today in the developing world is essentially the same as the pattern that existed three and four decades ago, when mortality began its precipitous decline.

Direct Effects of Patriarchal Structure

The direct causal relationships that link patriarchal structure, women's status, and fertility are illustrated in Fig. 2.1. Elements of patriarchal control combine to produce a particular degree of women's economic dependence on men, which, in turn, affects security target-setting in two ways. First, and most important, for a given level of risk (and availability of alternative sources of insurance), the dependence of women determines the relevance of sex of children in figuring security needs. Secondly, economic dependence may increase the demand for children as security assets over and above what it would otherwise be, because it introduces an additional source of risk. The security target—expressed in terms of desired number of surviving sons or children—in turn has implications for the level of fertility; the level consistent with a particular security target depends on levels of mortality and natural fertility. Other things being equal, the greater the chances of child survival, the lower the fertility necessary for achieving security goals. However, if the security target is high, improvements in mortality may simply facilitate the achievement of a security goal which had previously

---

[7] M. Cain, S. R. Khanam, and S. Nahar, 'Class Patriarchy, and Women's Work in Bangladesh', *Population and Development Review*, 5 (1979), pp. 405–38.

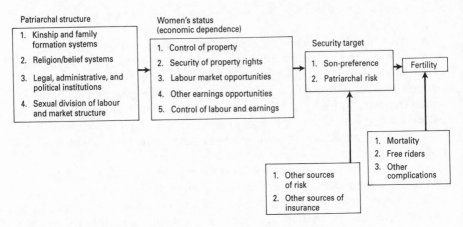

FIG. 2.1 Patriarchal structure. Women's status and fertility

been out of reach. Where conjugal ties are weak and the nuclear family unit lacks cohesiveness, the free-rider problem may 'short-circuit' the connection drawn between the security target and fertility.

Among the 'other complications' referred to in Fig. 2.1 are infertility, child-fostering, and the possibility of child default. Both extraordinary levels of infertility, and the institution of child-fostering are characteristic of sub-Saharan Africa. High levels of infertility introduce additional uncertainty concerning the achievement of reproductive goals into an environment where uncertainty about child survival is, in general, already great. The tenuous control over reproduction implied by the combination of a high incidence of infertility and high levels of mortality is antithetical to the notion of deliberate fertility limitation. While the incidence of fertility is by no means uniform throughout sub-Saharan Africa, it is high on average, and, at the upper end of the range, produces rates of childlessness among older women in excess of 30 per cent.[8] Child-fostering, as practised in much of sub-Saharan Africa, provides a means of diffusing and redistributing the costs of reproduction, and also of acquiring child services when reproduction fails. The significance of this institution in relation to reproductive behaviour, however, lies less with narrow cost and benefit considerations, than as a reflection of a social organization in which the conjugal bond is relatively weak, the primary corporate group is the lineage rather than the conjugal unit, and costs and benefits of reproduction must be evaluated from the perspective of this larger corporate group, rather than that of parents.

[8] O. Frank, 'Infertility in sub-Saharan Africa: Estimates and Implications', *Population and Development Review*, 9 (1983), pp. 137–44.

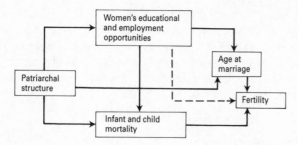

FIG. 2.2 Indirect effects of patriarchal structure on fertility

Indirect Effects of Patriarchal Structure

The indirect links between patriarchal structure and fertility are depicted in Fig. 2.2. The principal indirect effect operates through women's age at marriage, which is viewed as responding to both educational and employment opportunities, given a permissive patriarchal structure. In a similar way, and under similar conditions, infant and child mortality may respond to improvements in women's education, and, in turn, induce a response in fertility. Patriarchal structure thus operates as a covariate: the structure itself is assumed to remain relatively unchanged, but different structures either enable or inhibit other types of change. According to this view, evidence of marked improvements in secondary school enrolment of girls is less an indication of transformation in patriarchal structure than a reflection of the existence of a 'favourable' structure.

The arrow which connects educational and employment opportunities with fertility in Fig. 2.2 is broken, in order to indicate ambiguity of effect and subservience to the causal mechanism described in Fig. 2.1. Improvements in women's employment and education may initially serve to increase fertility, by disrupting traditional breast-feeding practices and thus reducing the period of post-partum amenorrhoea.[9] On the other hand, increased women's employment and education may raise the opportunity costs of children, and thus exert a negative influence on fertility. Education arguably has a number of other effects that combine to produce a negative influence on fertility. It may, for example, reduce the psychic and real costs of fertility regulation. However, security considerations are expected to take precedence, and the potential negative effects of women's employment and education should be evaluated in this context. Thus, an increase in opportunity costs

[9] M. Nag, 'The Impact of Sociocultural Factors on Breastfeeding and Sexual Behavior', in R. Bulatao and R. D. Lee (eds.), *Determinants of Fertility in Developing Countries* (New York, 1983), pp. 134–62.

will make children a more expensive form of insurance but, in the absence of change that affects the need for insurance or the availability of alternative forms of insurance, is unlikely to induce a fertility response. Similarly, while reduction in the costs of fertility regulation may well facilitate the achievement of fertility levels that are consistent with security targets, it will not override the determinant influence of these targets.

Empirical Application

The preceding discussion emphasized the theoretical importance of distinguishing the concept of women's economic status from the causally antecedent concept of patriarchal structure. Here we propose to use median age difference between once-married spouses as an indicator of patriarchal structure in a cross-national analysis of fertility.

The age difference between spouses (or partners in unions) has several attractive features as an indicator of patriarchal structure. In most cases, a large difference between the ages of spouses (men older than women) is associated with patrilineal kinship structure and patrilocal residence, while a small difference indicates bilateral kinship and greater flexibility in the residence pattern of newly married couples. A large difference represents a potentially powerful source of control by men over women, and may further reflect the kind of control that derives from the interaction of sex and age hierarchies. Moreover, the larger the age difference between spouses, the greater the probability of widowhood. Widowhood is a critical juncture in a woman's life, and, in societies where women's economic independence is curtailed, is the focal point of patriarchal risk.

Table 2.1 shows the median age difference between partners (excess of the man's age over that of the woman) by time elapsed since union for twenty-eight countries grouped by continent.[10] From the first column (time elapsed since union less than ten years), note that median age differences range from a low of 2.5 years in the Philippines to a high of 9.8 in Mauritania. The next three columns show the median age differences for successively shorter periods of time since first union, and thus provide a measure of change in age difference over the fifteen years that precede the date of the survey (in most cases the late 1970s). While some change is indicated, usually towards a narrowing of the age differences, the overall stability of median age differences through time is quite striking. For the most part, the rank order of countries is maintained in Columns 2–4 of Table 2.1, and inter-country variance in median age difference dominates inter-temporal

[10] J. B. Casterline and P. F. McDonald, 'The Age Difference between Union Partners', World Fertility Survey, WFS/TECH 2070.20; J. B. Casterline, L. Williams, and P. F. McDonald, 'The Age Difference between Spouses: Variations among Developing Countries', *Population Studies*, 40 (1986), pp. 353–74.

TABLE 2.1. *Median age difference between partners, by time elapsed since union, women in one union only* (years)

Country	Less than 10	10–14	5–9	0–4
Africa				
Ghana	7.6	9.5	8.2	7.2
Kenya*	7.1	8.0	6.9	7.3
Lesotho*	5.6	6.5	5.7	5.5
Sudan*	8.4	9.4	8.6	8.2
Nigeria[†]	9.7	—	—	—
Benin[†]	6.9	—	—	—
Mauritania[†]	9.8	—	—	—
Morocco[†]	6.5	—	—	—
Egypt[†]	6.2	—	—	—
Asia				
Syria*	6.1	6.8	6.2	6.0
Bangladesh*	9.1	10.1	9.3	9.0
Nepal*	3.8	4.6	4.1	3.6
Pakistan*	6.5	5.9	6.4	6.6
Sri Lanka*	4.8	6.1	5.3	4.3
Indonesia	4.9	5.3	5.2	4.7
Korea, S.	4.0	3.7	4.0	3.9
Malaysia: Malay	4.8	5.1	5.0	4.6
Chinese	3.9	3.6	3.9	3.9
Philippines	2.5	2.7	2.5	2.5
Thailand*	3.3	3.5	3.4	3.2
Yemen[†]	5.4	—	—	—
Americas				
Colombia	4.6	5.1	5.6	4.6
Paraguay	4.0	4.4	4.1	4.0
Peru	3.8	4.3	3.9	3.8
Costa Rica	3.0	3.7	3.6	2.4
Mexico*	3.0	3.5	3.2	2.9
Haiti	4.1	4.9	4.0	4.2
Jamaica*	4.1	3.3	3.8	4.9
Venezuela[†]	4.6	—	—	—

* Data relate only to women currently in union.
[†] Age diffence by duration not reported.

Sources: Casterline and McDonald, and ([†]) Casterline, Williams, and McDonald, both op. cit. in n. 10.

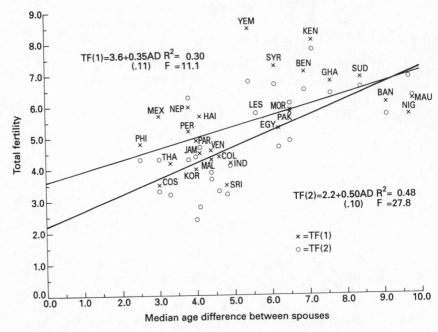

FIG. 2.3 Relationship between total fertility and age difference between spouses

variance. Median age differences between spouses are also remarkably invariant between socio-economic groups within countries.[11] For example, contrary to what might be expected, median age differences within the great majority of countries shown in Table 2.1 do not vary systematically with wife's years of schooling, husband's occupation, or wife's place of childhood residence (city, town, or village). With respect to its merits as an indicator of patriarchal structure, this invariance is reassuring.

In Fig. 2.3 total fertility (TF) is plotted against median age difference between spouses for the countries listed in Table 2.1. Two indices of total fertility are used; the first, designated by X, is that yielded by the World Fertility Survey (WFS) (referred to here as TF(1)), and the second, designated by O, is the estimate reported in the World Bank's 1987 *World Development Report* (referred to as TF(2)). Fig. 2.3 shows a positive relationship between median age difference and fertility. The slope of the regression line for TF(2), which reflects recent declines in fertility, is slightly steeper and the line fits better.

It is clear from Fig. 2.3 that the strong positive correlation between median age difference and fertility derives from the position of two clusters

---

[11] Casterline and McDonald, op. cit. in n. 10.

TABLE 2.2. *Regression analysis of total fertility*

	(1)	(2)	(3)	(4)	(5)
Age difference (0/1)	2.4	2.0	2.1	2.0	1.6
	(0.4)*	(0.4)	(0.4)	(0.4)	(0.4)
Infant mortality rate		0.01			
		(0.01)			
Log. GNP per head			−0.38		
			(0.22)		
Age at marriage				−0.16	
				(0.09)	
Girls' enrolment					−0.03
					(0.01)
Constant	3.9	3.2	6.5	7.3	5.0
R^2	0.65	0.69	0.69	0.69	0.76
F	49.1	28.2	27.8	27.9	40.1

* Numbers in parentheses are standard errors.

of countries on the plot: the cluster in the lower left, which contains primarily south-east Asian and Latin American countries, with both relatively low age differences and low fertility; and the cluster in the upper right, made up of African, south Asian (Muslim), and west Asian countries, with large age differences and high fertility. Within each cluster, however, no clear relationship between median age difference and fertility can be discerned. Therefore, the indicator of patriarchal structure appears to be able to distinguish, at best, two distinct regimes, one 'weak' and one 'strong'.

One measure of the effect of patriarchal structure on fertility can be obtained by regressing total fertility on median age difference between spouses, controlling for possible confounding variables. The results of these regressions are presented in Table 2.2. To facilitate interpretation, median age difference is transformed into a dichotomous variable, set equal to zero when the median age difference is less than five years, and equal to one when it is five years or more. These regression models incorporate successively as controls: infant mortality rate, logarithm of GNP per head, singulate mean age at first marriage (women), and girls' secondary school enrolment ratios.[12] The coefficients for mean age difference (the first row in Table 2.2) imply that a strong patriarchal regime is responsible for adding approximately

[12] Sources for infant mortality rate are S. O. Rutstein, *Infant and Child Mortality: Levels, Trends, and Demographic Differentials* (WFS Comparative Studies, 25; London, 1983), and J. Cleland and J. N. Hobcraft *Reproductive Change in Developing Countries* (Oxford, 1985); for GNP per head, *World Development Report* (1983), Table 1; for singulate mean age at marriage, UN, *Fertility Behaviour in the Context of Development: Evidence from the World Fertility Survey* (New York, 1987); for girls' secondary-school enrolment ratios, UNESCO, *Statistical Yearbook* (1981), Table 3.

TABLE 2.3. Regression analysis of total fertility

| | Median Age Difference | | | | | | | |
| | Less than 5 years (N = 15) | | | | 5 years or more (N = 13) | | | |
	(1)	(2)	(3)	(4)	(5)	(6)	(7)	(8)
Infant mortality rate	0.025 (0.005)*				-0.01 (0.01)			
Log. GNP per head		-0.51 (0.26)				-0.03 (0.43)		
Age at marriage			-0.22 (0.11)				-0.03 (0.16)	
Girls' enrolment				-0.035 (0.011)				-0.028 (0.022)
Constant	2.1	7.4	8.7	5.1	7.2	6.4	6.9	6.6
R^2	0.65	0.23	0.23	0.45	0.10	0	0	0.13
F	24.1	3.9	3.9	10.2	1.2	0	0	1.6

* Numbers in parentheses are standard errors.

two live births to total fertility. In Table 2.2 the more recent TF(2) is used as the dependent variable; the results when TF(1) is used are equally consistent, although the estimated coefficients for age difference are slightly smaller.

Another measure of the effect of patriarchal structure focuses on its role as a covariate. Where patriarchal structure is strong, mortality decline may simply facilitate the achievement of security targets that were out of reach previously, in which case one would not necessarily expect fertility to decline in response. In weak patriarchal regimes, however, where intrinsic security targets are already low, one would expect fertility to decline (perhaps with some lag) in response to a decline in mortality. Similarly, in weak patriarchal regimes there is greater inherent flexibility in women's age at marriage, education, and employment. These should prove more responsive to change in the course of economic development, and, through the channels described earlier, have an impact on fertility.

To test for the presence of interaction, the regression models of Table 2.2 were estimated separately for countries in which median age difference between spouses is less than five years (weak patriarchal regimes) and for those in which it is five years or greater (strong patriarchal regimes). The results are shown in Table 2.3 and are quite striking. In strong patriarchal regimes there is no measurable relationship between variations in GNP per head, infant mortality, median age at first marriage, or secondary school enrolment of girls, and fertility levels. In weak patriarchal regimes, on the other hand, the four predictor variables behave very much as expected: fertility is positively and significantly related to the infant mortality rate and negatively related to GNP, age at marriage, and girls' school enrolment ratios.

Preference for Sons

Societies in which women have little economic independence should generate a strong preference for sons because of women's need for security, particularly in old age. Quite apart from any other potential channel of influence, women's status should have fundamental implications for fertility by determining the extent to which the sex of children is relevant to planning for future security needs.

A recent analysis of preferences for the sex of children, in which WFS data were used, was focused on responses to the question 'Would you prefer your next (first) child to be a boy or a girl?' asked of all pregnant women and all currently married non-pregnant women who wanted at least one more child and considered themselves capable of having another.[13] As a

[13] J. Cleland, J. Verrall, and M. Vaessen, *Preferences for the Sex of Children and their Influence on Reproductive Behaviour.* (WFS Comparative Studies, 27; Voorburg, 1983).

TABLE 2.4. *Ratio of boy/girl responses to questions about sex preference*

Strong son-preference		Moderate son-preference		Equal-preference		Daughter-preference	
Pakistan	4.9	Lesotho	1.5	Kenya	1.1	Venezuela	0.8
Mauritius*	4.5	Sri Lanka	1.5	Indonesia	1.1	Jamaica	0.7
Nepal	4.0	Sudan	1.5	Peru	1.1		
Bangladesh	3.3	Morocco*	1.4	Guyana	1.1		
Korea	3.3	Thailand	1.4	Trinidad and			
Syria	2.3	Fiji	1.3	Tobago	1.1		
Yemen*	2.3	Malaysia	1.2	Colombia	1.0		
Egypt*	2.0	Dominican		Paraguay	1.0		
Jordan	1.9	Republic	1.2	Costa Rica	1.0		
		Mexico	1.2	Panama	1.0		
				Philippines	0.9		
				Haiti	0.9		

* Ratios for these countries were computed from the final WFS country reports.

summary indicator of preferences, the countries were ranked according to the ratio of 'boy' responses to 'girl' responses, after apportioning the occasionally large group of undecided women equally between the numerator (boys) and the denominator (girls). Four groups of countries were identified on this basis, ranging from 'strong son-preference' to 'daughter preference' (see Table 2.4).

Middle-eastern and south Asian countries dominate the strong-son-preference group; south-east Asian and sub-Saharan African countries are distributed between the moderate-son-preference and equal-preference group; while Latin American and Caribbean countries generally display equal preference. A more detailed analysis of preferences by parity (limited to parities 2–4) and existing sex composition of children shows that, within the strong-son-preference group, a net preference for girls occurs only among women who have no daughters. In the three other categories, preferences reveal a desire for a balanced sex composition. The desire to correct an imbalance is evident in both the moderate-son-preference and equal-preference groups; however, where a balance already exists, the moderate-son-preference group expresses a net preference for sons, while the equal-preference group exhibits no marked preference for either sex.

In Fig. 2.4, the sex-preference ratios are plotted against median age difference between spouses for the sample of countries for which both types of data are available. With several notable exceptions, it is possible to distinguish a rough correspondence between the measure of patriarchal structure and the degree of son-preference. Latin American, Caribbean, and south-east Asian countries are clustered in the quadrant to the lower left,

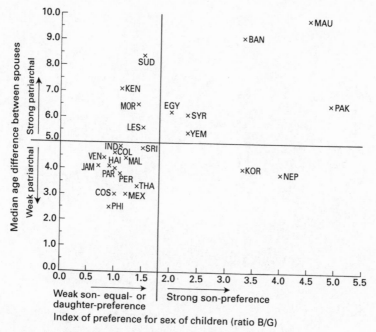

FIG. 2.4 Relationship between median age difference between spouses and preference for sex of children (ratio B/G)

with equal or weak son-preference and a relatively small age difference between spouses, and Muslim south Asian, middle eastern, and north African countries are located in the upper-right-hand quadrant. The tattered appearance of this plot is due largely to the small sample of countries from the latter region. The misfits in the figure are Korea and Nepal (low age differences between spouses, strong son-preference) and the African countries (large age differences between spouses, weak son-preference or indifference).

In Africa, the continuing importance of corporate kin groups and the institutions of bride-price and polygyny suggest that large age differences between spouses are more a reflection of lineage (and generational) control than of the economic subordination of women by men. Weak son-preference, or a preference for balanced sex composition, is consistent with this interpretation.

In Korea, it is likely that the material basis for son-preference has been substantially eroded by economic development and the consequent amelioration of risks, development of financial and insurance markets, and growth of social security and employee benefits.[14] This is not to say that the link between material security (particularly in old age) and reproduction has

[14] R. Repetto, T. H. Kwon, S. V. Kim, and D. T. Kim, *Economic Development, Population Policy and Demographic Transition in the Republic of Korea* (Cambridge, Mass., 1981).

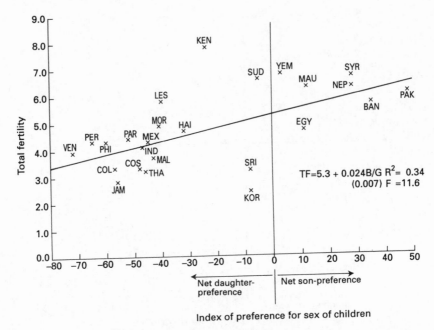

FIG. 2.5 Relationship between total fertility and preference for sex of children

been completely eliminated. The very strong son-preference that persists in Korea is, however, placed in a better perspective by noting that, of currently married, fecund, and non-pregnant women with one son and one daughter, 72 per cent indicated that they did not want any more children, and, of women with two sons and one daughter, 97 per cent said they wanted no more children.[15]

Although the population of Nepal is very heterogeneous, it contains two major cultural groups: Hindu Indo-Aryan and Tibeto-Burman (primarily Buddhist).[16] In kinship and women's economic status, the former, which is the numerically dominant cultural group (approximately 80 per cent of the total population), is akin to the strong patriarchal, 'north Indian' pattern. There is no ready explanation why the median age difference between spouses is low in Nepal; however, given women's relatively low economic status in the dominant group, it would seem that, in the aggregate, the country belongs with other strong patriarchal societies, as is suggested by the marked preference for sons.

In Fig. 2.5, total fertility is plotted against another measure of child sex

[15] Cleland, Verrall, and Vaessen, op. cit. in n. 13.
[16] G. L. Harris *et al.*, *Area Handbook for Nepal, Bhutan and Sikkim* (Washington, 1983).

preference: the difference between the percentage of women who want a son and the percentage of women who want a daughter among currently married fecund women who already have two living sons and one daughter, and who want more children.[17] For countries in the negative range, there is a net preference for daughters, and for those in the positive range, a net preference for sons. Because these women already have two living sons, and because the current sex composition of their children is unbalanced, this index represents a 'strong' test of son-preference. The sample of countries includes all those for which data on preference for the sex of children are available. With the exception of Korea, in countries with a marked preference for sons fertility is also high and relatively unyielding. Similarly, in all countries that tend towards a preference for balanced child sex composition (with the exception of sub-Saharan Africa) there has been a substantial fertility decline. As in the case of median age difference between spouses, the sex preference index of Fig. 2.5 is capable of distinguishing two distinct regimes: the cluster to the lower left, in which a strong preference for a balanced sex composition is evident, and the cluster to the upper right, where a net preference for sons persists.

Conclusion

The scope for cross-national quantitative analysis of fertility is sharply constrained by the meagre data that are available. The important conceptual distinction between women's economic status, on the one hand, and its structural determinants, on the other, and the need for independent indicators of both, greatly increase the demands on data. Indicators of women's economic status, even if they are well measured, cannot be used as indicators of underlying patriarchal structure. Incorrect functional form of statistical models is another important potential source of specification error and bias. A recent review of thirty-three cross-national studies of fertility in developing countries conducted between 1962 and 1981[18] showed that in all of them additive models instead of the required interactive form were used.

What is needed more than such cross-national analysis is research that can elaborate the elements of patriarchal structure in different settings, focused on the circumstances of women's economic vulnerability, and the role and importance of sons and daughters as sources of security. High priority should be given to intensive field-based work that can provide comment simultaneously on the economic relationships between parents and children

---

[17] Cleland, Verrall, and Vaessen, op. cit. in n. 13.
[18] P. Cutright, 'Statistical Models of Interrelations between Socioeconomic Development and Fertility in Less Developed Areas', paper prepared for the Fertility Determinants Project, Indiana University, Bloomington, 1983.

and between men and women, on family and kinship dynamics, and on the locus and criteria of reproductive decisions.

With respect to policy, the analysis here suggests that the task of fertility reduction in societies with strong patriarchal regimes is enormously more difficult than in those with weak ones. For example, in the weak patriarchal regime, the government can act to expand the educational sector and create educational opportunities with a reasonable expectation that such a policy will induce a fertility response, as age at marriage rises and various other channels of influence are activated. In the strong patriarchal regime, the government can expect resistance to school enrolment of girls, because it conflicts with the logic and inertia of patriarchal structure, and, to the extent that women's education is promoted, a weaker fertility response.

Recognition that the problem lies at the structural level, while a necessary step towards informed policy, does not make the problem less formidable or more amenable to policy intervention. Among societies with strong patriarchal regimes there are, as yet, no clear demographic success stories from which policy lessons might be drawn; nor are there many examples among these societies of concerted policy attacks on the institutional bases of women's economic dependence.

3 Urban Women's Autonomy and Natural Fertility in the Sahel Region of Africa

FRANCINE VAN DE WALLE AND ÉTIENNE VAN DE WALLE

The female sex does not hold in Africa that distinguished rank in society which it happily enjoys in Europe.[1]

The debate in the demographic literature over the place of women's status has grown enormously in sophistication during the last few years. It is now common to distinguish between those aspects of status that are connected to 'access to resources', and those that give 'control over resources'.[2] The focus on gender inequality makes it possible to avoid sterile comparisons of status in different societies, ascribed as part of the woman's roles as a wife and mother, rather than achieved through education or professional achievement.

The word *status* implies the orderly organization of individuals, as well as their own recognition of the rules that determine this organization. A fundamental problem in the use of this concept for analytical purposes by an outsider is the temptation to impose criteria and value judgements which are not acceptable to the members of the society that is being analysed. This risk was recognized by Lucy Mair in her classical discussion of African marriage:

The inferior status of women is believed to be evident in the institutions of polygyny, child betrothal, the inheritance of widows, and all procedures whereby women can be disposed of in marriage without their consent; in a division of labour which allots a large share of heavy work to women; and in the submissive behaviour expected of women towards their husbands, the generally recognized right of a man to beat his

[1] T. Winterbottom, *An Account of the Native Africans in the Neighbourhood of Sierra Leone; to which is added An Account of the Present State of Medicine Among Them* (London, 1803), p. 144.

[2] K. Oppenheim Mason, *The Status of Women: A Review of its Relationship to Fertility and Mortality* (Population Studies Center; Ann Arbor, Mich., 1984).

The authors wish to thank the Sahel Institute in Bamako for support and co-operation during the survey which is reported later in this paper. The project was funded by the International Research Award Programme on the Determinants of Fertility of the Population Council, financed by the Agency for International Development.

wife, and the fact that marriage often involves little companionship between spouses . . . it is too readily assumed, however, that any divergence from the pattern which is regarded as the ideal for Europeans must involve an inferior status for women.[3]

In this chapter we want to avoid connotations of 'inferior' and 'superior'. No society will freely admit that the status of its women is low. On the contrary, every society will praise its women for one reason or another, be it their beauty, their work, or their fertility. Rattray stated that it took him several years before he realized the social importance of women in Asante.[4] When he asked the elders why they had not told him about this, they replied: 'The white man never asked us this; you have dealings with and recognize only the men; we supposed the Europeans considered women of no account, and we know you do not recognize them as we have always done.'[5]

In Africa, women gain status as wives and mothers. The mother is the core of the family; she is praised by her daughters and her sons. It is to his mother that Camara Laye dedicated *L'Enfant noir*, the story of his childhood: 'Black woman, African woman, oh! you, my mother, I think of you . . . Black woman, African woman, oh! you, my mother, thank you, thank you for everything you did for me, your son, so far away and still so close to you!'[6] Goode has stressed the high emotional significance of the son–mother relationship in African society.[7]

Hence, fertility and woman's status are inextricably linked, and status is one of the results of fertility; conversely, fertility is one of the consequences of the condition of women in the agricultural economy.[8] People will point at the unequalled prestige attained by the mother of a large family, or at the authority and independence won by a senior wife who is universally respected and has control over her children, her co-wives, their children, and every one in the compound except the husband. Status is not a fixed concept. On the contrary, it evolves during the woman's life cycle and varies with the duties she performs at different stages of her career. For the young woman, her first progression in the hierarchy requires that she prove her fertility. Later, the cultural image of the mother as strong, nurturant, and wise develops as women hold their many roles and statuses during their lifetime. For example, in Bobo-Dioulasso, when a woman acquires a daughter-in-law, she is entitled to retire from housework and devote herself to her

[3] L. Mair, *African Marriage and Social Change* (London, 1969), p. 7.

[4] R. S. Rattray, *Ashanti* (London, 1923), p. 84.

[5] W. Bleek, *Sexual Relationships and Birth Control in Ghana: A Case Study of a Rural Town* (Amsterdam, 1976), p. 114.

[6] C. Laye, *L'Enfant noir* (Paris, 1954).

[7] W. J. Goode, *World Revolution and Family Patterns* (New York, 1970), p. 166.

[8] L. C. Kamuzora, 'Survival Strategy: The Historical and Economic Roots of an African High Fertility Culture', in É. van de Walle (ed.), *The Cultural Roots of African Fertility Regimes: Proceedings of the Ife Conference, February 25–March 1, 1987* (Ile-Ife and Philadelphia, 1987).

private concerns.[9] Fulton and Randall have commented about Bambara women in rural Mali: 'Personal satisfaction and sense of worth and autonomy are plain to see in women in the final phase of a successful demographic career, when influence over descendants has begun to counterbalance the official subservience to husbands and to men in general.'[10] Women gain status through reproduction and experience. Here, *status* denotes prestige, esteem, respect, influence, and power over one's domestic entourage.

Another central and more interesting issue is decision-making, or what is conveyed by the notion of *autonomy*. The notion is itself not free of ambiguity. Dyson and Moore refer to it 'as the capacity to manipulate one's personal environment.'[11] They make clear that 'autonomy is the ability . . . to obtain information and to use it as the basis for making decisions about one's private concerns and those of one's intimates. Thus, equality of autonomy between the sexes implies equal decision-making ability . . .' For Caldwell, 'Female autonomy is certainly not the same as female status, at least as measured by the potential for respect or reverence; indeed, it may be close to the opposite.'[12] A young woman may acquire some autonomy and yet enjoy no status at all, and the mother of a large family may have a high status and little autonomy. Autonomy benefits the mother and her children because it renders her capable of taking decisions alone. An autonomous young woman will decide by herself to look for help when her child is sick, she will treat her daughters in the same way as she treats her sons, she will take decisions at least in her feminine world. Autonomy has to do with 'control over resources', even when it is vicarious control, by the goodwill of a male household head, in the sphere of activity where he has delegated authority.

Although the distinctions between status and autonomy, between access to and control over resources, are standard in the literature, when push comes to shove, and the analyst attempts to describe the connection with fertility, the nature of the available information imposes a rather different focus. Fertility data of the kind gathered in the World Fertility Survey (WFS) come with simplistic independent variables: status, to all intents and purposes, is measured by levels of women's literacy, or labour-force participation. These are clearly important and meaningful variables. No doubt, they are also related to prestige and influence. But they do so in ways which

[9] F. van de Walle and N. Ouaidou, 'Status and Fertility among Urban Women in Burkina Faso', *International Family Planning Perspectives*, 11 (1985), p. 60.

[10] D. Fulton and S. Randall, 'Households, Women's Roles and Prestige as Factors Determining Nuptiality and Fertility Differentials in Mali', in J. C. Caldwell, A. G. Hill, and V. J. Hull (eds.), *Micro-Approaches to Demographic Research* (London, 1984), p. 203.

[11] T. Dyson and M. Moore, 'On Kinship Structure, Female Autonomy, and Demographic Behavior in India', *Population and Development Review*, 9 (1983), p. 45.

[12] J. C. Caldwell, 'Routes to Low Mortality in Poor Countries', *Population and Development Review*, 12 (1986), p. 202.

are different from traditional types of achievement, and are ultimately at odds with the old norms of natural fertility. They are, above all, a source of autonomy, because they allow the woman to take decisions for herself, and give her the means to treat more equally with other actors in society.

Is there nothing left to study, then, in those countries where only a small number of women have gone to primary school, let alone secondary school and college, and where labour-force participation is almost restricted to market activities and labour in the fields? We argue that the issue of women's autonomy continues to exert a major influence on fertility.

In everyday life there is a good deal of social distance between men and women in general, and husband and wife in particular. This is the issue of 'the world of women' separated from 'the world of men'. Some decisions may belong to women entirely, and it might plausibly be argued that they are 'separate but equal', free of interference within their own domain. Unfortunately, the dimensions of this world of women may be restricted, and subordinated in many ways to men's purposes. If mothers, for example, take fundamental decisions about the rearing of children, they may well take them for the benefit of their husband's kinship group. Besides, even within the world of women, an individual may be subject to the tyrannical authority of the mother-in-law, acting *in loco mariti*. True autonomy of the kind that is obtained by access to the market and financial independence opens doors beyond the world of women.

Our topic, then, is not really the status or the condition of women *per se*, but the extent to which women, and married women above all, are taking decisions which affect their own fertility. We will focus on how women's lack of autonomy, and, to a lesser extent, of power and prestige, influences their ability to control their lives, and mostly their fertility. The condition of women and their reproduction cannot be disentangled from the local culture. Natural fertility is still the norm in the two urban environments used for our case study. It is, therefore, convenient to treat the subject of this chapter, women's autonomy and fertility, systematically by using the device of the classification of the proximate determinants of fertility.

The Background of the Study

Bamako, the capital of Mali, and Bobo-Dioulasso, the second town of Burkina Faso, are situated in the Sahel region of French-speaking Africa. These are poor, dry, and landlocked countries. Bamako is 97 per cent Muslim; the Bambara constitute the main ethnic group, and their language is the language of common intercourse in Bamako. Bobo-Dioulasso is approximately 60 per cent Muslim, 30 per cent Christian; the remaining 10 per cent, who are mainly recent immigrants from the north, still adhere to traditional religion.[13] The main ethnic group is the Mossi, who immigrated from the

TABLE 3.1. *Selected characteristics of women who had a child in 1982 in Bobo-Dioulasso and 1983 in Bamako* (%)

Characteristics	Bobo-Dioulasso	Bamako
Muslim	60.5	96.6
Christians	29.7	1.0
Other	9.8	n.a.
Unmarried	7.7	15.5
In polygamous union	36.1	30.1
Wage-earners	2.6	6.5
No schooling	76.1	68.9
Primary school	18.1	15.0
Secondary school	4.9	9.9
Secondary +	0.9	5.5
Still breast-feeding at 2 years	18.4	47.0
Have heard of contraception*	15.8	12.2
Have used contraception*	12.9	2.9
Median age of child at resuming sexual relations (months)	12.0	3.3
Median age of child at weaning (months)	18.5	22.7
Median length of amenorrhea (months)	13.0	15.2

* In Bobo-Dioulasso traditional contraception is included.

plateaux north of Ouagadougou, and the Bobo constitute the indigenous group (see Table 3.1). Both sites, finally, are characterized by very low educational levels of women, and by minimum participation in wage-work.

The two towns have been the site of multi-round infant and child mortality surveys (known as EMIS). In Bamako 12,000 births, and in Bobo-Dioulasso 8,000 births, were recorded during one year, and then followed up for two years. The two surveys contain a wealth of data on the socio-economic and demographic characteristics of the mother. The periodic re-survey of women for twenty-four months made it possible to investigate their post-partum behaviour and the circumstances of the arrival of the next child. We used

[13] S. Coulibaly, 'Religion, Philosophy and Fertility: The Case of Upper Volta', in I. Pool and S. Coulibaly (eds.), *Demographic Transition and Cultural Continuity in the Sahel* (Ithaca, NY, 1977), p. 98.

this survey as a frame to select a small sub-sample of women who were still under observation, with their child alive, at the end of the two-year panel study.

In Bobo-Dioulasso (1983) and in Bamako (1984) we interviewed eighty women who had a child between approximately 25 and 27 months old. In Bobo, we selected forty Mossi women and forty Bobo women, and in Bamako we also selected eighty women, including a majority of Bambara and some Fulani, Sarakole, Malinke, and others. The sample was equally divided between younger women (less than 30 years old) and older women (30 years old or older). All women had a child of the same age. The project was aimed at gathering detailed information on the proximate determinants of fertility and on the women's perceptions of, and aspirations about, fertility and family life. By talking at length with these women, we gained plentiful information on their roles as mothers, and on their relations with their husbands.

The Proximate Determinants of Fertility

> We do not allow a girl to choose a husband for herself, we choose for her. Now the girls are giving us trouble in this respect, and the trouble arises through a thing called love. We parents do not comprehend this at all.[14]

We will discuss here 'the high-priority proximate determinants' of fertility.[15] These include those that are directly related to exposure to the risk of pregnancy—that is, the system of nuptiality, with early women's age at marriage, a large difference between ages of the spouses, and the polygyny that results. In a second section, we will consider abstinence, breast-feeding, and contraception together, because they are linked in what we call the ABC complex. We will try to relate every determinant of fertility to the behaviour of women and to local customs. The point is to show the link that exists between the condition of women, and particularly their autonomy, and high, uncontrolled fertility.

Exposure to the Risk of Pregnancy

The age at marriage is very low for women in the Sahel, as in much of west Africa, and this serves to maximize the time of exposure to the risk of fertility. Before marriage, girls are exposed to unwanted pregnancies, a

---

[14] Cape of Good Hope Blue Book, *Report and Proceeding of the Commission on Native Laws and Customs* (facsimile repr.; Cape Town, 1883), p. 304.

[15] J. Bongaarts, 'What can Future Surveys Tell us about the Proximate Determinants of Fertility?', *International Family Planning Perspectives*, 11 (1985), pp. 86–90.

circumstance that is dreaded by their own families but tolerated by society at large, where there are lots of young men willing to take advantage of unprotected girls. The danger reinforces the norm of early marriage for women. Polygyny can only exist on a large scale in societies where men marry at a much older age than women. Polygyny is possible because of the condition of women; it is a factor in high fertility, at least for the group, if not for the individual woman. It affects women's autonomy in contradictory directions, as we shall see presently.

Entry into Conjugal Union

Most women in Bamako and Bobo-Dioulasso do not take any decision about the timing of their marriage, and for many the choice of their future husband is left to their parents. In west Africa, 98 per cent of both men and women will marry. However, men spend a shorter time than women within marriage, because they marry at older ages.[16] Marriage, for a girl, is the time when she moves from the absolute authority of her parents to the absolute authority of her husband. The Sahelian women of Bobo-Dioulasso and Bamako marry young, and they wish their daughters to marry young. A survey during the early 1970s gave an average age at first union of 16.3 years for women in Bobo-Dioulasso.[17] In the multi-round survey, the mean age at first birth was 18.3. If we subtract the nine months of pregnancy plus the waiting time to conception, we obtain an age at marriage of around 17 years. Traditionally, among the Mossi, 17 is the preferred age for the marriage of a woman, and 15 and 19 are acceptable. Fourteen, 16, 18, and 20 are all considered inauspicious ages for a girl to marry.[18] In Bamako, the age at marriage appeared to be even younger, if we can trust the women we interviewed. Many said they wished their daughter would marry at 15, and certainly not later than at 17.

Knowledge of actual age is imperfect, and the normative age is often reported instead. In both Bamako and Bobo-Dioulasso, a majority of the women said they had married at 17. Seventeen is the norm for age at marriage, and also for age at first birth, which are often confounded. When asked about their age, most women would add 17 to the age of their first-born child:

INTERVIEWER. I would like to know your age, the age you have now.
WOMAN [*laugh*]. Do we know our age? I don't know my age. My birth certificate was lost and we never recovered it. I am over 20!
INTERVIEWER. How old is your first child?

[16] H. Ware, 'Female and Male Life-cycles', in C. Oppong (ed.), *Female and Male in West Africa* (London, 1983), pp. 6–31.
[17] Pool and Coulibaly, op. cit. in n. 13, p. 41.
[18] K. Mason, 'A Woman's Place: The Articulation of Structure by Co-Wives and Mothers among the Patrilineal Moose', Ph.D. thesis (University of Chicago, 1988), p. 73.

WOMAN. He must be at least 25 . . . if he is 25, I must be 17 plus 25, how much is that? (Mossi woman).

Another clue to early age at marriage was given by women who remembered their age at first menstruation, or linked it to a special event: 'I had seen my "washing" only once before I left my father's house for the owner of the courtyard's house' (Mossi woman). The use of the periphrase 'owner of the courtyard' in place of 'husband' is symptomatic of the distance between the spouses. A wife should never use her husband's first name. The fact that the husband is usually much older than his wife or wives reinforces gender inequality and men's superiority. In contrast to women, men marry late in the Sahel. The difference between the ages of husband and wife is wide, mostly in polygamous unions (although that is changing among young educated couples, who will often have met at school). In Bamako, the mean difference between the ages of husband and wife was 12.1 years, and 62 per cent of husbands were at least ten years older than their wives. We interviewed third and fourth wives who were ten and fifteen years younger than their husband's oldest child. This difference in age at marriage allows the surplus of women which makes polygyny possible. It also increases the authority of the husbands over their wives, who have often been given to them before they could make an informed choice.

The marriage of a young woman in the Sahel is often the result of a deal between her father and her future husband. It is an alliance between two families, and the woman is a pawn in this alliance. The woman's feelings are taken into account, for it is important that the alliance should last. Although wives today are almost always consulted on the choice of their husband, and have a right of veto, their young age and parental pressure hardly guarantee informed consent. The woman remains a member of her original family, the name of which she will continue to keep and to which she will return in case of dispute, divorce, repudiation, or the death of her husband. Her children do not belong to her, but are children of the family she entered by marriage, and belong to their father.

In our interviews, women were very eloquent when talking about their children, but they rarely mentioned the circumstances of their own marriages. In patriarchal societies, marriage is a traumatizing experience for the young woman, who is separated from her mother, her family, her home, and her friends. She joins a new family, where she is a stranger. She will have to work hard under the authority of her mother-in-law, who immediately adopts a dictatorial attitude to avenge herself for the treatment she once had to endure herself. Her co-wives, and every one in the compound, will test her and take advantage of her until she becomes their ally. She knows that she will never really belong to this house.[19] All the women we talked to

---

[19] D. Bazin-Tardieu, *Femmes du Mali* (Ottawa, 1975); R. Luneau, *Chants de femmes au Mali* (Paris, 1981); D. Paulme, *Femmes d'Afrique noire* (Paris, 1963).

reported how much they missed their mothers, even after many years of separation. But marriage is the door to child-bearing, and motherhood eventually confers on the woman a place in her new home. According to Bazin-Tardieu, the Malian woman finds in her marriage some emancipation, the confirmation of her status as a woman, and the promise of glory with many children.[20]

Parents have reasons for marrying their daughters early. We were struck in Bamako, and to a lesser extent in Bobo-Dioulasso, by the number of women who wanted their daughters to marry at 15 years of age and not later than at 17, even when they were at school. Mothers were questioned about the age at which they would like their daughters to marry: 'There is no question of age . . . when a man asks for her, she will be given away to that person.' (Bambara woman). Some women were reticent about school, for the good reason that 'school is the place where girls get a belly' (Bobo woman), or 'She will come back with something else than a diploma!' (Bambara woman). At least some women opted for school:

Ah! if she is in school . . . she must, first, face her studies and leave marriage alone, when she gets the 'papers' [certificate] she can look at marriage, it is not too late. But, if she is not in school, she has to be married as soon as possible, otherwise she will give birth to a *tampiri* [a child without a father]. (Mossi woman)

In Bobo-Dioulasso and Bamako the traditional insistence on virginity at marriage remains a lively concern of parents. Even though age at marriage is early, there is a risk of pregnancy outside marriage, and many young women, including schoolgirls, become pregnant. This usually precipitates the marriage to the father of the child. If the man leaves them as single mothers, this is a shameful experience for them and their family.

Girls, however, often assume a measure of pre-marital sexual freedom, and becoming pregnant is not an uncommon way of engaging the marriage negotiations between the two families. Some men will only marry women who have proved their fertility. Nevertheless, marriage remains the official door to motherhood, and illegitimacy is feared.

Nowadays, young urban women are caught between traditional and modern ways. They are faced with a dilemma: quit school and be given into marriage by their father, often to a much older man, sometimes as a second or third wife, or finish school without the certainty of finding a husband. There is a conflict between the two roads to feminine accomplishment: the traditional road to early marriage, and the new one through education and participation in the labour force. But each road has its own hurdles. School-girls run the risk of extramarital pregnancy, delayed marriage, and perhaps permanent celibacy. Many men are wary of overeducated women, who are too independent. And for many mothers a husband is, by any reckoning, a

[20] Bazin-Tardieu, op. cit. in n. 19, p. 90.

bigger asset for their daughters than schooling. Some mothers expressed the feeling that, if he wanted an educated wife, the man might pay for her education himself, but that they were not willing to run the risk of pregnancy that went together with schooling.

Polygyny

Polygyny continues to prevail in Bamako and Bobo-Dioulasso. In Bamako, *Le Code du mariage et de la tutelle* was promulgated in 1962, and constituted a great novelty for Mali (and for Africa). It included a provision which offered a choice between monogamy and polygamy. It is 'the man who takes the engagement not to contract another marriage before the dissolution of the previous one'.[21] This really means that the groom may choose (in principle with the consent of his fiancée) the form of his marriage, and commit himself for the future. Regrettably, the law does not mention the opinion of the other partner. According to our interviewers, men who signed up for monogamy continue to take second wives and threaten divorce when their spouses do not accept that decision.

In the Bobo-Dioulasso survey, 48 per cent of the women over 30 years old were in a polygamous union. Among the 160 women we interviewed, sixty were in polygamous unions. The institution continues to remain the norm for married life, and women are ambiguous about it. It has some aspects that limit, and others that enhance their freedom from marital authority and the drudgery of lonely household labour. Most women said they got along very well with their co-wife or co-wives. Among monogamous wives, many said they wanted a co-wife. The most important reasons for wanting a co-wife were companionship, help, and freedom to trade and to visit one's mother. Educated women were most often opposed to polygyny.

A Mossi woman summarized the disadvantages of being an only wife: 'If you are alone, every day you cook, you sweep the courtyard, you wash, you don't have time to trade, to make money, you never rest, you cannot go to the village to visit your mother.' Sometimes the first wife even takes the initiative in suggesting that a second wife, who will be burdened with the most tiresome jobs in the household, should be procured. Besides, a co-wife is often a companion. Many women call their co-wives 'my little sister' or 'my big sister', depending on age and rank. Kathryn Mason has reported how rural Mossi co-wives help each other, and enjoy each other's company.[22] We were often told in Bamako and in Bobo-Dioulasso that being alone was 'sad and not good'. Men are rarely home, and women dread solitude combined with loads of work. Men and women live in two separate worlds; spouses have usually little to say to each other, their relations are discreet,

---

[21] Ibid., p. 103.
[22] Mason, op. cit. in n. 18, p. 85.

they are not supposed to express their feelings for one another.[23] Finally, it would seem that polygamous wives are more free, less dependent, and have more time for a private life of their own; in sum, they have more autonomy. Jealousy is, of course, not unknown, but from the women's point of view it is always the fault of the husband, who treats his preferred wife, often the youngest or the most recent, differently.

The institution of polygyny has undeniable positive effects on individual women and their sense of freedom. In the aggregate, it is part of a system where women are subjected to external authority—that of the husband, of the first wife, of the mother-in-law—largely because it is predicated on a large age difference between spouses, and sets the interests of women and their children against those of other women and children. (To be fair, the Sahelian systems that we observed take great pains to ensure the harmony of the compound, and to mix children with minimum distinction among lines of half-siblings. This is not the case among the Yoruba, for example, who practise strict division among co-wives. Goody has noted that the word for co-wife, in most languages of west Africa, means 'the jealous one' or the rival.[24])

As for the effects on women's autonomy, we must distinguish between the individual and the aggregate effects of polygyny on fertility. Much research has been published on the effect of polygyny on the fertility of individual women, and the results suggest that it is slightly lower than in monogamous unions; the main effect, among the Sereer of Senegal, is due to the large age difference between partners and the decline in the fertility of older men.[25] The survey in Bobo-Dioulasso showed about the same timing for resumption of sexual relations after a birth for monogamous and polygamous wives. The percentage of women who had resumed intercourse within six months of birth was 26 per cent for monogamous, and 29 per cent for polygamous wives. After one year it was 50 per cent for both groups. Polygyny is regulated by rules and conventions, one of them being that cooking and sleeping with the husband go together. According to Luneau, the Bambara see a close relation between the two, since 'the woman has two roles, she is the one who gives life and nourishes the family'.[26] After menopause, the Bambara woman does not cook any more, and for many women having sexual relations becomes indecent. The effect of lowering the fertility of individual women should not lead us to believe that polygyny is anything but a fertility-maximizing strategy for society as a whole. It maximizes the time

[23] P. Erny, *Les Premiers pas dans la vie de l'enfant d'Afrique noire* (Paris, 1972).
[24] J. Goody, *Production and Reproduction: A Comparative Study of the Domestic Domain* (Cambridge, 1976), p. 43.
[25] M. Garenne and É. van de Walle, 'Polygyny and Fertility among the Sereer of Senegal', *Population Studies*, 43 (1989), pp. 267–83.
[26] Luneau, op. cit. in n. 19, p. 113.

spent in unions by women, by making possible a very young age of brides, and the absorption of widows and divorced women as second wives.

Thus, polygyny, autonomy, and fertility are linked. Early marriage, little choice on the part of the woman, wide difference between ages of spouses, sharing a husband with other wives, do not confer a high status on the woman. The young wife has no option but to gain status through reproduction. On the other hand, polygyny grants some freedom and power to the women in their own world.

In sum, nuptiality in general plays an important role in curtailing women's autonomy. It is symbolic that women who have eschewed the bonds of marriage and conducted their sexual life outside the traditional forms are often called *free women*. It is particularly in cities that free unions have flourished, and they have sometimes afforded women opportunities and bargaining positions that they did not possess previously.[27] The effect of these changes on fertility are difficult to ascertain. It may well be that extramarital relations are one of the paths through which fertility control is making progress in sub-Saharan Africa.

The Abstinence–Breast-feeding–Contraception Complex

> A mother should not go to her husband while she has a child she is suckling. If she does, the child gets thin, he dries up, he won't get strong, he won't be healthy. If she goes after one year, the child won't get strong, but if she goes after two years it is nothing, he is already strong before that, it does not matter if she conceives again after two years.[28]

Women's autonomy in matters of reproduction is likely to be a crucial issue in any discussion of gender inequality, because the woman's role as a mother is simultaneously irreplaceable and necessary for the man's own ends. The question of who has control over reproduction has been a focus of recent anthropological literature on Africa, from Boserup to Meillassoux, from Goody to Lesthaeghe.[29] The consensus seems to be that reproductive powers are valued, and are not controlled by women themselves. The subordinate status of women is a result of the economic conditions of traditional agriculture, and it has been aggravated by foreign influences.[30]

---

[27] K. Little, *African Women in Towns: An Aspect of Africa's Social Revolution* (Cambridge, 1973).

[28] M. F. Smith, *Baba of Karo: A Woman of the Muslim Hausa* (London, 1954), p. 148.

[29] E. Boserup, *Woman's Role in Economic Development* (New York, 1970); C. Meillassoux, *Femmes, greniers et capitaux* (Paris, 1977); Goody, op. cit. in n. 24; R. Lesthaeghe, 'On the Social Control of Human Reproduction', *Population and Development Review*, 6 (1980), pp. 527–48.

[30] Kamuzora, op. cit. in n. 8, p. 315.

Hence the potential of domination and exploitation, and the inevitability of conflict between the sexes.

Karen Oppenheim Mason has suggested that the recent concern for women's status in theories of fertility decline is linked to the recognition that the interests of the members of the couple and the family may not coincide, and, therefore, that the incentive to reduce fertility may originate in different motivations for each sex.[31] In a regime of natural fertility, too, there is conflict between the spouses on each of the proximate determinants. This is particularly true in the area of the most important interval variables that we call the ABC complex: abstinence, breast-feeding, and contraception. The partner who controls the ABC complex largely controls fertility.

By marriage, the man and his kinship group acquire rights over the woman's powers of reproduction. This includes sexual rights of the husband, which are tempered by the woman's reasonable claim to periods of abstinence in the interest of her own health and that of the new-born baby. This is obviously an area of conflict between husband and wife, and in all parts of Africa it is strongly regulated by tradition. There is a fairly·widespread (although, as we shall see, by no means universal) consensus that the period of breast-feeding is a period of sexual abstinence. The duration of breast-feeding and of abstinence may be declining, and contraception has slowly been making its way as a substitute mechanism for birth-spacing. In this section, we review systematically the interrelations between women's control over fertility, as they are mediated through the ABC complex.

Sexual Abstinence

In Bobo-Dioulasso we encountered a typical culture of long abstinence, motivated by a concern for the health of the child. The Burkinabe women whom we interviewed gave us two main reasons for abiding by the taboo while breast-feeding a baby. First, they feared pregnancy, and, secondly, they believed that their milk would become polluted by sexual relations. The sperm (or blood in the local culture) of the man, particularly if he is not the father of the baby, would contaminate the milk of the woman, and the baby at the breast would suffer from diarrhoea and vomiting. Besides, 'allowing one's body some time to rest' and 'spacing pregnancies' were felt to be of first importance for the health of the mother and her ability to carry further pregnancies to term.

Marital abstinence is mostly a woman's business, and sexual relations have, without question, more important consequences for the woman than for the man. Still, it is always the husband who takes decisions about the sexual life of his wife or wives, and he will often press for the early resumption of relations. It is an area of conflict between men and women.

[31] Mason, op. cit. in n. 2, p. 4.

The nursing woman is in a position where she wants to please her husband and keep him, and, at the same time, she is afraid that intercourse will spoil her milk and that her baby will fall sick. Her choices are, either to refuse the husband, who will look elsewhere if there is no co-wife; to accept the husband but 'wash herself well' between intercourse and feeding the baby; or, the most modern way, which needs the participation of the husband, to practise *coitus interruptus*. The last choice was mentioned only two or three times during our interviews.

Informal conversations with women seem to suggest that wives (with the exception of educated women) almost never ask their husband for sexual relations, because 'it is indecent if it comes from the woman'. The decision is generally the husband's. The wife has to accept; she can only refuse if she has a good reason. Some women with a child at the breast said they preferred to be beaten, rather than to agree. Besides, in Bamako, many women to whom we talked used aphrodisiacs and simulated pleasure in order to please their husbands.

It is likely that the intercourse taboos following a birth lasted longer in the past, if one can trust the reports of earlier anthropologists. Delobsom related that the Mossi 'must rely on the mother's milk to feed their babies and must, therefore, wait two to three years before resuming sexual relations with a nursing mother'.[32] In Bobo-Dioulasso the median interval between birth and resumption of sexual relations was twelve months, according to the EMIS Survey of 1983. Even more striking is the transformation of the post-partum taboo in Bamako. Henry reported in 1910 a sexual taboo upward 'of three to four years completed' among the Bambara of Mali.[33] The mean length of abstinence following the birth of a child is now three months among the Bambara of Bamako.

The Islamic rule which prohibits sexual relations during the forty nights that follow the birth of a child has become a norm which almost dictates the resumption of sexual activity at the end of that time.[34] It is linked to the unclean state of the woman after parturition or during menstruation; any idea of spacing births and protecting the baby has been pushed into the background. A Bambara woman explains: 'When you give birth, before going back to the husband, you wait the 40 days, that is when your belly's aches are soothed and when all the blood of the delivery has flowed out of your body.'

---

[32] Cited by R. Schoenmaekers, I. H. Shah, R. Lesthaeghe, and O. Tambashe, 'The Child-Spacing Tradition and the Post-Partum Taboo in Tropical Africa: Anthropological Evidence', in H. Page and R. Lesthaeghe (eds.), *Child-Spacing in Tropical Africa: Traditions and Change* (London, 1981), p. 53.

[33] J. Henry, *L'Âme d'un people Africain: Les Bambara, leur vie psychique ethnique, sociale, religieuse* (Munster, 1910), p. 188.

[34] É. van de Walle and F. van de Walle, 'Postpartum Sexual Abstinence in Tropical Africa', paper presented at the IUSSP Seminar on the Biomedical and Demographic Determinants of Human Reproduction, Johns Hopkins University, 1988.

The diffusion of the forty-day norm is observed in much of the sub-Saharan belt where Islam is spreading. Undoubtedly, it suits the men to resume relations sooner. Paradoxically, religion gives them leave to invade an area where the women used to exert control according to custom. The idea is expressed powerfully in a passage of *Baba of Karo*, the memoirs of an old Hausa woman:

But if her husband desires her, then in the day she carries her child, at night she carries her husband—this is what pleases Allah. He does not like argumentative women. But it is not right that she should sleep with her husband for two years; if he insists she should wear the kolanut charm. As you know, there is medicine to make the pregnancy 'go to sleep', but that is not a good thing.[35]

Allah does not like argumentative women! That the woman should wear the 'kolanut charm' hints at contraception, which could substitute for abstinence as a spacing mechanism. And 'put the pregnancy to sleep' is a reference to abortion.

If Islam is a powerful solvent of post-partum traditions, there are other forces at work, more in line with gender equality, that go in the same direction. It is arguable that the practice of abstinence is only possible in cultures where the conjugal link is weak, where polygyny exists, where a single wife is never sure of remaining her husband's only partner, and mostly where the extended family prevails and emotional ties between husband and wife constitute a potential threat to the solidarity of the patrilineal group.

In Bamako and in Bobo-Dioulasso, during the evening, one is struck by the absence of men in the family compound, where women and children are relaxing, chatting, and joking. Wives take the nightly absences of men for granted. There are apparently more love affairs than are admitted, on the part of men, and on the part of young women. According to Luneau, 'there is not a Bambara man nor a Bambara woman who did not have, at least once, a lover'.[36]

Excision is practised almost universally in Bamako. It is the prerogative of older women to make decisions about this. The Senegalese feminist Awa Thiam inveighs against the custom: 'An excised woman is often reduced to the state of vagina and reproducer . . . her pleasure would constitute a danger for the man . . . but the paradox is that the men prefer women who are not excised.'[37]

A new view of the couple, and of romantic love and companionate marriage, is making headway, as elsewhere in Africa. The Caldwells have described how 'the practice of post partum abstinence now constitutes the

---

[35] Smith, op. cit. in n. 28, p. 148.
[36] Luneau, op. cit. in n. 19, p. 132.
[37] A. Thiam, *La Parole aux négresses* (Paris, 1978), p. 90.

major crisis of the Ibadan family' and 'the potential that the abstinence period possesses for destroying marriages':

Many of [the husbands] do not expect to have to go outside to find their pleasures, and many put increasing pressure on apprehensive and confused wives for an early resumption of sexual relations . . . The wife is afraid of alienating her husband's affection, of losing him altogether, or of his bringing home a new wife . . .[38]

The resumption of sexual relations is often the subject of negotiations between more equal partners. At the same time, a more scientific view of biological mechanisms is diffused by the media and the medical establishment. The idea that sperm poisons the milk is questioned, as are notions about the uncleanliness of the nursing mother.

Breast-Feeding

Karen Oppenheim Mason has discussed the relationship between breast-feeding and the status of women by considering the effect of education and employment.[39] Participation in the labour force has a mechanical effect on the intensity of breast-feeding, because it is difficult to combine the demands of the two activities. The persistence of traditional, prolonged, on-demand breast-feeding in our two urban communities is only possible because very few women work in the modern sector (2.6 per cent in Bobo-Dioulasso and 6.5 per cent in Bamako), and those who have jobs benefit from very liberal policies. The Burkinabe and Malian legislations grant a maternity leave of three months to women working in the formal sector. When the woman returns to work, she is entitled to go home in the middle of the day to feed her baby. Moreover, a survey in Bamako showed that women with babies, and mothers of large families, were known for their absenteeism.[40]

In this chapter we are concerned with another line of relationship between breast-feeding and women's autonomy. At first sight, breast-feeding is uniquely part of the woman's domain. The mother lives in symbiosis with her child; until it is weaned, the baby is always with her, on her back during the day, in her bed at night, at her breast day and night. In Bamako and Bobo-Dioulasso, the mother alone takes the decisions about breast-feeding, giving supplementary food, and weaning. Some respondents were breast-feeding children who were 27 months old during our interviews. Extended breast-feeding on demand is still the rule, with the few exceptions of women working in the modern sector.[41] This link between mother and child may be

[38] J. C. Caldwell and P. Caldwell, 'The Limitation of Family Size in Ibadan City, Nigeria: An Explanation of its Comparative Rarity Derived from In-Depth Interviews', in É. van de Walle, op. cit. in n. 8, pp. 243–45.

[39] Mason, op. cit. in n. 2, pp. 50–51.

[40] Bazin-Tardieu, op. cit. in n. 19, pp. 147–49.

[41] F. van de Walle, 'The Diversity of Fertility Behavior: Bobo-Dioulasso, Bamako, Yaoundé and Ngayokheme', in É. van de Walle, op. cit. in n. 8, pp. 215–31.

at the root of the love, respect, and devotion that her adult sons and daughters will express to her during her lifetime.

In our study sites, the decision to wean was taken solely by the mother, who often did not tell her husband about it. There is extremely little knowledge about the physiological effect of lactation on post-partum amenorrhoea, and no conscious use of breast-feeding to space births, except to the extent that the husband will stay away from the nursing mother. Usually, the child is weaned with a new baby in mind. The main reason for weaning is the beginning of a new pregnancy. Most women agree than one cannot feed two at the same time, because 'the child in the womb will take the blood from the breast' (Bobo woman; the concepts of blood, milk, and sperm are often related). Moreover, the milk of a pregnant woman will deteriorate: 'it will make the child sick; the child will vomit and will have diarrhoea' (Mossi woman). Some older women said they had never weaned a child, and the child was said to 'wean itself'. Then, in many cases, no conscious decision is taken and the child refuses the breast when it has had enough, or when it becomes ashamed because older siblings are making fun of it. The mean ages at weaning were respectively 21 and 19 months for Bobo-Dioulasso and Bamako.

Customs relating to weaning differ widely in Africa, and the authority of the mother in the process is not as general in other places as it is in Bamako and Bobo-Dioulasso. In Ngayokheme, in the Sahel region of Senegal, the husband orders his wife to remove her child from the breast without advance notice, usually 'when the child has [lived through] two rainy seasons'.[42] In a rural setting of Zimbabwe, the child's grandmother or aunt must endorse the parents' decision to wean. A woman cannot terminate breast-feeding without instruction from mother and/or sister-in-law, 'for to do so would imply that the woman is getting involved in extra-marital sex'.[43]

Contraception

Even though contraception is the proximate determinant that best explains fertility differentials among populations today,[44] it was not an important one among the Sahelian women.

Several observers have noted that men's opposition to contraception in sub-Saharan Africa is often based on a fear that the wife will gain sexual autonomy. Olusanya, for example, noted the fear of Yoruba parents that their daughters will misbehave, and the fear of Yoruba husbands that their wives will take lovers, if they can rely on methods other than abstinence to

[42] Ibid., p. 221.
[43] M. Mhloyi, 'The Proximate Determinants and their Socio-Cultural Determinants: The Case of Two Rural Settings in Zimbabwe', in É. van de Walle, op. cit. in n. 8, p. 138.
[44] Bongaarts, op. cit. in n. 15.

avoid births.[45] Mhloyi reported from Zimbabwe that 'modern contraception is still not acceptable', even for men of the young generation; approximately 60 per cent of that group 'perceive it as a practice by prostitutes'.[46] When asked what they would do if they found their wives using contraception without their knowledge, they responded: 'If my wife is using contraception without my knowledge it means that she must be having extra-marital sex, she can only do that at her home' (young man Chipinge).

Similar fears were expressed by some of our male respondents in Bobo-Dioulasso. They were often not opposed to contraception as such, but expressed clear reservations about free access by their wives. It was a subject that men might discuss, but was clearly unsuitable for women's conversation. We asked a man, who had enumerated all the modern methods of contraception, whether the idea of using one of these could appeal to one of his wives. He answered: 'Neither I, nor my wives, will ever do that. These matters are discussed outside the home; my wives would never dare to talk about that' (Bobo man). Husbands flaunted their own ability to 'count' (i.e. to use the rhythm method), but believed that their wives would be incompetent to do so. We were surprised to find out that men were much more knowledgeable than women about modern contraception and were better informed about family planning than their wives thought they were. Among the twenty-five husbands interviewed, five had, at one point, used family planning on their own initiative. They claimed to be responsible for contraceptive decisions in the family.[47] Family planning was still a very new notion in Bobo-Dioulasso at the time of our survey.

In Bamako, concern for family planning developed from needs expressed by urban dwellers, and as early as 1969 the Union des Femmes Maliennes was aware of the growing social problem of unwanted pregnancies and inadequately spaced births and anxious that something should be done. In 1972 a pilot project was begun, the first one in western French-speaking Africa. Yet contraception is little used, and the problems encountered elsewhere in Africa exist here, too. There is widespread awareness of contraception, but only few women want or dare to use it. Moreover, the large difference between the ages of the spouses in both Bamako and Bobo-Dioulasso limits communication between spouses, and with it the acceptance of contraception. Finally, women do not take decisions in domains where they cannot act by themselves. The public health establishment has clearly recognized that women have no independent right of access to contraception, and a woman needs the authorization of her husband to receive help from a

[45] P. O. Olusanya, 'Nigeria: Cultural Barriers to Family Planning among the Yorubas', *Studies in Family Planning*, 37 (1969), pp. 13–16.

[46] Mhloyi, op. cit. in n. 43, p. 145.

[47] F. van de Walle and B. Traoré, *Attitudes of Men and Women towards Contraception in Bobo-Dioulasso* (African Demographic Working Paper, 13; Population Studies Center, University of Pennsylvania, 1986).

family planning clinic in Bamako and in Bobo-Dioulasso. This is yet another sign that men claim the right to control fertility, and that they feel that it would subvert their authority if women were able to have independent access to contraception.

In sum, the systematic review of the proximate determinants of fertility, and how they allow decision-making power to the women, provides a picture of rather limited autonomy. The husband keeps control over married life and the couple's sexuality and reproduction. Most women face their situation in good spirit; they do not worry much or argue about their status or their dependence on their husbands, nor do they challenge their role in the family compound. If they have been successful at giving their husband and his family several sons, they find a place among their in-laws. Women often have good relations with their co-wives and enjoy their company; they share the same life and the same problems. With age and many children, women gain status and authority and find more time and freedom to do what interests them.

Conclusion

The question of women's autonomy in matters of reproduction must be answered in detail by looking at the various proximate determinants of natural fertility. On all counts, it appears that the women do little more than inhabit, and to some extent administer, a domain which belongs to the men. They are at a disadvantage in contracting unions, because of their lack of authority, which is compounded by the large difference between their age and that of their spouses. The security provided by marriage is a compensation for the lack of freedom it entails. Furthermore, the male regulates the ABC complex jealously.

4 Changing Family Ties, Women's Position, and Low Fertility

EVA M. BERNHARDT

Does the emancipation of women inevitably lead to a situation in which too few children are born? This question was already of concern to early advocates of women's rights, such as Mary Wollstonecraft and John Stuart Mill.[1] They seem to have agreed, however, that this worry for the future of the human species was unwarranted.

When, around the turn of the present century, women struggled for the right to vote and for other civil and economic rights, fertility was generally high, so that the possible fertility-inhibiting effect of women's emancipation was rarely used as an argument in opposition to emancipation. Lower fertility, at the time, was often regarded as equivalent to social progress. During the 1960s concern over the impending population explosion in Third World countries became prominent. Raising the status of women—for example, by giving them education and stimulating an interest in things other than producing children—was often suggested as one method of slowing down population growth in the less developed countries.[2] The corresponding argument has also been used for the developed countries. As late as 1972 one of the contributors to the Report of the American Commission on Population Growth and the American Future strongly recommended improvements in the status of women as one method of lowering fertility in the United States, which at that time was still fairly high.[3] During the last ten years or so, fertility has declined in most industrialized countries to levels insufficient to ensure long-term population replacement, whilst there has been a substantial increase in the labour-force participation of women. Concern over the possible negative effect of a too far-reaching emancipation of Western women on the birth rate has since come to predominate both in academic and non-academic debates.

---

[1] M. Wollstonecraft, *A Vindication of the Rights of Women* (London, 1792); J. S. Mill, *The Subjection of Women* (London, 1869).

[2] See, e.g., J. Blake, 'Demographic Science and the Redirection of Population Policy', in M. C. Sheps and J. C. Ridley, *Public Health and Population Change: Current Research Issues* (Pittsburgh, 1965), pp. 41–69.

[3] S. Keller, 'The Future Status of Women in America', in C. Westoff and R. Parke (eds.), *Commission on Population Growth and the American Future* (Washington, 1972), pp. 267–88.

Norman Ryder, for example, has stated that 'our past success at population replacement, throughout all of human history, has been conditional on the discriminatory treatment of women'.[4] If such discriminatory treatment were to cease, or at least to be sharply reduced, the inevitable result would be below-replacement fertility. This view seems to have been shared by another American demographer, Nathan Keyfitz: 'Low fertility is the ultimate natural outcome of gender equality.'[5] Thus, in the judgement of these two distinguished scholars, there is no way in which it is possible to achieve both sex equality and sufficient fertility.

Ridley has pointed to the conceptual problem encountered in any discussion of the roles and status of women.[6] Status or position is a relative term which implies some kind of ranking. The 'role' concept, on the other hand, refers to actual or expected patterns of behaviour, which are associated with a particular social position. According to Mason,[7] most definitions of women's status focus on one of three basic dimensions of gender inequality: inequality in prestige, inequality in power, and inequality in access to or control over resources. The concept remains elusive, however, since it is empirically as well as conceptually a multidimensional phenomenon. Moreover, the degree of gender inequality may differ at different stages of a woman's life cycle.

The object of this chapter is to try and clarify the issue of how changing family ties and changes in women's position in society are related to below-replacement fertility. By 1978 indices of net reproduction were below unity in most Western European countries and in the non-European English-speaking countries overseas. Thus, there is at present a decade's experience of below-replacement fertility. It is beyond the scope of this chapter to provide an overall presentation of recent fertility trends. These have been documented for Europe by Blayo,[8] and for the United States, Canada, Australia, and New Zealand by Preston.[9] As fertility levels in the socialist countries of Eastern Europe have generally stayed at or above replacement levels, these countries will be omitted from the discussion which follows.

It is my object to discuss the question of gender equality and fertility in such a way that it can be generalized to all countries in which fertility is

---

[4] N. B. Ryder, 'The Future of American Fertility', *Social Forces*, 26 (1979), pp. 359–70.

[5] N. Keyfitz, 'The Family that does not Reproduce itself', in K. Davis, M. S. Bernstam, and R. Ricardo-Campbell (eds.), *Below Replacement Fertility in Industrial Societies: Causes, Consequences, Policies*, Supplement to *Population and Development Review*, 12 (1986), pp. 139–54.

[6] J. C. Ridley, 'On the Consequences of Demographic Change for the Role and Status of Women', in Westoff and Parke, op. cit. in n. 3, pp. 289–304.

[7] K. Oppenheim Mason, *The Status of Women: A Review of its Relationship to Fertility and Mortality* (Population Studies Center; Ann Arbor, Mich., 1984).

[8] C. Blayo, 'La Fécondité en Europe depuis 1960: Convergence ou divergence?', in Central Statistical Office of Finland, *European Population Conference 1987, Plenaries* (Helsinki, 1987), pp. 47–112.

[9] S. Preston, 'The Decline of Fertility in Non-European Industrialized Countries', in Supplement to *Population and Development Review*, 12 (1986), op. cit. in n. 5, pp. 26–47.

below replacement level. However, I shall draw extensively on the situation in Sweden, both because it is the country with which I am most familiar, and also because Sweden provides an interesting example, as it is in many ways a pioneer in the field of gender equality. I shall begin by discussing gender roles in the context of the family, and proceed to an examination of the position of women outside the family—that is, primarily the increase in the labour-force participation of women in Western societies and its implication for gender equality, and for fertility.

Cohabitation and Family Formation

In all societies almost the whole of reproduction occurs within the framework of the family. The term *family* may have different meanings in different societies, but child-bearing by single individuals outside any kind of family unit remains a marginal phenomenon. This is true even in a country like Sweden, where nowadays almost half of all children are born outside marriage. Most of these 'illegitimate' children are born to parents who are living together in a non-marital union (and of whom a substantial proportion will marry shortly after the birth of the child). Child-bearing by unmarried, non-cohabiting women has in fact decreased in Sweden during recent years.[10]

It is, therefore, natural to begin a discussion of below-replacement fertility with an examination of the contemporary family. For a penetrating discussion of the family in Europe today, and its prospects for the future, the reader is referred to Hoffman-Nowotny,[11] and for two different views on the contemporary Swedish family to Hoem and Hoem[12] and Popenoe.[13] Hoffman-Nowotny contended that, despite the general decline in marriage rates, the propensity to form couples—that is, to live in partner-relationships—has remained fairly stable, at least in the European context. In those countries in which marriage rates are lowest, above all in Sweden and Denmark, marriage has to a very large extent been replaced by cohabitation. Pair-bonding as such has, therefore, hardly decreased in popularity; indeed, one would suspect that, on an annual basis, more couples are formed than ever before, since breakdowns in relationships are to a large extent followed by new partnerships, though not necessarily by marriage.[14] If such new(?)

---

[10] E. Bernhardt and B. Hoem, 'Cohabitation and Social Background: Trends Observed for Swedish Women Born between 1936 and 1960', *European Journal of Population*, 1 (1985), pp. 375–95.

[11] H. J. Hoffman-Nowotny, 'The Future of the Family', in Central Statistical Office of Finland, op. cit. in n. 8, pp. 113–200.

[12] B. Hoem and J. Hoem, 'The Swedish Family: Aspects of Contemporary Developments', *Journal of Family Issues*, 9 (1988), pp. 397–424.

[13] D. Popenoe, 'Beyond the Nuclear Family: A Statistical Portrait of the Changing Family in Sweden', *Journal of Marriage and the Family*, 49 (1987), pp. 179–83.

[14] Results from the Swedish Fertility Survey have shown that the proportion of women who,

TABLE 4.1. *Sexual unions, marital and non-marital, by sex and age, Sweden, 1975, 1980, and 1985*

Age group	% of population in marital or non-marital union			% non-marital of all unions		
	1975	1980	1985	1975	1980	1985
MEN						
20–24	26.9	23.3	21.3	70.8	80.5	86.2
25–29	61.6	55.4	50.5	35.5	50.7	61.4
30–34	75.0	71.9	66.6	14.6	25.8	36.6
35–39	79.0	76.9	74.0	7.6	13.9	22.3
40–44	79.8	78.0	76.5	5.5	8.9	14.6
45–49	78.9	78.1	77.0	4.6	6.8	10.8
WOMEN						
20–24	50.5	45.8	40.3	56.8	69.3	77.9
25–29	74.9	70.7	65.3	22.7	36.9	48.1
30–34	76.9	79.2	75.7	9.5	18.0	25.2
35–39	81.1	80.5	78.2	5.6	10.2	17.1
40–44	82.6	80.4	77.9	4.4	7.3	9.4
45–49	81.7	80.1	77.6	3.9	5.9	9.2

Source: Census.

forms of relationship as 'living apart together' (or 'commuter marriages' as they have been called)[15] are included, the proportion of persons of reproductive age who are truly single would be even smaller.

This does not mean that the proportions of those who live outside any form of sexual union are negligible. The figures in Table 4.1 from the Swedish censuses of 1975, 1980, and 1985 show that, even among men and women in their thirties, between 25 and 30 per cent lived outside a sexual union, and the proportions have been increasing over time. Nevertheless, given the relatively high level of the divorce rate,[16] it seems remarkable that

at any given age, have experienced more than one partner-relationship (marriage or consensual union) has increased dramatically in recent cohorts, but that the average length of time lived in a partner relationship has increased as well; see Statistiska Centralbyran, *Kvinnor och barn: Intervjuer med Kvinnor om familj och arbete* (Stockholm, 1982).

[15] We use the term 'commuter marriage' to denote a man and a woman (married or unmarried) who live together in a stable relationship, but maintain separate households, either because they work in different places or like 'to have a place of their own', or for some other reason. The prevalence of this type of relationship in different countries is not known.

[16] The dissolution rates of non-marital unions are even higher.

TABLE 4.2. *Cohabitation, by different marital status groups, sex, and age, Sweden 1985* (%)

Age group	Never married	Currently married	Divorced	Widowed
		MEN		
20–24	19.0	92.0	21.7	—
25–29	39.2	94.9	28.5	15.0
30–34	44.4	96.2	34.6	27.2
35–39	42.2	96.9	35.1	34.9
40–44	33.3	97.1	34.0	27.1
45–49	23.2	97.5	31.3	23.9
		WOMEN		
20–24	34.8	92.4	27.2	13.5
25–29	49.8	95.4	33.0	27.7
30–34	52.2	96.5	33.3	31.1
35–39	46.1	97.0	32.1	31.1
40–44	34.2	97.4	29.4	26.6
45–49	24.2	97.8	26.8	22.8

Source: Census.

the proportion of the population over the age of 30 who live in a sexual union has remained fairly stable. However, among those who currently live in a union, the proportion who are not married is increasing. Nor is it the case that all those who are living in a non-marital union have not been married previously. As may be seen from the figures in Table 4.2, a substantial proportion of the population of reproductive age, irrespective of marital status, lives with a partner. In fact, among cohabiting men and women in their forties, more are divorced than never-married: they are people who are trying a different form of relationship after having been divorced. When it comes to formal remarriage, the rates for men are clearly higher than those for women. Analysis of data from the Swedish Fertility Survey has shown that highly educated women whose first sexual union has broken down are about 30 per cent less likely to enter a new relationship than women with less education. Women whose first union was a formal marriage are more likely to have another try, and the same is true of childless women when compared with those who had children.[17] The increasing proportions

[17] R. Larsson, 'Analys av svenska kvinnors benägenhet att inga nytt samboende efter det forsta parforhallandets upplösning' (University of Stockholm, Department of Demography, 1986).

of relationships that are not formal marriages may have substantial effects on the overall fertility rate, if cohabitation and marriage are not equivalent as regards their reproductive function. Swedish data show that the fertility of cohabitants is lower than that of married persons.[18] This may partly have been due to selection, however, because women or couples with lower fertility intentions may have chosen non-marital forms of cohabitation in preference to formal marriage, or, in the contemporary Swedish context, they may feel less inclined to formalize their informal union by marrying. As Hoffman-Nowotny has put it:

The reluctance to marry can be interpreted among other things as the result of low fertility aspirations, in other words, as low aspirations for forming a family. That is to say, the rapidly falling marriage rates are not the cause, but rather the consequence of a decreasing willingness to form a family.[19]

He points to the Nordic countries—primarily Sweden and Denmark—where there is 'an increasing disassociation of fertility and marital status', whilst in most other European countries marriage follows after a shorter or longer period of pre-marital sexual relations, because the couple have made up their mind to start a family—that is, to have children.

Although in a country like Sweden marriage is no longer considered to be an absolutely necessary precondition for the arrival of a child, this does not mean that there is a complete disassociation between fertility and marital status. Results from the Swedish Fertility Survey of 1981 show that, for 40 per cent of the women who had a first child while cohabiting, the first demographic event after the birth was marriage, before they had a second child or separated.[20] Moreover, it has been shown that pregnancy continues to be related to marriage, as cohabiting women who become pregnant are four times more likely to marry than those who do not.[21] This means that pregnancy or childbirth still tends to trigger a change in marital status. Formation of a couple-relationship can no longer be automatically interpreted as an indication of an intention to have children. Most young men and women, when they start living together, have not yet made a decision about this. Cohabitation is a way of life, in which the automatic connection with child-bearing has been broken. Beginning a relationship (which may or may not turn into a marriage), and having a child, are two separate decisions in contemporary Swedish society.

[18] C. Etzler, *Education, Cohabitation and the First Child: Some Empirical Findings* (Stockholm Research Reports in Demography; 1987).
[19] Hoffman-Nowotny, op. cit. in n. 11.
[20] B. Hoem, *Ett barn är inte nog* (Stockholm Research Reports in Demography, 25; 1985).
[21] Hoem and Hoem, op. cit. in n. 12.

A Psychoanalytic Theory of Reproduction

Marriage (including cohabitation) and parenthood have tended to become two distinct institutions. Liljestrom has argued that this process has exposed the asymmetry between motherhood and fatherhood more clearly than before.[22] The consequences of asymmetrical parenthood for the Oedipal drama and for the reproduction of gender roles in the next generation have been discussed by Chodorow.[23] According to her, women come to want and need primary relationships with children, because they experience heterosexual relationships in a triangular context, and strive to recreate the triangular relationship that they have experienced as children. The first carer—the omnipotent mother—is the same for boys and girls, but the crucial difference is that this first object of identification for girls is the parent of the same sex, whilst for boys it is the opposite. According to psychoanalytic theory, a boy will resolve his Oedipus complex by repressing his attachment to his mother, while a girl, in order to attain her proper heterosexual orientation, must transfer her primary object-choice to her father and to men. Chodorow's hypothesis is that, partly because fathers in the contemporary family are comparatively unavailable physically and emotionally, a girl retains her pre-Oedipal tie to her mother and adds to that her Oedipal attachment to the parent of the other sex. This results in a triangular psychic structure being created in women, in which men are not the exclusive object: 'heterosexual relationships are on the model of a nonexclusive second relationship to her, whereas for the boy they recreate an exclusive primary relationship.'[24] 'These different psychic structures are formed in early childhood as an unavoidable result of the social organization of parenting.'[25] Later, explicit role-training tends to intensify this effect.

Chodorow is primarily concerned with the negative effects of the social organization of parenting on the personality structures of men and women. She sees women's primary parenting role as the basic reason that underlies the system of sexual inequality which is still characteristic of Western society. Her argument is that the development of a nurturing personality orientation leads women to assume the care of children, and this, in turn, perpetuates gender roles and sexual inequality. Thus, she discusses the *social* organization of parenting and its consequences, and not why people in most societies become *biological* parents. Nevertheless, it can be argued that the psycho-

[22] R. Liljestrom, 'Gender Systems and the Family', in Kamerman and Kahn (eds.), *Sociology: From Crisis to Science?*, ii (London, 1986), pp. 132–49.

[23] N. Chodorow, *The Reproduction of Mothering: Psychoanalysis and the Sociology of Gender* (Berkeley, Calif., 1978).

[24] Ibid., p. 198.

[25] Empirical evidence for men's primary interest in a partner-relationship is found in clinical studies reported by Chodorow, which have shown that men are frequently jealous of their own children, whom they regard as competitors.

logical need for nurturing and for providing child care is of great significance for biological reproduction in that it provides a strong motivation to have children. Without becoming a biological parent it is difficult, in contemporary society, to have close and regular contact with children.

Caldwell has asserted that after 'the economic divide [i.e. the reversal of the intergenerational wealth flow] economic rationality dictates zero fertility. This does not happen . . . for social and psychological reasons.'[26] I would like to argue that the psychological mechanisms, which, according to Caldwell, prevent (or have at least so far prevented) fertility from falling to zero or close to zero, spring from the psychic structures created in early childhood through the processes explained by Chodorow. Previously, there were many other (mainly economic) reasons for having children. But, with the reversal of the intergenerational wealth flow, the level of fertility has come to depend on psychological factors. The possibility of controlling reproduction means that child-bearing can nowadays be avoided. Since child-bearing continues to a not insignificant extent, it must have some attraction. One may speculate that it is women's need for children (to create a triangular relationship) that has, so far, prevented the birth rate from falling far below replacement level. This does not mean that men do not either like or want children. Many men certainly do, but their desire cannot be compared with women's deep psychological need to become mothers.

A Structural Theory of the Family

There is, however, nothing to suggest that women's need to become mothers is eternal. Because children in early childhood are cared for exclusively by women, and this results in a psychic disposition towards motherhood (but not towards fatherhood), this does not mean that this has always been the case, or will continue to be the case. Although these processes are very slow to change, it is possible that eventually women, exposed to the growing strains of role relationships in the family system, may become less inclined to accept their ascribed role of primary parent to the next generation. Hoffman-Nowotny thinks that it is likely that 'the continuing aspirations of many women to fulfil their traditional role through motherhood' will diminish in importance in the course of time.[27]

According to the structural theory of the family, this process is related to the weakening of the structural basis of marriage and the family, which, in turn, follows from the gradual transformation of our social system from 'community' to 'society'. In a society, 'social positions and life chances are less ascribed, but are achievable, at least in principle'.[28] On a cultural level,

---

[26] J. C. Caldwell, *Theory of Fertility Decline* (London, 1982).
[27] Hoffman-Nowotny, op. cit. in n. 11.
[28] Ibid., p. 166.

a 'society' is characterized by the ideology of democracy, equality, and participation. Adult individuals are increasingly likely to live alone and to follow an individualized life-style, since 'the individual in "societal" structures is much less dependent on the family for the fulfilment of existential needs and requirements for survival than was the case in "community" structures'.[29] The same point has been made by Goode.[30] The increasing complexity of living arrangements today is the result of this reduced dependence on the family. Individuals make their own decisions, freed from many of the constraints that were characteristic of the old 'community' structure. In comparison with marriage, cohabitation is a 'weak' institution in which the partners enjoy greater personal autonomy and freedom of individual choice. This also implies less built-in oppression of women, which is probably why Hoffman-Nowotny has argued that ' "improvement" in the societal position of women is another (and probably one of the most important) determinants of the decline in the traditional family, and the rise of other life-styles'.[31]

The individual has increasingly become the basic unit in our society. The family is a subsystem of the 'community' type, and cannot in the long run coexist with a predominantly 'societal' structure and culture. Therefore,

there is little reason to believe that the family as we know it can and will survive as the mainstream model for future living patterns. The traditional family, which has become a universal and quasi-natural phenomenon in Europe, is not just changing, but proceeding towards its dissolution.[32]

These statements are probably true, and I see no reason for regret in them.[33] The essential feature of the conventional nuclear family is the predominance of men and the subordination of women. In the 'ideal' Western family there is a pronounced division of labour by sex, and an authoritarian allocation of power within the family. According to conventional psychological and sociological theory, the early symbiosis between mother and child creates a need for protection and sustenance, which is provided by the husband/father. This is supposedly at the base of the marriage contract in a 'traditional' family. It is typical of the industrialized society, where the workplace and home are separated.

It has often been said that the family has ceased to be a unit of production

---

[29] Ibid., p. 168.

[30] W. Goode, 'Individual Investment in Family Relationships in the Coming Decades', *Tocqueville Review*, 6 (1984), pp. 51–83.

[31] Hoffman-Nowotny, op. cit. in n. 11, p. 173.

[32] Ibid., p. 177. Popenoe has discussed developments in Sweden in these terms (op. cit. in n. 13).

[33] This does not mean that there are not some aspects of the breakdown of the traditional family which raise problems: e.g., men's failure to transfer income to their children after the parents have divorced or separated. This is a serious problem in many countries, e.g., in the United States.

and has, instead, become a unit of consumption. However, as Caldwell has pointed out,[34] what exists today is rather a two-tiered mode of production. We live in a non-familial capitalist economy, but a familial mode of production continues to exist within the family. Domestic production has not ceased completely. In spite of the existence of labour-saving devices and many commercial products that were formerly produced in the home, a great deal of physical and mental work is undertaken within the domestic unit, even today. The overwhelming part of this (unpaid) domestic work continues to be done by women. In addition to these traditional domestic tasks, women are increasingly engaged in paid work outside their homes. The family system based on the traditional breadwinner–housewife model, therefore, begins to break down. In this chapter we shall discuss the probable consequences of this breakdown for reproduction.

Changing Gender Roles within the Family

Have gender roles within the family changed as a result of women's increasing participation in market work? Ryder has asserted that 'there is now evolving a much different form of the family, particularly one that is egalitarian with respect to the division of labour by gender'.[35] In this egalitarian family, the wife's influence increases relative to that of her husband. It seems to be a prevailing notion among family sociologists that egalitarian sex roles and sexual behaviour are incompatible with large families, and perhaps even with small ones.[36] Thus, egalitarian couples would tend either to remain childless or to have minimum-sized families. Höhn has expressed a different opinion,[37] and I tend to agree with her: there is no automatic connection between egalitarian sex roles and abstention from, or severe restriction of, child-bearing. The relationship could as well be in the other direction.

Mott and Mott have studied what they have called 'prospective life style congruence' among American adolescents,[38] by which they seem to mean awareness of potential role conflicts for working mothers. A high level of

[34] Caldwell, op. cit. in n. 26.
[35] N. B. Ryder, 'Fertility and Family Structure', in UN, *Fertility and the Family: Proceedings of the Expert Group on Fertility and the Family* (New York, 1984), pp. 279–319.
[36] Keller, op. cit. in n. 3; B. E. Cogswell and M. B. Sussman, 'Changing Roles of Women: Family Dynamics and Fertility', in H. Y. Tien and L. Bean (eds.), *Comparative Family and Fertility Research* (Leiden, 1974), pp. 9–26; J. H. Scanzoni, *Sex Roles, Lifestyles and Childbearing* (London, 1975); K. Davis, 'Wives and Work: The Sex Role Revolution and its Consequences', *Population and Development Review*, 10 (1984), pp. 397–417; B. E. Chapman, 'Egalitarian Sex Roles and Fertility in Canada', paper presented at a Colloquium on the Family in Crisis, University of Ottawa, Nov. 1986.
[37] C. Höhn, 'Erwerbstätigkeit und Rollenwandel der Frau', *Zeitschrift für Bevölkerungswissenschaft*, 8 (1982), pp. 297–317.
[38] F. L. Mott and S. H. Mott, 'Prospective Lifestyle Congruence among American Adolescents', *Social Forces*, 63 (1984), pp. 184–208.

congruence means that high fertility expectations go together with high scores on an attitude scale that measures traditional sex roles (mothers ought not to work, husbands need not share the housework, etc.), and conversely. A high and significant correlation was found between sex-role attitude and expected family size, particularly among white girls who expected to have more than thirteen years of education. Even in this group, however, those who scored lowest on the attitude scale expected an average of 2.2 children. Thus, egalitarian sex roles were associated with an expected fertility which would be sufficient for replacement.

Repeated cross-sectional studies on time-use in the United States[39] have shown moderate increases in the amount of time devoted to housework by men. According to Robinson, men's increased participation in housework has occurred in two phases: from 1965 to 1975 their share increased mainly because women dramatically cut down the amount of time they spent in housework as more of them took paid jobs and had fewer children, and between 1975 and 1985 the pattern changed, mainly because men spent more time doing the cleaning and the cooking. Men did 15 per cent of the housework in 1965, and 33 per cent in 1985.

Studies of the relative contribution made within the family have often shown a reduction in inequality when the wife holds a job. However, it has been argued that husbands of both employed and non-employed women contribute about the same amount of time to housework, but that, because employed wives spend less time on housework, the base decreases and the relative contribution of the husband increases.[40] In that sense, the division of household tasks has become less unequal in families in which the wife works outside the home. Spitze, who has studied longitudinal adjustments to change,[41] found that changes in wives' hours of work or earnings led to adjustments in task division over a two- to three-year period, 'although the unequal starting point for that division leads one to question economists' views of its rationality'.

Barnett and Baruch have studied the factors that determine fathers' participation in family work and differentiate between different forms of paternal involvement.[42] They found that, in two-earner families, the number of hours that the wife worked each week exerted a strong influence. Longer hours worked by the wife increased the likelihood of the father's interaction with his child(ren), as well as involvement in child-care tasks and in 'feminine' home chores. In single-earner families, fathers' attitudes towards the quality

[39] J. Vanek, 'Time Spent in Housework', Scientific American, 231 (1974), pp. 116–20; J. P. Robinson, 'Who's doing the housework?', American Demographics (Dec. 1988), pp. 24–8.

[40] J. H. Pleck, 'The Work–Family Role System', Social Problems, 24 (1977), pp. 417–27.

[41] G. Spitze, 'The Division of Task Responsibility in US Households: Longitudinal Adjustments to Change', Social Forces, 64 (1986), pp. 689–701.

[42] R. C. Barnett and K. G. Baruch, 'Determinants of Fathers' Participation in Family Work', Journal of Marriage and the Family, 49 (1987), pp. 29–40.

of the fathering they had received as youngsters was the most consistent predictor.

There seems to be increasing interest in studying the role and behaviour of fathers in the family context. Sandquist, commenting on the results of a number of such studies carried out in Sweden, has stated that 'the conclusions of such studies usually stress the inequalities between women and men . . . but emphasis on remaining inequalities may obscure the important changes which have occurred'.[43] In a recent time-use study in Sweden it was shown, for example, that 'child-care tasks in general are shared quite equally between the parents, whilst most household tasks are heavily sex-typed'. It was shown that fathers made extensive use of parental leave in Sweden (the so-called 'daddy-days': ten days' leave at the time of birth); this opportunity was used by 85 per cent of fathers. They also used parental insurance for short-term child care (mostly to enable one parent to stay away from work when the child is ill). In 45 per cent of the cases the father made use of this facility—thus, this task was divided almost equally between fathers and mothers. Sandquist interprets this as meaning that, 'at workplaces all over Sweden, the idea of a father's responsibilities to his child taking precedence over his responsibilities at work is becoming commonplace'. She points out that those aspects of the parental insurance scheme that imply role-sharing rather than role reversal have become the most popular. Fathers use only 5 per cent of the days within the first nine months of the child's birth,[44] since this part of the scheme would require a more definite reversal of roles, that is the father staying at home, instead of the mother, as the prime carer of a new-born baby.

Is there any reason for believing that role-sharing or role reversal in the family will affect fertility levels? This is difficult to answer, as the effect might go in either direction, because, as a result of role-sharing, women, too, find it easier to combine paid work and motherhood, and this might make them more inclined, for example, to have three rather than two children. On the other hand, it has been argued that men's involvement in household chores and child care might decrease their interest in having (additional) children. Unfortunately, there is very little evidence on this very critical point, and, in addition, the long-term effects may be very different from the short-term ones.

Women's Position Outside the Family

Any statement about improvements in the position of women usually implies that their status has been raised to a level closer to that of men. The role

[43] K. Sandquist, 'Swedish Family Policy and Attempts to Change Paternal Roles', in C. Lewis and M. O'Brien (eds.), *Reassessing Fatherhood* (London, 1986), pp. 144–60.

[44] However, 20 per cent of the fathers made use of the provision allowing them to take at least one month's leave.

model, the social status to which women aspire, is that of equality with men. In conventional (men-dominated) social theory, the definition of gender equality is expressed in terms of equal opportunities, which means that women's access to education, different occupations, promotion, earnings, or political office should be the same as that of men. The idea is that women should expand their roles, whilst those of men remain unchanged.

Feminist writers have opposed the idea that women are seen as unequal, 'needing only a few more reforms to allow them to catch up with men'.[45] Women are oppressed because of their reproductive role. Other writers have pointed out that the sexes are interdependent,[46] so that the status and opportunities enjoyed by one sex cannot change without affecting those of the other. Ridley has emphasized that any discussion of the proper roles of women also implies a discussion of the proper roles of men.[47] It is, of course, this realization which underlies the recent upsurge of studies of the extent to which husbands/fathers participate in housework and child-rearing. The interdependence also means that, if women's roles were to change, so would those of men. This means, for example, that their role as breadwinners has considerably diminished as a consequence of the increased labour-force participation of their wives.

There can be no doubt that women's position in Western societies has changed in many ways during the post-war period. The most crucial aspect of this change, which is perhaps the dynamic between many of the other changes, has been the increased involvement of women in paid work outside their homes. The percentage of women (and particularly of married women and/or women with children of pre-school age) is often equated with the status of women. The higher the percentage of women who are gainfully employed, the higher is the status of women in that country. According to this definition, Swedish women unquestionably enjoy the highest status in the world, or at least in the part of the world which contains the industrialized market economies, and they are closely followed by women in Finland and Denmark.[48]

Women and Gainful Employment

In an analysis of trends in women's labour-force participation in Sweden between 1965 and 1980, Gustafsson and Jacobsson found that the most important explanatory factor behind the substantial increase in the proportion

[45] S. Firestone, *The Dialectic of Sex* (London, 1970).

[46] e.g., Keller, op. cit. in n. 3.

[47] Ridley, op. cit. in n. 6.

[48] OECD, *The Integration of Women into the Economy* (Paris, 1985); E. Bernhardt, 'Fertility and Employment', paper contributed to the Symposium on Population Change and European Society, European University Institute, Florence, 7–10 Dec. 1988.

of economically active women was the increase in women's wages.[49] Women's real wages increased relative to husbands' after-tax earnings, as a result of both the introduction of compulsory separate taxation in 1971 and the dramatic decreases in sex differentials in pay, which were, in part, associated with increases in women's education. This does not mean that full equality of incomes between the sexes has been achieved. Between the ages of 25 and 55 the average annual income for women is two-thirds or less of the corresponding income for men. The main reason is not the wage differential as such, but the fact that almost half the employed women work part-time.[50] Norway seems to head the league, with the highest proportion of part-time workers (54 per cent), followed by Sweden, Denmark, and the Netherlands.

This means that, although Swedish women participate in the labour force to a greater extent than women in most other industrialized countries, their labour-force attachment is of a different kind from that of men. Moreover, the Swedish labour market is supposed to be one of the most sex-segregated in the world.[51] Of course, part-time work is most common among women who have children of pre-school age (61 per cent), but, even among women without children below the age of 17 years, 36 per cent were working part-time.[52] Most women do not leave the labour market completely when they become mothers, but enter a special category of the working force, the part-time employed. They have one foot in their home and one in the labour market. Such a 'combination strategy' would normally entail at least one year's interruption of work in connection with childbirth, and then a de-escalation to part-time work.

An important question relates to the long-term consequences for earnings, careers, and satisfaction with life situation and with the life-course choice that these women make at the time when they have their first birth. One might suspect that, although a 'woman who pursues a "combination strategy" is not completely economically dependent on her husband, she has, nevertheless, largely suppressed her own (long-term) economic and other interests during the phase of her life when she has small children'.[53]

[49] S. Gustafsson and R. Jacobsson, 'Trends in Female Labour Force Participation in Sweden', *Journal of Labour Economics*, 3 (1985), pp. 256–74.

[50] Gustafsson found that the earnings of Swedish women were between 80 and 84 per cent those of men, when schooling and labour-force history were controlled (S. Gustafsson, 'Male–Female Lifetime Earnings Differentials and Labour Force History', in G. Eliasson, B. Holm, and F. Stafford (eds.), *Studies in Labour Market Behavior: Sweden and the United States* (Stockholm, 1981)), see also US, Bureau of the Census, CPS P-60, No. 161.

[51] See OECD, op. cit. in n. 48, for an overview of occupational segregation by sex in OECD countries.

[52] *Swedish Labour Force Survey* (1985).

[53] E. Bernhardt, 'The Choice of Part-Time Work among Swedish One-Child Mothers', *European Journal of Population*, 4 (1988), pp. 117–44. Newell and Joshi found that occupational downgrading was relatively common in England, in connection with a first birth, particularly for women who de-escalated to part-time work (M. Newell and H. Joshi, *The Next Job after the First Baby: Occupational Transition among Women born in 1946* (London, 1986)).

In modern industrialized societies there is generally a negative relationship between fertility and women's employment, but the causal direction is far from clear. No doubt, fertility exerts a negative influence on labour-force participation, in the sense that the birth of a baby has a dramatic and immediately inhibiting effect on the labour-force participation of the woman who has just become a mother. This effect tends to be temporary, however, and decreases as the child grows older. On the other hand, the effect of fertility on employment is much more debatable.[54] Traditionally, it has been supposed that the impossibility (or near-impossibility) of combining paid employment with motherhood will have caused many women with career ambitions to restrict their fertility. Paid employment and motherhood seem to have become somewhat less incompatible though, as a result of the introduction of part-time work and the increased availability of institutionalized child care. From a feminist point of view, it may be argued that the incompatibility between work and motherhood is mainly a consequence of existing gender structures in society and the consequent power relations within marriage. Women in countries with modified gender structures would, therefore, seem to stand a better chance of achieving a birth rate near replacement level.

Women as Supplementary Workers

Returning to Mason's definition of the status of women, it would seem that labour-force participation of women captures the dimension (or at least part of the dimension) that is associated with control over resources. Without wishing to deny the importance of household production, it seems to be participation in market work that gives access to economic resources, which, in turn, is closely related to power and prestige (the other two dimensions of the definition). However, this seems to be true only when women take part in economic activities outside their home in their own right. As Goode has pointed out, women used not to work as independent persons in earlier times.[55] When they held paid jobs outside their home, they were legally, or at least morally, obliged to hand their pay over to their husbands.

Writing in 1974 about the status of women in the developed world, Blake has argued that most women have not, in fact, achieved an independent occupational status.[56] Women are supplementary workers, and work part-time precisely because their work does not interfere (so much?) with their primary status as housewives and mothers. According to Oakley, one of

[54] For a thorough discussion of the relationship between fertility and employment, see Bernhardt, op. cit. in n. 48.

[55] Goode, op. cit. in n. 30.

[56] J. Blake, 'The Changing Status of Women in Developed Countries', in *The Human Population* (San Francisco, 1974), pp. 136–47.

the characteristics of a true housewife is that her domestic duties take precedence over other roles and activities.[57] Another way of expressing this is to describe the social identities of women as grounded in the familial roles of wives and mothers.[58] Economists tend to explain the prevalence of part-time work among women in terms of underlying sex differences between the productivity of market work and domestic work respectively. Women allocate relatively more time to domestic work than men, because their productivity is higher in that sphere. This effect is strengthened by a progressive tax system, such as exists in Sweden.[59]

Occupational demands and expectations continue to be based on the assumption that the worker is an individual who is relatively free of domestic and family responsibilities. As women who are mothers cannot meet this expectation, they must make adjustments in their personal situation—for example, by working part-time and/or limiting the sizes of their families, if they wish to combine the two roles. Liljestrom has discussed the increasing economic individuation of women.[60] It would be interesting to undertake a comparative study of variations in the degree of individuation of women in different countries and different social classes in the industrialized world. Lesthaeghe has pointed to what he has called the 'underlying dimension of modernization: the increasing centrality of individual goal attainment'.[61] In that sense, men were probably the first to become 'modern', but women are perhaps 'modernizing' now, although in most countries they still have a long way to go.

There is, however, an intrinsic problem connected with the 'modernization' of women. Since the conditions of working life have been determined on the basis of a male worker model (i.e. an individual man without domestic obligations),[62] women are only able to enter the men's world of economic production on equal terms if they can become like men in the sense that they are unburdened by household duties and child care. Otherwise, they simply cannot compete. Davis has stated that 'there is nothing in the modern workplace that encourages either marriage or reproduction'.[63] This would seem to be an understatement. It is, therefore, probably no coincidence that in all countries, with the intriguing exception of Finland,[64] in which

[57] A. Oakley, *Housewife* (London, 1974).

[58] Cogswell and Sussman, op. cit. in n. 36.

[59] For an economist's view of the growth of part-time work in Sweden, see M. Sundstrom, *A Study of the Growth of Part-time Work in Sweden* (Stockholm, 1987).

[60] Liljestrom, op. cit. in n. 22.

[61] R. Lesthaeghe, 'A Century of Demographic and Cultural Change in Western Europe: An Exploration of Underlying Dimensions', *Population and Development Review*, 9 (1983), pp. 411–36.

[62] Apart from the financial obligation to support his family. This was, incidentally used as a strong argument for the 'family wage', which the trade unions fought for to raise the level of wages of their members (and, incidentally, to keep female competitors out).

[63] K. Davis, 'Low Fertility in Evolutionary Perspective', in Supplement to *Population and Development Review*, 12 (1986), op. cit. in n. 5, pp. 48–68.

[64] Economic activity rates of Finnish women are high, but only 8 per cent work part-time.

women's labour-force participation rates are high, a high proportion of employed women also work part-time.

Moen has studied the changing situation of employed parents in Sweden between 1968 and 1981.[65] She argues that the Swedish cultural milieu provides both emotional and structural supports for those who combine employment and parenting, and that this support (particularly structural support) has increased over time. This would explain why there has been a decline in the proportion of working mothers who report psychological distress. Nevertheless, mothers continue to experience higher levels of fatigue, exhaustion, and psychological strain than fathers. In her discussion of recent pro-natalist policies in Western Europe, McIntosh has pointed to the introduction of the right to extended post-confinement leave (which could, in principle, also be used by fathers) as one of the few successes achieved in attempts to lessen the conflict between parenthood and work. According to her, 'Sweden has elaborated the only really successful labor market policy for parents.'[66] In a recent Swedish study of women who returned to work after childbirth, it was shown, however, that women often encountered considerable difficulties in making use of the rights and benefits that the law officially provided for them.[67]

A comparative study of different degrees of incompatibility between work and motherhood which would take account of differences in institutional frameworks and public policies in different countries might be useful for an understanding of differences between fertility levels that exist today in different low-fertility countries. It is worth noting, for example, that total fertility in Sweden has increased quite substantially since 1983 to a value of 2.0 in 1988, the highest figure in Western Europe, with the exception of Ireland. There have also been slight increases in some other countries (for example, Denmark and what was West Germany), but fertility in these countries is still well below replacement level. In many other countries, fertility levels seem to have become more stable during recent years, but there is so far no indication of an increase which would compensate for the extremely low levels of fertility of the late 1970s and early 1980s.

Unchanged Sex Roles or Ideational Change?

Is there a danger of painting an 'exaggerated picture of the emerging modern woman—well-educated, career-oriented, financially independent'?

The Netherlands provide an exception in the opposite direction: low economic activity rates, but a high proportion of part-time workers (OECD, op. cit. in n. 48).

[65] P. Moen, 'The Unevenness of Social Change: Employed Parents in Sweden', paper presented at the National Conference on Family Relations, Atlanta, Georgia, Nov. 1987.

[66] A. C. McIntosh, 'Recent Pro-natalist Policies in Western Europe', in Supplement to *Population and Development Review*, 12 (1986), op. cit. in n. 5, pp. 318–34.

[67] C. Calleman, L. Lagercrantz, A. Peterson, and K. Wilderberg, *Kvinoreformer pa männens villkor* (Lund, 1984).

Easterlin has maintained that 'the large majority are doing much the same type of work for the same type of pay as in the past, that is, they are in jobs traditionally held by women and earn considerably less than men'.[68] According to him, women's aspirations today are not very different from those of the past: to find a husband who can support them, to give birth to children, and to be a 'good mother'. The reason that underlies the increasing labour-force participation of women is economic pressure created by the decline in relative incomes: a couple's material aspirations are higher than their earnings potential (or, rather, the earnings potential of the husband). When relative earnings begin to rise again during the 1990s as a result of the entry of the smaller cohorts of the 1970s into the labour market, Easterlin predicts that marriage and birth rates will rise again.[69] In his view, women will then return happily to their primary tasks of homemaking and child-rearing.

The changes in sex-role attitudes recorded in various surveys have generally shown a definite trend towards more egalitarian conceptions of women's roles, as well as increasing acceptability of men's involvement in domestic tasks which used to be regarded as appropriate for women.[70] Easterlin interprets this as just a matter of 'cognitive consonance'—that is, young men and women favour ideological developments that are consistent with their behaviour. It is difficult to deny that he may have a point there; it is an inherent weakness of attitude surveys that respondents tend to give answers that are socially acceptable. If behaviour were to change, either voluntarily or as a result of external pressures, individuals will tend to bring their expressed attitudes in line with their behaviour. In Easterlin's view, 'deep at heart', neither men nor women have really changed their views about the proper roles of the two sexes. What counts for a man is his success at work and his ability to support a family, while crucial for a woman's personal fulfilment is her maternal role.

While there may be some truth in this point of view (more in some countries and classes than in others), it seems to me that Easterlin has underestimated the forces of change. Preston, in discussing changing values and falling birth rates, has predicted that, 'as the costs of adhering to a particular value system rise, behavior increasingly departs from the ideal

---

[68] R. A. Easterlin, *Birth and Fortune* (New York, 1980).

[69] The relevance of Easterlin's hypothesis has been questioned by many writers. See, e.g., Ryder, op. cit. in n. 4; C. F. Westoff, 'Fertility Decline in the West: Causes and Prospects', *Population and Development Review*, 9 (1983), pp. 99–104. Adherents of the 'New Home Economics' school of thought pioneered by Becker and Mincer have argued that relative income is not the dominant factor that explains fertility movements in the United States. In their view, the decline of fertility was primarily due to a rise in women's wages. See J. Ermisch, 'The Relevance of the Easterlin Hypothesis and the New Home Economics in Fertility Movements in Great Britain', *Population Studies*, 33 (1979), pp. 39–58.

[70] See, e.g., K. Mason, J. L. Czajka, and S. Aerber, 'Changes in US Women's Sex-Role Attitudes, 1964–1974', *American Sociological Review*, 41 (1976), pp. 573–96; A. Thornton, D. F. Alwin, and D. Camburn, 'Causes and Consequences of Sex-Role Attitudes and Attitude Change', *American Sociological Review*, 48 (1983), pp. 211–27.

and eventually erodes the legitimacy of this value system'.[71] In other words, even if in the beginning only a minority of the population were convinced of the importance of egalitarian sex roles; in the long run behavioural changes, such as the increased labour-force participation of married women, will induce ideational changes. This is not to deny the importance of economic factors of the type that Easterlin has discussed. Such factors may, indeed, 'produce period fluctuations that are superimposed on long-term (and often cohort-driven) ideational effects'.[72] It may well be true that, if economic pressures were reduced, some women would prefer not to work outside their home. This would be true primarily for women 'in unrewarding, boring, and blocked mobility jobs, such as service and menial office work [who] may choose pregnancy and child care to escape from an unpleasant situation'.[73] This would not necessarily result in increased fertility, however. In Sweden, the difference between the fertility of employed and non-employed women has decreased over time, because the fertility of housewives has declined.

The Post-Child Years

The question may, of course, be asked why women should be privileged to use marriage and child-bearing as an escape from wage work. In any case, as Keller has pointed out, 'small families simply do not fill a lifetime'.[74] As mortality declines and the period of child-bearing and child-rearing is reduced, what will women do in their post-child years?[75] Neither individual couples, nor society at large, can really afford a situation in which women are kept at home from the period of their marriage, or the arrival of the first child, for the rest of their lives. Both Ryder and Demeny have expressed grave doubts about the economic and political feasibility of enacting child subsidy schemes of an order that would be sufficient fully to compensate the mother for her lost income during the time that she stays at home to care for her children.[76] McIntosh has expressed similar scepticism.[77]

The idea that some kind of annual wage should be paid to the mother–housewife usually refers to a limited period of her life, when she has small

[71] S. H. Preston, 'Changing Values and Falling Birth Rates', in Supplement to *Population and Development Review*, 12 (1986), op. cit. in n. 5, pp. 176–95.

[72] R. Lesthaeghe, 'Value Changes and the Dimensions of Familism in the European Community', *European Journal of Population*, 2 (1986), pp. 225–68.

[73] Cogswell and Sussman, op. cit. in n. 36.

[74] Keller, op. cit. in n. 3.

[75] Davis, op. cit. in n. 36.

[76] Ryder, op. cit. in n. 4; P. Demeny, 'Pronatalist Policies in Low-Fertility Countries: Patterns, Performance and Prospects', in Supplement to *Population and Development Review*, 12 (1986), op. cit. in n. 5, pp. 335–58.

[77] McIntosh, op. cit. in n. 66.

children. After this period is over, she is supposed to return to the labour market, thus following the model envisaged by Myrdal and Klein.[78] They recommended a domestic period of ten years for all mothers, and a working life consisting of two phases, before and after they have had children. Women were not supposed to lose anything by following this pattern; they could return to the labour market in the same positions they had previously occupied and continue where they had left off. However, this 'separate-but-equal' ideology has not been successful in this context, and women have come to realize this. Women who have left the labour market and have then returned can compare their position with that of women who have worked continuously, and will often find that they have lost considerable ground.

This so-called depreciation from labour-force interruption[79] is perhaps a major concern to only a minority of women. Nevertheless, I would argue that, in most countries, women have become increasingly unwilling to accept these negative effects of their transition to motherhood. The 'combination strategy' followed by an increasing number of Swedish women[80] can be interpreted as one method of trying to reduce these negative effects. The 'professionalisation of motherhood' would be another solution to this dilemma, as Keyfitz, for example, has suggested.[81] Ridley has also discussed this idea of 'a society in which a minority of women specialize in child-bearing and child-rearing, with the vast majority of women participating, like men, throughout their adult lives in economic activities'.[82] Neither Keyfitz nor Ridley indicates how these specialized mothers would be selected. What is more serious perhaps is that such a system would deny the joys and benefits of parenthood to a majority of the population. In my view, this would be a very high price to pay for the possibility of achieving replacement fertility and (partial) gender equality. Would anyone really want to live in such a society?

Below-Replacement Fertility and Women's Liberation

At present, birth rates in almost all Western European countries are insufficient to ensure full replacement of the population. With a few exceptions, such as Easterlin,[83] all commentators predict that this situation will continue.[84]

---

[78] A. Myrdal and V. Klein, *Women's Two Roles* (London, 1956).
[79] See, e.g., J. Mincer and S. Polachek, 'Family Investments in Human Capital Earnings of Women', *Journal of Political Economy*, pt. II (1974), pp. 76–108.
[80] Bernhardt, op. cit. in n. 48.
[81] Keyfitz, op. cit. in n. 5.
[82] Ridley, op. cit. in n. 6.
[83] Easterlin, op. cit. in n. 68.
[84] Ryder, op. cit. in n. 4; Westoff, op. cit. in n. 69; C. F. Westoff, 'Perspectives on Fertility and Nuptiality', in Supplement to *Population and Development Review*, 12 (1986), op. cit. in n. 5, pp. 155–70; Lesthaeghe, op. cit. in n. 61.

Great strides have supposedly been made in the emancipation of women, and the prime evidence for this is the increase in their labour-force participation. The presumption is that there is some form of connection between the two.

There is no doubt that the role of mother–housewife as a lifelong career is on its way out. However, although an increasing number of (married) women now participate in the labour force, most women are probably still not members in their own right and do not pursue their own independent economic interests. Many employed women still do not earn a living wage.[85] Occupationally and otherwise, working mothers are frequently discriminated against, so that the goals of the women's liberation movement are far from realized.

Shulamith Firestone, one of the leading feminist writers, has asserted that at the heart of women's oppression are their child-bearing and child-rearing roles. Therefore, the only way to achieve 'freedom from biology' is the realization of artificial reproduction. Only when this is achieved, can women be liberated. Despite recent developments in reproductive techniques such as surrogate mothers, *in vitro* fertilization, etc., most children are still born as a result of the old procreative process. In spite of this, sexuality has effectively become divorced from reproduction as a result of modern contraception, abortion, and contraceptive sterilization. Child-bearing has become one of a number of possible options for women. It is quite feasible to refrain from child-bearing and child-rearing without having to refrain from sexual relations inside or outside a stable relationship.

There has been a 'de-institutionalization' of the family,[86] but, in spite of this, practically all child-bearing occurs within a family framework, whether 'de-institutionalized or not'.[87] Although the average size of families has shrunk, increased socialization has, at least in part, made up for decreased reproduction, as developmental psychologists have stressed the crucial role of the mother for the development and growth of her children. Thus, women have fewer children, but spend more time mothering them.[88]

The achievement of gender equality has often implicitly been taken to mean that women would behave more like men, especially by being more economically active. Egalitarian sex roles may involve 'a bit more washing up and child minding for the husband', but the most revolutionary part of the transformation is the increased labour-force participation rate of wives

[85] Skrede has pointed out that in Norway only one-quarter of married women have incomes that are high enough to be considered sufficient for self-support (Kari Skrede, 'Shaping Women's Lives: The Impact of Recent Social Change in Norway', paper presented to the Conference on Life Course, Family, and Work held in Lysebu, Norway, Feb. 1986).

[86] Lesthaeghe, op. cit. in n. 61.

[87] Not only are most children born to a two-parent family, but they continue to live with their natural parents. It has been shown in a Swedish study that, even when they had reached the age of 16 years, 72 per cent of all children were living with both their natural parents.

[88] J. Mitchell, *Women's Estate* (Harmondsworth, 1971).

and mothers. Even if the so-called integration of women into the economy has been only partial and incomplete, it has probably been the *sine qua non* for raising women's previously inferior position in society. The gender gap has closed, in the sense that women have adopted certain aspects of 'male behaviour'. Overall, however, the man's role, as it exists at present, is an impossible model for human beings, as it does not include child-bearing or child-rearing (except in a very subsidiary form). It cannot be generally adopted, since in the long run it would lead to an extinction of the population. Thus, if 'elimination of discrimination by gender' were to mean treating women like men, this would be a self-defeating strategy from the point of view of population replacement.

Germaine Greer has pointed to the enormous sacrifices many women make when they have children, and for which they are to expect no reward or recompense.[89] The extent of the sacrifice is, of course, related to the degree of the woman's interest in an independent occupational career. Therefore,

the closer women draw in social and economic status to the male level, the more disruptive childbirth becomes. In order to compete with men, the Western woman has joined the masculine hierarchy and cultivated a masculine sense of self. The acknowledgement of her pregnancy means that she has to step down from all that and enter the psychological equivalent of a birth hut.[90]

To the extent that women become liberated from the traditional feminine gender role by adopting masculine perceptions and aspirations—i.e. by role reversal, rather than by role extension—these consequences seem likely. During the early stages of the women's liberation movement there were, no doubt, some women who emphasized the importance of overcoming the limitation of the concept of 'self' that was constructed during the early process of socialization.[91] In other words, women are handicapped by their sex-typed upbringing, and can get nowhere, if this is not overcome.

These matters are related to the discussion of women's so-called 'success avoidance'. According to Markus, women's relative 'disinterestedness' in the socially prescribed and normatively fixed forms of success is connected with 'the everyday life activities [which] the majority of adult women are involved in: the activities of mothering and/or housekeeping'. She seems to argue in favour of the 'subversion of the achievement principle', in the sense that women should not strive to reach 'up' to the masculine standard, but should try to convince men to reach 'down'.

How can men 'reach down'? Ryder, in discussing the parity norm as an assessment of the costs and benefits of children, has argued that, although

[89] G. Greer, *Sex and Destiny* (London, 1984).
[90] Ibid., p. 12.
[91] M. Markus, *Women, Success and Civil Society. Submission to or Subversion of the Achievement Principle* (Haverford, Pa., 1985).

time spent on child-rearing is from one point of view a cost, since it represents opportunities foregone, it can also be seen as a benefit, 'since it is the vehicle through which many of the satisfactions of child rearing are delivered'.[92] In other words, a large part of the pleasure derived from having children results from the time one spends with them. This would seem to be true for men as well as for women. However, the way in which parenting is socially organized today means that many fathers spend relatively little time with their offspring.

Perhaps this is less true of Sweden than of other Western countries, but the extent of part-time work among women with children of pre-school age in particular, and the relative absence of such work among fathers of young children, indicates clearly that, even in Sweden, women are the primary parents. Höhn has taken the Scandinavian countries as examples of how high economic activity rates for women are compatible with family life 'as a result of the spread of equality between the sexes and egalitarian partner relationships'.[93] It seems to me that she is painting somewhat too rosy a picture of the situation in Scandinavia. Nevertheless, the emphasis on role-sharing between parents, and the conscious efforts on the part of the government to promote equality of the sexes,[94] have resulted in a relatively egalitarian sex-role structure, possibly unrivalled in the Western world.[95]

McIntosh and Demeny seem to agree that Swedish family and labour-market policies are mildly pro-natalist in practice, though not in theory.[96] Hoem and Hoem have pointed out that the Swedish birth rate has increased since the early 1980s, in particular for women between the ages of 25 and 35.[97] In the general context of below-replacement fertility in Western societies, Swedish fertility has remained relatively high, despite all the factors that would seem to encourage the contrary (a high frequency of consensual unions, and high labour-force participation of women amongst others). Hoem and Hoem are convinced that 'a closer scrutiny would continue to demonstrate the advantages for the level of reproduction of the advanced Swedish-type set of policies that aim to mitigate the direct costs and opportunity costs of childbearing'.[98]

[92] Ryder, op. cit. in n. 35.

[93] Höhn, op. cit. in n. 37.

[94] See, e.g., R. Liljestrom, 'Sweden', in S. B. Kamerman and K. Kahn (eds.), *Family Policy* (New York, 1978), pp. 19–48; S. Gustafsson, 'Equal Opportunity Policies in Sweden', in G. Schmid and R. Weizel (eds.), *Sex Discrimination and Equal Opportunity* (Berlin, 1984), pp. 132–54.

[95] For a presentation of the Swedish policy of 'pursuit of sexual equality', see A. C. McIntosh, *Population Policy in Western Europe: Responses to Low Fertility in France, Sweden and West Germany* (London, 1983).

[96] McIntosh, op. cit. in n. 66; Demeny, op. cit. in n. 76.

[97] Hoem and Hoem, op. cit. in n. 12. This increase is not exclusively or even primarily the result of compensation for the previous postponement of births among women who were in their early or middle twenties during the 1970s. When we look at parity-specific rates, second and third birth rates have increased more than first birth rates.

[98] Hoem and Hoem, op. cit. in n. 12.

The Social Organization of Parenting: An Alternative Model

Swedes have had the advantage of a government-approved continuous emancipatory movement. This has resulted in a combination of relative gender equality, and a birth rate near replacement level. However, it is difficult to be convinced that the present circumstances will suffice permanently to raise fertility to full replacement level. According to Ryder, 'people make choices how they can best achieve an optimum quality of life under prevailing circumstances'.[99] I would like to argue that children contribute to the quality of life, and that the conflict between individual and group interests that is often mentioned is apparent rather than real. The question that should be asked is how 'prevailing circumstances' could be changed. What are the prevailing circumstances that prevent individuals from realizing a quality of life that includes children as an important part?

Demeny has proposed the introduction of the 'Nuclear Family Inc.', presumably with the husband as president.[100] This would do away with the last remnants of the 'community' structure. I do not think that the rules of the economic world should be introduced into the family. Höhn and others have pointed to the need to create working conditions that are more family-oriented; Pleck has called this 'crossover'.[101] The woman's work role is vulnerable to family demands. For husbands, the work–family boundary can be crossed mostly from the other side: demands from work impinge on family time. To achieve full gender equality both roles must be symmetrically permeable to work and family demands. I would argue that this would also be beneficial from the point of view of increasing birth rates, since it would constitute a step towards more egalitarian parenthood away from the present situation, where motherhood is primary, and fatherhood secondary.

Why is this important? In the current debate on low birth rates and pro-natalist policies, many have argued in favour of upgrading motherhood, the importance of social rewards for responsible parenthood, and the need for a positive reinforcement of family life. If men were to become more actively involved with their children at an early stage, women could more easily combine child-rearing and gainful employment. It would also presumably create a psychic disposition for fatherhood in the next generation, equal to the psychic disposition towards motherhood which already exists among women. Without this, there is probably no chance of achieving replacement-level fertility. The best that can be hoped for is constraints on further decline, in circumstances such as exist in Sweden. A restructuring of the social institutions of motherhood and fatherhood in combination with a transformation of the conditions of working life would make full gender equality compatible with fertility sufficient to ensure replacement.

[99] Ryder, op. cit. in n. 4.
[100] Demeny, op. cit. in n. 76.
[101] Höhn, op. cit. in n. 37; Pleck, op. cit. in n. 40.

5 The Status of Women and the Position of Children: Competition or Complementarity?

GHISLAINE JULÉMONT

For more than a quarter of a century researchers and policy-makers have taken an increasing interest in the position of women, the functions and roles that they perform in the family, and their position in society as a whole, including their access to the labour market and to education. In the developed as well as the less developed countries, an understanding of women's preferences and choices has become a matter of prime importance, for these preferences and choices will shape the future of the family as an institution in developed countries, and also the national, regional, and perhaps even the global, demographic future in less developed countries.

This view may, within limits, hold true of developed countries. In less developed countries, however, the responsibility that we would like to see women take upon themselves does not yet seem to be within their grasp. Of course, it has been shown in many studies that there is a relationship between the length of women's education and, for example, the number of live births they have. General fertility rates by educational status have been published by the United Nations in 1986.[1] Except in Bangladesh, and even more so in Kenya, a negative relationship appears to have been established between the length of women's schooling (particularly where this exceeds three years of primary education) and their subsequent fertility. However, it is possible to cite a number of counter-examples. In Bangladesh, a slight negative relationship between schooling and fertility was found only where the length of schooling exceeded six years. Practically the same is true of Kenya, and a similar relationship was found in Ghana.[2] In all these cases, the effect of the decline in fertility was so small relative to the high level of existing fertility that it is not really possible to consider the length of women's education as one of the principal determinants of fertility.

[1] UN, Education and Fertility: Selected Findings from the World Fertility Survey (New York, 1986).

[2] C. Safilios-Rothschild, 'Female Power, Autonomy, and Demography', in R. Anker, M. Buvinic, and N. H. Youssef (eds.), Women's Roles and Population Trends in the Third World (London, 1982), pp. 117–32.

The same is true of the participation of women in the workforce in the modern economic sector. At the World Fertility Survey Conference held in Wembley in 1980 a participant from an African country reported that information collected in her country suggested that women's participation in the labour force appeared to have a positive effect on family size, to the extent that women in the labour force had the opportunity of finding cheap outside help to perform their domestic tasks, and that their own incomes provided financial assets which made it possible for them to meet the costs of a larger number of children. It is likely that, in the long run, as other participants in the conference argued, and as Jacobson has also reported when analysing the length of girls' schooling,[3] it may well prove to be negatively related to fertility. However, the negative effect remains questionable, since it depends entirely on the development process.

Even though, during the Wembley Conference, observation was not focused on the positive relationship between women's labour-force participation and fertility, this factor is of considerable importance. It provides a new element in explaining the persistence of high fertility in a number of less developed countries, in spite of the attempts that have been made in those countries to promote family planning.

If it were true that women in less developed countries desire to have many children irrespective of their economic status, the contention that high fertility persists only because women have no other means at their disposal to acquire a status in society, and that consequently they have no strong incentive to limit the number of children they bear, becomes untenable. In those cases where the economic status of women is maintained (or even improved) instead of being reduced, they will produce large families, not merely because children provide additional labour to support the family (as is the case in poorer families), but rather because a greater number of children is an outward indicator of wealth, which will raise the whole family's social status. In such cases, arguments that are couched in terms of individualist values will be irrelevant.

These examples are put forward to show that factors used to indicate the status of women which are based on recent changes in developed countries do not necessarily apply in countries that are less developed, and may, indeed, yield contradictory results there, or be irrelevant. Indicators of social status are always the product of a specific social situation and cannot necessarily be universally applied.

The demographic changes that occurred in industrialized countries during the nineteenth and the beginning of the twentieth centuries did not initially result in an improvement in the status of women. On the contrary, they occurred when women were being increasingly confined to their homes and

---

[3] J. Jacobson, *Planning the Global Family* (Washington, 1987), p. 43.

excluded from participation in economic life, which was linked to the industrial development that was becoming ever more important. It was only during the second half of the twentieth century that factors associated with women's status came to acquire greater importance for demographic change.

This new trend is the product of a conflict between individualist and family values that had previously existed in society. Women's adherence to, and increasing acceptance of, these individualist values largely fostered research in modern contraceptive technology. The use of new contraceptive methods gives women autonomy and a real power of making decisions about their own lives, and enables them to achieve recognition as full adult members of society without any reference to their marital or reproductive status.

Philippe Ariès, in order to characterize the demographic changes that have been observed in industrialized countries,[4] distinguished between two types of contraceptive behaviour that might be adopted by married couples. The first type, which he termed 'ascetic', was particularly prevalent during the nineteenth and first half of the twentieth centuries, and was designed to limit the number of children in order to improve their future opportunities. The second type, which he called 'hedonist' and which he regarded as being characteristic of the decline of fertility after the mid-1960s, was designed to provide greater opportunities for self-fulfilment for both members of the couple, self-fulfilment which would have been restricted by the arrival of children.[5] In the first, 'ascetic', type of behaviour, children, though they might be fewer in number, remained the essential primary objective of marriage. The second, 'hedonist', Malthusian type of behaviour could only occur when accompanied by an 'extension of life' (to use Kingsley Davis's very apposite expression),[6] and necessarily implies a range of choices.

Keeping this distinction in mind, I propose to analyse the different roles played by women during these two evolutionary phases of the demographic transition. Because the evolution from 'ascetic' to 'hedonist' behaviour implies a change in the value given to children, this distinction will also prove to be useful in elucidating a number of important elements for the implementation of family planning in less developed countries.

The Status of Women and Children in Developed Countries

It is generally stated that in countries of the Third World the economic status of women deteriorated significantly during the process of development,[7]

---

[4] P. Ariès, 'L'Enfant: La Fin d'un règne?', in 'Finie la famille? Traditions et nouveaux rôles', *Autrement*, 3 (Paris, 1975), p. 172.

[5] It goes without saying that extra-marital sexual relations are, with very few exceptions, of the 'hedonist' type.

[6] K. Davis, 'Wives at Work: Consequences of the Sex Revolution', *Population and Development Review*, 10 (1984), p. 409.

[7] See, e.g., K. B. Ward, *Women in the World System: Its Impact on Status and Fertility* (New

and it has been claimed that this did not happen in the industrialized countries.[8] However, if there is any aspect of the history of these two groups of countries which is similar, it is this one. As I have already indicated, when industrial development and urbanization began in the West, they were accompanied in the capitalist economies—and to a lesser extent in planned economies as well—by a deterioration in women's status. It is only during the later stages of development that their situation improved, and that the trend was to some extent reversed.

Changes before 1950

The Dimensions of the Decline in Women's Status. We begin by noting that, in some social groups in Western countries, the decline in women's status preceded industrialization. It coincided with the early stages of capitalism, which seemed to be accompanied by a restructuring of functions and roles within the family. Industrialization and urbanization were powerful forces which resulted in a wider diffusion throughout society of a type of family that already existed among the ruling classes.

In a controversial book, Philippe Ariès has analysed the emergence of the modern family, by considering the position occupied by children.[9] He makes the point that childhood used to be regarded as a 'special' period of life, a view which was first found during the sixteenth century. This view is characteristic of a special type of family, which gradually brought about the emergence of an area of 'private life'. This area was the preferred domain of domestic activities and gradually became separated from that of economic activities, so that life was fragmented into two separate sections.

The concept of the 'special' nature of childhood, which Ariès has described in very positive terms, was the first sign of a division accentuated by the creation of artificial barriers between children and adults, that were represented as being 'natural', and later extended to society as a whole.[10] They were the outward sign of a development which contained within itself the seeds of both future evolution and potential conflict.

York, 1983), p. 11; A. Michel, 'Multinationals and Inequalities', *Current Sociology*, 71 (1983), pp. 86 ff.

[8] E. Mueller, 'The Allocation of Women's Time and its Relation to Fertility', in Anker, Buvinic, and Youssef, op. cit. in n. 2, pp. 81–82.

[9] P. Ariès, *L'Enfant et la vie familiale sous l'Ancien Régime* (Paris, 1960); trans. as *Centuries of Childhood: A Social History of Family Life* (New York, 1962); page references in subsequent notes are to the English translation.

[10] The strict discipline to which children were subjected during this period has led some writers to interpret the same facts in a different way. They tend to regard the modern family and school as a sort of prison for children. Though at first sight these two interpretations seem very different, they are not necessarily mutually exclusive. The concept of childhood in which the child is regarded as an alien in the world of adults, contains, as do all concepts of dissimilarity, both an interest in and a rejection of children.

Ariès used his study of attitudes to childhood to point to what at the time appeared to be a new phenomenon—the increased social importance of the conjugal family consisting of a couple and their children, and the consolidation and extension of the power of the husband within the family. He stressed that attitudes towards children formed part of the attitudes towards the family as a whole.[11] The husband's authority could be exercised only at the expense of other members of the family, who became totally subordinate to him. Other authors have noted,[12] as Ariès himself has reported (though he makes no further use of these notions), that in France, as in other European countries during the same period, 'the wife's power steadily diminished';[13] that, 'beginning in the fourteenth century, we see a slow and steady deterioration of the wife's position in the household'; and that finally during the sixteenth century 'the married woman is placed under a disability, so that any act she performs without the authority of her husband or the law are null and void'. 'This development strengthens the husband's power and he is finally established as a sort of domestic monarch.'[14] Contemporary laws also stressed paternal authority,[15] and Petot concluded: 'While lineal ties weakened, the husband's authority in the home became stronger, and his wife and children were more rigorously subject to him.'[16] This new social unit was both fashioned by the laws and reflected in them, and became the foundation of the modern state and its power.[17] It is not, therefore, surprising that it should also have been characteristic of the social group on which this power was based—the urban bourgeoisie.

There is not sufficient space in this chapter to describe the entire social context of the period, though this would be the only means of fully understanding the type of family which has become the model for our system of morals. It is sometimes forgotten that this system originated mainly in the bourgeoisie. It was also members of this type of family who, during the nineteenth century, a period when the husband's authority had reached its apogee, adopted a form of reproductive behaviour that was both rational and voluntarist.

---

[11] Ariès, op. cit. in n. 9, pt. III, ch. 2.

[12] See, especially, J. Flandrin, *Le Sexe et l'occident: Évolution des attitudes et des comportements* (Paris, 1981); G. Duby, *La Société aux XIe et XIIe siècles dans la région du Mâçonnais* (Paris, 1953); M. Petot, 'La Famille en France sous l'Ancien Régime', in *Sociologie comparée de la famille* (Paris, 1955).

[13] Duby, as cited by Ariès, op. cit. in n. 9, p. 355.

[14] Petot, as cited by Ariès, op. cit. in n. 9, p. 356.

[15] Flandrin, op. cit. in n. 12, pp. 76 ff.

[16] Petot, as cited by Ariès, op. cit. in n. 9, p. 356. Some observations he made on clothing are also suggestive. Ariès noted that the clothes worn by both girls and boys at the time resembled those worn by women. During the second half of the eighteenth century, little boys only stopped wearing dresses with collars after they had reached the age of 4 or 5 years (Ariès, p. 158). An analysis of manuals on etiquette shows that, after the eighteenth century, women ceased to be mentioned in these books, as if, Ariès adds, 'their role had become less important at the end of the Middle Ages and the beginning of the modern period'.

[17] Ariès, op. cit. in n. 9, pt. III, ch. 1.

Changes in the Position of Children. Returning to attitudes towards children, we note that the view that 'the child was not ready for life and had to be subject to special treatment, a sort of quarantine before he was allowed to join the world of adults'[18] was the base for the development of schools, which became the 'normal instrument of social initiation and of progress from childhood to manhood'.[19] They replaced the old method of 'transmission by direct apprenticeship from one generation to another'.[20] Children were withdrawn from daily life and enclosed in a world of their own—at first in schools (it was during this period that boarding schools became more common) and later, towards the end of the nineteenth and the beginning of the twentieth centuries, within the family itself, at a time when it became an outward sign of social mobility for the wife to be engaged solely in running her household and bringing up her children.[21] Children, as it were, ceased to belong to the present and became instead a projection (of their parents' personalities?) into the future. This new conception of the child as a future adult coincided with a change in the conception of time, and a new consciousness of the importance of individualist values in the establishment of the family. It may have been this new 'social invisibility' of children, and it was certainly the educational care given to them (with all its attendant hopes for the future), and which was often inspired by affection,[22] that made each child valuable and precious to its parents. It also resulted in the acceptance of family limitation when the increasing severity of social competition made this form of conduct seem desirable. In this context, Ariès has mentioned that this type of education, was at first mainly characteristic of the middle levels of society—the middle classes.[23]

Conclusion. Our argument has suggested that the desire to limit one's family, and therefore to have recourse to contraception, was less related to

[18] Ibid., p. 412.

[19] Ibid., p. 369.

[20] Ibid., p. 367.

[21] This led Flandrin to write that 'this development . . . separated children at school from the world of adults and resulted in the infantilisation of a large part of society' (Flandrin, op. cit. in n. 12, pp. 143–44).

[22] It has been suggested that Ariès's study led to the conclusion that, from this time, the family became enclosed and emotionally focused on the children (see C. Andrew, 'Women and the Welfare State'. *Canadian Review of Political Science*, 17 (1984), pp. 667–83). However, I doubt whether this conclusion is correct. This is shown by the justification that Ariès gives to corporal punishment throughout childhood. 'The concept of the separate nature of childhood, of its difference from the world of adults, began with the elementary concept of its weakness which reduced it to the level of the lowest social strata' (Ariès, op. cit. in n. 9, p. 262). This conclusion was confirmed by Flandrin (op. cit. in n. 12, p. 229), who showed that there was a reduction of interest in children during the eighteenth century, and that their position deteriorated at that time (p. 209). He also underlined the close connection that existed between the status of women and that of children (p. 365).

[23] This is an important point, which has been neglected by Ariès. If attitudes towards children had been based solely on affection, there would have been no reason to treat boys and girls differently in the first instance. As Ariès himself has said, 'boys were the first "specialized" children' (op. cit. in n. 9, p. 58).

the objective status of women than to the desire to improve the life chances of one's children.[24] This resulted in a gap between the life-styles of different generations, a development that could occur only in an open society in which social inequalities, though evident, were not regarded as immutable.

It could be objected that the results of almost all studies of fertility in developed countries have shown that economically active women—and particularly those who worked outside their own households—had smaller families than others. Without wishing to deny this fact, it seems to me that there are two principal difficulties in interpreting this phenomenon. The first is that this relationship is based on relatively recent data. The proliferation of fertility surveys, even in developed countries, occurred during the 1960s, and the relationship between fertility and women's economic status which was shown in their results is the product of a further development, which I shall examine later. Secondly, the interpretation of survey data—as, indeed, of all statistical information—is to some extent dependent upon one's perspective.

The decline in fertility has been so large that it can only have been achieved by the widespread practice of contraception on the part of women, irrespective of their economic status. For instance, in Belgium the average family contained between two and three children only, at a time when three-quarters of women of reproductive age were economically inactive. Ninety per cent of all couples had used contraception at some time during their marriages, and 80 per cent were practising contraception at the time of the survey—the most popular methods were withdrawal and rhythm. This would suggest that their mental attitudes remained close to those we have described.[25]

Recent Developments

We return to the attitudes towards childhood, as described by Ariès. His analysis suggests that these attitudes should have been accompanied by similar attitudes towards gender, and it is remarkable that an author of Ariès's insight should have been blind to this aspect.[26]

---

[24] I believe that it is important to distinguish between a woman's objective social status and her subjective feelings about this status. As late as 1966, when the first fertility survey was carried out in Belgium among women aged below 40, it was regarded as a sign of social distinction to return one's status as 'economically inactive', and most women attempted to do so. It was only among the better-off sections of the population, in which girls as well as boys had access to modern education, that this status was less esteemed.

[25] J. Morsa, G. Julémont, and P. Guilmot, 'Une enquête sur la fécondité', vol. i in the selection of papers published in *Population et famille* (Brussels, 1976). See also G. Julémont, 'Une enquête sur la fécondité, xvi. Attentes au souhaits (1966, 1970, 1975). Quelques aspects de changement', *Population et famille* (1979).

[26] Thus, he wrote that 'the concept of the family, the concept of class, and perhaps elsewhere the concept of race, appear as manifestations of the same intolerance towards variety, the same insistence on uniformity' (Ariès, op. cit. in n. 9, p. 415). They are all different aspects of the

The analysis shows that the system of social inequality, which was characteristic of the old society, was reproduced within the family itself as it has been structured since the sixteenth century. As almost absolute power was gradually yielded to the husband, men's supremacy became institutionalized in industrial society[27] during the nineteenth and twentieth centuries, when children were relegated to a world of their own at the same time as women were enclosed in an area reserved to themselves. This process was analogous to the introduction of a class or caste system into the family.[28]

For the child, segregation during childhood consisted of a period of compulsory subordination. However, this period was transitory, even though, as time passed, the length of education required before adult status could be achieved increased, and the barriers to achievement became higher.[29] Segregation by sex, however, implied a permanent state of subordination, which during the eighteenth and even during part of the nineteenth century became a kind of 'socio-economic death'.[30] On marriage, a woman ceased to have an identity separate from that of her husband and could obtain recognition only through his status.[31] In fact, sexual segregation went beyond the mere differentiation of roles by gender that were observed. It resulted in enclosing women within a sphere of activities of no economic value, the social utility of which was recognized only, when it seemed desirable to retain them in this situation or cause them to return to it. In the writings of economists, such as Friedrich Engels or John Stuart Mill, who discussed these subjects during the nineteenth century, it is possible to recognize the contempt with which women's activities were usually regarded.[32] Though these two authors are generally considered as being among the foremost

---

same phenomenon. But when he discusses the fact that little boys were treated 'like little girls who were not distinguished from women', he gets over the difficulty by doing a U-turn, and states that this is one of the yet unexplored areas of social consciousness about age and sex, and that up to the present, only the feeling of class consciousness has been explored (ibid., pt. I, ch. 4).

[27] L. Peattie and M. Rein, *Women's Claims: A Study in Political Economy* (Oxford, 1983).
[28] In a book that is still quoted, Gunnar Myrdal pointed to the situation in the United States in 1940, when there were similarities between racial segregation, sexual segregation, and the caste system; in these three instances, the barriers were practically insurmountable (G. Myrdal, *An American Dilemma* (New York, 1945), pp. 22, 103).
[29] Flandrin, op. cit. in n. 12, p. 146.
[30] A. Michel, *Le Féminisme* (Paris, 1979), has used the term 'civil death'. From the strictly legal point of view, this description is probably better.
[31] Many social scientists have adopted what is socially a very conservative view of this phenomenon. Though they may be correct in describing the situation, the fact that they accept it uncritically as 'normal' or 'typical' does not help to modify it.
[32] F. Engels, *The Origin of the Family, Private Property and the State* (London, 1884); J. S. Mill, *The Subjection of Women* (London, 1869). Contempt for women's activities can also be found in the writings of some feminist authors. It is particularly pronounced in Simone de Beauvoir, *The Second Sex* (London, 1956). Though de Beauvoir is generally regarded as a feminist, she could just as easily be characterized as 'male', because she accepts the perceived inferiority of women as a fact of nature. Her suggested remedy is that women should enter the world of men and accept masculine values.

advocates of women's rights, in fact they tended to stress the absurdity of women's activities. It is only recently that female authors have pointed to the importance of domestic work for the maintenance of the economy, even though economists recognize only activities that possess an economic value.[33]

It is hardly surprising that this opposition between the two worlds (the men's world of economics, and the women's of domesticity), which is becoming more and more extreme, has led to a revolt among women who see themselves as being refused recognition as individuals. The history of feminism is well known, and I shall not deal with it here.[34] I would, however, stress that the emergence of industrial society has, at least in the West, been accompanied by the appearance of individualist values, such as autonomy and the search for self-fulfilment. Though such values may have existed previously, they were only latent. The new values which emerged suddenly and were strongly accentuated were reserved to those who had themselves participated in the development of industrial society: collectivist values continued to operate only within the family. Men, to the extent that they participated in both these worlds, therefore, shared two concurrent value systems. Women, however, confined as they were to the household, had access only to the traditional values. Only after girls had begun to attend school and received the same education as boys were the doors to that other system of values opened to them. The renunciation of the new value system, exclusively inherent in marriage for women, came to be regarded as an intolerable injustice from that time onwards.

Awareness of this forbidden world resulted in what has been called the 'woman problem'. The socio-economic implications of women's position differ in different societies, classes, or social groups in which both men and women share the same system of collectivist values. In such societies, the conditions of men and women remain much more alike. Though women may continue to occupy a subordinate position, their status seems to cause them less resentment and evokes less protest than a situation in which men are able to participate in an open society, but women are confined to a closed sub-society. This situation leads to the establishment of a so-called 'dualist society', although this concept appeared much later and in a different context. A situation in which women are aware of the existence of a different society, live in it, but are excluded from any real power or decision-making is a worse fate than to be cloistered, in the literal and figurative senses of this term.

Modern Contraception and its Social Significance. The struggles of some women have gradually resulted in their gaining autonomy and the right to

---

[33] To cite only two, see Michel, op. cit. in n. 30, and Anker, Buvinic, and Youssef, op. cit. in n. 2.
[34] See particularly the synthesis in Michel, op. cit. in n. 30.

be mistresses of their own lives. These victories were 'democratized' and extended to other women after the 1960s when modern methods of contraception came into use. As a result of this new technology, women gained self-determination and, for the first time, were able to make decisions about their own lives. These new opportunities were not only connected with the spectacular liberalization of sexual behaviour among younger women which began in the 1960s—this was only an obvious manifestation of this change. Those who would confine the consequences of modern contraception to this area conceal the implications of this new technology for women's economic behaviour and, indeed, for the entire social and familial culture; implications that are at present admittedly potential rather than fully realized. This change, which they are trying to dismiss, is, indeed, the beginning of a true revolutionary process.

At the level of the family, these conclusions are similar to those drawn by J. Block from an analysis of the crisis in the contemporary American family, which could be extended to other western countries. Block argued that the present crisis in the American family 'has proceeded from the consistent extension of the voluntarist principles of autonomy, choice and mutuality— universally approved standards of our liberal society—to the last traditional institution [the family]'.[35] He adds:

if we extend the principles of autonomy and voluntarism to the husband and wife, making the maintenance of the marital bond a matter of choice and refusing to allow a husband to exercise authority over his wife, why should we be surprised to find children demanding as their right their own autonomy and freedom of choice and refusing to accept the authority of parents.[36]

Just as in the past women and children have been equally oppressed, so today their joint revolt represents two facets of the same revolution.

Although sexual permissiveness is less important in itself than as an aspect of profound social changes on the global scale, the study of pre-marital sexual relations makes it possible to establish a link between the autonomy gained by women and the liberty gained by children. It provides a method of approach to the study of the social and economic implications of the introduction of modern contraceptive methods.

Though Belgium has lagged behind even its closest geographical neighbours in its acceptance of sexual permissiveness, the survey which I conducted in the French-speaking part of the country in 1976–77 among young women who were between the ages of 18 and 29 years on 1 January 1976 has yielded

[35] There are different opinions about this. Some authors believe that changes in the family have lagged behind other social changes, whereas others think that they have preceded them (see especially the work of P. Laslett on this point). I regard the first point of view as providing a more correct assessment of the situation.
[36] J. E. Block, 'New Shapes in Family Life', *Dissent* (1981), pp. 350–57, as cited by Peattie and Rein, op. cit. in n. 27.

some interesting results that support my thesis.[37] For instance, young women who had their first sexual relations without necessarily intending to marry at the time saw these as a *rite de passage* that enabled them to leave the world of children, without as yet fully entering that of adults, who, to them, represented the authority that they wished to throw off. They regarded their sex lives as a means of self-assertion, and used their sexuality in increasing numbers and at ever earlier stages of their lives. Those who engaged in numerous or long-lasting relationships without intending to marry were so conscious of this objective of self-fulfilment that the motivation to avoid pregnancy prevailed and led them to behave in a consistent manner. Thus, 75 per cent had used oral contraceptives, if not during their first sexual experience, then at least on subsequent occasions.[38] In marriage, the use of modern contraception became the norm; it was used by more than 70 per cent of all couples. Current use at the time of the survey was estimated at 50 per cent.[39] In this respect the behaviour of married women who were less than 30 years old before 1 January 1976 differed from that of their older contemporaries who were interviewed in the third round of the three-round survey which began in 1966. The younger women tended to use the more efficient methods of contraception from the beginning of their marriages, so that their reproductive behaviour consisted of a succession of 'active' decisions.[40] Whereas older women tended to use modern contraceptives to stop further increases in the size of their families after they considered these to be complete, younger women demonstrated that they were prepared to make decisions about their lives, at least as far as reproduction was concerned, and recent changes in the life-styles of teenagers suggest that this attitude is becoming more common. For them, children are no longer a natural consequence of marriage, but represent rather one of a number of possible consequences, which had not only to be desired, but to be chosen deliberately.

Social and Economic Implications of Modern Contraception. The economic and social implications of the new power which modern contraception has given to women are immense, even though their full potential has not yet been fully realized. It seems that not even women themselves have fully appreciated the significance of this change, as most feminist writers (or, at

---

[37] G. Julémont, 'Une enquête nationale sur la fécondité, xix. Relations sexuelles et contraception: Évolution de leur signification sociale', *Population et Famille*, 53 (1981–82), pp. 105–29, and 'Relations prénuptiales et prévention de la grossesse', ibid., 50–51 (1980), pp. 119–36.

[38] Julémont (1980), op. cit. in n. 37, p. 120.

[39] Based on Tables 9 and 10 in Julémont (1981–82), op. cit. in n. 37, pp. 113–25.

[40] In the sense used by H. Leibenstein, 'Economic Theory and Fertility Behaviour: A Speculative Essay', *Population and Development Review*, 7 (1981), pp. 377–78. See also J. Ladrière, *Les Enjeux de la rationalité: Le Défi de la science et de la technique aux cultures* (Paris, 1977), p. 129.

least, those who have written in French) are preoccupied with celebrating the victory of sexual liberation, as if this were the only important aspect of this change, whereas it is, in reality, only subsidiary. The implications of this new sexual independence for women's economic position are a different matter. It is now possible for women, married or unmarried, sexually active or not, to follow an occupational career just as men do, untrammelled by the establishment of and care for a family. Those with professional ambitions can be confident that they will be able to avoid both pregnancy and child-birth and, once they have found self-fulfilment outside the domestic sphere like their male partners, they may regard having children as less necessary for their own satisfaction. These new attitudes have been responsible for the second phase of the decline in fertility which has occurred after the baby-boom period that followed the Second World War in the United States at the end of the 1950s, and in Europe during the mid-1960s.

Taken to its logical extreme, this could mean that women might decide to abandon their reproductive functions and the associated activities of child-rearing altogether. In the present state of morals, this could mean that, in the absence of large-scale immigration, their societies would become extinct, unless an alternative solution were found. That such alternative solutions are possible appears to be confirmed by recent advances in embryology, genetics, and biotechnology.[41]

If women wish to exploit this situation, it is urgent that they should act now, lest they be deprived of the advantages at present in their reach. Their power to decide and negotiate whether to have an (additional) child is considerable, even though, as Sullerot has put it, 'having been accustomed even during periods when feminism was active to stress the negative aspects of their roles', women have not yet sought to use these powers in a conscious or organized manner.[42] I would add that women have not yet shown them-selves to be capable of using these powers, because—particularly during periods when feminism was active—too many of them have thought of themselves as second-rate and 'defective' men.[43] Their efforts were devoted to aping the masculine model as closely as possible, rather than to affirming their own proper identity, which they have been conditioned to regard as inferior.

What matters, in addition to reproduction, need to be negotiated? Given the still-prevalent patriarchal structure of the family and of society, only

---

[41] We need only to read the debates in the Parliamentary Assembly of the Council of Europe to realize that the obstacles to artificial reproduction of human beings are now purely ethical. *The Brave New World*, described by Aldous Huxley during the 1930s, is no longer a Utopia, but could easily become a reality.

[42] E. Sullerot, *Le Fait féminin: Qu'estce qu'une femme?* (Paris, 1978), pp. 500, 506.

[43] This term has been used by Peattie and Rein, op. cit. in n. 27, p. 112. To my mind, this view finds its clearest expression in Simone de Beauvoir, *The Second Sex*. It would be difficult to find a clearer denial of the role of women than is given in this book, which is often presented as a feminist classic. To my mind, it is nothing more than an apology for men's supremacy.

women are faced with the dilemma of having to choose between their economic and their familial role at the time of giving birth, or when bearing and bringing up their children. Thus, the division of tasks within the family, and its reorganization at the institutional level, should be the subject of negotiation. Some scholars and reformers have used the term 'equity revolution', which implies a 'major and permanent change in the nature of the family as a social organization'.[44] This change can properly be called a revolution,[45] because it would entail 'repercussions not only for women's roles and identities, but also for the roles, identities and life experiences of men and children'.[46] If the family is to survive, it must succeed in transforming itself, and this implies a complete reorganization of tasks within the family, or an increased institutionalization of child-rearing, or both. These two changes are not mutually exclusive, but rather complement one another. They could mean that some aspects of life which have become private will return to the public domain.[47] Democratization of the family, as of society as a whole, implies the removal of barriers between the individual and society.

The Current Position of Women—The Reality. Peattie and Rein have provided some observations, taken from a variety of sources, relating to the gap between theory and practice in this area. They have pointed to the absence of evidence that 'a substantial renegotiation of the family decision structure' or the redistribution of domestic tasks between the sexes is taking place. Housework continues to be the exclusive responsibility of women, irrespective of whether they work outside their homes or not. Where men have agreed to renegotiate, the discussion is focused on tasks with which a certain amount of social prestige is associated, such as recreational tasks concerned with their children's leisure activities. But they have so far obstinately refused to take on the more routine and humdrum domestic tasks.[48]

The principal change that has occurred in the work of women outside their homes during the last twenty years has been the increase in the proportion of married women in the labour force who have young children and are living with their husbands. However, a closer look at these figures suggests that this economic revolution has been more apparent than real. In the United States today (and also in some other western countries for which statistics are available, such as Denmark, France, Great Britain, and Italy), and probably throughout the western world, women continue to

[44] OECD, *The Equity Revolution*, as cited by Peattie and Rein, op. cit. in n. 27.

[45] This was stressed by Jean Morsa in his report to the Third European Population Conference (see J. Morsa, 'Constitution et dissolution des familles: Structures familiales', Council of Europe, Document EPC82 (2)). See also Julémont (1980), op. cit. in n. 37, pp. 126–27.

[46] OECD, op. cit. in n. 44.

[47] Sullerot speaks of the 'politicisation of the private domain', and Peattie and Rein of 'redrawing of the line between the natural, and the subject of policy' (op. cit. in n. 27, p. 118).

[48] Peattie and Rein, op. cit. in n. 27, pp. 71–72.

arrange their participation in economic activities to fit in with their domestic responsibilities, either by taking part-time employment or by abandoning their careers—either temporarily or permanently.

As a consequence, women tend commonly to continue to be regarded as making only a subsidiary contribution to household expenses, as their incomes tend to be lower than those of men. Even though their earnings may play an important part in determining the household's level of living, they generally contribute less than their male partners do. In a society in which the monetary contribution is of primary importance for the determination of economic status, women's contribution remains secondary.

In terms of status, an economic revolution for women is far from having been achieved, and the difference between the economic positions of men and women has not been closed, even though its size may have been somewhat reduced.[49]

At this point it may be worth recalling Sullerot's remark that, as women have become able to enter the economic sphere more easily, the value of work as a measure of social status has gone down.[50] In the renegotiations that women are urged to undertake, this is an important feature to be taken into account. If the determination of status and the balance of powers are to be changed, it is not sufficient merely to allow women to enter economic life; they must also concede or delegate domestic tasks that have traditionally been theirs. All tasks and roles must be re-examined and re-evaluated.

Conclusion. A number of conclusions follow from this analysis. Although many of the suggested solutions to the problems of women that have been put forward in the developed countries have not succeeded in improving their status, but have resulted in a continuation of the status quo, we shall briefly discuss some of them in order to make the ideas more concrete.

As regards reproductive behaviour, the link between the availability of traditional or modern contraceptives and the position of women is neither simple nor automatic. Modern contraceptive techniques have been important in bringing about the indispensable autonomy which was needed before a renegotiation of tasks and roles could be undertaken in favourable conditions, but contraception remains what Judith Blake and Kingsley Davis have called an explanatory 'intermediate variable'.[51] This is probably part of the reason why women have failed to recognize the powers that these modern techniques have given them.

It is also imperative for women to recognize that they will not improve their own position or status by lowering the position of children, especially within the family, by regarding them as simple objects, or by abandoning

[49] Ibid., pp. 61–69.
[50] Sullerot, op. cit. in n. 42, p. 491.
[51] K. Davis and J. Blake, 'Social Structure and Fertility: An Analytical Framework', *Economic Development and Social Change*, 4 (1956), pp. 211–35.

their prerogatives and the essential role they themselves play in the reproductive process. To do so would be to give away some of the most important trump cards that they at present hold.

As regards institutions, two principal conclusions emerge. First, the creation of part-time jobs reserved to women is no solution to the crisis in the contemporary family. On the contrary, such a policy would sharpen and exacerbate existing inequalities, and carry within it the seeds of future conflict. The correct solution must rather lie in restructuring the use that both men and women make of their time through the introduction of more flexible working hours for both sexes that will be compatible with rearing a family. In this context, new attitudes to the value of work are important, provided that they apply to both sexes equally, and are replaced by a higher valuation of other activities, such as leisure. Following this change of view, the value in exchange of tasks will become less important than their value in use.

The setting-up of nurseries to care for very young children of working mothers is not sufficient either. A wide variety of specific aids is needed to assist in housework and child-rearing and to free couples from the routine and repetitive work that these tasks at present involve, so as to make time available for a more creative use of their energies and for the expression of affection. It must, however, be emphasized that these aids will benefit women only if there is full economic equality between husbands and wives, and the repetitive and irksome domestic tasks which are at present exclusively carried out by women to ensure the welfare of their families do not become occupations that are reserved for women. If this were to happen, women would feel—and rightly so—that they have been deceived and will again retreat into their families and households.[52] In an individualist society such as ours, such a retreat would represent an irreparable failure, unless women were to arrive at a point where they could renegotiate the constraints of reproduction in terms of power based not on the number of children they have borne, but rather on the responsibilities and use of inventions which are an essential part of child-rearing today.

Implications for Less Developed Countries

Our analysis has led us to certain conclusions which are in accord with the work of other authors. For instance, K. B. Ward amongst others has

---

[52] It is in this way that the reconstitution of the family—in the modern sense of the term—can be explained, with a separation of domestic work, to be done by women, and economic activities, to be carried out by men—as has happened in the kibbutzim of Israel. It was the women themselves, shut away in the less prestigious occupations, who reconstituted a domestic domain which provided them with a higher status. See E. Ben Rafael and S. Weitman, 'The Reconstitution of the Family in the Kibbutz', *European Journal of Sociology*, 25 (1984), pp. 1–27.

suggested that a family-planning programme has no chance of being successful unless it is preceded (or at least accompanied) by a take-off in economic development.[53] She focused attention on the structure of employment offered to women, because she considers fertility to be a matter for individual decisions taken mainly by women, as has recently been the case in industrialized societies. However, it appears that this is a question of the structure and the amount of employment offered in the formal sector to the labour force as a whole—that is, to both men and women. In a stagnant economy, the effect of women's activity on fertility (even in the formal sector) could be positive—resulting in larger numbers of children because a large family will be the only outwardly visible indicator of wealth. Moreover, considering the situation in individualist terms in countries where only a collectivist system of values is shared by both sexes, will probably give no indication of what would actually happen.

To achieve a change in the valuation of children at the individual as well as the collective levels, it is necessary to find a solution to the problem of daily survival. It is only when the present is regarded as being to some extent secure, when the child is no longer regarded as an indispensable economic support for its family, that it becomes possible for parents to plan for the future and to try and shape it differently from the past. In other words, the problem is one of increasing awareness and of extending the area in which individuals feel that they can exercise free will and freedom of choice. Only when this situation has been achieved will children—representing a potential future—be regarded as a class of dependants, and the social, economic, and family costs of rearing them be properly evaluated.

Though I am less familiar with the economic sphere, it seems to me that modern technology, foreign aid, and investments, as they are applied in the less developed world today, 'actually have negative consequences for long-run economic growth'.[54] The conditions for the beginning of economic development in the contemporary Third World are very different from what they were in the industrialized countries a century or so ago. Industrial development today does not create employment, particularly not for unskilled or less skilled workers, that would mop up the supply of excess labour. Nor is emigration, which used to be an important outlet for excess labour, and which was so important in the West during the nineteenth and twentieth centuries, available today. By disturbing the traditional economic structure in which every individual had his or her own social position and value, industrialization today leads to unemployment and underemployment with all the painful consequences that follow from them. It is rather through developments based on employment of the labour force to which everyone, men as well as women, can contribute in accordance with their abilities and

---

[53] Ward, op. cit. in n. 7, pp. 152–53.
[54] Ibid., p. 10.

needs that awareness of the future which is necessary for the reduction of fertility can be achieved.

In the beginning, using Ariès's terminology, users of contraception will be 'ascetics'. In order that contraception should become acceptable in societies in which sexuality has not acquired the same negative connotation as in western Christian societies, the methods must be both certain and efficient. So that they should be used efficiently, it will be necessary to create a strong motivation to avoid pregnancy, through the desire to realize a common purpose that is based on the idea of a common good.

Our analysis has suggested that, if contraception is only an intermediate variable that connects the status of women with voluntary birth control, the status women occupy is not by itself sufficient to explain the reduction in fertility either. All successful examples of development go to show that women's entry into the labour force outside their own households, followed by an improvement in their economic status and the reduction of their fertility, are different aspects of the same social transformation. Improvements in women's education mark the beginning of an improvement in their status and, therefore, play an important part in this process. However, if the status of women is defined in terms of their 'access to economic resources relatively to that of men, their economic status is not modified greatly'.[55] It is even possible, as was the case in Europe and Japan, that a reduction in fertility could precede an improvement in women's status, and that changes in status would reinforce and amplify the size of the fertility reduction. To put it in extreme terms, improvements in women's status, far from being a cause of fertility reduction, are more likely to be a consequence thereof. Whatever the truth may be, both these phenomena are merely symptoms of a more profound social change, that politicians and policy-makers will need to understand and foster.

Conclusion

When I began this study I assumed that the situation of children within the family was inversely related to that of women.[56] But it would appear that the relation between these two phenomena is more complex than appears at first sight. The beginning of the concept of childhood, as Ariès has described it, may be regarded as being simultaneously an improvement in and a deterioration of the status of children. It was an improvement, because the educational care that accompanied the segregation of children rendered them more precious in themselves, if only on account of the hopes invested in them. Attention and care given by parents to their children increased and

---

[55] Ibid., p. 19.

[56] A similar hypothesis has been presented by E. Varikas, 'Genèse d'une conscience féministe dans la Grèce du XIXe siècle, 1887–1907', thesis presented to the University of Paris VII, cited by C. Dauphin, *et al.*, 'Culture et pouvoirs des femmes', *Annales ESC*, 41 (1986), p. 281.

could be seen as the origin of the public expression of what has been called 'affection'. But education is a two-edged weapon; it has also resulted in a deterioration of children's status, because children came to be seen as a class of dependants. They were regarded as inferior, incapable of making decisions for themselves, and needing to be guided or socialized to conform to rules imposed by adults. They had no social rights or entitlements of their own, other than the right to education or instruction until they had passed the barrier that separated them from the adult world. In practice, it was a situation open to all kinds of abuses.

Ariès showed that children lost some of their freedom during this period of transition. We may consider, as Ariès has done, that this loss was in the children's own interest, but it is also possible that it resulted in the formation of a new out-group, deprived of all rights reserved to members of the in-group—a recipe for potential conflict. The revolt of the young during the 1960s was no accident.

Although I do not rely overmuch on the history of feelings and attitudes, as I believe this requires criteria which are specific in space and time, it is likely that the part of family life expressed in affection for children has become more important, whilst at the same time the feeling of equality on which such affection should be based has disappeared. The young of today are trying to overcome the constraints that have been imposed on them by this segregation. In their efforts to do so, they will undoubtedly make mistakes, which will result, once again, in both an improvement in and a deterioration of the status of children, for children must—willingly or unwillingly—necessarily experience this period of dependency.

The relegation of children to a dependent class has coincided with a similar relegation of women into a dependent caste, which has divided the adult world into two groups, the able and the disabled, the strong and the weak, the whole and the defective. The division based on gender cannot be overcome. The problems, as Gunnar Myrdal has shown, are similar to those that arise from a division into ethnic or racial groups. Just as a black person cannot become white, so a woman cannot turn into a man. The fact that only men continue to be considered as fully able adults is a recipe for oppression, and the fact that such oppression may be an expression of affection, as some historians of conjugal love have held, does not alter the situation in any material way. There are two ways of escaping from this oppression: assimilation, or the achievement of a separate identity. The struggle for the former is endless and does not result in any redistribution of power—those who retain power need only introduce a slight change in the rules of the game; so, for example, when occupations become predominantly feminine, they tend to lose prestige, and conversely. The latter solution—based on achieving a separate identity—seems more promising but will take much longer unless women become more aware of their power and initiate a true revolutionary process.

6 Women's Position and Child Mortality and Morbidity in Less Developed Countries

JOHN CALDWELL AND PAT CALDWELL

This chapter will be focused on the situation of adult women—almost invariably mothers—and the resulting impact on the health of children of either sex. It would be a very different chapter if it had been entitled 'Women's Status and Health', in which sex differentials in morbidity rather than of child mortality would be discussed. Yet, these two topics are related in at least two ways. First, the kind of disadvantage which results in the higher mortality of women is often the same as that which prevents mothers from optimizing the health care of their children. Secondly, unnecessarily high mortality of girls in childhood almost invariably results in unnecessarily high overall child mortality, because differences between the mortality of the two sexes are unlikely to reduce the deaths of boys as much as they increase the deaths of girls. Accordingly, we shall briefly examine certain sex differentials in mortality in the next section.

There are a number of problems associated with the study of child health in less developed countries. The first is that very little satisfactory statistical work has been done on morbidity, and nearly all the evidence cited relates to child mortality. The second is that the impact of external conditions on infant mortality is not as great as it is on child mortality.[1] The reason is that breast-feeding dominates mortality during the first year of life; it usually provides both milk and protection by maternal antibodies, regardless of the mother's education or social status. This problem is compounded by the greater number of studies of infant rather than child mortality, and may be one of the reasons why differentials in child mortality by mother's status are sometimes not found. The third difficulty is that mortality estimates for many countries in the Third World are obtained by indirect techniques, which blur real differences between mortality at different ages. Indeed, the problem goes further, in that estimates of life expectancy at birth are frequently based on child mortality, so that there is usually a high correlation between the figures compiled by international agencies of infant mortality

[1] A. Palloni, 'Mortality in Latin America: Emerging Patterns', *Population and Development Review*, 7 (1981), pp. 623–50, esp. pp. 641 ff.; J. N. Hobcraft, J. W. McDonald, and S. O. Rutstein, 'Socio-economic Factors in Infant and Child Mortality: A Cross-National Comparison', *Population Studies*, 38 (1984), pp. 193–224.

rates, child death rates, and life expectancies at birth (e.g. in the *World Development Report*).

There are obvious problems in using definitions of women's status which will satisfy everybody. We shall concentrate on eight elements.

1. *Autonomy*. This refers to a woman's control over resources, and her ability to make decisions on her own and to act upon these decisions.[2] The issue is confused, because there are different types of autonomy, of which the most significant here is sexual autonomy and its implications for various degrees of seclusion.[3]

2. *Kinship*. This may refer to the type of residential family, or to emotional and economic ramifications that go beyond residence. It may also refer to the distinction between involvement in a monogamous or polygynous marriage.

3. *Education*. The measure of education we use is almost always either the number of years of full-time formal education received, or recognized educational levels, or qualifications attained.

4. *Social Status*. This is usually defined operationally, not by any concept of social class, let alone class of origin, but by occupation, usually that of the husband.

5. *Work*. The measure used here is whether the woman works outside the home or not, with outside work usually defined as paid work, and excluding labour on family land.

6. *Income*. In the rare cases where this is measured, the measure used is generally family income, although there are problems in sub-Saharan Africa where the two spouses may have separate budgets, or where there are polygynous households. Problems also arise from the existence of joint families.

We shall also pay some attention to *ethnicity*, *culture*, and *radicalism*.

Women's Position and Mortality

There has recently been a renewal of interest in differences between the mortality of men and women, especially in south Asia.[4] In addition, there

---

[2] C. Safilios-Rothschild, 'Female Power, Autonomy, and Demographic Change in the Third World', in R. Anker, M. Buvinic, and N. H. Youssef (eds.), *Women's Roles and Population Trends in the Third World* (London, 1982), pp. 117–32; T. Dyson and M. Moore, 'On Kinship Structure, Female Autonomy, and Demographic Behaviour in India', *Population and Development Review*, 9 (1983), pp. 45–46.

[3] P. Caldwell and J. C. Caldwell, 'Kinship Forms, Female Autonomy, and Fertility', paper presented to the Rockefeller Foundation Workshop on Status of Women and Fertility/Mortality, Bellagio, 6–10 June 1988.

[4] B. Miller, *The Endangered Sex* (Ithaca, NY, 1981); Social Science Research Council Workshop on Differential Female Mortality and Health Care in South Asia, Dhaka, 4–8 Jan. 1987.

are data from the World Fertility Survey (WFS) for more than forty less developed countries, which provide information on age-specific mortality.[5] These data confirm the view that mortality of boys during the first year of life is usually higher than that of girls, when the year as a whole is considered. Other information suggests that in many countries this is due to the domination of infant mortality by neonatal mortality, and obscures the fact that girls' mortality is often higher than boys' during the second half, or even during most of the first year of life.[6] However, in every survey taken in south Asia (Bangladesh, Nepal, Pakistan, Sri Lanka), the Middle East, and north Africa, except Tunisia (Egypt, Jordan, Morocco, Syria, Sudan, Turkey, Yemen AR), and in about half the Latin American surveys, the mortality of girls was found to be higher than that of boys between 1 and 5 years of age. In east and south-east Asia, girls' mortality was higher than boys' at this age in the Philippines; during the last three years of this age range, it was higher also in Korea and Thailand. Only in sub-Saharan Africa was the mortality of girls generally lower than that of boys. In India, the Sample Registration System makes it possible to compare the mortality of the two sexes over the whole age range.[7] This comparison clearly distinguishes between two different types of disadvantage suffered by females. The first occurs at ages below 10 years and seems to have been due to relative neglect, rather than positive discrimination, in that there is no excess mortality of girls between the ages of 10 and 14 years, when girls are better able to fend for themselves. The second hump of excess mortality is found among women aged between 15 and 34 years, and is explained by high maternal mortality, because the excess disappears after the thirtieth birthday in those states in which child-bearing on average ceases at an earlier age. A similar bimodal distribution has been found for the Matlab area of Bangladesh.[8] Two points should be noted. First, women's high mortality during their reproductive years has a biological component, in that it has been falling during recent years as fertility has declined. Secondly, this biological component is clearly affected by the social context. The very high levels of anaemia that have been found may be related to the distribution of food, although they are also inevitably affected by family poverty. High maternal mortality is sustained by low proportions of women giving birth with trained attendants and at appropriate health facilities. These are marks

[5] S. O. Rutstein, 'Infant and Child Mortality: Levels, Trends and Demographic Differentials', in WFS, *Comparative Studies* (London, 1984); P. Caldwell and J. C. Caldwell, 'Gender Implications for Survival in South Asia', Health Transition Working Paper, No. 7. Health Transition Centre, Australian National University, Canberra, 1990.

[6] S. D'Souza and L. Chen, 'Sex Differentials in Mortality in Rural Bangladesh', *Population and Development Review*, 6 (1980), pp. 257–70.

[7] Caldwell and Caldwell, op. cit. in n. 5.

[8] International Diarrhoeal Diseases Research Centre, Bangladesh, data presented to the Social Science Research Council Workshop on Differential Female Mortality and Health Care in South Asia, Dhaka, 4–8 Jan. 1987.

of national poverty, but also evidence of political priorities and the priorities of men in individual communities. It should also be noted that the difference between the life expectancies at birth of the two sexes has probably now disappeared in India,[9] but this owes a good deal to the substantial excess mortality of men at ages above 40. There are also cultural differences, as is shown by lower excess mortality of women in the south at all ages, and, indeed, by the absence of any significant excess in any age group in Tamil Nadu.[10] Evidence of the strong social component in both humps of excess mortality of females is provided by Langford's demonstration that the excess in Sri Lanka began to disappear very rapidly in the non-reproductive, as well as the reproductive, age groups after 1953,[11] a year of political ferment inducing social change.

There is other evidence of the relative neglect of girls which has resulted in raising the general level of child mortality, and which is related both to their own position and to that of their mothers. Indeed, we found that one of the indicators of the higher status of women in rural south India was the ability to treat their daughters as well as they did their sons.[12] In Bangladesh it has been shown that, once adjustments have been made for relative requirements, girls, especially those less than 5 years old, receive less food—especially during periods of shortage—than boys, and are more stunted; moreover, the likelihood that they will be brought even for free treatment for diarrhoea is only two-thirds that of boys.[13] It has been argued that the relative neglect of daughters, in both Bangladesh and India, is primarily economic,[14] rather than cultural, particularly among the poor, but it is clear that it is specific aspects of the culture that make the economic value of sons relatively so much greater.

Recent General Studies of Women's Position and Child Health

Flegg has used macro-data to examine inequality of income, illiteracy, and medical care as determinants of infant mortality in forty-six less developed

[9] T. Dyson, 'Excess Female Mortality in India: Uncertain Evidence and a Narrowing Differential', paper presented to the Social Science Research Council Workshop on Differential Female Mortality and Health Care in South Asia, Dhaka, 4–8 Jan. 1987.
[10] Caldwell and Caldwell, op. cit. in n. 5.
[11] C. M. Langford, 'Sex Differentials in Sri Lanka: Past Trends and the Situation Recently', paper presented to the Social Science Research Council Workshop on Differential Female Mortality and Health Care, Dhaka, 4–8 Jan. 1987.
[12] J. C. Caldwell, P. Reddy, and P. Caldwell, 'The Social Components of Mortality Decline: An Investigation in South India Employing Alternative Methodologies', *Population Studies*, 37 (1983), pp. 185–215.
[13] L. C. Chen, E. Huq, and S. D'Souza, 'Sex Bias in the Family Allocation of Food and Health in Rural Bangladesh', *Population and Development Review*, 7 (1981), pp. 55–84.
[14] M. A. Koenig and S. D'Souza, 'Sex Differences in Childhood Mortality in Rural Bangladesh', *Social Science and Medicine*, 22 (1986), pp. 15–22; J. Pettigrew, 'Child Neglect in Rural Punjabi Families', *Journal of Comparative Family Studies*, 17 (1986).

countries.[15] Taking the proportion of women who are illiterate as an indicator of mothers' education, he identified this as the second most important factor among those he studied. A drop of 1 per cent in illiteracy among women had an impact on the infant mortality rate double that of a rise of 1 per cent in the number of medical practitioners, and three times that of a rise of 1 per cent in the number of nurses. On the other hand, the importance of women's literacy was only three-fifths that of income (as measured by the effect of greater equality of incomes).

Hobcraft, McDonald, and Rutstein examined data from twenty-eight surveys taken in less developed countries as part of the WFS[16] to determine what socio-economic factors were most important for infant mortality in developing countries. They found that both mothers' and fathers' education, particularly the former, were of predominant importance, especially in Latin America, east Asia, and south-east Asia. Fathers' occupation (probably a proxy for income and, to some extent, social class) was less, but still substantially, significant, and mothers' work status and urban–rural residence were relatively unimportant.

In an important study undertaken for the United Nations, socio-economic differences in child mortality were studied for fifteen less developed countries with reasonably comprehensive data.[17] Seven were in Africa (Ghana, Kenya, Lesotho, Liberia, Nigeria, Sierra Leone, and Sudan; unfortunately all anglophone, with six being former British colonies); five were in Asia (Indonesia, Nepal, South Korea, Sri Lanka, and Thailand) and provided a reasonable distribution, except for south-west Asia and the exclusion of the two giants, China and India; and three (Chile, Jamaica, and Peru) were in central or south America. Child mortality was measured by the proportion of children who had died, and the authors concluded, from a comparison with the average loss of women of the same marriage duration and age elsewhere, that the most important factor was mothers' education. Child mortality fell by 6.8 per cent for each additional year of schooling (and by 3.8 per cent when all other variables were controlled—an excessive degree of control, as the authors noted, because many of these other variables were influenced by the mothers' education). Only two other variables proved to be important: ethnic variation and fathers' education. The former is a clear indicator of the significance of cultural factors and probably has two main components: the position of women, and interpretations of child care. The latter is probably a measure of income, although the extent to which family attitudes to the position of children and the role of child care also change with fathers' education should not be underestimated.

[15] A. T. Flegg, 'Inequality of Income, Illiteracy and Medical Care as Determinants of Infant Mortality in Underdeveloped Countries', *Population Studies*, 36 (1982), pp. 441–58.
[16] Hobcraft, McDonald, and Rutstein, op. cit. in n. 1.
[17] B. Mensch, H. Lentzner, and S. Preston, *Socio-economic Differentials in Child Mortality in Developing Countries* (UN, New York, 1985).

In the United Nations study the authors found that economic factors, and even the availability of piped water and flush lavatories in the household, only exercised a weak influence on child mortality. They concluded:

Our results tend to emphasize the importance of socio-cultural variables relative to socio-economic ones. The very considerable impact of mother's education and ethnicity points above all to the potential importance of child care practices in determining levels of child mortality. It is reasonable to suppose that these practices are generally improved by school attendance both for the specific hygienic practices learned, and for the general changes in outlook and break with resistance to innovations that invariably results. Similarly, it seems likely that much of the impact of ethnicity represents variation in child care practices, perhaps particularly those practices surrounding the event of birth itself.[18]

Caldwell, when exploring the 'Routes to Low Mortality in Poor Countries',[19] examined the health experience of ninety-nine less developed countries with populations exceeding one million, listed in the *World Development Report*.[20] The characteristic that was found to correlate most closely with low levels of child mortality was the proportion of girls in primary school almost a quarter of a century earlier. The real relation, of course, is between child health and mothers' schooling. Once again, fathers' schooling was shown to be important, whereas the ratio of medical practitioners in the population was much less significant, with even less impact (in descending order of importance) being exercised by food intake, the proportion of nurses in the population, and finally income per head. One other factor which was almost as strongly correlated with low child mortality as mothers' education was the practice of some form of fertility control by the parents. This may partly serve as a measure of the care taken of children, once family growth is curtailed, but the most likely cause is that the curtailment of family size and greater care for children both originate in a new view of the importance of the child.[21] In the study, countries were also identified in which mortality was unexpectedly low and those in which it was unexpectedly high, relative to income per head. In the former group were Sri Lanka, China, Burma, Jamaica, India, Zaire, Tanzania, Kenya, Costa Rica, Ghana, and Thailand. It was also pointed out that the situation in the Indian state of Kerala was even better than in Sri Lanka. Countries in which child mortality was relatively high in relation to average income were Oman, Saudi Arabia, Iran, Libya, Algeria, Iraq, Yemen AR, Morocco, Ivory Coast, Senegal, and Sierra Leone. Difficulties have clearly been experienced in the oil-rich states in converting relatively recent wealth into good health, but, even when they are excluded, it is obviously disadvantageous to health to belong to the western wing of

[18] Ibid., p. 289.

[19] J. Caldwell, 'Routes to Low Mortality in Poor Countries', *Population and Development Review*, 12 (1986), pp. 171–220.

[20] World Bank, *World Development Report, 1984* (New York, 1984).

[21] J. C. Caldwell, *Theory of Fertility Decline* (London, 1982).

Islam (Mauritania to Pakistan), probably largely because of the limited autonomy enjoyed by women in this area. The other major contrasts between the two groups are the higher proportion of educated women among the superior health achievers, and the greater proportion of women who practised family planning. Clearly, there are links between these three factors. The author also examined some of the countries in which most success had been achieved in terms of low levels of child mortality relative to average income, and concluded that a relatively autonomous position of women, a comparatively high level of women's education, and a tradition of radicalism could all be identified in them.

The situation in a number of countries has also been analysed in some regional studies. Palloni has studied the situation in Latin America[22] and concluded that mothers' education played the major role in determining child mortality, although the effect of income was equally important for determining mortality during the first year of life. Martin *et al.* examined three Asian countries (Philippines, Indonesia, and Pakistan) and concluded that both mothers' and fathers' education were of primary importance for child survival, and that such factors as sanitation, piped water, and electricity were also significant.[23]

There have also been a number of studies of India, a country which is of interest because its size and division into numerous states make possible the kind of analyses which are often employed on a global scale to compare different countries. Schultz has shown that differences between the mortality of the two sexes in childhood were smaller in areas in which girls were more likely to earn income when they grew up.[24] This is, of course, an index of women's autonomy, whilst indicating at the same time one way in which such autonomy achieves lower child mortality. Dyson and Moore have demonstrated that women's autonomy was greater and child mortality lower in the south of India than the north.[25] Jain also showed the importance of literacy among adult women, which he related to an increased chance of a birth being attended by trained medical personnel, and a greater likelihood of children being immunized.[26]

Measures of women's autonomy, when related to child mortality, are as yet largely confined either to geographical comparisons, or to contrasting women in terms of such characteristics as religion or education. So far,

[22] Palloni, op. cit. in n. 1.

[23] L. G. Martin, J. Trussell, F. R. Salvail, and N. M. Shah, 'Co-variates of Child Mortality in the Philippines, Indonesia and Pakistan: An Analysis Based on Hazard Models', *Population Studies*, 37 (1983), pp. 417–32.

[24] T. P. Schultz, 'Women's Work and their Status: Rural Indian Evidence of Labour Market and Environmental Effects on Sex Differences in Childhood Mortality', in Anker, Buvinic, and Youssef, op. cit. in n. 2.

[25] Dyson and Moore, op. cit. in n. 2.

[26] A. K. Jain, 'Determinants of Regional Variation in Infant Mortality in Rural India', *Population Studies*, 39 (1985), pp. 407–24.

decision-making power, freedom of movement, or sexual freedom have not been related in quantitative terms to child survival.

Nor has there been much quantitative work to test the kinship situation. Straus and Winkelmann have shown that the middle classes in Bombay were more likely to live in nuclear families, and the working classes in families that were neither nuclear nor joint, but were often aggregated fragments that bore testimony to misfortune or migration.[27] They showed that decisions in the middle classes were more likely to be shared between spouses, in contrast to the situation among the working classes, where decisions were generally husband-led, though there was a significant minority in which they were wife-led. The authors did not investigate health decisions; however, this was done in depth for twenty-nine families in Uttar Pradesh.[28] Thirteen of the twenty wives said that they had no power to call in a medical practitioner because they were illiterate and were not used to taking initiatives outside the home, and therefore felt that they were ill-suited to make decisions about treatment (the investigators apparently agreed). In a situation in which few women had received any education at all, the researchers identified the characteristics which allowed seven women to call in medical practitioners as earning money, nuclear residence, and older age.

Most work has been done on parents' education, especially that of the mother. Preston has provided data for the United States in the late nineteenth century which show that at that time wide educational differences did not result in large differentials in child mortality, a finding that he explained in terms of lack of knowledge about health, even among the middle classes.[29] Caldwell has questioned this interpretation in the light of Australian historical research, and has suggested that the difference was so narrow because of inability on the part of the medical system to produce much to help even those parents who were sufficiently well educated to persist, and rich enough to have the necessary resources.[30] Three generations later, Chase and Nelson used data for New York in 1968, and found marked infant mortality differentials by mothers' education.[31] Work in Malaysia showed a marked impact of mothers' education on infant mortality, but found that fathers' education and income had little significance, suggesting a strong cultural

---

[27] M. A. Straus and D. Winkelmann, 'Social Class, Fertility and Authority in Nuclear and Joint Households in Bombay', *Journal of Asian and African Studies*, 4 (1969).

[28] M. E. Khan, R. Anker, S. K. G. Dastidar, and S. Bairathi, *Inequalities between Men and Women in Nutrition and Family Welfare Services: An In-Depth Enquiry in an Indian Village* (ILO Population and Labour Policies Programme, Working Paper, No. 158; Geneva, 1987).

[29] S. H. Preston, 'Resources, Knowledge, and Child Mortality: A Comparison of the US in the Late Nineteenth Century and Developing Countries Today', in IUSSP, *Proceedings of the International Population Conference, Florence, 1985* (Liège, 1985), iv. 373–88.

[30] Caldwell, op. cit. in n. 19.

[31] H. C. Chase and F. G. Nelson, 'Education of Mothers, Medical Care and Condition of Infant', in H. C. Chase (ed.), *A Study of Risks, Medical Care, and Infant Mortality*, Supplement to *American Journal of Public Health* (1973).

impact on child survival.[32] In neighbouring Thailand, Frenzen and Hogan found mothers' education to have a strong impact on infant mortality, but this disappeared as a determinant after controls were introduced for fathers' social class, mothers' health information, and whether births were wanted or not.[33] A more satisfactory interpretation might regard the close relation between these factors and mothers' education as partly explaining its origin, and partly forming its elements, so that it is hardly possible to talk of the disappearance of mothers' education as a significant influence on mortality. In Sri Lanka, Trussell and Hammerslough analysed WFS data to show that parents' education dominated the socio-economic determination of child mortality, but that fathers' education was more important than that of the mothers.[34]

There are a series of studies on mainland south Asia. Bairagi established from data for Companyganj in Bangladesh that both income and mothers' education were important influences on child mortality and were interrelated, so that at very low income levels mothers' education had little impact because their capacity to deal with the situation was severely restricted, but that, as income increased and more choices became available, the benefit to the child of having a literate mother became ever greater.[35] In Kerala, Nag assessed the situation that arose from more frequent and better use of health facilities by mothers, caused by their higher levels of education and by the partly associated conviction of even poor mothers of their rights to health provision for themselves and their children.[36] Gulati put forward a similar argument for Kerala fisherwomen, but also maintained that their education had made them aware of the existence of health facilities and convinced them of their value.[37]

In the Middle East, Kohli and Al-Omain demonstrated that, in almost wholly urban Kuwait, mothers' education was of foremost importance, both among the native population and in the immigrant communities.[38] In rural

---

[32] J. DaVanzo, W. P. Butz, and J. P. Habicht, 'How Biological and Behavioural Influences on Mortality in Malaysia Vary during the First Year of Life', *Population Studies*, 37 (1983), pp. 381–402; J. DaVanzo, 'Infant Mortality and Economic Development: The Case of Malaysia', in IUSSP, *Proceedings of the International Population Conference, Florence, 1985* (Liège, 1985), ii. 79–92.

[33] P. D. Frenzen and D. P. Hogan, 'The Impact of Class, Education, and Health Care on Infant Mortality in a Developing Society: The Case of Rural Thailand', *Demography*, 19 (1982), pp. 391–408.

[34] J. Trussell and C. Hammerslough, 'A Hazards-Model Analysis of the Covariates of Infant and Child Mortality in Sri Lanka', *Demography*, 20 (1983), pp. 1–26.

[35] R. Bairagi, 'Is Income the Only Constraint on Child Nutrition in Rural Bangladesh?', *Bulletin of the World Health Organization*, 58 (1980).

[36] M. Nag, 'Impact of Social and Economic Development on Mortality: Comparative Study of Kerala and West Bengal', *Economic and Political Weekly*, 18 (1983), pp. 18–21.

[37] L. Gulati, 'Fisherwomen on the Kerala Coast: Demographic and Socio-economic Impact of a Fisheries Development Project', in ILO, *Women, Work and Development* (Geneva, 1984).

[38] K. L. Kohli and M. Al-Omain, 'Levels and Trends of Infant, Foetal, and Childhood Mortality and their Determinants: A Case Study of Kuwait', *Population Bulletin of ECWA*, 22–3 (1982), pp. 93–118.

Jordan, Edmonston also showed that mothers' education, together with access to maternity and child health programmes, were important for infant mortality, and health facilities for child mortality.[39] In Peru, Young, Edmonston, and Andes showed that there were marked differentials in infant and child mortality by mothers' education, and none at all by the existence or non-existence of health institutions.[40] Pebley and Stupp found in Guatemala that the substantial impact of mothers' education on infant mortality was achieved partly because, among more educated women, there were not the same levels of excess infant mortality caused by births to mothers of very young or very old ages, or after unusually short birth intervals.[41] In sub-Saharan Africa, Oyeka demonstrated that mothers' education was an important determinant of child mortality in rural areas, but that income was the main determinant in urban areas.[42]

Compared with the recent stress on mothers' education, little work has been done on other socio-economic determinants of child mortality. This is particularly true of social class, which has usually been defined inadequately by reference to either education or husband's occupation. There is some evidence for the importance of this factor, in that the middle classes have easier access to and receive greater attention from the health services. This was found to be true in Ibadan by Okediji,[43] and in the Punjab by Gupta, who concluded that 'mothers with high socio-economic level and low birth order were found to be the most common acceptors of hospital-based obstetrical care during childbirth'.[44] Schultz used Indian data to show that the excess mortality of girls was lower when there were significant levels of women's participation in wage work outside the household.[45] He concluded that the lower mortality of boys was a function of the greater demand for sons. Differences were also smaller in other situations where the traditional peasant, largely subsistence, and illiterate culture had been modified by irrigation, higher school attendance of girls, or residence in towns. He concluded that, if culture is important, it operates through the existence of a market for female labour, and that Indian Muslims are different only in that

[39] B. Edmonston, 'Community Variations in Infant and Child Mortality in Rural Jordan', *Journal of Developing Areas*, 17 (1983), pp. 473–89.

[40] F. W. Young, B. Edmonston, and N. Andes, 'Community-Level Determinants of Infant and Child Mortality in Peru', *Social Indicators Research*, 12 (1983).

[41] A. B. Pebley and P. W. Stupp, 'Reproductive Patterns and Child Mortality in Guatemala', *Demography*, 24 (1987), pp. 43–60.

[42] I. C. A. Oyeka, 'Development and Investigation of a Patt Model of Child Mortality Determinants in Ghana', Ph.D. Dissertation, University of Michigan (Facsimile University Microfilms International, Ann Arbor, Mich., 1977).

[43] F. O. Okediji, 'Nigeria: Socio-economic Status and Attitudes to Public Health Problems in the Western State: A Case Study of Ibadan', in J. C. Caldwell, N. O. Addo, S. K. Gaisie, I. Igun, and F. O. Olusanya (eds.), *Population Growth and Socioeconomic Change in West Africa* (New York, 1975).

[44] S. C. Gupta, 'Social Correlates of the Mother's Intra-Natal Health Behaviour', *Journal of Family Welfare*, 32 (1986), p. 48.

[45] Schultz, op. cit. in n. 24.

their women are less likely to work outside the home. This, of course, merely places the impact of culture a further step back—back, in fact, to women's autonomy.

It has been shown in a series of studies that, whatever the autonomous or educated mother may want to do, family income can modify the use she makes of the health services. This has been demonstrated for the Philippines, Indonesia, and Pakistan by Martin *et al.*,[46] and for Bangladesh by Bairagi.[47] In India, Shariff has shown that poor mothers waited longer to see what happened in the course of their children's illness before using their money and time in seeking treatment,[48] while in Senegal Garenne and van de Walle found that cost was a factor in making the decision whether to use modern medicine or traditional treatment.[49]

Perhaps the clearest demonstration of the importance of cultural factors is provided by the substantial differences between child mortality in different ethnic groups in the same country, which persist even after other variables have been controlled. This has been shown for Malaysia.[50] Such patterns are also found throughout sub-Saharan Africa, where it is not clear whether they indicate differences between the positions of women or those of children, or interactions between the two. In an area of the west African savannah, where there was little in the way of access to health services or education, Hilderbrand *et al.* found clear differences between child survival rates in different ethnic groups, which suggests differences in the nature and level of child care.[51] This again shows that culture, rather than economic determinants and the level of health facilities, is important, but that the role played by women remains uncertain, except perhaps in so far as there is more or less pressure on them to devote themselves to child care, or to take the blame for child deaths.

There are no published studies of the impact of kinship–family type, marriage type, or relationships within the family on child mortality. Further study would be warranted, because women's autonomy is controlled by family type and position in the family.

[46] Martin *et al.*, op. cit. in n. 23.

[47] Bairagi, op. cit. in n. 35.

[48] A. Shariff, 'Some Cultural Factors Associated with Morbidity and Mortality in South India: A Village-Level Investigation', mimeo, Institute for Social and Economic Change, Bangalore, 1986.

[49] M. Garenne and F. van de Walle, 'Knowledge, Attitudes and Practices Related to Child Health and Mortality in Siné-Saloum, Senegal', in IUSSP, *Proceedings of the International Population Conference, Florence, 1985* (Liège, 1985), iv. 267–78.

[50] DaVanzo (1985), op. cit. in n. 32.

[51] K. Hilderbrand, A. G. Hill, S. Randall, and M. L. van Eerenbeemt, 'Child Mortality and Care for Children in Rural Mali', paper presented to the National Institute for Research Advancement and IUSSP Seminar on Social and Biological Correlates of Mortality, Tokyo, 24–27 Nov. 1984.

Assessing the Evidence

We shall now draw some general conclusions from the rather heterogeneous evidence, and draw on some of our own research experience in attempting this integration.

Although women's education may not be our fundamental concern, in that an educated woman's later experience cannot be derived completely from her training, and may be replicable in other ways, nevertheless most of the confirmed results come from this area. It seems to be beyond doubt that improved education of mothers does quite dramatically reduce infant and child mortality. The effect of mothers' education rather than fathers' education is most pronounced when levels of women's education are relatively low. Where there is relatively little difference between the sexes in this respect, fathers' education may be of equal importance to that of mothers, as is the case in Sri Lanka. There is still a tendency to regard the effect of fathers' education as contributing to child health only through the enhanced income brought in by higher qualifications. It is likely that this conclusion will prove to be wrong, and that with more education the father's direct parental role becomes more important. The impact of mothers' education on child mortality increases with the age of the child, the major dividing line being drawn after weaning, when what influences the child is generally a matter of parental choice, and there is none of the (partly automatic) care provided by the mother's milk and its antibodies. Thus, studies in which attention is confined to infant mortality underestimate the contribution made to child survival by women's education.

The real issue is how mothers' education achieves its impact on child health. The conclusion of the majority of studies appears to be that it operates, wholly or largely, through educated mothers making better use of modern health services.[52] While no one would deny that this symbiotic relationship with modern medicine is important, there is another significant body of research in which it is claimed the mothers' education changes a whole range of health-improving behaviour, of which the optimal use of modern medicine is but one aspect. Mothers' schooling has been found to reduce child mortality in circumstances in which there is practically no access to modern medicine.[53] Where there is neither education nor modern medicine, different styles of child care appear to produce very different levels of mortality.[54] This implies that, if education can affect the type of

[52] Frenzen and Hogan, op. cit. in n. 33; Nag, op. cit. in n. 36; Gulati, op. cit. in n. 37; E. van de Walle, A. Palloni, A. Lomas, L. Kephart, and J. Marcotte, 'A Model for Incorporating the Effects of AIDS in Population Projections', paper presented to the IUSSP Seminar on Mortality and Society in Sub-Saharan Africa, Yaoundé, 19–23 Oct. 1987.
[53] I. O. Orubuloye and J. C. Caldwell, 'The Impact of Public Health Services on Mortality: A Study of Mortality Differentials in a Rural Area of Nigeria', *Population Studies*, 29 (1975). See also Caldwell, op. cit. in n. 19.
[54] Hilderbrand *et al.*, op. cit. in n. 51.

care given by the mother, it could also achieve an impact even without modern medicine. In Peru it was found that child mortality varied markedly with mothers' education, but not with the presence or absence of medical institutions,[55] although it is not clear whether the more educated women were more likely to travel to distant facilities. Preston has implied that, if late-nineteenth-century Americans had fully understood the germ theory of disease, they could have taken a range of protective actions against the risk of mortality.[56] Sloan reached a similar conclusion after studying four societies in the Third World.[57]

Educational attainment may be associated with such preventive health measures as isolating ill from healthy children, preventing accidents in the household, securing inoculations and antenatal care, separating animals' quarters from those of the family, maintaining appropriate food storage, and cleaning food utensils. The educated mother is more likely to seek health information and treatment from scientific, rather than from indigenous or folk sources.

Some research results modify the picture by introducing other equally important factors that have little to do with women's position. Palloni, in his study of Latin America, gave equal emphasis to the impact of income.[58] In Bangladesh, Bairagi emphasized the greater importance of income change at very low levels of income.[59] Mothers' education has been shown to have a relatively greater impact in rural than in urban areas.[60] The authors mention the greater demographic heterogeneity in the towns, more individual initiative, and easier access to health services, as well as the greater role played by money. There may be another factor which is more directly related to the role of women, the lesser importance of restricting kinship bonds, which enables younger women to make their own decisions. Ware has related the higher level of survival of babies of educated mothers at birth to the mothers' better physical condition and the babies' higher birthweights.[61] There may be another reason for the high neonatal (and maternal) mortality in cultures of seclusion: the reluctance to have a woman attended at birth by male medical practitioners, even in countries where, for exactly the same reason of seclusion, nearly all such practitioners are men.

In our collaborative research in rural south India we used both anthropological and survey techniques to explore many of these factors, but it

[55] Young, Edmonston, and Andes, op. cit. in n. 40.

[56] Preston, op. cit. in n. 29.

[57] F. Sloan, *Survival of Progeny in Developing Countries: An Analysis of Evidence from Costa Rica, Mexico, East Pakistan, and Puerto Rico* (Santa Monica, Calif., 1971).

[58] Palloni, op. cit. in n. 1.

[59] Bairagi, op. cit. in n. 35.

[60] Oyeka, op. cit. in n. 42; Mensch, Lentzner, and Preston, op. cit. in n. 17.

[61] H. Ware, 'Effects of Maternal Education, Women's Roles, and Child Care on Child Mortality', in W. H. Mosley and L. C. Chen (eds.), *Child Survival: Strategies for Research*, supplement to *Population and Development Review*, 10 (1984), pp. 191–214, at p. 195.

remains very difficult to give relative weights to their importance. Our work was carried out in a rural area, where there was access to free, or nearly free, health services, although ease of access and time costs varied with the distance of the family's residence from the health centre, which might range from almost nothing to ten kilometres. In these circumstances, there were very considerable differences between child mortality by mothers' education, but once that factor had been controlled, family income, and even caste, had no impact at all. Accordingly, much of the research was focused on how mothers' education achieved its impact. Amongst those mothers who lived close to the health centre, there were no significant differences between the use made of it by those with different levels of education; but, as distance from the centre increased, educated women were more likely to take sick children, or to insist upon their husbands taking them for treatment. There were differences in the quickness of response to sickness by women with different levels of education. The major reason was that uneducated women were not accorded the right by their husbands' kin either to identify sickness, or to take action against it. Educated daughters-in-law saw themselves as primary actors in these matters, and were recognized as such by their less well educated affines. They also saw themselves as belonging to a world of schools and health centres, rather than traditional medicines and home cures. There were other important factors. Educated women demanded more attention for their children at health centres. However, we decided that the most important factor was the interaction between the educated mother and the health system. Educated mothers were more likely to follow the instructions given them, and to persist with treatment. They were much more likely to report back when the child's condition did not improve. Less educated women, especially those of low social status, were apprehensive about informing medical personnel that the prescribed treatment had not been effective, partly because they thought they were accusing their superiors of being wrong, and partly because they feared that they would be blamed for not having properly followed instructions. Educated mothers were more likely to have their children immunized, partly because they had a more continuing relationship with the health services. Low levels of education were associated not only with failure to report the unsatisfactory progress of an illness, but also with failure to return to the health centre as instructed, or to persist with immunization. The reasons appear to be, first that such mothers often thought that, if a treatment existed, it should work the first time, and, secondly, that the first visit had proved costly in terms of fees, medicines bought, time wasted, and wages lost.

However, our experience showed that there was a range of other reactions to education which should also have had an impact on child survival. Educated mothers were more careful about hygiene, provided a better share of food for children including girls, recognized the need for rest when children were clearly sick, and understood the need to allocate an unusually high proportion of family resources to food during famines. There is also a factor which is harder to measure. The women were surer of themselves and more convinced that they should act quickly to identify illness and to do something about it.

The whole question of women's autonomy was bound up with education, at least among younger women. Traditionally, they were subordinate not only to men, but also to their mothers-in-law. In the great majority of cases which we investigated, the young mothers were the first to notice illness of their children, yet, by tradition, they could not act upon this recognition, nor, in many cases, could they even be the first to draw attention to it. Even a few years' schooling rapidly changed this situation.

The position in Kerala and Sri Lanka is one which is found in societies in which women have for long enjoyed greater autonomy and, partly as a result, have during recent times been provided with high levels of schooling. This has resulted in greater sensitivity to illness among children, and a greater determination to find a cure. In Sri Lanka, in almost half the episodes of illness we investigated, the mother alone took action to seek treatment, whereas in rural India the analogous figure was only 10 per cent. Such mothers were often assisted by the fact that they, too, earned some income which could be used to meet expenses.

The Total Picture

The question is whether women's position *as women* affects the mortality of their children. The issue is not whether they share poverty with their entire families, or whether this places their children at greater risk. It is confused because there are really two questions and types of data: one refers to the situation of relatively less privileged women in a given society, the other to the position of women in a society in which all women lack autonomy. Our concepts and measures of autonomy are far from satisfactory. Clearly, the education women receive will affect their autonomy, both in the way in which they see themselves and in the way society allows them to behave, but education cannot be identified with autonomy.

The evidence when entire societies are contrasted is relatively clear. Where women must depend on men or on their husbands' relatives for decisions, and where they cannot take decisions about treatment and proceed to health facilities with their sick children, child mortality rates are unusually high. In the wealthier Arab states, the conversion of oil money into health facilities has been markedly unsuccessful in reducing infant and child mortality.[62] In all Muslim areas, from Pakistan westward, child

---

[62] Caldwell, op. cit. in n. 19.

mortality is higher than would be predicted from income levels and health resources. Clearly, this is in part a direct result of a relative lack of mothers' autonomy, and in part an indirect result because lack of such autonomy keeps women's educational levels low.

Similarly, a comparison of child mortality levels in less developed countries leaves no doubt that levels of parents' education, especially those of mothers, are a potent force for reducing child mortality. Indeed, the level of girls' schooling a decade or two earlier is a far better indicator of child mortality than either income or the provision of health services.

Clearly, these two elements are strongly interrelated. The areas in which females are forbidden autonomy contains the peasant societies of the Old World, stretching from north Africa to the Indian subcontinent and, in the past at least, to China; these are the societies where women's sexual indiscretions brought shame on their families. We have discussed elsewhere the reasons why settled peasant societies tend to restrict women's sexual autonomy.[63] There was felt to be a need for seclusion to varying degrees which restricted women's access to education, work outside the home, and such activities as taking the children for medical treatment. Where this was not the case, as in the uxorilocal societies of south-east Asia, the lineage societies of sub-Saharan Africa, and the neo-local societies of north-west Europe, there were fewer difficulties with regard to women's education, women's work outside the home, and most other aspects of their autonomy.

There remain two basic problems. The first is conceptual. There is difficulty in defining autonomy. The type of lack of autonomy which restricts women's movement and education is a denial of sexual autonomy. This is not absolute, and may be associated with such control over much of the household that husbands hardly feel at home there. Nevertheless, among younger women the safeguarding of their sexual *mores* and reputation may mean such control over them by husbands and mothers-in-law that their belief in themselves, and their capacity to make decisions about child health and many other matters may be severely impaired.

The second problem is one of method. Much of our concern about women's autonomy and education is based upon contrasts between societies, but research is most often undertaken within a society. The link between the two may only be tenuous. Furthermore, we possess few measures of autonomy, except the ease with which females can receive an education, or work outside their home. Thus, there is the problem that both these

---

[63] J. C. Caldwell and P. Caldwell, 'Family Systems, their Viability and Vulnerability: A Study of Intergenerational Transactions and their Demographic Implications', paper presented to the IUSSP Committee on Family Demography and the Life Cycle, Seminar on Changing Family Structures and Life Courses in Less Developed Countries, Honolulu, 5–7 Jan. 1987; J. C. Caldwell, 'Family Change and Demographic Change: The Reversal of a Generation Flow', in K. Srinivasan and S. Mukerjee (eds.), *Dynamics of Population and Family Welfare* (Bombay, 1987).

measures are used as indices of autonomy, whilst at the same time we wish
to relate them to an independent measure of autonomy. When comparing
societies and defining women's autonomy more strictly as sexual autonomy,
we have experimented with using the risk to life of pre-marital pregnancy,
or detected sexual activity, and we have recently collected the necessary
data for this measure in Sri Lanka.

In this chapter we have said little about mortality change, or about
morbidity. We have reasonably firm evidence about mortality differentials,
but the lack of successive studies means that we do not know whether these
differentials within specific societies narrow or widen as mortality falls. We
do know that infant and child mortality have fallen furthest (when income
per head was controlled) in those societies in which women's position has
been higher in terms of such measures as autonomy and education. It is
probably reasonable to assume that, a century ago, child mortality levels in
less developed countries in which women were fairly autonomous were not
as different from those in other similar countries, as is the case at present.
Certainly, child mortality levels in Sri Lanka were very high only half a
century ago. The situation appears to be that child mortality transition has
occurred earlier and more rapidly where women occupy a superior position
(at least, as measured by sexual autonomy). There is practically nothing in
the literature on child mortality differentials by mothers' position, let alone
by change in their situation.

Summary

In this chapter we have surveyed recent research on the relation between
women's position and the mortality and morbidity of their children. The
'position' of women has been defined in terms of autonomy, education,
work for wages, and other measures. Two types of research have been
identified: that in which women's position and child mortality in different
societies are compared, and that in which the positions of individual women
in the same society are contrasted. Most research with implications for
autonomy has been a comparison between societies.

The majority of recent analyses has been based on census or survey data
for individual countries, focused on mothers' education. There is little
doubt that the level of mothers' education is a major determinant of child
mortality in most less developed countries. Its impact is probably greater on
childhood than on infant mortality, because breast-feeding has a levelling
effect on the latter. In most countries, fathers' education is also important: it
may not merely be a proxy for income, but may have some parallels with
mothers' education.

The major contemporary argument is over the way in which mothers'
education achieves its effect. A majority has concluded that it does so solely

because of an enhanced ability to use modern health services. Others have claimed that their evidence shows that a whole range of behaviour, mostly connected with child care, plays a role.

Finally, it is noted that there are difficulties in approaches which identify different aspects of the position of women. In societies in which men, or whole families, limit the sexual autonomy of women, the latters' power to make their own decisions, to move freely, attend school, work outside their homes for wages, and seek immediate treatment for sick children is restricted. The result is a relatively higher infant and child mortality than would be predicted by the society's income levels or distribution of health services.

7 Sex Differentials in Adult Mortality in Less Developed Countries: The Evidence and its Explanation

JOSEPH E. POTTER AND LETITIA P. VOLPP

Differences between the death rates of females and males have received substantial attention from demographers and other social scientists in recent years. There are a variety of reasons for this interest. Mortality is an objective, measurable indicator of the relative health of men and women, and health, which is increasingly viewed as an important determinant of the quality of life, is regarded as being primarily socially determined, rather than driven by exogenous natural or biological forces. Moreover, there is a wide variation in the experience of different human populations. We are all struck by the size of this variation and compelled to provide an explanation.

The organizers of this conference have requested two papers on sex differentials in mortality: one on infant and child mortality, and the second on adult mortality. The separation between the two is by no means clear-cut. Demographers have usually drawn the line at the fifth birthday, but the determinants of mortality in early childhood (ages 1–4 years) may be very similar to those of mortality in later childhood and adolescence, especially where overall mortality is high, and there is a differential in favour of males. Moreover, morbidity in childhood, for which age-specific mortality between the ages of 1 and 4 years may be a good proxy, could have consequences for mortality in adult life. For these reasons, it is inevitable that there will be a considerable overlap between the chapters.

We shall begin by briefly reviewing the available data relating to adult mortality in less developed countries and assess their coverage and quality before going on to review the general conclusions that may be drawn about the pattern of sex differentials. In the section that follows we shall take up the various ways in which discrimination against females has been found to contribute to the excess mortality of women, and the factors that underlie this discrimination. In the final section we consider the issues that relate to maternal mortality and to current thinking about its social determinants.

Data on Adult Mortality

In contrast to the situation twenty years ago, much less is known about adult mortality in less developed countries than about infant and child mortality. Adult death rates are almost always estimated from conventional data provided by civil registration and censuses in which coverage is often both incomplete and uneven, and which suffer from age misreporting. Indirect methods and surveys have made a much smaller contribution to the estimation of adult mortality than to that of child mortality. Though notable progress has been achieved in developing indirect methods for the estimation of adult mortality, these often require data that are not regularly collected, for example questions on orphanhood. Where indirect methods are feasible, they usually refer to a period far removed from the date of the census or survey, and depend on fairly strong assumptions about the shape of the mortality curve. In surveys, there is the additional difficulty that a large sample is needed and that retrospective information must be collected about the mortality of members of a household, who may not have been directly related to the person answering the questionnaire.

When the United Nations and OECD set out to assemble a reliable set of life tables from less developed countries during the late 1970s in order to construct a new set of model life tables, the final set that passed their tests for internal and external consistency consisted of only thirty-six tables from twenty-two countries, almost exclusively from Latin America and Asia. Sub-Saharan Africa was not represented at all, and there was only one life table from north Africa. A more recent attempt to collect relatively reliable life tables from less developed countries produced seventy-eight national life tables for the period 1945–81.[1] The regional coverage was more even, with thirteen African life tables complementing the thirty-seven from the Americas, and the twenty-eight from Asia. Nevertheless, the scarcity of good data from sub-Saharan Africa on adult mortality was reflected in the recognizably lower quality of life tables from that region.[2]

But even the quality of some of the presumably reliable life tables that passed the more stringent tests of the first exercise can be questioned. For instance, when one investigator set out to test whether the apparently distinctive age pattern of mortality found in the life tables that had been used to construct the new 'Chilean' model was an artefact of reporting errors, she was able to demonstrate convincingly that, at least for females, the difference between this model and Coale's and Demeny's 'West' model was largely the product of age misreporting.[3]

---

[1] UN, *Model Life Tables for Developing Countries* (New York, 1982).
[2] L. Heligman, 'Sex Differentials in Survivorship in the Developing World: Levels, Regional Patterns and Demographic Determinants', in *Population Bulletin of the United Nations* (1987).
[3] C. E. Florez-Valderrama, 'Destabilized Population Techniques for Analyzing Adult

TABLE 7.1. *Life tables used for the study of sex differentials in mortality*

Country	Year	Life expectancy of males at age 10	Life expectancy of females at age 10	Ratio of males' to females' death rates for age group				
				5–14	15–24	25–44	45–64	65–84
Africa								
Tunisia	1968–69	56.4	56.7	1.139	0.970	0.879	1.157	0.974
Latin America								
Chile	1951–53	52.0	55.7	1.118	1.087	1.264	1.426	1.254
	1959–61	54.7	59.8	1.236	1.344	1.482	1.538	1.315
	1969–71	55.4	61.1	1.369	1.777	1.844	1.685	1.265
Colombia	1963–65	55.6	58.3	1.279	1.599	1.204	1.176	1.140
Costa Rica	1962–64	59.7	61.6	0.840	1.535	1.199	1.190	1.125
	1972–74	62.6	65.7	1.309	1.852	1.683	1.429	1.122
El Salvador	1970–72	57.7	62.4	1.091	1.863	1.719	1.365	1.195
Guatemala	1963–65	50.5	51.6	1.016	1.003	1.053	1.138	1.050
Guyana	1959–61	55.1	58.8	1.293	1.071	0.997	1.391	1.471
Honduras	1960–62	46.7	49.4	1.053	1.315	1.266	1.108	1.112
	1973–75	52.9	56.3	1.106	1.705	1.490	1.176	1.016
Mexico	1969–71	57.5	61.2	1.170	1.581	1.435	1.371	1.122
Peru	1969–71	58.8	62.5	1.230	1.129	1.075	1.411	1.356
Trinidad and Tobago	1920–22	40.1	42.6	1.055	0.884	1.146	1.403	1.250
	1945–47	50.2	52.4	1.002	0.858	0.999	1.315	1.320
	1959–61	57.0	60.5	1.608	1.349	1.128	1.330	1.407

	Period							
Far East Asia								
Hong Kong	1960–62	57.8	65.2	1.295	1.338	1.389	2.088	1.928
	1970–72	59.7	66.9	1.395	1.431	1.872	2.106	1.812
	1976	61.1	67.9	1.348	1.789	1.776	1.972	1.852
Korea, Republic of	1971–75	52.8	60.0	1.004	1.213	1.212	2.074	1.990
Singapore	1969–71	57.9	64.0	1.308	2.185	1.474	1.845	1.652
South Asia								
India	1970–72	53.3	51.9	0.784	0.582	0.764	1.123	0.967
Iran	1973–76	59.5	60.8	0.852	0.878	0.967	1.220	1.111
Israel								
Jewish population	1948–49	60.5	62.2	1.336	1.515	1.071	1.266	1.065
	1960–62	63.4	64.9	1.418	1.915	1.201	1.208	1.075
	1971–73	62.4	65.0	1.409	2.240	1.501	1.393	1.155
non-Jewish population	1971–73	60.4	63.2	1.314	1.597	1.857	1.422	1.056
Kuwait	1974–76	60.2	64.4	1.511	1.927	1.706	1.623	1.301
Bangladesh (Matlab)	1974 and 1976 average	56.1	56.4	0.721	0.523	1.036	1.216	0.999
Philippines	1969–71	56.4	61.0	1.268	1.718	1.584	1.440	1.165
Sri Lanka	1945–47	48.5	46.8	0.882	0.694	0.776	1.167	0.990
	1952–54	58.6	57.4	0.893	0.661	0.683	1.135	0.997
	1962–64	59.7	59.9	1.004	0.842	0.841	1.210	1.010
	1970–72	59.4	62.2	1.009	1.131	1.199	1.495	1.165
Thailand	1969–71	54.4	57.9	1.050	1.262	1.177	1.376	1.306
Average				1.159	1.343	1.276	1.416	1.252

Sources: Calculated at the United Nations Population Division, and reported in United Nations (1983). See Annex V of United Nations op. cit. in n. 6 (1986).

The importance of 'quality', or freedom from errors caused by misreporting or omission, of course, depends on the weight of the demands that will be placed upon the data. Unfortunately, to assess differentials in mortality by sex and age is a tall order—the appraisal may be especially vulnerable to errors such as differential age misreporting by sex. The usual techniques used to overcome difficulties posed by deficient data, which involve imposing strong assumptions about the age pattern of mortality (which are inherent in the use of model life tables), are of no use in this instance. Indeed, it could be argued that the readiness of demographers to believe that model life tables encompass most observed human experience may occasionally have served to distract attention from sex differentials and their variation by age.

In spite of these shortcomings, the major conclusions drawn from the data collected by the United Nations and OECD are probably only subject to minor qualifications. The expectations of life at birthday 10, and the ratios of men's to women's death rates in five broad 'adult' age groups are shown in Table 7.1 for the thirty-two life tables in the original collection. The first broad generalization from these data is that life expectancy at birthday 10 tends to be greater for females than for males, and that this difference increases as mortality declines. This result parallels that obtained for life expectancies at birth by Heligman for the same life tables,[4] and for the larger life-table collection of seventy-eight tables.[5] But what is more striking than the trend in these data is the deviation from the average relationship, particularly in three south Asian life tables (India 1970–72, and Sri Lanka 1945–47 and 1952–54) which show a differential in favour of males. More broadly, the deviations from the 'expected' relationship vary systematically by region. Women are at greatest advantage in the Far East, at smallest advantage in south Asia and north Africa, and in an intermediate position in Latin America.

In a search for an understanding of the factors that shape sex differentials in mortality, age is particularly important. The relative position of women in society may vary somewhat over the life cycle,[6] and, in the absence of even moderately reliable data on causes of death for countries in which mortality is highest, age is also an indicator of the aetiology of adverse sex differentials.

Mortality Data: The Cases of Chile and Argentina', unpublished doctoral dissertation, Princeton University, 1982.

[4] Heligman, op. cit. in n. 2.

[5] UN, 'Patterns of Sex Differentials in Mortality in Less Developed Countries', in A. Lopez and L. T. Ruzicka (eds.), *Sex Differentials in Mortality: Trends, Determinants and Consequences* (Canberra, 1983), pp. 7–32.

[6] Relative improvements, where they occur, are apt to appear only after the end of child-bearing; see, e.g., J. Vallin, 'Sex Patterns of Mortality: A Comparative Study of Model Life Tables and Actual Situations with Special Reference to the Case of Algeria and France', in Lopez and Ruzicka, op. cit. in n. 4, pp. 443–76; H. Ware, 'Differential Mortality Decline and its Consequences for the Status and Role of Women', in UN, *Consequences of Mortality Trends and Differentials* (New York, 1986), pp. 113–25.

Heligman has offered the following classification by age of the dominant causes of death in 'typical' less developed countries.[7]

Age group	Dominant causes of death
5–14	Respiratory diseases, infectious and parasitic diseases
15–44	Accidents, suicides, violence, maternal deaths
45+	Cardiovascular diseases, neoplasms

The sex ratios of age-specific mortality in Table 7.1 show that, in the three life tables in which the differential in life expectancy at birthday 10 favours males, women's death rates only fall below, or equal those of males after the age of 45. Relative excess mortality of women is greatest during the early child-bearing years (15–24). A substantial excess mortality of women in these age groups is also found in a number of the other life tables. On the other hand, in the life tables which show the largest overall advantage of males, the excess mortality of men is usually exceptionally pronounced in this same age group. The presumed explanation in terms of causes of death is that maternal mortality is responsible for the disadvantage suffered by women where it exists, and that high death rates from accidents and violence account for the men's disadvantage that is found in many life tables at these ages.

The final observation relating to Table 7.1 concerns the erosion over time of the excess mortality of women in the life tables for Sri Lanka and, to some degree, for Chile, Costa Rica, and Trinidad and Tobago. Here the relationships identified for the cross-section of all life tables can be seen for the development of mortality in individual countries. The ratio of the mortality of males to that of females increases with increasing life expectancy, and the change is particularly pronounced during the early child-bearing years.

The problem is to examine how these patterns are related to the changing conditions of women. In doing so, we shall focus on the two most immediately troublesome aspects of the data: first, the excess or unusually high mortality of women in the countries of south Asia and north Africa throughout the life cycle, but particularly between the ages of 5 and 14 years; and, secondly, the disadvantage in survival suffered by women during their child-bearing years which results from maternal mortality. This concentration on the adverse experience of women in certain regions or countries necessarily deflects attention from the question how the excess mortality of men in other parts of the Third World is related to the position of women in society. Although relatively little research has been undertaken on this

[7] Heligman, op. cit. in n. 2.

topic, it is important, because it stresses the complex, multidimensional nature of the relationship between the status of women and survival. In particular, as Garcia and de Oliveira have suggested, the sexual division of labour that has led to the differential in the incidence of accidents, and the norms and values which have led to an extremely high incidence of homicide and other types of violence among men in many less developed countries, are by no means causes for satisfaction.[8]

Explanations for the Excess Mortality of Women

Hypotheses that have been advanced to account for the excess mortality of women in developing countries have most often been focused on various aspects of social, economic, and cultural discrimination against them. The most common explanation put forward is discrimination against females, particularly female children, in the allocation of food and health care within the household. When mortality is high, infectious diseases aided by undernutrition are the leading causes of death. At the societal level, higher mortality of females is associated with poor overall nutritional levels.[9] Nutritional, medical, and emotional stunting of females throughout the life course manifests itself in higher mortality of women.

Reports of sex differentials in access to health care include the Khanna study in Punjab, in which it was shown that female members of the community had received medical attention less frequently than males before dying, and that the little care that was given to women was provided by practitioners who were, on average, less competent.[10] In a study of child mortality in rural Punjab it was found that, when treatment was sought, it was delayed for more than twenty-four hours for 44 per cent of the female children, compared with 23 per cent of the male children.[11] In nutritional field studies it has been shown that kwashiorkor is four to five times more common among girls than among boys, but that, among children hospitalized on account of the disease, boys outnumbered girls by between 47 and 53 to one.[12] And in Bangladesh it was found that, whereas incidence of field diarrhoea was comparable between boys and girls, among those who were

---

[8] B. Garcia and O. de Oliveira, *Differencial por sexo de la mortalidad Mexicana: Algunos hallazgos y sugerencias para investigaciones posteriores* (El Colegio de Mexico, Centro de Estudios Demograficos y de Desarollo Urbano, DT-87-05; 1987). For an interesting explanation of why women enjoy such a large advantage in life expectancy over men in industrialized countries, see Vallin, Chapter 9 in this volume.

[9] L. T. Ruzicka and H. Hansluwka, 'Sex Differences in Mortality: Effects on the Family Life Cycle and Fertility', in Lopez and Ruzicka, op. cit. in n. 4, pp. 311–34.

[10] J. B. Wyon and E. J. Gordon, *The Khanna Study: Population Problems in Rural Punjab* (Cambridge, Mass., 1971).

[11] B. Bhatia, 'Traditional Practices Affecting Female Health and Survival: Evidence from Countries of South Asia', in Lopez and Ruzicka, op. cit. in n. 4, pp. 165–78.

[12] Ibid.

brought to a treatment facility the number of boys exceeded that of girls by 66 per cent.[13] Visaria studied fifty-eight deaths of children under 5 years old in the Kachoh Project. Of twenty-seven girls who had died, 30 per cent had been treated only with home remedies, 48 per cent had received treatment from a medical practitioner in the village or a nearby village, and the remaining 22 per cent were taken to district headquarters. In contrast, nearly 80 per cent of the boys had been taken to an urban centre.[14]

Marked differences in the allocation of food within the family were also found by Chen, Huq, and D'Souza,[15] who noted a consistent and systematic discrimination against females of all ages in family decisions on investment and consumption. Among children less than 5 years old, boys consumed 16 per cent more calories than girls; among those aged between 5 and 14 years, the difference was 11 per cent; among those of child-bearing age (15–44), it was 29 per cent. In many households the tradition of sequential feeding was practised; where all members of the family ate simultaneously, marked sex differentials in the quality of food consumed were noted.[16] Sen and Sengupta have also noted the poorer nutritional status of girls in all socio-economic strata in two west Bengal villages.[17]

Das Gupta found that recent data suggest that relative deprivation of medical care for females may be more important than differences in nutrition as an explanatory factor in sex differentials in mortality.[18] However, discrimination in the allocation of food and other familial investments affects a woman throughout her life.[19] Women who are poorly fed to begin with are seldom able to meet the heavy additional nutritional demands caused by pregnancy and lactation. Undernourished, and generally weakened by the biological burdens of excessive reproduction, they fall victims to the maternal depletion syndrome and become increasingly vulnerable to death in childbirth, or to infections and anaemia.[20] Later in her life course, as a woman approaches the end of her reproductive period, her role changes to that of mother-in-law and grandmother. She faces a high probability of being widowed, because of the large differences between the ages of

[13] L. C. Chen, E. Huq, and S. D'Souza, 'Sex Bias in the Family Allocation of Food and Health Care in Rural Bangladesh', *Population and Development Review*, 7 (1981), pp. 55–84.

[14] L. Visaria, 'Sex Differences in Nutritional Status and Survival during Infancy and Childhood: Review of Available Evidence', paper presented at the Conference on Women's Position and Demographic Change in the Course of Development, Asker, Oslo, 15–18 June 1988.

[15] Chen, Huq, and D'Souza, op. cit. in n. 13.

[16] Ibid.

[17] A. Sen and S. Sengupta, 'Malnutrition of Rural Children and the Sex Bias', *Economic and Political Weekly*, 18 (1983).

[18] M. Das Gupta, 'Selective Discrimination against Female Children in the Punjab', *Population and Development Review*, 13 (1987), pp. 77–100.

[19] Indeed, the mortality of women from undernutrition is relatively small, compared with the number whose growth is inhibited, who live under the constant threat of sickness, or who lack the strength and stamina to realize their capabilities (see Bhatia, op. cit. in n. 11).

[20] Bhatia, op. cit. in n. 11.

spouses.[21] Widows rarely remarry, and are normally excluded from access to their husbands' property. A widow is also expected to waive her legal rights to part of her inheritance in favour of her son, in whose house she must seek shelter and protection. In very poor, landless families widows may be reduced to begging.[22]

What seems to underlie this differential allocation of resources in favour of males is a patriarchal society in which men are enabled to dominate women through a set of social relations with a material base. The base is built on men's control over property, income, and women's labour. The structural elements reinforce each other and include aspects of the kinship system, political system, and religion.[23] Often there is patrilocal marriage whereby a newly married woman is removed to her husband's locality, and thenceforth produces only for his family. In such societies, daughters are a poorer investment than sons, whose wives will bring additional labour, as well as dowries, to the family.

The way in which patrilocal marriage affects the excess mortality of women is suggested by a comparison of north and south India. In the north, where the excess mortality of women is high, large dowries are paid and the expenses of the marriage are met by the bride's family. 'Wife givers' are socially and ritually inferior to 'wife takers', and the dowry is used to secure a suitable husband for the daughter. Sons are perceived as means of acquiring dowries.[24] In south India, where child mortality is roughly equal for the two sexes, the situation is not so clearly weighted against women. In some groups, bridewealth is paid by the groom's family to that of the bride, whilst in others bridewealth and dowries are exchanged. When bridewealth is paid in the south, it is generally smaller, and its purpose is to secure the welfare and security of the bride, and it often remains her property; or that of the newly married couple.[25] Dyson and Moore have suggested that north Indian kinship rules result in a lower autonomy of women and greater discrimination against girls.[26] Besides north Indian exogamy, greater distance between the natal and marital homes, lower age at marriage, lower labour-force participation of women, higher illiteracy of women, and more extensive practice of purdah are all posited as contributing to higher excess mortality of women.[27]

[21] M. Cain, S. R. Khanam, and N. Shansun, 'Class, Patriarchy and Women's Work in Bangladesh', *Population and Development Review*, 5 (1979), pp. 405–38.

[22] Bhatia, op. cit. in n. 11.

[23] Cain, Khanam, and Shansun, op. cit. in n. 21.

[24] C. Makinson, 'Sex Differentials in Infant and Child Mortality in Egypt', unpublished doctoral dissertation, Princeton University, 1986; B. D. Miller, *The Endangered Sex: Neglect of Female Children in Rural North India* (Ithaca, NY, 1981).

[25] Makinson, op. cit. in n. 24.

[26] T. Dyson and M. Moore, 'On Kinship Structure, Female Autonomy, and Demographic Behaviour in India', *Population and Development Review*, 9 (1983), pp. 35–60.

[27] Bride-burning, where husbands and in-laws murder wives or induce them to commit suicide when their families fail to meet demands for sufficient dowry, is occasionally mentioned

Conscious Discrimination

Whether the parental actions that result in the stinting of female children are the result of conscious decisions is a matter of some controversy. Some authors appear to be reluctant to believe that excess mortality of women could result from anything but deeply ingrained views about the separate nutritional, medical, and other needs of boys and girls. The assumption is that there is a generalized tendency to give preferential treatment to boys, which is rooted in the low value given to females in south Asian societies. The implication of this assumption is that discriminatory behaviour need not occur at a conscious level. Parents may simply have internalized certain norms that lead them to give better care to their sons than to their daughters, and excess mortality of girls may be an unintended consequence. Acceptance of this cultural hypothesis appears to stem in part from a reluctance to accept the idea that people will make economic cost-benefit decisions about their children. Krishnaji has claimed that conscious calculation is suspect as an explanation for the observed variation in the sex ratio of mortality, because it is difficult to believe that this actually occurs, especially among the poor, for whom work is directly related to day-to-day survival, and for whom long-run calculations may not be relevant.[28]

Waldron, too, has stated that parents do not apparently engage in conscious discrimination against girls; rather, she suggests, sex discrimination may be embodied in cultural beliefs—for example, that girls are hardier, or that too much of a certain type of food may be bad for girls.[29] Miller has emphasized a strong preference for sons, rather than a clear dislike for daughters.[30] In her view, the problem is that son-preference is so strong in some areas of India and among some classes that daughters must almost logically suffer in order that the families' perceived and culturally manifested needs are satisfied.

Das Gupta has provided the strongest critique of the unconscious cultural explanation.[31] She claims that Punjabi society falls somewhere on the spectrum between generalized neglect of females and a deliberate failure to

as the most extreme consequence of the economic exchanges that take place within the kinship system. Dowry murders are allegedly most often masked as 'cooking accidents'. The figure of 300 married women between the ages of 18 and 30 who died of burns during the first half of 1987 in New Delhi has been quoted as an indication of the possible incidence of this phenomenon. See S. Sirohi, 'Bride Burning over Dowries', *Telegraph*, 22 Feb. 1988; M. Kishwar and R. Vanita (eds.), *In Search of Answers: Indian Women's Voices from Manushi* (London, 1984). Payment of dowry has, in fact, been illegal in India since 1961, but is still widespread.

[28] N. Krishnaji, 'Poverty and the Sex Ratio: Some Data and Speculations', *Economic and Political Weekly*, 22–3 (1987).

[29] I. Waldron, 'Patterns and Causes of Excess Female Mortality among Children in Developing Countries', *World Health Statistical Quarterly*, 40 (1987), pp. 194–210.

[30] Miller, op. cit. in n. 24.

[31] Das Gupta, op. cit. in n. 18.

provide crucial inputs for life to specific categories of females. She notes that in the Punjab, excess mortality of girls tends to be increasingly sharply concentrated among girls born to mothers who already have one or more surviving daughters; discrimination is thus not merely based on gender-linked practices, but is closely related to the family-building strategies of individual parents. Sex differentials by birth order were found to be far stronger than those by socio-economic status. Moreover, these differentials showed a remarkable persistence in the face of socio-economic development, and the decline of mortality and fertility. In fact, declining fertility appeared to strengthen such selective discrimination. Interestingly, women's education was associated with lower child mortality, but stronger discrimination against girls of higher birth orders. Das Gupta suggested that the reason for this was that young educated women were under greater pressure not to have more than one surviving daughter than uneducated, older women, whose fertility was higher. Amin recently conducted a multivariate analysis of data from another Punjabi setting that provides support for this thesis.[32] She found that, whilst the mortality of first daughters was lower than that of sons, the mortality of second or higher-order daughters was substantially higher. Education appeared to allow mothers to use resources more effectively in a preferential manner to benefit the children who were more highly valued.

   Das Gupta has suggested that the strong underlying preference for sons is rooted in the material, as well as the structural, bases of patriarchy. Excess mortality of women appears to be the outcome of women's structural marginalization in this culture, which results in their being of low value to their parents. This pattern seems to be linked to patrilineal descent, which is the organizing principle of Punjabi Jat kinship, political system, and spatial distribution. It may operate through a convergence of interests at several levels to put a premium on sons and discriminate against daughters. Son-preference is in the interest of the lineage, whose continuity depends on sons alone; it is also in the interest of the household, for whom daughters are transitory members. For each individual, brothers and sons are more valuable than sisters and daughters: a girl values her brother more than her sister, because the former will do much for her throughout life, while the latter will effectively disappear after marriage. As Das Gupta has pointed out, people's position in society is determined not only by the contributions they make to the economic process, but also by their rights of ownership and their powers of decision-making. When women are conceived as transitory components, the vessels whereby the men of the lineage reproduce

[32] S. Amin, 'The Effect of Women's Status on Sex Differentials in Infant and Child Mortality in South Asia', paper presented at the Conference on Women's Position and Demographic Change in the Course of Development, Asker, Oslo, 15–18 June 1988.

themselves, and when married women can do almost nothing for their natal kin, they are less valued.[33]

Clark has suggested that excess mortality of women forms part of an overall reproductive strategy which, in most cases, reflects strategic calculations of social units that are considerably larger than the household.[34] While the household participates in its own micro-level political economy, which encompasses gender relations, it faces constraints and incentives from within the larger political economy, which affects its reproductive options.

A more recent manifestation of son-preference which may shed some light on the question of consciousness and excess mortality of women has been documented in India, although there has as yet been little systematic reporting on the issue. The spread of amniocentesis for pre-natal sex determination began in Punjab, Haryana, and western Maharashtra. When the All-India Institute of Medical Sciences introduced the techniques, it was found that seven out of eight parents who came for the test did so with the specific purpose of aborting the foetus if it was found to be female. The Institute was flooded with requests for abortions when the woman was found to be carrying a female foetus. Some of the clinics that have mushroomed during the last few years proclaim through advertisements that the birth of a son is the primary purpose of the test.[35] In one study of 700 women who underwent amniocentesis, 95 per cent of those who were carrying a female foetus opted for abortion, whereas none of the women who were carrying a male foetus did so.[36]

Women's Autonomy

It has often been suggested that an increase in women's autonomy would lead to a reduction in discrimination against them, and thus to a lower excess mortality. Autonomy has been defined by Dyson and Moore as the capacity to manipulate one's personal environment.[37] Autonomy means the ability—technical, social, and psychological—to obtain information and to use it as the basis for making decisions about one's private concerns and those of one's intimates. Caldwell has pointed out that women's autonomy is not the same as women's status, at least as measured by the potential for respect or reverence; indeed, the opposite may be closer to the truth.[38]

[33] Das Gupta, op. cit. in n. 18.
[34] A. W. Clark, 'Social Demography of Excess Female Mortality in India: New Directions', *Economic and Political Weekly*, 22 (1987), pp. 12–21.
[35] M. Kishwar, 'The Continuing Deficit of Women in India and the Impact of Amniocentesis', in G. Corea *et al.*, *Man-Made Women: How New Reproductive Technologies Affect Women* (Bloomington, Ind., 1987).
[36] Visaria, op. cit. in n. 14.
[37] Dyson and Moore, op. cit. in n. 26.
[38] J. C. Caldwell, 'Routes to Low Mortality in Poor Countries', *Population and Development Review*, 12 (1986), pp. 171–220.

Dyson and Moore have claimed that societies in which women possess high personal autonomy compared with men are typically characterized by one or several of the following features: freedom of movement and association of adult and adolescent females; post-marital residence patterns and norms that do not rupture or severely constrain social intercourse between the woman and her natal kin; the ability of females to inherit or otherwise acquire, retain, and dispose of property; and some independent control by females of their own sexuality (e.g. in the choice of marriage partners). Caldwell has added that women's autonomy is greatest when both society and women themselves have little doubt about a woman's right to make decisions and to battle for her own and her children's rights in the public arena.

Greater autonomy makes it likely that sex differentials in education will be narrower. It also makes it more likely that a mother will make her own decision that something must be done when she identifies a child as being sick, that she will venture outside the home to seek help, that she will struggle to obtain adequate treatment from physicians and nurses, and that she will understand the advice she is given and take responsibility for carrying it out. And such autonomy will make it more likely that girls will receive the same treatment as their brothers. Extended education of women will be more acceptable in some cultures than other interventions that affect women's position more broadly; but this sometimes has the consequence that substantial inputs into education do not result in the impact on women's health that might be anticipated from experience elsewhere.[39]

Covariates of the Excess Mortality of Women

Women's labour-force participation and socio-economic level have both been suggested as material factors within the patriarchal structure that either contribute to or reduce excess mortality. It might be expected that a higher socio-economic status would result in a reduction of excess mortality; larger resources might enable families to distribute them more equitably. In addition, they might mask any inequities that would result in an excess mortality of women in conditions of scarcity. Lower excess mortality of women might also result from a reduction of son-preference brought about by a higher socio-economic status and concomitant education. 'Westernization' and the improved status of women might lead to a reduction in son-preference and reduce the excess mortality of women. On the other hand, a more equal ratio might be expected among the poor, because in poor families women tend to participate more actively in the labour force, and are, therefore, valued; also property-transfer mechanisms, such as

[39] Ibid.

bridewealth and dowry, could only have a weak effect, as there is not much property to be transferred.[40]

Makinson examined sex differentials in infant and child mortality in Egypt.[41] Covariates that reflected differences between the circumstances of households, such as parental education and father's occupation, appeared to have little or no effect on sex differentials. In fact, Makinson suggested that modern facilities and practices might have been adopted sex-selectively to the detriment of girls, and that this development could lead to an increased excess mortality of women, at least in the near future. Bairagi also noted that a simple improvement in the level of household resources was unlikely to improve sex differentials.[42] Increased discrimination against girls was associated with an increase in income following a recent famine in Africa; an improvement in household resources benefited males more than females. In addition, the differential was larger in the higher socio-economic groups.

Chen, Huq, and D'Souza similarly found unexpected excess mortality of women among wealthy landowning families in Matlab, Bangladesh.[43] Weinberger and Heligman, in examining data for south and west Asia, found that excess mortality of women was present in all social groups.[44] Higher mortality of girls was found as frequently among educated, urban parents and among gainfully employed mothers, as among the uneducated, rural, and economically inactive.[45]

Krishnaji found a more balanced sex ratio in poor households, though he cautions that it would be hasty to conclude that there is less discrimination against females among the poor.[46] It is possible that discriminatory practices, especially those that relate to nutrition and health care, are more effective among the landowning classes than among the poor, given the very low standard of living of the latter. In their examination of two west Bengal villages, in one of which there had been land reform, Sen and Sengupta found much sharper sex discrimination in the village with the better overall nutritional record. In the two villages, the mortality of girls was broadly similar; the economic benefits seem to have been enjoyed primarily by the boys.[47]

Agarwal has added a number of important qualifications to the theory that sex differentials would be smaller among the poor: where there

[40] B. Agarwal, 'Women, Poverty and Agricultural Growth in India', *Journal of Peasant Studies*, 13 (1986).

[41] Makinson, op. cit. in n. 24.

[42] R. Bairagi, 'Food Crisis, Nutrition and Female Children in Rural Bangladesh', *Population and Development Review*, 12 (1986), pp. 307–16.

[43] Chen, Huq, and D'Souza, op. cit. in n. 13.

[44] M. B. Weinberger and L. Heligman, 'Do Social and Economic Variables Differentially Affect Male and Female Child Mortality?', paper presented to the 1987 Annual Meeting of the Population Association of America, Chicago.

[45] Ibid.

[46] Krishnaji, op. cit. in n. 28.

[47] Sen and Sengupta, op. cit. in n. 17.

is high and sustained underemployment among women, the trend could be reversed.[48] There are additional dimensions in intra-household inequities in the burden of poverty, such as time devoted to work and rest by women compared with men, and the nature of women's domestic work, particularly their specific responsibilities for collecting fuel, fodder, and water in conditions of increasing deforestation and ecological deterioration. The nature of women's work in agriculture which exposes them to specific health hazards, the seasonal variation in poverty, sexual exploitation arising from poverty, the caste dimension, and violence within the family will all affect women differentially.

The mechanisms that connect women's participation in the labour force to excess mortality are, of course, related to those that mediate socio-economic status. One suggestion is that the labour demands on women may lead to their excess mortality;[49] the type of work employed women do in India is often physically more demanding than that done by employed men. Because they have received training or formal education, some men have been able to move into skilled or semi-skilled jobs, whilst most women, being untrained and uneducated, remain in unskilled work in the unorganized sector of the economy that requires heavy manual labour. In addition, women have been pushed into manual labour through loss of jobs in indigenous industry. A higher percentage of employed women (51 per cent) than of employed men (21 per cent) is found in agricultural work.[50]

Conversely, it has been argued that women's participation in the labour force may reduce their excess mortality. Agarwal has suggested that, as labour-force participation of women increases, there would be less tendency to discriminate against them; when women contribute their labour, they will be perceived as being more valuable.[51] But, she cautions, this tendency could be modified or even reversed when the differential between men's and women's earnings is high, or where the productive work done is not visible, especially economically.

Differences in treatment may, in fact, be related to the low participation of female workers in income-generating activities. These are perceived as being men's work; women's work in the field is regarded as being an integral part of their household duties. Women do not make managerial decisions in production, nor do they market the final product or control the resulting cash.[52] Thus, as men are more likely to be employed and to earn higher wages, and as sons are more likely to provide security in old age, and as

[48] Agarwal, op. cit. in n. 40.

[49] B. Iseley, 'Social Correlates of Sex Differences in Mortality in a Small Area of South India', unpublished doctoral dissertation (University of Oregon, 1981); R. Dixon, 'Women and Human Rights', *Populi*, 11 (1984).

[50] Iseley, op. cit. in n. 49.

[51] Agarwal, op. cit. in n. 40.

[52] Das Gupta, op. cit. in n. 18.

women's involvement in household industry and family agriculture is not recognized by the family as being important, men are perceived as being economically more valuable.[53]

Structural Change and Excess Mortality of Women

It has been suggested that the monetization of agriculture has led to a devaluation of women's work and resulted in excess mortality. The reversal from an excess mortality of men to one of women in India in about 1920 lends credence to this theory. Iseley has suggested that women lost their economic roles, because Western development experts imported the assumption that women should not work outside the home, particularly in agriculture. Development has primarily produced services for men. They have been trained in new farming methods to produce cash crops; they were provided with credit and gained land-tenure rights that once were communal. As a result, many women lost economically productive roles, and the relative status of their remaining work declined, as men, trained to use the new techniques, became more productive. Between 1911 and 1971 the proportion of women in the organized labour force declined from 34 to 12 per cent. This reduction was caused primarily by the elimination of lower-status jobs, which were more frequently held by women than by men. Jobs such as weaving and commercial food processing have also been lost, as indigenous small-scale industry has been replaced by large-scale industry.[54]

Johansson's historical data offer strong support for this theory.[55] She examined data from European or European-settled countries which indicated that there was a widespread and pronounced excess mortality of women during the early and middle phases of European economic development in the nineteenth century. She found no clear patterns of excess mortality of women in pre-modern agriculture, when women and girls were important. As economic modernization spread, primarily in agriculture, it gave specific cash values to various forms of farm production. Since wives and daughters were disproportionately involved in production for household consumption, whereas men and boys were disproportionately involved in producing for the market, the labour contributions of women and girls were perceived as being less valuable to the family economy, relative to those of men and boys. Household resources available for investment were, therefore, concentrated on sons. This resulted in a demographic pattern in which

---

[53] Iseley, op. cit. in n. 49.
[54] Ibid.
[55] S. R. Johansson, 'Deferred Infanticide: Excess Female Mortality during Childhood', in G. Hausfater and S. B. Blaffer-Hardy (eds.), *Infanticide: Comparative and Evolutionary Perspectives* (New York, 1984).

agricultural development was accompanied by declining child mortality for both sexes, but where the death rates of boys fell faster than those of girls, until an excess mortality of women emerged from these differential rates of decline. By the late nineteenth century, agrarian Europe was generally characterized by an excess mortality of women below child-bearing age.

Wherever development has led to modern forms of industrialization and urbanization, it has generally created an abundance of paying jobs for young girls. In the cities and regions in which young women found remunerative employment, excess mortality of women was eliminated. However, once most urban women were married and subject to the rigours of child-bearing, excess mortality of women persisted.[56]

The Far East provides recent examples of dramatic structural transformations—both socialist and capitalist—that seemed to have little influence on discrimination linked to patriarchal structure. Since 1949, the Chinese government has repeatedly reiterated its commitment to sexual equality and has made substantial efforts to undermine the social, economic, and psychological bases of men's supremacy. The Marriage Law of 1950 repudiated the traditional family structure that had oppressed women, and established a marriage system based on free choice of partners, monogamy, and equal rights for both sexes. The law prohibited concubinage, child betrothal, infanticide, and the exaction of gifts or money as a condition of marriage. The Marriage Law of 1980 stipulates that a husband may become a member of his wife's family, and that daughters, as well as sons, are responsible for supporting their parents in old age.[57]

Despite these laws, there is incontrovertible evidence of the persistence of son-preference in almost every part of China. Couples with one daughter are less likely to have obtained a one-child certificate than couples with one son, and having received a certificate they are more likely to violate its provisions by having a second child. Couples without a son are less likely to use contraception than couples with at least one son, and pregnant women without a son are less likely to have an abortion than those with at least one son.[58] The persistence of son-preference, especially in rural areas, strongly suggests that, despite legal sanctions, traditional social structures persist; in

---

[56] Ibid. The excess mortality of women often peaked during late adolescence and the early twenties, reflecting the importance of tuberculosis in the overall pattern of cause-specific mortality. During the late nineteenth century, pulmonary tuberculosis was the leading killer in most European countries, and it seems likely that nutrition played some part. The peasant 'feeding rule' required women to prepare the food, but to serve it first to the males of the family. If the rule were followed, there might not have been much food left for the women and girls. Meat may have been especially scarce. As the family's diet improved, young girls were the last to benefit. Because the postulated patterns of discrimination were passive, rather than active, they could be expected to produce a mortality pattern in which the survival chances of girls gradually fell behind those of boys, as parents did less to ensure the girls' survival.

[57] F. Arnold and L. Zhaoxiang, 'Sex Preference, Fertility and Family Planning in China', *Population and Development Review*, 12 (1986), pp. 221–46.

[58] Ibid.

fact, Wolf has claimed that the Chinese experience proves that socialism and patriarchy can co-exist.[59] It might be thought that, with a higher level of mortality, there might be excess mortality of women in China; in fact, there have been persistent rumours of the reappearance of infanticide of girl babies in rural areas.[60] Compared with other systems, socialist societies appear to satisfy many of the basic requirements of human life better, and tend to draw women into non-traditional production. However, the structures of gender subordination within families, social consciousness, and the political leadership have proved remarkably resistant to change.[61]

Taiwan provides an example of son-preference that has persisted in the face of rapid structural transformation, manifested here through capitalist-based sexual stratification. Greenhalgh has reported that economic development has provided tools to intensify already entrenched systems of gender inequality.[62] Her interpretation is that the emergence of capitalism profoundly threatened men's position of dominance, both by destroying the old institutions that had supported it, and by creating new institutions, such as the labour market, that removed women and children from patriarchal control and gave them individual means of support. Threatened by this loss of control, men took active, if unconscious, steps to maintain their gender-based power. The lesson is that social systems do not merely persist, but are actively perpetuated by individuals whose interests are bound up with their continuation, and who possess the resources and mechanisms necessary to protect them.[63]

Maternal Mortality

It is worth singling out mortality caused by complications of pregnancy, attempts at abortion, and childbirth. In the first place, where there is excess mortality of women between the ages of 15 and 50, and where reasonably reliable data on cause of death are available, the total difference between the mortality of the two sexes at these ages is usually accounted for by maternal mortality. This may be seen in the graphs presented by Chen, Huq, and D'Souza, and by Vallin.[64] Moreover, it gives cause for concern even in situations where death rates from all causes in this age range are in balance, or favour women. Virtually the whole of this mortality from a risk

[59] M. Wolf, *Revolution Postponed: Women in Contemporary China* (Stanford, Calif., 1985).
[60] Arnold and Zhaoxiang, op. cit. in n. 57.
[61] G. Sen and C. Grown, *Development Crises and Alternative Visions: Third World Women's Perspectives* (New York, 1987).
[62] S. Greenhalgh, 'Sexual Stratification and the Other Side of "Growth with Equity" in East Asia', *Population and Development Review*, 11 (1985), pp. 265–314.
[63] Ibid.
[64] L. Chen, M. C. Gesche, S. Ahmed, A. I. Chowdhury, and W. H. Mosley, 'Maternal Mortality in Rural Bangladesh', *Studies in Family Planning*, 5 (1974); Vallin, op. cit. in n. 6.

which is borne exclusively by women is in some sense unnecessary. Death rates related to child-bearing are infinitesimal in developed countries in comparison with those experienced in most less developed countries.

The major causes of maternal deaths in less developed countries today are the same as were experienced in industrialized countries fifty years ago: haemorrhage, infection, toxaemia, and obstructed labour.[65] Added to these age-old complications are those caused by illegal abortions, which may be considerably more prevalent in contemporary less developed countries than they were in the historical experience of the now developed countries. The degree to which maternal mortality is socially determined, and the extent to which 'excess' maternal mortality has resulted from the type of discrimination reviewed in the preceding section are questions that do not seem to have been extensively studied, at least explicitly. At one extreme there is the opinion, apparently not unusual among medical practitioners, that a large fraction of maternal mortality derives less from the failures and inadequacies of modern medical infrastructure than from ignorance, traditional belief systems, and the generally low position of women in society. One of the most forceful statements to this effect has been made by Harrison, the author of an extensive report on a survey of 22,774 consecutive hospital births in Zaria, northern Nigeria. He concludes:

It must be obvious from this study that unsuccessful childbearing in an area like Northern Nigeria is due overwhelmingly to socioeconomic and cultural features rather than to existing deficiencies in the maternity services.

Large numbers of women are born into a cycle of deprivation where they will remain uneducated, where their religion and culture encourages child marriage so that they may begin their childbearing while still children themselves; and where they are systematically neglected, both physically and emotionally. Moreover, they may be denied access to medical care when they need it, and the consequent damage by neglect is compounded by inappropriate and exceedingly harmful traditional medicine.[66]

In his view, relatively little can be accomplished by unilateral improvements or extensions of the modern medical system in the absence of fundamental social change, beginning with universal formal education.

Assessments of the 'quality' of traditional childbirth practices do, of course, differ. Ethnographers, for instance, have frequently arrived at a more nuanced and sympathetic judgement of the trade-offs involved in choosing between modern and traditional birth attendants. They stress the different logistic and economic obstacles to the use of hospital facilities, as

[65] A. Rosenfeld and D. Maine, 'Maternal Mortality: A Neglected Tragedy. Where is the M in MCH?', *Lancet*, 13 July 1985.
[66] K. A. Harrison, 'Childbearing, Health and Social Priorities: A Survey of 22,774 Consecutive Hospital Births in Zaria, Northern Nigeria', *British Journal of Obstetrics and Gynaecology*, 92, Supplement No. 5 (1985).

well as the loss of personal autonomy and family and community support.[67] Moreover, anthropologists have frequently concluded that, when provided with the opportunity, women are more than willing to make the economic and 'cultural' sacrifices that are required to obtain the greater health security that can be provided by Western medical practice.[68]

Yet, from the fragmentary evidence, it would seem that the position of women in society—and in particular various forms of discrimination against them—does have a substantial influence on the risk of dying from maternal causes. There are three principal ways in which discrimination and absence of women's autonomy are mediated. First and foremost is through a woman's control, or lack thereof, over the timing and number of her pregnancies. The risk of dying from causes related to pregnancy is, of course, directly related to the number of pregnancies experienced, and there are additional risks associated with pregnancies that occur at the very early and the very late stages of a woman's reproductive period, as well as those that may result from very high parity, a series of short birth intervals, or a poorly performed abortion.

The second way is through women's access to the health services. Restrictions on mobility, limited access to cash, and absence of decision-making authority may all prevent a mother from making use of medical services that are available, either for preventive ante-natal care, or in case of a recognizable complication of pregnancy or delivery. Women's access to male medical practitioners in much of south Asia is known to be limited by purdah,[69] and, even in the less restricted cultural setting of rural Malaysia, the preservation of feminine modesty has an important bearing on the decision, generally taken by the husband, to move the parturient woman to hospital.[70] Indeed, choice of the type of birth attendant and place of delivery seems to be 'influenced, particularly in Hindu culture, by the view that confinement is ritually unclean and ceremonially impure. . . Women are delivered in the worst and darkest corner of the house.'[71]

The third route of impact, further removed from the immediacy of sexual activity and the exigencies of child-bearing, but which may still be of major importance, is the effect on maternal mortality of stunted growth, low haemoglobin levels, and other nutritional deficiencies brought on by discrimination in the allocation of food. Nutrition in childhood, throughout reproductive age, and during pregnancy seems to be related to maternal mortality. Not only does height seem to be an important indicator of risk,[72]

---

[67] C. Laderman, *Wives and Midwives: Childbirth and Nutrition in Rural Malaysia* (Berkeley and Los Angeles, Calif., 1983).

[68] M. A. Muecke, 'Health Care Systems and Socializing Agents: Childbearing the North Thai and Western Ways', *Social Science and Medicine*, 10 (1976).

[69] Bhatia, op. cit. in n. 11.

[70] Laderman, op. cit. in n. 67.

[71] Bhatia, op. cit. in n. 11, p. 173.

[72] Rosenfeld and Maine, op. cit. in n. 65.

but nutritional supplements during pregnancy appear to have a measurable positive effect on reproductive outcome, including cephalo-pelvic disproportion among teenage mothers.[73]

Contemporary discussions of maternal mortality are more apt to focus on service programmes and technology than on patriarchy and the position of women in society. In contrast with the perception regarding interventions to promote child survival, there is ample recognition of the limitations of inexpensive community medicine that can be delivered by untrained personnel. Only a fraction of the complications of pregnancy and childbirth can be expected to be averted by preventive measures, such as screening during antenatal care. And some of the most common complications, such as haemorrhage and obstructed labour, are rarely managed adequately without a relatively sophisticated infrastructure, and/or highly trained personnel. In a number of recent papers, the focus has been on methods of overcoming these constraints with appropriate technologies and service delivery systems.[74] This is a legitimate problem. But, in the emerging effort to *do something* about maternal mortality,[75] it is important that the social nature of the phenomenon be further explored by researchers, and taken into account by those responsible for providing services.

Conclusion

The mortality and morbidity of adults in less-developed countries is not a well-developed or well-funded field of social science research. Mortality and morbidity have received only a fraction of the attention given to fertility, and it is, indeed, fertility research that has, somewhat serendipitously, generated much of the data for the study of the mortality of infants and children. There has been no such rich uncle to fund research on adult mortality, and it is no exaggeration to state that very little effort has been devoted to collecting the data necessary for investigation of the social determinants of this phenomenon.

Yet, in spite of these limitations, a fairly well-defined picture of the determinants of sex differences in adult mortality seems to emerge. Much of what has been learnt about sex differentials in infant mortality seems to carry over, and there can be no doubt that discrimination and autonomy

[73] Harrison, op. cit. in n. 66.

[74] B. Winikoff, 'Medical Services to Save Mothers' Lives: Feasible Approaches to Reducing Maternal Mortality', background paper prepared for the International Safe Motherhood Conference, Nairobi, 10–13 Feb. 1987; D. Maine, A. Rosenfeld, M. Wallace, A. M. Kimball, B. Kwast, E. Papiernik, and S. White, 'Prevention of Maternal Deaths in Developing Countries: Program Options and Practical Considerations', background paper prepared for the International Safe Motherhood Conference, Nairobi, 10–13 Feb. 1987.

[75] B. Herz and A. R. Measham, 'The Safe Motherhood Initiative: Proposals for Action', paper prepared for the International Safe Motherhood Conference, Nairobi, 10–13 Feb. 1987.

matter for adults as well. In south Asia, as elsewhere, there are inequities of economic and political structures between classes, sexes, and ethnic groups which are often the historical legacy of colonial domination. Post-colonial developments have, in some cases, increased these inequities, and women's lives have, as a result, become increasingly uncertain. Their vulnerability has been further reinforced by systems of traditional sex-based subordination which have typically limited their access to and control over productive resources, such as land and labour, imposed sexual division of labour, and curtailed women's physical mobility.[76]

Further research is, of course, needed. One question that seems amenable to comparative study concerns the links between the excess mortality of women in childhood and maternal mortality. As more information on the latter subject becomes available, it should be possible to substantiate or refute the thesis that maternal mortality is high relative to the general level of mortality, where child mortality of girls is high relative to that of boys. Comparative ethnographic research could illuminate the links between the two phenomena. Another perplexing question concerns the processes that drive the declines in the excess mortality of women, such as have occurred in Sri Lanka and China. Does the reversal of advantage between the sexes reflect increased efforts on the part of government and other agents to curb abuses? Is it due to a change in the disease environment? Or does it result from a decrease in the strength of son-preference related to changes in the position of women within the family and the larger society? At present, we can only speculate about the relative importance of these different influences.

[76] Sen and Grown, op. cit. in n. 61.

8 The Condition of Women and the Health and Mortality of Infants and Children

ANTONELLA PINNELLI

Infant and Child Health and the Position of Women in Developed Countries

It is common to use infant mortality and morbidity as indicators of health conditions, on the assumption that a link exists between these variables. This link may have been more obvious in the past, when infectious diseases were the principal cause of high mortality, and tended to affect weaker organisms.

As the situation changed, the link between mortality, morbidity, and health became less obvious. Today, infant mortality is largely the result of perinatal causes and congenital defects, and tends to be heaviest during the period immediately following birth. After the first year of life, accidents, rather than illnesses, are the leading causes of death among children. But perinatal conditions and accidents are also the chief reasons for infant morbidity, so that mortality rates retain their value as negative indicators of health, for they also provide information about those survivors who have experienced the highest frequency of handicaps or disabilities. Morbidity, on the other hand, is no longer as good an indicator of infant health, for illness is now often a transitory affair which has little or no effect on the child's permanent health status, or its psychological well-being, a concept which is now included in the context of general health.[1]

Thus, any attempt at an analysis of infant health has become much more complex than in the past, given the need to use indicators that cover aspects other than merely physical ones, but which relate to the quality of life, and are, therefore, more difficult to define, as well as harder to obtain.

The health of a child is closely related to the status of its mother, whose health is of primary importance. It plays a decisive part in determining the outcome of the pregnancy, and the vitality, weight, and other characteristics of the infant. The recent improvement in infant health can in large part be

---

[1] M. Okolski, 'Relationship between Mortality and Morbidity Levels According to Age and Sex, and their Implications for Organizing Health Care Systems in Developed Countries', in UN, *Consequences of Mortality Trends and Differentials* (New York, 1986).

attributed to an improvement in the health of women, which has resulted from higher standards of general hygiene, nutrition, etc. Reduced discrimination against women in matters of nutrition and access to care, better social protection during pregnancy and in childbirth (prohibition of exposure to a toxic working environment, more widely available maternity and child welfare services), as well as lower fertility rates, have all played a part.

The other link between women's status and the health of children is the woman's ability to care for her children, as care is usually the mother's responsibility.

Women are considered a key health resource and take particular responsibility for general health through their contribution to the health of their families. This consists of teaching health care to the coming generation, creating a home environment—ranging from cleanliness to nutrition—that is conducive to health, and ensuring that children are immunized, given treatment when they are ill, and taken for medical advice when necessary. Women are also responsible for the control of family size—too many or too closely spaced pregnancies lead to health risks for both mother and infant—as well as for the health of other children in the family, especially the very young, who may still be dependent on maternal feeding and care.[2]

Women's education has been considered to be particularly important in helping to increase their capacities in these areas. Improvement in the condition of women within the overall framework of economic and social change has thus been a fundamental factor in raising health levels.

However, though modernization has reduced and eliminated some of the risks of the past, it has created new ones linked to employment (contact with toxic substances, work-related illness, pace of work, noise, vibration), urbanization (stress, mental illness, violence), industrialization of food production resulting in contamination with toxic substances, air and water pollution, greater use of motor vehicles, and new personal habits that have developed in modern society (smoking, excessive consumption of alcohol, overeating, excess of fat and sugar in the diet, less physical activity and exercise). Inevitably, these factors will affect the health of infants either directly or through their effects on the mothers' health and life-style.

The link between infant health and women's status thus becomes more complex: the more women are involved in modernization, the greater will be the extent to which they take part in masculine life-styles, and the higher the risk that toxic substances will affect the foetus during pregnancy. At the same time, however, improvements in economic status and education contribute to more successful pregnancies, and also to improvements in child-rearing. Thus, a potentially negative factor operates at the same time as the more positive ones, whose effects are continuing.

---

[2] WHO, 'Having a Baby in Europe', *Public Health in Europe*, 26 (1985).

Infant and Child Mortality Trends and Structures

Before beginning an analysis of the relationship between infant health and the position of women, we must take a brief look at recent trends in infant health and at geographical differences. Even though this objective might seem limited, it soon proves to be too ambitious to carry out with the information available. Indicators such as health, morbidity, or the quality of life cannot be generally applied or standardized. The only data that are compatible, both geographically and over time, are those which relate to mortality.

At this stage, we shall not consider late foetal mortality, because the statistical data are neither continuous nor sufficiently complete to make possible a suitable historical and geographical reconstruction. In the age group that we are considering, from birth to adolescence, mortality has become increasingly rare, although trends differ at different ages.

The data used are national mortality statistics by cause, provided by WHO data bank.

1–14 Years

Between the ages of 1 and 14 years mortality has fallen to such low levels that almost no geographical differences can any longer be discerned. Mortality rates at these ages are lower than at any other stage of life. During the 1950s and 1960s the fall was particularly steep in countries in which the initial levels were still relatively high. However, during the 1960s the pace of reduction slowed down, and it has been suggested that a biological limit had been reached, which would be difficult to breach.[3]

Mortality differences between the two sexes were still considerable. 'Accidents, traumas, and violence' were the chief causes of death between the ages of 1 and 4, and between 5 and 14 years. As individuals in these age groups neither work nor drive, it has been suggested that the sex differential in mortality can be attributed to gender-related attitudes in the family and in society in general which encourage more reckless and aggressive behaviour, projected outside the domestic hearth, for boys.[4]

When the figures are updated in line with what has happened during the 1980s, a number of interesting changes become apparent (see Table 8.1). The fall in mortality in this age group resumed during the early 1970s, and the reduction has been sharper and more pronounced for boys than for girls. The ratio between the medians of the probabilities of dying for boys and girls increased, until it reached a value of about 1.40 at the beginning of the 1970s, since when it has remained stable with only a very slight reduction during the early 1980s. A trend towards greater geographical uniformity that

---

[3] G. Caselli and V. Egidi, *New Trends in European Mortality* (Strasbourg, 1981).
[4] UN, *Selected Demographic and Social Characteristics of the World's Children and Youth* (New York, 1986).

TABLE 8.1. *Probability of dying, by age and sex, 1950–1984* (×1,000)

Year	Min	Q₁	Median	Q₃	Max	Relative spread*	RVM†	Mortality/ sex ratio at median
			Males aged 1–14 years					
1950–54	10.67	13.25	15.30	24.51	64.02	0.74		1.28
1955–59	8.48	10.91	12.47	17.54	50.08	0.74	−18.5	1.29
1960–64	7.80	9.43	10.43	12.53	39.41	0.53	−16.4	1.34
1965–69	6.73	8.65	9.51	10.11	25.20	0.30	−8.8	1.37
1970–74	5.61	8.17	8.37	8.82	20.98	0.08	−12.0	1.40
1975–79	4.74	6.37	6.93	7.40	13.39	0.15	−17.2	1.41
1980–84	3.37	5.16	5.67	6.22	10.88	0.19	−18.2	1.39
			Females aged 1–14 years					
1950–54	7.71	9.95	11.98	22.34	60.58	1.03		
1955–59	6.02	7.80	9.19	15.02	47.35	0.79	−23.3	
1960–64	5.61	6.72	7.37	9.60	35.32	0.39	−19.8	
1965–69	4.58	6.03	6.59	7.41	21.59	0.21	−10.6	
1970–74	4.09	5.42	6.00	6.37	16.47	0.16	−8.9	
1975–79	3.38	4.44	4.91	5.45	9.98	0.21	−18.2	
1980–84	2.50	3.61	4.12	4.57	7.50	0.23	−16.1	
			Males aged 0–1 year					
1950–54	22.56	31.32	41.97	62.64	122.72	0.75		1.27
1955–59	19.13	26.88	33.60	50.11	101.91	0.69	−19.9	1.27
1960–64	17.54	23.38	29.47	37.34	84.63	0.47	−12.3	1.28
1965–69	14.33	19.23	24.85	30.14	66.40	0.44	−15.7	1.28
1970–74	11.82	15.18	19.95	28.20	50.81	0.65	−19.7	1.29
1975–79	8.99	11.08	16.20	19.07	37.52	0.49	−18.8	1.28
1980–84	7.26	9.44	12.30	14.48	32.64	0.41	−24.1	1.27
			Females aged 0–1 year					
1950–54	17.18	24.23	32.97	52.83	110.20	0.87		
1955–59	14.77	20.99	27.02	41.41	93.87	0.76	−18.0	
1960–64	13.40	17.80	23.11	29.77	78.02	0.52	−14.5	
1965–69	10.84	14.62	19.43	23.24	66.06	0.44	−15.9	
1970–74	9.00	11.50	15.40	21.08	45.18	0.62	−20.7	
1975–79	6.97	8.47	12.50	15.93	33.91	0.60	−18.8	
1980–84	5.90	7.28	9.50	11.04	28.98	0.40	−24.0	

Note: For the countries considered, see Table 8.2, excluding Luxembourg, Malta, German Democratic Republic, USSR, Israel, Greece, and Romania.

* Relative spread is $\dfrac{Q_3 - Q_1}{\text{median}}$.

† RVM = Relative variation of the median per 100.

Source: WHO, *World Health Statistics Annual* (Geneva, 1986).

culminated during the early 1970s has been replaced by a situation in which geographical differences are once again becoming apparent.

The nature of this change becomes clearer when we consider the probabilities of dying at these ages in individual countries. The steeper fall in mortality was not a universal phenomenon; it did not occur in eastern or southern Europe. In the countries in which the decline was steepest, it was also greater for boys than for girls.

To conclude: a new trend in mortality levels and geographical differences has appeared in an age group in which we would not have expected any new surprises, and the differences which are sex-linked provide some interesting material for speculation about the relationship between health and the position of women. The trend towards reduced sex differentials in some countries (the ratio of boys' to girls' mortality fell from 140–55 in 1970–74 to 120–35 in 1980–84 in the Netherlands, Denmark, Sweden, Austria, Northern Ireland, and Belgium) followed the more rapid decline in the mortality of boys. This suggests that there may have been a reduction in the difference between the behaviour expected of the two sexes in childhood.

After the 1960s, education, inspired by a more egalitarian approach, became more widespread as well as less aggressive and violent as far as boys were concerned, and greater freedom of expression was permitted to girls. Moreover, urban life-styles have probably increasingly confined children's activities to their homes. If this were so, some degree of 'feminization' may have entered into boys' education, and contributed to some reduction in their mortality.

The First Year

The situation relating to the first year of life is quite complex. Analyses that go back to the early 1970s show that mortality during the first year of life has declined overall, and that the size of the decline was independent of the initial level and of the level of development of the country concerned. The pace of the decline slowed during the 1960s, and the reduction was greater for post-neonatal than for neonatal mortality, so that infant mortality tended increasingly to be concentrated in the neonatal period. Causes of death were predominantly linked to conditions of perinatal origin, particularly low birthweight and congenital abnormalities. There was a marked reduction in the incidence of infectious and respiratory illness, which remained important only in countries in which infant mortality continued to be relatively high. Deaths from congenital abnormalities are not linked geographically to mortality levels.

An analysis of more recent data offers a number of interesting novelties. Since the early 1970s the pace of decline of infant mortality has been greater than during the 1950s. Geographical variations reappeared during the 1970s, but became less important during the last quinquennium con-

TABLE 8.2. *Infant mortality in the main developed countries, 1984–1986* (per 1,000 live births)

Country	Abbreviation	Rate	Year
Iceland	ICE	5.4	1986
Japan	J	5.5	1985
Sweden	S	5.9	1986
Finland	SF	6.5	1986
Switzerland	CH	6.8	1986
Netherlands	NL	7.7	1986
Norway	N	7.8	1986
Denmark	DK	7.9	1985
Luxembourg	L	7.9	1986
France	F	7.9	1986
Canada	CN	7.9	1985
Federal Republic of Germany	D	8.6	1986
Ireland	EIR	8.7	1986
Spain	E	9.0	1984
German Democratic Republic	DDR	9.2	1986
Belgium	B	9.5	1986
United Kingdom	UK	9.5	1986
Italy	I	9.8	1986
Australia	AUS	9.8	1986
Austria	A	10.3	1986
United States of America	USA	10.4	1986
New Zealand	NZ	10.8	1985
Israel	IL	11.4	1986
Greece	G	11.8	1986
Malta	M	13.6	1985
Czechoslovakia	CS	13.9	1986
Bulgaria	BG	14.7	1986
Portugal	P	15.9	1986
Poland	PL	17.5	1986
Hungary	H	19.0	1986
Yugoslavia	YU	23.3	1986
USSR	U	25.4	1986
Romania	R	25.6	1985

Note: The abbreviations in the second column are used in Figs. 8.1 and 8.2.

Sources: WHO, *World Health Statistics Annual*, (Geneva, 1987); A. Monnier, 'La Conjoncture démographique', *Population*, 4–5, (1988).

sidered (1980–84). Thus, the 1970s would again appear to have been a turning-point.

Sex-related differentials were a little higher than 30 per cent, and did not change much during the period considered, except for a slight reduction after the beginning of the 1970s. A detailed geographical analysis shows that at the beginning of the 1950s infant mortality was lowest in the United States, New Zealand, Sweden, Norway, and England and Wales, and highest in eastern and southern Europe. This situation had changed by the beginning of the 1980s, when it was lowest in the Scandinavian countries, the Netherlands, Switzerland, and Japan, and highest in eastern Europe, and, among the southern European countries, in Portugal (Table 8.2). These changes followed different rates of decline throughout the period, even though initial levels may have been the same.

During the thirty-five-year period under discussion lower rates of decline were found during the 1950s in some countries (Canada, United States, Scandinavia except Finland); in others the slowdown continued into the 1960s (Austria, Belgium, Scotland, Australia, the Federal Republic of Germany, Switzerland, England and Wales, Northern Ireland, Hungary); in some (Bulgaria, Poland) it is still continuing today.

In some countries the decline was more pronounced throughout the 1970s and slowed again during the first half of the 1980s (the United States, Italy, Scandinavia), whereas in others it continued at the same pace (Canada, United Kingdom, Federal Republic of Germany, Hungary).

The decline in infant mortality during the 1970s and 1980s was due almost entirely to a fall in mortality during the first week of life, which had originally seemed to be the most difficult to control. Mortality at this age decreased by more than 80 per cent in Scandinavia, the Netherlands, the Federal Republic of Germany, the United States, and Australia, and by between 60 and 80 per cent in most of the other countries. At present this mortality accounts for half or more of total infant mortality, except in a few countries (Bulgaria, Romania, New Zealand).

As regards sex differentials, there were two trends: in some countries the difference between the mortality of boys and girls increased at first, and a decrease followed (the United States, Scandinavia, Japan, Australia, and the Federal Republic of Germany); in others it increased throughout the period (Bulgaria, Italy, Poland, Spain, and Portugal).

The increased difference between the mortality of the two sexes could reflect the gradual disappearance of residual forms of discrimination against girls in care, attention, and nutrition, which would reveal the biological advantage of females. A smaller differential at a time when infant mortality is again falling as a result of a reduction in early neonatal deaths would, at first sight, seem to run counter to this biological law, particularly as mortality linked to perinatal conditions (low birthweight and congenital abnormalities)

TABLE 8.3. *Distribution of deaths during the first five years of life, by age* (%)

	All countries	Romania (Type A)	Italy (Type B)	France (Type C)
0–6 days				
1.1. Infectious diseases	0.1	0.0	0.2	0.1
1.2. Diseases of the respiratory system	0.3	0.1	0.7	0.1
1.3. Congenital abnormalities	9.3	3.9	10.1	7.0
1.4. Perinatal conditions	29.7	13.7	45.2	12.5
1.5. Accidents	0.1	0.0	0.1	0.1
1.6. Other, ill-defined conditions	1.9	0.2	0.5	14.4
7–27 days				
2.1. Infectious diseases	0.3	0.3	0.2	0.2
2.2. Diseases of the respiratory system	0.8	3.2	0.7	0.1
2.3. Congenital abnormalities	3.2	3.0	3.9	4.1
2.4. Perinatal conditions	4.5	3.4	6.1	4.3
2.5. Accidents	0.1	0.2	0.0	0.2
2.6. Other, ill-defined conditions	1.4	1.0	0.4	1.7
28–364 days				
3.1. Infectious diseases	2.5	4.4	1.1	1.1
3.2. Diseases of the respiratory system	5.5	25.7	3.2	1.3
3.3. Congenital abnormalities	6.5	6.9	7.0	6.9
3.4. Perinatal conditions	1.7	0.3	2.4	2.6

TABLE 8.3. (*cont.*)

	All countries	Romania (Type A)	Italy (Type B)	France (Type C)
3.5. Ill-defined conditions	8.0	0.0	1.9	15.1
3.6. Accidents	2.0	1.7	1.1	4.3
3.7. Other	5.0	8.2	2.3	4.5
1–4 years				
4.1. Infectious diseases	1.0	1.0	0.7	0.8
4.2. Neoplasms	1.7	1.5	2.1	2.4
4.3. Diseases of the respiratory system	1.9	7.8	1.5	0.9
4.4. Congenital abnormalities	2.4	2.7	2.7	2.7
4.5. Accidents	6.0	8.3	3.0	7.1
4.6. Other, ill-defined conditions	3.9	2.5	2.9	5.5
TOTAL	100.0	100.0	100.0	100.0
0–6 days	41.4	17.9	56.7	34.2
7–27 days	10.3	11.1	11.4	10.5
28–364 days	31.2	47.2	19.1	35.9
1–4 years	16.9	23.8	12.8	19.4
TOTAL	100.0	100.0	100.0	100.0

Note: The numbers in the left-hand column are used in Fig. 8.1.

Source: WHO. Geneva.

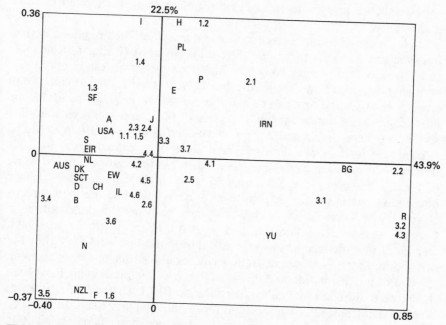

FIG. 8.1 Structure of mortality by age and cause of death (Results of the simple correspondence factor analysis in relation to the first factorial plane)

has been reduced. This suggests an effect which is not a positive result of efforts to reduce mortality further.

Recent Age- and Cause-Specific Mortality

We shall consider four age groups: 0–6 days, 2–27 days, 28–364 days, and 1–4 years, and shall group causes of death in such a way as to highlight the more important ones in each group, without excessive disaggregation. A more detailed breakdown would have led to problems of comparability between different countries as a result of different methods of diagnosis, and changes in the International List of Classification of Causes of Death.

The most important causes of death between birth and fifth birthday are (in decreasing order of importance): perinatal causes and congenital abnormalities during the first week of life; ill-defined causes and congenital abnormalities after the first month; accidents after the first year; respiratory disease and 'other causes' between the first and eleventh month of life; perinatal causes between the first week and the first month of life (see Table 8.3, Col. 1).

To summarize the information for individual countries, we applied a correspondence analysis to the tabulations of sex–age specific mortality in each country.[5]

Three groups of countries seem to present a profile which is quite different from the one generally prevailing (Fig. 8.1). Group A (Bulgaria, Romania, and Yugoslavia) is distinguished by a higher frequency of respiratory illness between the second week and the fourth year of life, and of infectious diseases between the first month and the end of the first year of life. Both these phenomena can be attributed to low hygienic and sanitary conditions which have been eliminated in most developed countries. Group B (Italy, Hungary, Poland, Spain, Portugal, and Ireland) is characterized by high frequency of perinatal causes and respiratory diseases during the first week of life. In this group the more general problems which have led to high infant mortality in the past appear to have been overcome, but others more closely linked to conditions at childbirth have remained. In the countries in Group C (France, New Zealand, and Norway) the main features are a high frequency of ill-defined causes of death during the first week and after the first month of life, and deaths from accidents and perinatal causes between the end of the first month and the first birthday. This profile may have been due more to different methods of certification (the high frequency of deaths of perinatal origin after the first month of life supports this explanation), rather than to any real differences in the structure of mortality. In addition to data which relate to all the countries considered, Table 8.3 also contains information for three countries (one from each group) which emerged from the correspondence analysis. This makes it easier to verify the differences found between the structures. It should be noted that similar profiles correspond to similar distributions of outcomes during the first five years of life. Profiles in Group A contain a higher frequency of deaths between the end of the first month of life and the first birthday, whereas Profile B contains more deaths during the neonatal period. However, levels of mortality can differ between groups.

The Geography of Infant Health, Modernization, and Women's Status

Having sketched an outline of recent trends and features of infant and child mortality in the developed countries, we now ask whether the picture that emerges represents infant health, and whether it is associated with the status of women in the countries concerned within the framework of their own overall development.

We know that different morbidity patterns correspond to different mortality levels. A high level of mortality at later periods of infancy is generally the result of infectious diseases, and a sign of deterioration in infant health.

[5] M. Greenacre, *Theory and Application of Correspondence Analysis* (London, 1984).

Thus, a fall in infant mortality at later periods of infancy may be taken as an indicator of improved infant health. Where levels of mortality are near the average, even though mortality may be concentrated during the first week of life, it is likely that conditions at delivery and confinement are below standard. This could imply worse health among the survivors, compared with countries in which such risks are lower. We can thus use mortality figures for a broader interpretation of the situation than is generally done.

We shall use age-specific mortality in four age groups: 0–6 days, 7–27 days, 28–364 days, and 1–4 years, as negative indicators of infant health. To these we have added another variable, the frequency of babies of low birthweight, which is an index of the present and past health of the mother, and of the new-born infant's chances of survival, and its future health.

For a geographical analysis of the association between modernization, the status of women, and infant health we used a number of indices that were related to the socio-economic situation and to the state of the health services, as well as indices of women's status. We employed the framework proposed by Oppong[6] and Oppenheim Mason,[7] with simplifications which were made necessary by the type of information available in different countries. The variables relate to the twenty-two developed countries for which there was a complete set of data.

The first group of indices describes socio-economic and health conditions in the country concerned, and relates to economic conditions (gross domestic product (GDP)), urbanization, communications, life expectancy, and availability of health services and personnel. These indices represent aspects of the environment to which infants' and mothers' health are related. We expect this association to be positive.

A second group of variables describes the position of women. The indices used here are fertility, and the proportion of women in their teens who are married. We would expect women's status to be more traditional where both fertility and the percentage of teenagers who are married are high. High educational attainment is the best index of women's higher status. Two other indices are women's labour-force participation, as well as their participation in the national legislature. The latter represents participation in the power structure of their society. Other indicators which will be negatively related to women's status are maternal mortality, and mortality at reproductive ages. We also use the ratio of mortality rates of males to those of females at reproductive ages and in childhood. These are regarded as representing differences in the life-style and behavioural models for each sex.

The association between these indices and infants' and mothers' health

[6] C. Oppong, *A Synopsis of Seven Roles and Status of Women: An Outline of a Conceptual and Methodological Approach* (Geneva, 1980).
[7] K. Oppenheim Mason, *The Status of Women: A Review of its Relationship to Fertility and Mortality* (Population Studies Center; Ann Arbor, Mich., 1984).

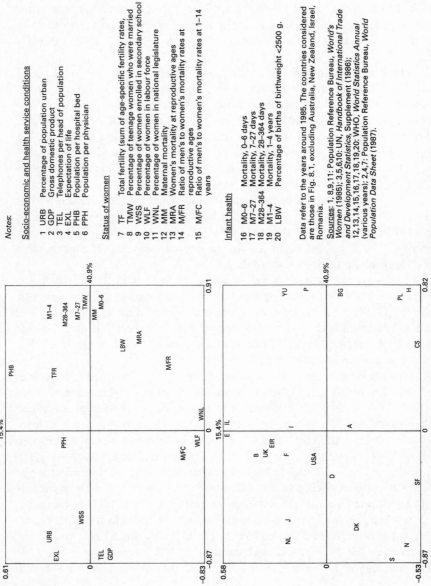

Notes:

Socio-economic and health service conditions

1	URB	Percentage of population urban
2	GDP	Gross domestic product
3	TEL	Telephones per head of population
4	EXL	Expectation of life
5	PHB	Population per hospital bed
6	PPH	Population per physician

Status of women

7	TF	Total fertility (sum of age-specific fertility rates,
8	TMW	Percentage of teenage women who were married
9	WSS	Percentage of women enrolled in secondary school
10	WLF	Percentage of women in labour force
11	WNL	Percentage of women in national legislature
12	MM	Maternal mortality
13	MRA	Women's mortality at reproductive ages
14	M/FR	Ratio of men's to women's mortality rates at reproductive ages
15	M/FC	Ratio of men's to women's mortality rates at 1–14 years

Infant health

16	M0–6	Mortality, 0–6 days
17	M7–27	Mortality, 7–27 days
18	M28–364	Mortality, 28–364 days
19	M1–4	Mortality, 1–4 years
20	LBW	Percentage of births of birthweight <2500 g.

Data refer to the years around 1985. The countries considered are those in Fig. 8.1, excluding Australia, New Zealand, Israel, Romania.

Sources: 1, 8,9,11: Population Reference Bureau, *World's Women* (1985); 3,5,6,10: UN, *Handbook of International Trade and Development Statistics*, Supplement (1986); 12,13,14,15,16,17,18,19,20: WHO, *World Statistics Annual* (various years); 2,4,7: Population Reference Bureau, *World Population Data Sheet* (1987).

FIG. 8.2 Infant health, women's status, and modernization (Results of the principal components factor

can be ambiguous. Whereas a positive association between favourable environmental conditions, the socio-economic and demographic status of women, and mothers' health would be expected, the nature of the association with the other indices is not so obvious, as the indices themselves are ambiguous. Similarity between men's and women's working conditions may mean a deterioration in the situation of women, particularly if their role as workers is coupled to their traditional roles in the home and in the family, and if there are no alternative arrangements for child care. A lower excess mortality of men can imply greater parity between the sexes in a number of Western countries, where it is associated with low infant and women's mortality (Switzerland, the Netherlands, and Japan), or a residual of social disadvantages suffered by women (as is the case, perhaps, in Yugoslavia and Italy).

We used principal components analysis as our method. No attempt was made to establish dependency relations between the variables considered, because of the possible ambiguity of the indices chosen, and also because the analysis was carried out at an ecological level, which is not easily adapted to considerations of causality. We preferred to extract the principal factor from a sufficiently large number of indices to represent the complexity of the topic and the issues involved, and allowed for interactions between the different indices. The results suggest a first component which could be defined as modernization and welfare (expectation of life, GDP, communications, and urbanization), all of which were positively correlated, and infant mortality, which was negatively correlated with this factor ($r \geq |0.65|$). The second component represented sexual equality (women's labour-force and political participation and excess mortality of males in infancy). These variables were correlated with the second component.

The first result to note is that infants' and mothers' maternal health, and the general level of health of the population, are subsumed under 'welfare'. The only aspect that characterizes women's status specifically is the low percentage of teenagers who are married; the other indices are less strongly correlated. Modernization and infant and maternal health appear to be completely independent of the degree of equality achieved by women (the two factors being orthogonal). In Fig. 8.2 it is possible to distinguish two situations in which infant health is worse: in the first, mortality after the first month of life is high; in the second, early neonatal mortality is high. It is in countries in the second situation that two other indices of maternal and infant health are associated—the percentage of babies of low birthweight, and women's mortality at reproductive ages—and these characterize areas that differ from those we have described previously. It should be noted that a relatively high frequency of babies of low birthweight is not confined to the poorer countries, in which overall survival conditions are worse.

There are a number of variables which do not have an effect on infant health:

1. Availability of physicians and hospital services. This is consistent with the results from other studies.[8] This finding does not contradict the picture that has emerged. Health services are a key resource for treatment when members of the population fall ill, but the overall state of a population's health depends on those who remain well. The factors that render a particular disease more or less frequent are generally external to the provision of health services.[9]

2. Higher labour-force participation by women. This confirms that, as we speculated above, a reduction of discrimination against women in work or politics is not associated with changes in socio-economic development, nor in maternal and infant health.

3. Marked sex differentials in mortality in childhood or at reproductive ages. This phenomenon can be considered as a transitional situation between socio-cultural conditions that were disadvantageous to females and where a reduction in discrimination did not result in women assuming traditionally masculine roles, but where there was greater respect for the difference between the sexes, and a healthier life-style on the part of men.

In the lower section of Fig. 8.2, the position of individual countries is represented by their co-ordinates in the factor plane: eastern Europe and Portugal are characterized by less modernization, less welfare, and lower infant survival; in these countries high mortality, particularly during the first week of life, is found in Poland, Hungary, and Czechoslovakia, and is associated with a higher frequency of babies of low birthweight, lower late neonatal and post-neonatal mortality, larger sex differentials in mortality, higher labour-force and political participation rates among women, and greater availability of health services with respect to others (Yugoslavia, Portugal, and Bulgaria).

As health and socio-economic conditions improve, we find the optimum situation—in which a high level of socio-economic development is associated with higher survival—in Scandinavia, the Netherlands, and Japan. There is a marked difference between Scandinavia and the other countries. In Scandinavia, women's labour-force participation as well as their participation in the legislature is much stronger, and health services are more developed. The ratio between the mortality of the two sexes is also larger.

There are obvious difficulties in providing an unambiguous definition of women's position. The situation may be described as good where women enjoy full access to education and a high level of welfare, where maternal and infant health are satisfactory, fertility is lower, and late marriage results in an extended period of training. However, such a situation can exist in societies in which women participate in the labour force and in government,

---

[8] F. Pampel and V. Pielai, 'Patterns and Determinants of Infant Mortality in Developed Nations', *Demography*, 23 (1986), pp. 525–41.
[9] S. L. Barron and A. M. Thompson, *Obstetrical Epidemiology* (London, 1983).

as well as in societies in which their role is more marginal. Could this be a matter of personal choice?

Moreover, what we have described as a favourable health situation can exist where the ratio of mortality rates of the two sexes is high as well as where it is low. Excess mortality of boys is somewhat higher in countries in which the labour-force participation rate of women is higher, and where one might expect life-styles of men and women to be more alike. Thus, even when women wish to participate in paid employment and the power structure, they do not need to assume the more damaging life-styles of men. Is there a model in which participation in the labour force is not marginal, but which is compatible with both health and maternity? Finally, the role played by health services appears somewhat ambiguous; given that improvement in health is possible, both where such services are widespread and where they are more limited, what is the most favourable situation not merely for survival, but also for quality of survival and the experience of maternity?

So far we have used an ecological approach. Such analyses can only be exploratory and cannot establish causal relationships between different variables, which must be verified by other means.[10] However, our indices can suggest hypotheses which can be verified by other more direct ones, and which could be used to explore further the factors that are related to infant health.

Aspects of Women's Position and Infant Health

Socio-Economic Status

We have shown that there are different dimensions of women's status which are not necessarily correlated, nor linked to an improvement in infant health, but that welfare and modernization were so linked. If we look at studies at the individual level, it has been shown in a review of the links between the mother's socio-economic condition on one hand, and infant morbidity and the use made of health services on the other,[11] that disabilities are more frequent among the children of poorer women, that the number of disabilities they suffer from is larger, and that handicaps such as dental caries, visual impairment, lead poisoning, or incomplete immunizations are more frequent among them than among children of wealthier women. Illness is not only more frequent; it is also more severe and has a greater impact through limitation of activities caused by acute diseases (influenza, rheumatic fever, gastroenteritis, parasitic disease), or through disability

[10] L. I. Langbein and A. J. Lichtman, *Ecologic Inference* (Beverly Hills, Calif., 1978).
[11] L. Egbuono and B. Starfield, 'Child Health and Social Status', *Paediatrics*, 69 (1982), pp. 550–6.

caused by chronic disease. Hospitalization is also more frequent, and stays in hospital are longer.

Children of women who come from a lower socio-economic stratum are more often affected by visual impairments which remain uncorrected, as well as by otitis and iron deficiency. Psychological and psychosomatic morbidity is also both more serious and more frequent among the children of poorer mothers.

The use that is made of health services acts as an intermediate variable between socio-economic conditions and illness. Economically deprived women tend to have recourse to medical care less often and later in the child's illness, when it has already reached a serious stage, as they tend to underestimate the importance of symptoms. This form of behaviour can distort the results of enquiries into child health and lead to relationships which may be difficult to interpret, or which are U-shaped,[12] or a positive relationship may appear between morbidity indices and socio-economic conditions[13] when the survey is based not on clinical examination but on the statements made by the mother, or when statistics are based on numbers who use health facilities.

The use the mother makes of health services is important: the more frequently she consults a physician and undergoes a diagnostic examination, the more frequently will the physician be consulted about the health of her children. This can happen, both when they suffer from illness, or as a result of personal attitudes which are influenced by their higher socio-economic status,[14] and medical treatment may be sought even when the illness is mild. Overmedication has become a new problem for the children of wealthier women, as has overfeeding which causes obesity, overhousing which leads to social isolation, and overeducation which increases the risk of some children being considered as retarded.[15]

Women's Health

We have shown that there is a very close association between the health of mothers and that of their children. Women who were born or grew up in conditions of deprivation in wartime or during a period of economic

---

[12] M. G. Kovar, 'Health Status of US Children and Use of Medical Care', *Public Health Reports*, 97 (1982), 3–15; L. N. Edwards and M. Grossman, 'Income and Race Differences in Children's Health in the Mid-1960s', *Medical Care*, 20 (1982), pp. 915–30; D. B. Dutton, 'Socio-economic Status and Children's Health', *Medical Care*, 23 (1985), pp. 142–56.

[13] R. Cillis, 'Fattori della salute infantile secondo l'indagine ISTAT del 1983', thesis submitted to the Department of Demographic Sciences, University La Sapienza, Rome, 1988.

[14] B. Starfield, *The Effectiveness of Medical Care* (Baltimore, 1985); Dutton, op. cit. in n. 12; Cillis, op. cit. in n. 13; D. Mechanic, 'The Influence of Mothers on their Children's Health Attitudes and Behaviour', *Paediatrics* (1964), pp. 444–53.

[15] WHO, *Problems of Children of School Age (5–9 Years): Report of a Working Group* (Copenhagen, 1976).

depression can, in their turn, give birth to weaker children. This interpretation is confirmed by an inexplicably high incidence of low birthweight and serious congenital abnormalities experienced in certain countries during specific periods. An example is Scotland during the 1960s, when women born during the economic depression, whose mothers had suffered dietary deprivation in childhood, reached reproductive age themselves.[16] The disastrous effects of maternal malnutrition have become apparent in those parts of Europe which were particularly affected by the war, and in the immediate post-war period in Germany, when food was no longer available from the previously occupied countries.

A cohort effect could have contributed to the reduction in the pace of infant mortality observed in several countries during the 1960s (years when the cohorts born during and immediately after the Second World War reached peak reproductive age) and also to the rapid decrease in infant mortality during the 1970s, when mothers had grown up during periods when nutrition was better and welfare more universal. This speculation has been made explicit for Italy,[17] where an increase in the frequency of babies of low birthweights was observed until the early 1970s, and was followed by a gradual reduction during the slowdown and later acceleration in the rate of decline of foetal and infant mortality.

Demographic Behaviour

The Decline of Fertility. Our previous analysis suggested that the pace and timing of fertility decline were related to the status of women, and closely associated with infant health. High fertility is usually associated with a longer fertile period, as reproduction begins earlier and lasts longer, the proportion of children of high birth orders increases, and birth intervals are generally shorter. Births which occur very early or very late in a woman's reproductive period, primiparity, or very high parity, and short birth intervals have all been recognized as high-risk factors which lead to unfavourable outcomes of pregnancy.[18] The transition from high to low fertility usually involves a concentration of births at ages where risks are reduced, and to longer birth intervals, with a potentially favourable effect on pregnancy outcome. Several authors have shown that, in some countries and at certain times, the decrease in infant mortality has been assisted by a

---

[16] D. Baird, 'The Epidemiology of Low Birth Weight: Changes in Incidence in Aberdeen, 1948–72', *Journal of Biosocial Science*, 6 (1974), pp. 323–41.

[17] A. Pinnelli, 'Rapport à l'OMS sur les raisons du déclin récent de la mortalité féto-infantile en Italie', Dipartimento di Scienze Demografiche. *Materiali di studi e ricerche*, 2 (1983).

[18] The literature on the subject is extensive; see WHO, *A WHO Report on Social and Biological Effects on Perinatal Mortality* (Geneva, 1979).

change in the distribution of births by birth order which resulted from lower fertility.[19]

Teenage and Older Mothers. Both early and late motherhood are now much rarer than they used to be. However, because such pregnancies tend to occur among women of low socio-economic status and with little education, the chances of an unfavourable outcome are higher than they were in the past. These conditions have repercussions on the condition of children Mortality among children of these women is higher, children of low birth-weight are more frequent, and the quality of survival is worse. Among healthy children, behavioural problems are more frequent at school age irrespective of the socio-economic status of the mother. Younger mothers often display a series of negative behavioural features towards their children (less physical contact, less time spent with them, less verbal communication) and this may well lead to problems at later stages of development.[20]

The solution must lie in preventing pregnancy among younger women through the use of contraception.

More recently, late pregnancy (among women over 35 years old) has emerged as a phenomenon which is linked to an improved women's condition. Women who postpone reproduction to this stage of their lives are often highly educated, of high socio-economic status, generally live in towns, are capable of controlling their own fertility, and are eager for professional self-fulfilment.[21] Some writers consider that the higher age of the

[19] O. Meirik, B. Smedby, and A. Ericson, 'Impact of Changing Age and Parity Distribution of Mothers on Perinatal Mortality in Sweden, 1953–1975', *International Journal of Epidemiology* 8 (1979), pp. 361–4; N. M. Morris, J. R. Udry, and C. I. Chase, 'Shifting Age-Parity Distribution of Births and Decrease in Infant Mortality', *American Journal of Public Health*, 65 (1975) pp. 359–62; M. Gendell and E. Hellegers, 'The Influence in the Changes of Maternal Age Birth Order and Color on the Changing Perinatal Mortality', *Health Service Reports*, 88 (1973) pp. 733–42; G. Masuy Stroobant, *Les Déterminants de la mortalité infantile: La Belgique d'hier et d'aujourd'hui* (Louvain la Neuve, 1983); J. F. Forbes and R. M. Pickering, 'Influence of Maternal Age, Parity and Social Class on Perinatal Mortality in Scotland', *Journal of Biosocial Science*, 17 (1985), pp. 339–49; J. Hellier, 'Perinatal Mortality, 1950 and 1973', *Population Trends*, 10 (1977), pp. 13–15; H. C. Chase, *A Study of Infant Mortality from Linked Records Comparison of Neonatal Mortality from Two Cohort Studies* (1972); Pinnelli, op. cit. in n. 17.
[20] E. R. McAraney, R. A. Lawrence, H. N. Ricciuti, J. Polley, and M. Szilagyi, 'Interactions of Adolescent Mothers and their One-Year-Old Children', *Paediatrics*, 78 (1986), pp. 585–90; G. T. Arline, 'On Teenage Childbearing and Neonatal Mortality in the United States', *Population and Development Review*, 13 (1987), pp. 245–79; I. L. Horon, D. M. Strobino, and H. M. MacDonald, 'Birth Weights among Infants Born to Adolescent and Young Adult Women' *American Journal of Obstetrics and Gynecology*, 146 (1983), pp. 444–45; C. A. Miller, 'La mortalità infantile negli Stati Uniti', *Le Scienze*, 205 (Sept. 1985), pp. 10–17; B. Blondel M. Kaminski, M. J. Saurel-Cubizolles, and G. Breart, 'Pregnancy Outcome and Social Conditions of Women under 20: Evolution in France from 1972 to 1981', *International Journal of Epidemiology*, 16 (1987), pp. 425–30.
[21] Forbes and Pickering, op. cit. in n. 19; Z. A. Stein, 'A Woman's Age: Childbearing and Childrearing', *American Journal of Epidemiology*, 121 (1985), pp. 327–42; M. P. Kernoff 'Re-evaluating the Medical Risks of Late Childbearing', *Women and Health*, 11 (1986), pp. 37–60.

mother is associated with poor outcomes of pregnancy, such as miscarriages, premature births, low birthweight, perinatal mortality, and congenital abnormalities, but others have regarded the evidence as inconclusive.[22] Whatever may be the truth, the spread of this new type of demographic behaviour involves higher costs, not only in economic terms, but also psychologically; in fact, late pregnancies are particularly closely monitored, increasingly tending to medicalize birth, i.e. to treat pregnancy not as a natural event but rather as an illness.

Abortion. The power to control their own fertility is a fundamental aspect of women's status. Amongst fertility-control methods, abortion has been studied on account of its possible negative influence on women's health and on the health of subsequent children. Repeated abortions may damage a woman's reproductive system and increase the likelihood of future unsuccessful pregnancies. This hypothesis might explain the higher percentage of children of low birthweight and of consequent high neonatal mortality in some eastern European countries, where induced abortion has been used on a massive scale as a means of fertility control.[23] However, this does not seem sufficient to explain the high incidence of low birthweight in Hungary, which occurs also among first pregnancies.[24] Abortion in western European countries was legalized later than in eastern Europe, and abortion rates have not been as high, since abortion is used mainly to eliminate conceptions following early sexual activity among young, unmarried girls, or to stop fertility once the desired number of children has been attained. Therefore, any assessment of the impact of legal abortion on reproductive health in western countries is likely to be favourable, as it has eliminated unwanted pregnancies among women in high-risk categories, such as teenagers, unmarried women, or older mothers.[25]

Births Outside Marriage, One-Parent Families, and Step-families. Increases in women's education, independence, and participation in the labour force have contributed to the emergence of new patterns of demographic behaviour. The increased proportion of births which occur outside marriage in many countries is an obvious result of the spread of new family-building habits and of reproduction outside the legal institution of marriage. It is, therefore, possible that the negative association between illegitimacy and infant survival in the past could become weaker in the future as a result of

[22] Stein, op. cit. in n. 21; Kernoff, op. cit. in n. 21.

[23] C. Davies and M. Feshbach, *Rising Infant Mortality in the USSR in the 1970s* (US Bureau of the Census, Washington, 1980); V. Bodrova and R. Anker, *Working Women in Socialist Countries* (Geneva, 1985); H. Herlemann, *Quality of Life in the Soviet Union* (Boulder, Col., 1987).

[24] WHO, op. cit. in n. 15.

[25] Starfield, op. cit. in n. 14; R. J. Gandy, 'An Estimate of the Effect of Abortions on the Stillbirth Rate', *Journal of Biosocial Science*, 11 (1979), pp. 173–8.

the changed social significance of this condition, and will be linked to the instability of this type of union.

Increases in the frequency of divorce and of extramarital cohabitation in many countries have resulted in the existence of two different types of family which might affect infant health: one-parent families, and step-families. Growing up in a one-parent family may be more risky for a number of reasons: the family's standard of living may be lower, the single parent may have to work harder and longer to meet the family's economic needs, the child may suffer from lack of contact with an adult of a sex different from that of the single parent, and there may be prolonged periods of suffering or aggressiveness and quarrels between the parents. When the single parent is the father, the child may suffer from his lack of experience in child-rearing.

Usually, non-custodial parents tend to lose touch with their children and are excluded or substituted by a new partner of the single parent. Such events lead to a discrepancy between the actual and the legal situation, which is designed to provide the child with a network of blood-relations. Instead, the parent's role is redefined as a 'social' and not necessarily as a 'genetic' parent, but we do not yet know to what extent such a situation is socially or emotionally acceptable.[26] Nor have the long-term effects of parental separation and remarriage on the health of children been adequately documented as yet. The World Health Organization (WHO) has devoted a seminar to this problem.[27]

Women's Employment

Our ecological analysis showed that women's participation in the labour force and in the power structure seemed to be independent of other aspects of women's status and that they were not linked to infant health. This result is due to the fact that women's activity rates are very high both in countries in which infant mortality is low (e.g. Scandinavia), and in those in which it is high (e.g. eastern Europe). However, an analysis at the individual level confirms these results.

The belief that some types of work are harmful for reproductive health has resulted, during the last hundred years, in some countries, in legislation being passed designed to protect women's health. Their access to certain types of work has been limited, as have their working hours (prohibition of work with toxic substances, night work, and work on Sundays or public holidays; maternity leave both before and after the confinement; reductions in working hours for breast-feeding mothers, etc.). This has resulted in men and women being treated differently, but may also have contributed to the

---

[26] R. Chester, P. Diggory, and M. B. Sutherland, *Changing Patterns of Child-bearing and Child-rearing* (London, 1981).

[27] WHO, *Children and Family Breakdown* (Copenhagen, 1986).

marginality of women's position in work and careers. However, it has protected the health of women and children and has made it easier to combine the roles of mother and worker.

During the 1970s, encouraged by the women's movement, attempts were made to prove scientifically that some aspects of work might have a negative effect on reproductive outcomes, not only in terms of higher infant mortality, but also through an increased frequency of miscarriages, stillbirths, congenital abnormalities, and mortality from malignancies. The link could come about in two ways, the first connected with the work itself (fatigue, position, etc.), the second concerned with contact with toxic substances at the workplace. The analysis has also been extended to include the father's occupation, in order to identify any influences that might exist between the working environment and spermatogenesis.

The results of studies of the first hypothesis are not conclusive, probably because there is a form of self-selection that ensures that women can perform certain activities only if they are already healthy, because the toll taken by housework should not be underestimated,[28] and also because having a job will increase a woman's income and make it possible for her to enjoy a better standard of living, diet, and medical care.[29]

As regards the second hypothesis, it has been demonstrated in many studies that the outcomes of pregnancies of women who are exposed to toxic substances in the workplace will more frequently be unfavourable, but there are also other studies that do not confirm this theory. There are problems of comparability between different studies, as well as differences in their sources, design, and method. Industrialization has released many chemical substances into the environment, and into the workplace in particular. Some are mutagenic, teratogenic, or carcinogenic for animals, but little has been done to study systematically their effects on man, or on reproductive health in particular.[30] It is also possible that the interests of industry which

---

[28] P. Romito and F. Hovelaque, 'Changing Approaches in Women's Health: New Insights and New Pitfalls in Prenatal Preventive Care', *International Journal of Health Services*, 17 (1987), pp. 241–58.

[29] C. Muller, 'Health and Health Care of Employed Women and Home Makers: Family Factors', *Women and Health*, 11 (1986), pp. 7–26; D. Maffioli, *Lavoro e maternità: Relazione tra il lavoro della donna e le gravidanze, il parto, e il prodotto del concepimento* (Rome, 1980).

[30] A. Ericson, M. Eriksson, B. Kallen, and R. Zetterstrom, 'Maternal Occupation and Delivery Outcome', *Acta paediatrica Scandinavica*, 3 (1987), pp. 512–18; B. S. Zuckerman, D. A. Frank, R. Hingson, S. Morelock, and H. L. Kayne, 'Impact of Maternal Work outside the Home During Pregnancy on Neonatal Outcome', *Paediatrics*, 77 (1986), pp. 459–64; K. Hemminki, P. Mutanen, I. Saloniemi, and K. Luoma, 'Congenital Malformation and Maternal Occupation in Finland: Multivariate Analysis', *Journal of Epidemiology and Community Health*, 35 (1981), pp. 5–9; K. Hemminki, I. Saloniemi, T. Partanen, and H. Vaino, 'Childhood Cancer and Parental Occupation in Finland', *Journal of Epidemiology and Community Health*, 35 (1981), pp. 11–15; J. Gofin, 'The Effect on Birth Weight of Employment During Pregnancy', *Journal of Biosocial Science*, 11 (1977), pp. 259–67; S. E. Arundel and L. M. Kinnier-Wilson, 'Parental Occupations and Cancer: A Review of the Literature', *Journal of Epidemiology and Community Health*, 40 (1986), pp. 30–36.

has been responsible for the pollution of the environment do not favour reaching the obvious conclusion in this field.

Although work *per se* may not be the factor that influences the outcome of a pregnancy, there are some indications which make it possible to evaluate the effect of the increase in women's employment. During the 1970s and 1980s women's participation in the labour market increased to more than 5 per cent in public services and part-time work,[31] occupations which are easily compatible with success in limited reproductive activity.

The situation in eastern Europe is different. Women's labour-force participation has also increased in these countries, from initial levels that were already high at the beginning of the 1960s. At the beginning of the 1980s, women's labour-force participation rates exceeded 70–80 per cent and women were assigned to all types of industrial work. The division of work between the sexes at the workplace is more equal than in market economies, and working hours are similar for both sexes. But certain discriminations persist, for example in earnings (wages are low where there is a greater concentration of women in the labour force), and in the division of household tasks. In eastern Europe an employed woman will normally give the same amount of time to domestic work as the man gives to leisure. The lives of working women in eastern Europe are, therefore, more oppressive than in the west.[32] The condition of female workers and their children has been made worse by the progressive weakening of the family network, in which grandmothers used to play a fundamental part. This has been caused by the decline in co-residence and the prolongation of work beyond the age of retirement (encouraged since the mid-1960s in the USSR) and also because the role of a *babushka* is becoming increasingly less attractive to elderly women.[33]

We conclude that, while features of increased labour-force participation by women seem compatible with an improvement in infant health in western countries, doubts remain as far as eastern European countries are concerned.

Women's Life-Styles

In their desire to achieve gender equality, women adopted a number of typically masculine behavioural patterns, such as drinking and smoking both of which are known to damage health. Can these habits endanger the health of their children? Much attention has been devoted to this problem and there is a suspicion that attempts are being made to show that women are themselves in some way responsible for unfavourable results which are actually due to different causes.[34]

---

[31] OECD, *L'Emploi et le chômage des femmes dans les pays de l'OCDE* (Paris, 1984).
[32] See Bodrova and Anker, op. cit. in n. 23; ILO, *Women, Work and Demographic Issues* (Geneva, 1984); OECD, op. cit. in n. 31.
[33] Herlemann, op. cit. in n. 23.
[34] Romito and Houelaqxe, op. cit. in n. 28.

That smoking can harm the foetus has been known since 1957, when Simpson discovered that the birthweights of infants born to women who smoked during pregnancy tended to be lower than those of infants whose mothers did not smoke. This finding has been confirmed by other studies. However, women smokers often belong to groups which are at higher-than-average risk for other reasons, e.g. socio-economic status, age, and parity. Smoking will accentuate their disadvantaged position and will also decrease the advantages enjoyed by women of higher status.[35]

Failure to take these and other possible selection factors into account could, on the other hand, conceal relationships which have been well established[36] between a large number of negative results that range from miscarriage and foetal death to complications during pregnancy associated with the highest neonatal mortality rates.[37] Some authors also believe that the subsequent development of the child will be affected, though others do not share this view.[38]

The negative effect of alcohol consumption during pregnancy has also been well established, and its extent will depend on the amount of alcohol consumed. Moderate consumption causes low birthweight,[39] but higher consumption decreases not only birthweight but also height of the child, and head circumference, and can cause mental retardation which is often accompanied by cardiac abnormalities and hyperactivity, a very serious toxic effect which has been called the Foetal Alcohol Syndrome.[40]

Part of the higher infant mortality in eastern Europe can perhaps be attributed to the excessive consumption of alcohol by women.[41] The reproductive risks associated with this type of behaviour must be recognized, but they are symptoms of a more general *malaise*. Nor must the many other risk factors that do not depend on personal choice be neglected, such as

[35] D. Elbourne, C. Pritchard, and M. Danucey, 'Perinatal Outcomes and Related Factors', *Journal of Epidemiology and Community Health*, 40 (1986), pp. 301–8.

[36] M. B. Meyer, J. A. Tonascia, and C. Buck, 'The Interrelationship of Maternal Smoking and Increased Perinatal Mortality with Other Risk Factors', *American Journal of Epidemiology*, 100 (1975), pp. 443–52; H. Goldstein, 'Smoking in Pregnancy', *British Journal of Preventive and Social Medicine*, 31 (1977), pp. 13–17.

[37] R. J. Simpson and N. G. A. Smith, 'Maternal Smoking and Low Birth Weight: Implications for Antenatal Care', *Journal of Epidemiology and Community Health*, 40 (1986), pp. 223–7.

[38] J. B. Hardy and E. D. Mellits, 'Does Maternal Smoking during Pregnancy have a Long-Term Effect on the Child?', *Lancet*, 23 Dec. 1972, pp. 1332–6.

[39] R. R. Little, 'Moderate Alcohol Use during Pregnancy and Decreased Infant Birth Weight', *American Journal of Public Health*, 67 (1977), pp. 1154–6.

[40] V. Chernik, R. Childiaeva, and S. Ioffe, 'Effects of Maternal Alcohol Intake and Smoking on Neonatal Electroencephalogram and Anthropometric Measurements', *American Journal of Obstetrics and Gynecology*, 146 (1982), pp. 41–7; P. May, R. Hymbaugh, J. Aase, and J. Samet, 'Epidemiology of Fetal Alcohol Syndrome among American Indians of the Southwest', *Social Biology*, 30 (1983), pp. 374–87.

[41] Herlemann, op. cit. in n. 23; Davies and Feshbach, op. cit. in n. 23; Okolski, op. cit. in n. 1; M. Feshbach, 'On Infant Mortality in the Soviet Union', *Population and Development Review*, 10 (1984), pp. 87–102.

those related to the environment, pollution at the workplace, poverty, the possible effects of drugs, and inadequacy of treatment.

Women and Medical Care

The ecological analysis in the discussion of infant health suggested that the availability of health facilities and medical personnel is not necessarily associated with better health for infants and mothers. The role of medical care in reducing infant mortality has been overestimated: improvements in social and economic conditions and in the standard of women's education, the concentration of births at ages and parities which are at lower risk, linked to the decline of fertility are all factors that could be partially responsible for falling infant mortality. Moreover, completely different practices in the supervision of pregnancy, the management of labour, and neonatal care are associated with equal survival rates. We shall consider the extent to which medical practice in childbirth has changed the way in which women give birth, in the absence of any scientific proof that overmedication has led to better results.[42]

The evidence suggests that pregnant women consider themselves to be in a potentially dangerous situation, and feel safer by giving birth in hospital, where they tend to accept the procedures decided by the obstetrician, even when they find them unpleasant and do not understand their reasons or possible consequences. Emotional repercussions are not normally taken into account, even though it has been recognized that certain practices damage the relationship between mother and child—for example, the separation of mother and baby immediately after birth, or breast-feeding at fixed times, both of which fit in with the hospital routine, but do not necessarily lead to successful breast-feeding. There is also the use of drugs to induce birth, which appears to be associated with an increased frequency of idiopathic hyperbilirubinemia in the child, and which necessitates its separation from the mother. The use of analgesics induces sleepiness and suckling problems in the child.

The need has been expressed to modify a system of care which treats all pregnancies as 'at risk' and has resulted in losing sight of the real nature of pregnancy, delivery and a normal baby. The need to give the woman an active part in defining her health requirements and choosing how to be treated has been recognized, so that the emotional aspect of maternity, and not just the need for survival, is taken into consideration.[43]

Whilst perinatal care has led to excessive medicalization of pregnancy and childbirth without any scientific justification, there can be no doubt that

[42] WHO, op. cit. in n. 2; J. M. L. Phaff (ed.), *Perinatal Health Services in Europe* (London, 1986).
[43] WHO, op. cit. in n. 2.

developments in neonatal care have had a positive effect on infant survival, largely because of the increased rate of survival of babies of low birthweights. The high cost of intensive neonatal care, however, raises a problem: limited budgets have meant that greater efforts have been made to reduce the incidence of mortality among these babies than to prevent low birthweights in the first place. If Sweden is taken as a point of reference (conditions of infant survival have been good there for a long time), the difference between the mortality of babies of low birthweight in that country and other European countries is not large. Differences are, however, marked for babies of normal weight, and between the frequency of babies of low birthweights.[44] The position is similar in the United States, as is shown by the results of record linkage study for the birth cohort of 1980, which dealt with differences between the mortality of blacks and whites.[45]

These data illustrate a strategy which encourages the survival of high-risk children but neglects the need to prevent risks and the care of children who show no signs of being at any particular risk. They illustrate the way in which efforts to treat the child 'at risk' have resulted in losing sight of the 'normal child'. Prevention of risks would be a strategy which could improve infant survival by improving the condition of women—by endeavouring to eliminate social inequalities, and raise the working, living, and health conditions of women.

Women's Condition and Infant Health in eastern Europe

In the preceding sections we have repeatedly focused on the negative aspects of the status of women, conditions of childbirth, and infant survival in eastern Europe and the USSR. In particular, the decline in mortality in the USSR has not slowed down as it did in other developed countries; during the 1970s infant mortality increased continuously. Those who have argued that this was an artefact caused by an improvement in the quality of the data[46] have not convinced other authors,[47] who have traced the deterioration of health, not only of children but also of men of reproductive age, to conditions in the country.

A fall in the life expectancy of males at the ages of 1 and 30 years and an increase in the mortality of adult men has been recorded not only in the USSR, but in other eastern European countries (Czechoslovakia, Hungary,

---

[44] A. Pinnelli, 'Infant Survival in Italy: Recent Trends', *Genus*, 42 (1986), pp. 125–39.

[45] C. J. R. Hogue, J. W. Buehler, L. T. Strauss, and J. C. Smith, 'Overview of the National Infant Mortality Surveillance (NIMS): Project Design, Methods, Results', *Public Health Reports*, 102 (1987), pp. 675–81.

[46] E. Jones and F. W. Grupp, 'Infant Mortality Trends in the Soviet Union', *Population and Development Review*, 9 (1983), pp. 213–46.

[47] N. Eberstadt, 'A Comment'; *Population and Development Review*, 10 (1984), pp. 91–8; Feshbach, op. cit. in n. 41.

Poland), at a time when rapid progress was made in the West and in Japan. The mixture of nationalities in the population of the USSR, compared with other Eastern European countries, may help to explain the position there, but the causes are probably similar in all countries: a cohort effect, deteriorating health services, overcrowding, a low standard of living, alcohol consumption, excessive recourse to abortion, oppressive conditions of women's lives as a result of their dual role, lack of alternative arrangements for child care.

The way to improve conditions of infant health in these countries is complex and must include a review of the position of women in the family and in society.

Conclusion

The first point which needs comment is the unsatisfactory nature of data relating to aspects of infancy, other than survival. The difficulty in identifying and collecting objective indicators of health or sickness in no way justifies this omission. The only possible explanation is lack of interest and sensitivity to the needs of a part of the population—infants and children—which has no power and can only submit passively to changes in social and health policies.

This absence of interest could perhaps be justified by the fact that, except during the period immediately following birth, and only for children who suffer unfavourable conditions, mortality and morbidity are lower at that stage of life than at any other. However, marked geographical differences persist, and social and health interventions have not been successful in bringing about greater equality or uniformity. Excessive medication at birth and in infant care, which has been a characteristic feature during recent years in most developed countries, has been shown to be unnecessary and unjustified on scientific grounds. Moreover, this has caused primary prevention to be neglected, so that social risk factors have not been reduced, and the emotional aspects of childbirth and child-rearing have not been taken into account.

The aspects neglected are those which most affect the health and economic status of women, and which prevent women from experiencing maternity in an active and informed manner. Overmedication of children by well-to-do mothers is a reverse aspect of this problem, as is the mother's unconscious complicity in delegating problems of varying nature to the medical authorities.

Research has shown repeatedly that the welfare of the child and the mother are more than ever inseparable, and that survival is still linked to conditions at birth. Moreover, certain aspects of women's status are related to improvements in maternal and child health, whereas the influence of others is doubtful. Positive aspects are welfare, education, moderate fertility. More doubtful ones include life-styles, work patterns that resemble those of men, and family models which have become more fragile as a result of the greater independence enjoyed by women.

The crisis in the Welfare State is a serious threat to the health of mothers and children, because budget cuts have resulted in primary prevention being the first to fall by the wayside. This tends to be the aspect of the welfare services which does most to eradicate social inequalities.[48] The ageing populations of the developed countries devote more resources to care for the old, and fewer to care for future generations, for whom families have become more fragile and offer fewer guarantees of stability and welfare than used to be the case. This break in intergenerational solidarity has resulted in a renewed risk of poverty for infants, and for women who want to become mothers.[49]

[48] Miller, op. cit. in n. 20.
[49] S. H. Preston, 'Children and Elderly: Divergent Paths for American Dependents', *Demography*, 21 (1984), pp. 435–7.

9 Social Change and Mortality Decline: Women's Advantage Achieved or Regained?

JACQUES VALLIN

Part of the excess mortality of men has always been considered to be biological. Different writers have estimated the importance of this biological contribution differently; some have even regarded the XY configuration of chromosomes that characterizes males as an inferior version of the XX configuration that characterizes females—a view which puts men at a relative disadvantage to women in the determination of human longevity.[1] Whilst it is possible to be sceptical about so determinist a theory, the hypothesis that there exists a biological factor which is responsible for part of the difference between the mortality of men and women cannot be disregarded altogether, even though there are many considerations that point to this excess mortality being a reflection of socio-cultural and environmental factors. We must, therefore, ask whether in the beginning 'God did not create woman as a more vigorous creature than man.

However, where information is available about past populations, or about present populations in which mortality is high, it is almost universally found that life expectancies at birth for the two sexes are nearly equal (this is the result of an excess mortality of women in adolescence and early adult life and an excess mortality of men at higher ages), or that women suffer from an excess mortality which reduces their life expectancy below that of men. At some levels of social and economic development, the theoretical generosity with which nature appears to have endowed the female sex has been nullified by the actions of men, who reduced women to an inferior status, or even by nature itself, which has limited the hazards of reproduction to them.

Economic and social progress has been characterized by a reduction of the difference between the social status of the two sexes and of the hazard associated with maternity. Even during the early stages of the demographic transition it was clear that women were more long-lived than men. Does this mean that the improvement in their status enabled them to regain the

---

[1] F. Lenz, 'Die Übersterblichkeit der Knaben im Lichte der Erblichkeitslehre', *Archiv f. Hygiene*, 93 (1940), pp. 126–50; N. Federici, 'La mortalità differenziale degli due sessi e le su possibile cause', *Statistica*, 10 (1950), pp. 274–320.

innate biological advantage? Though the answer to this question is likely to be in the affirmative, it does not provide a complete explanation for the relationship between the status of women and the difference between the mortality of the two sexes. We know that this difference can be caused by a variety of social factors, the effects of which are superimposed on those of biology. The improvement in the status of women may have enabled them to benefit from their innate advantage, which had previously been nullified by the social disadvantages from which they suffered. This would explain why, since the beginning of the nineteenth century, and particularly in Europe, excess mortality of men has continued to increase well above the level which could be accounted for by the biological difference between the two sexes.

However, this explanation would not suffice at a time when changes in the status of women, though allowing them to benefit from advantages that had previously been reserved for men, also resulted in their participation in forms of behaviour which were associated with a higher risk of dying, and which had hitherto been largely confined to men: drinking, smoking, driving motor vehicles, working outside their homes. Perhaps new hypotheses should be framed; it could be that the risks of these activities are not the same for men as for women, or that the effects of this new type of behaviour will only become fully apparent in the long run, or similar risks may produce different results for men and for women.

It is questions of this type that I propose to consider in this chapter, and, though it may not be possible to provide a definitive answer, it will be possible to point to certain problems in this field.

More Vigorous but at Greater Risk of Dying

It is difficult, perhaps impossible, to measure the relative influence of the genetic and the socio-cultural factors that underlie the differences between the mortality of different human groups. How can we isolate the effects of genotype from socio-cultural factors, when genetic variations between individuals may well be larger than those between groups? How are differences between the mortality of two groups to be interpreted, when the very constitution of these groups may have affected mortality through the effects of selection? These are but two questions to which it is difficult to provide an answer. As regards sex, we know at least that mankind is divided into two genetically distinct groups by the Y-chromosome, which characterizes an individual throughout his or her life, is determined at conception, and thus cannot select in a population for health. Is it, therefore, possible, that, as Pressat has written,[2] 'there exists a reference level which

[2] R. Pressat, 'Surmortalité biologique et surmortalité sociale', *Revue française de sociologie*, 14 (1983), pp. 103–10.

enables us to separate those parts of the excess mortality of men that are due to biological, and to social and behavioural causes respectively'. This would not be easy, because gender itself has resulted in socio-cultural differences, the effects of which are very difficult to assess, it is, therefore, difficult to measure how much of the difference in mortality was due to them and how much to biology.

A Probable Natural Advantage

Many demographers have argued that, at the outset of life, women are biologically superior to men, and they have given different reasons for their view.[3] In a study of the continuous increase in the excess mortality of men that has resulted in a difference of six years between the life expectancies at birth of the sexes, Madigan wrote in 1957: 'not only [are] sociocultural pressures less important than biological factors in relation to the mortality differentials of the sexes, but they are of comparatively small importance in this respect.'[4] He based this extreme view on a comparison of mortality in two religious communities consisting of monks and nuns respectively, in which, according to him, conditions of life were identical. The slight excess mortality of women which he observed at the beginning of the century had, during the previous fifty years, been continuously eroded and replaced by an excess mortality of men, similar to that observed in the general population. Believing that the only difference between the two communities was the biological one of sex, he concluded that, in the population as a whole, as well as among the religious, the emergence of an excess mortality of men could be explained almost entirely by a reduction in the prevalence of infectious diseases, as resistance to these diseases—and particularly to tuberculosis—was lower among women, and by the increased importance of neoplasms and cardiovascular diseases as causes of death, diseases to which, by contrast, women were more resistant than men. The author made little of one important social difference between the two communities—the consumption of tobacco.[5] Nor did his argument allow for the possibility that, even though both monks and nuns were subject to similar rules, their life-styles may have been different. But these qualifications do not refute the thesis of a biologically determined excess mortality of men, which must be retained as a partial explanation of the excess mortality

---

[3] See Lenz and Federici, op. cit. in n. 1.
[4] F. C. Madigan, 'Are Sex Mortality Differentials Biologically Caused?', *Milbank Memorial Fund Quarterly*, 35 (1957), pp. 202–23.
[5] According to a contemporary study by the American Cancer Society, 54% of the excess mortality of men aged 35 and over who were smokers can be attributed to smoking. Smoking is particularly important in increasing the risk of dying from cancer or cardiovascular disease.

that has been observed, even though it may not be its most important component. Other writers have also attempted to assess its importance.[6]

In 1952, Bourgeois-Pichat proposed to generalize the distinction that he had suggested existed between 'endogenous' and 'exogenous' mortality in early childhood,[7] and calculated a life table which would correspond to the biological limits of human mortality. In that table, women's life expectancy at birth of 78.2 years exceeded that of men, which was 76.3 years, by 1.9 years.[8] However, his 'endogenous' mortality was not the same as mortality from wholly biological causes—and even less like mortality from genetic causes. It included those morbid processes against which medicine at the time was powerless, or almost powerless. In 1952 these were mainly neoplasms and cardiovascular diseases. Bourgeois-Pichat believed that medical progress would result in increasing life expectancy. When he repeated his calculations twenty-five years later, using the same concepts, he arrived at a figure of 80.3 years for women and 73.8 years for men, a sex difference of 6.5 years,[9] considerably larger than a quarter-century earlier. In actual fact, during this period the 'hard rock' of mortality was eroded, and women profited from this progress more than men. These changes could have been brought about by medical progress or by changes in behaviour, and it is probable that changes in behaviour affected the two sexes differentially. The increase in the difference between life expectancies probably overestimates the biological component.

Pressat estimated that women's inborn advantage resulted in a life expectancy two years higher than that of men. As effective medical treatment barely existed in the pre-industrial period, he suggested that differences between the life expectancies of the two sexes at that time were almost entirely biological. He was confirmed in this view by the fact 'that as at present the mortality of boys during the first year of life in the Western cultural area, where the only factor that could cause differential mortality is biological, is between 25 and 30 per cent higher than that of girls' and 'that a maintenance of this difference throughout life would produce a moderate difference [between life expectancies at birth] of the order of . . . two years'.[10] This argument, based on sex differences in infant mortality, has for some time been recognized as being the most convincing.[11] Extrapolation to

---

[6] e.g. G. Herdan, 'Causes of Excess Mortality in Men', *Acta genetica et statistica medica*, 3 (1952), pp. 351–75.

[7] J. Bourgeois-Pichat, 'La Mesure de la mortalité infantile', *Population*, 6 (1951), pp. 381–94.

[8] J. Bourgeois-Pichat, 'Essai sur la mortalité biologique de l'homme', *Population*, 7 (1952), pp. 233–48.

[9] J. Bourgeois-Pichat, 'Future Outlook for Mortality Decline in the World', in *Prospects of Population: Methodology and Assumptions* (Papers of the ad hoc Group of Experts on Demographic Projections, 1977), pp. 227–66.

[10] Pressat, op. cit. in n. 2.

[11] S. Shapiro, 'The Influence of Weight, Sex, and Plurality on Neonatal Loss in the United States', *American Journal of Public Health*, 44 (1954), pp. 142–53.

older ages is, of course, more hazardous. Here we merely note that there exists a consensus of opinion which agrees that women enjoy an innate advantage of lower mortality, but that this advantage is slight and difficult to measure.

The Consequences of Initial Unfavourable Conditions

In spite of women's innate advantage, in the past they have generally suffered higher mortality than men, and this continued to be true until recently in the less developed countries.

Maternal Mortality. It is well known that women suffer a higher mortality than men at reproductive ages. This has been adequately documented for Europe in the past,[12] and has been measured in France by the study of a representative sample of parish registers by Louis Henry.[13] During the eighteenth and the beginning of the nineteenth century, women's age-specific mortality rates between the ages of 20 and 45 years exceeded those of men by between 5 and 20 per cent, depending on age group and period,[14] and this was also true of the less developed countries until relatively recently.[15]

This excess mortality of women was largely caused by maternal mortality. In this sense it may be regarded as biological, as only women are exposed to the risk of pregnancy and childbirth. Thus nature takes away with one hand some of the advantages she has bestowed on women with the other. But maternal mortality is not entirely biological; the risks of dying in pregnancy or childbirth will be related to the social and economic circumstances of women and the nature of their reproductive lives, which, in turn, is closely linked to their social status, and to their fertility, which also depends on the socio-cultural status of females. It is a masculine society that has curtailed some of the advantages that women enjoyed. In eighteenth-century France the expectation of life of a woman on her twenty-fifth birthday differed little from, and was even slightly lower than, that of a man of the same age. Excess mortality of men at ages over 50 was not sufficient to compensate for women's excess mortality between the ages of 25 and 45 years.

Mortality at Young Ages. The importance of the social status of women is particularly marked when we consider their excess mortality at young ages, for this differential can be explained only by a difference in the behaviour of parents, and of society as a whole, to the two sexes.

---

[12] D. Tabutin, 'La Surmortalité féminine en Europe avant 1940', *Population*, 34 (1978), pp. 121–48.
[13] Y. Blayo, 'La Mortalité en France de 1740 à 1829', *Population*, 30 (1975), pp. 123–42.
[14] Ibid.
[15] See Potter and Volpp, Chapter 7 in this volume.

Excess mortality of girls was apparent in Europe in the past, and appeared to be marked between the ages of 1 and 4, and 5 and 9 years. This excess appears to have increased during the nineteenth century.[16] In France, more detailed statistics show that, after 1889, females still suffered from an excess mortality over males, between the ages of 4 and 17 years, and that this did not disappear finally until the Second World War, though by then it was limited to a smaller age group.[17] Tabutin has stressed the role played by mortality from infectious diseases in causing this excess. Tuberculosis, in particular, was important in this respect, and the excess mortality of girls and young women from this cause more than compensated for the higher mortality from accidents and violence suffered by men at these ages. He linked the excess mortality of women to the unfavourable conditions of life of girls during this period: they were given less care, and standards of hygiene and nutrition for them were lower as the result of an anti-feminist ideology,[18] which regarded them as being intrinsically less valuable than boys.[19]

This low valuation of the female sex lies at the base of its excess mortality and can still be found today in a number of less developed countries. The most flagrant examples are found on the Indian sub-continent.[20] In Bangladesh, the mortality of girls between the ages of 1 and 4 years is 50 per cent higher than that of boys, and the principal reason is differential access to nutrition, and differences between the care given to boys and girls.[21] Similar attitudes can be found in a number of other cultures. Excess mortality of girls is particularly prevalent in Muslim countries during the 1960s.[22] In Algeria the mortality of girls exceeded that of boys from the age of three months onwards, but this excess was confined to deaths from 'exogenous'

---

[16] Tabutin, op. cit. in n. 12.

[17] Ibid.; see also J. Vallin, 'Tendances récentes de la mortalité française', *Population*, 38 (1983), pp. 77–106.

[18] This ideology was developed by such writers as Jean Jacques Rousseau, Auguste Comte, Honoré de Balzac, and even by the socialist, Proudhon, who claimed to have established 'scientifically' that a woman's worth was only $\frac{8}{27}$ that of a man (see Tabutin, op. cit. in n. 12).

[19] The way in which this ideology permeated the thought of the past has been illustrated by Armengaud, who has quoted two anecdotes from Legouve's *L'Histoire morale des femmes* (1849): 'ask a peasant about his family, and he will reply: "I have no children, I only have girls", and the Breton farmer whose wife had given birth to a daughter will still say today "My wife has miscarried"' (A. Armengaud, 'L'Attitude de la société à l'égard de l'enfant au XIXe siècle', *Annales de démographie historique* (Enfants et sociétés) (1973), pp. 310–11).

[20] L. C. Chen, E. Huq, and S. D'Souza, 'Sex Bias in the Allocation of Food and Health Care in Rural Bangladesh', *Population and Development Review*, 7 (1981), pp. 55–70; M. Das Gupta, 'Selective Discrimination against Female Children in India', *Population and Development Review*, 13 (1987), pp. 77–100.

[21] Chen, Huq, and D'Souza, op. cit. in n. 20.

[22] A. Adlakha and C. M. Suchindran, 'Infant and Child Mortality in Middle Eastern Countries', in IUSSP, *Proceedings of the International Population Conference, Florence 1985* (Liège, 1985), ii. 367–76; T. Haffad, 'Les Différences de mortalité selon le sexe et leurs conséquences', doctoral dissertation (Paris, 1984).

causes; 'endogenous' mortality was considerably higher among boys.[23] The explanation lies entirely in the lower degree of care that is given to girl children.[24] Even in sub-Saharan Africa, where the statistics are insuf- ficiently detailed to make it possible to distinguish between the different causes of infant mortality, it is likely that the absence of a difference between the infant mortality rates of the two sexes is associated with the less favour- able treatment given to girl babies, whose mortality would otherwise almost certainly be lower than that of boys.[25]

The relationship between the social status of women, the valuation of females, and the excess mortality of little girls is seen particularly clearly in China, where traces of the old practice of infanticide of girl babies have persisted, and where the practice has probably been given new life by the one-child family policy.[26] In Anhui province, where infant mortality rates for girls exceed those of boys by 12 per cent, Zhang has estimated that infanticide, which was responsible for 60 per cent of all infant deaths accounted for this exceptionally high excess mortality of girls during the first year of life.[27]

Thus, the social disadvantages to which women were subjected for a long time in Europe masked, and continue to mask in developing countries today, the theoretical biological advantage in longevity that they enjoy. In India,[28] Bangladesh,[29] Pakistan,[30] and Sri Lanka,[31] the cumulative disadvantage suffered by women which begins at young ages and continues throughout their reproductive lives resulted in a lower life expectancy at birth compared with that of men until the end of the 1960s. In Algeria, to- wards the end of the 1970s, the excess mortality of men at ages 50 and over

[23] J. Vallin, 'Un fait social: La Surmortalité des petites filles en Algérie', *Actes du 3e Colloque de Démographie Maghrébine* (Tunis, 24–28 April 1978), i.

[24] Ibid.; N. Ferry, 'La Femme et l'enfant en milieu rural algérien: Étude sociologique et médicale de la maternité et du premier âge', thesis for the degree of MD (University of Lille, 1979).

[25] K. Gbenyon and T. Locoh, 'Les Différences de mortalité entre garçons et filles', G. Pison, E. van de Walle, and M. Sala-Diakanda (eds.), *Mortalité et société en Afrique* (Paris, 1989), pp. 221–44; English translation entitled 'Mortality Differences in Childhood by Sex in Sub-Saharan Africa', in *Mortality and Society in Sub-Saharan Africa* (Oxford, 1992) pp. 230–52.

[26] G. Calot and G. Caselli, *La Mortalité en Chine d'après le recensement de 1982*, i *Analy selon le sexe et l'âge au niveau national et provincial* (Paris, 1988).

[27] W. Zhang, et al., 'Yinger xingbili shitiao yao qieshi jiuzheng' (Effective measures must taken against the abnormal masculinity at birth), *Sheshui* (Society), 2 (1983), quoted by Cal and Caselli, op. cit. in n. 26.

[28] S. Ragharavarachari, S. K. Biswas, A. K. Biswas, and S. S. Bawa, *The Population India* (New Delhi, 1974).

[29] L. Bean and R. M. Khan, *Mortality Patterns in Pakistan* (Karachi, 1967); F. Yusu 'Abridged Life Tables for Pakistan and its Provinces', paper submitted to the IUSSP Conference Sydney, 1967.

[30] M. Afzal, '1972 Census: Population Expected and Actual', *Pakistan Development Review* 12 (1973), pp. 122–33; Yusuf, op. cit. in n. 29.

[31] Sri Lanka, Department of Census and Statistics, *The Population of Sri Lanka* (Colombo 1974).

led to life expectancies at birth being equal for the two sexes. In eighteenth-century France, where the absence of modern medicine resulted in mortality being less affected by social inequalities, the slight excess mortality of males during the first year of life, coupled with a high infant mortality rate, was sufficient to reduce men's life expectancy at birth below that of women. However, the higher mortality of women below the age of 45 meant that life expectancies at the first birthday were about equal for the two sexes, or even lower for women.

From Regaining an Original Advantage to New Advantages

During the last two centuries in Europe, and more recently but also much more rapidly in developing countries, women have achieved, or are achieving, a completely new social status in society, and no longer need to feel envious of men. Attitudes to children, both by individual parents and by society, have been considerably modified, and children of both sexes are more highly valued than previously.[32] Little girls now have the same access to nutrition, hygiene, and medical facilities as their brothers, and need not, therefore, die earlier, but are able to enjoy the innate advantage that nature has granted them. Reductions in fertility and improvements in the care given to women in pregnancy and childbirth have reduced the only bio-logically sex-linked disadvantage in respect of mortality from which women used to suffer. However, recent changes in mortality have gone well beyond the stage in which women merely regained their original advantage. They have resulted in giving women a new privileged status in relation to longevity. We shall consider how this has come about by looking at statistics of mortality in France.

Women's Excess Mortality Eliminated; Men's Excess Mortality Increases Spectacularly

In France women's life expectancy at birth does not seem to have been lower than that of men, even under the *ancien régime* (see Table 9.1). Between 1740 and 1860, however, the advantage enjoyed by women was small, and the differences between life expectancies fluctuated irregularly between 0.6 and 2.4 years. Commonly, the difference was smaller than the two years at which Pressat has estimated the biological advantage of women, and which was not completely nullified by their lower social status, quite apart from the higher mortality of men from non-biological causes, such as

---

[32] J. Vallin and A. Lery, 'Estimating the Increase in Fertility Consecutive to the Death of a Young Child', in S. H. Preston (ed.), *The Effects of Infant and Child Mortality on Fertility* (New York, 1978), pp. 69–90.

TABLE 9.1. *Life expectancy at birth, by sex, France, 1740–1986* (years)

Year	Life expectancy at birth		Difference
	Women	Men	
1740–49	25.7	23.8	1.9
1750–59	28.7	27.1	1.6
1760–69	29.0	26.4	2.6
1770–79	29.6	28.2	1.4
1780–89	28.1	27.5	0.6
1790–99	32.1		
1800–09	34.9		
1810–19	37.5		
1820–29	39.3	38.3	1.0
1835–37	40.7	39.2	1.5
1845–47	41.9	40.7	1.2
1855–57	40.1	37.7	2.4
1861–65	40.6	39.1	0.9
1877–81	43.6	40.8	2.8
1898–1903	48.7	45.3	3.4
1908–13	52.4	48.5	3.9
1920–23	55.9	52.2	3.7
1928–33	59.0	54.3	4.7
1933–38	61.6	55.9	5.7
1946–49	67.4	61.9	5.5
1952–56	70.9	64.7	6.2
1960–64	74.3	67.2	6.9
1966–70	75.2	67.7	7.2
1973–77	77.0	69.1	7.9
1984–86	79.5	71.3	8.2

accidents and violence. Since 1860, however, the difference has increased very considerably from 2.8 years in 1877–81 to 8.2 years in 1984–86. It is now four times as large as the supposed biological advantage of two years. Even if this estimate were incorrect, it is clear that during the last hundred years women have done much better than merely regain this advantage, or, what at first sight appears to be the same thing, that men have lost more than can be accounted for by the removal of inequalities in the treatment of women. This impression is confirmed when we consider the ratios of men's age-specific mortality rates to those of women (Fig. 9.1).

In order to appreciate this change, we shall consider the consequences of the two hypotheses put forward by Pressat. He has suggested, in the first

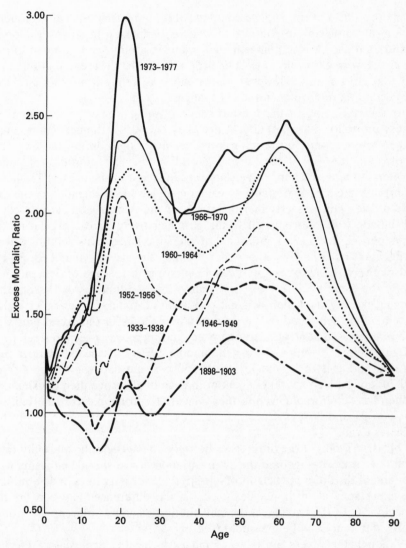

FIG. 9.1 Changes in excess mortality ratios of men by age between 1898–1903 and 1973–77
Source: INSEE

place, that the excess mortality of boys in infancy is essentially caused by biological factors. In the second place, he assumes that, in the absence of other disturbing factors, the same excess mortality would apply throughout life. In fact, the excess mortality of male babies during their first year of life has been almost constant at between 25 and 30 per cent since the beginning of the present century, and we could use this figure as an indicator of men's biological handicap. In contrast to what is happening in some developing countries today, it would appear that infant mortality, concentrated during the first few weeks of life, has been little affected by differential attitudes to boy and girl babies.[33] However, the situation is different at other stages of life, where there have been radical changes.

At the beginning of the present century young women still suffered an excess mortality, but mortality at ages beyond 40 was higher among men, and at ages beyond 50 the difference was larger than during the first year of life. On the eve of the Second World War excess mortality of young women had almost completely disappeared (except at the ages of 13 and 14 years), but the excess mortality of young men was lower than during the first year of life. This suggests that the status of the two sexes in society could still influence the mortality of young girls negatively. However, during the same period, the excess mortality of men increased considerably among adults and was as high as 60 per cent between the ages of 40 and 60. By the end of the war the excess mortality of men up to the age of 35 years was nearly the same as during the first year of life, so that it would seem that women had regained their original biological advantage, whereas at higher ages men had continued to lose ground. After the 1950s the excess mortality of men increased at an accelerating pace, and there was a second steep peak at ages around 20 years. During the middle 1970s it exceeded 200 per cent between the ages of 18 and 75, it was 250 per cent between the ages of 60 and 70, and as high as 300 per cent at the age of 20. Since then the situation of men has deteriorated even further. We are far from an excess mortality of between 25 and 30 per cent at these ages, where the excess is nearly ten times as large.

Our description of the differences between the age-specific mortality rates of the two sexes has ignored the large variation of age-specific mortality with age, and of the different weights of age-specific mortality rates in determining life expectancy at birth. By decomposing the differences between the life expectancies of the two sexes, the contribution made by different age groups to this difference can be measured (see Fig. 9.2).[34]

Although the excess mortality of males during the first year of life has remained relatively constant, the fall in infant mortality has meant that its weight in the difference between life expectancies at birth has greatly diminished. At the beginning of the present century, when the difference came to 3.3 years, 1.46 years, or nearly half the excess, could be attributed

---

[33] An analysis of fertility following the loss of an infant has shown that recently the desire to replace a lost child did not depend on its sex (see ibid.).

[34] R. Pressat, 'Perspectives de réduction de la surmortalité masculine dans les pays ayant une faible mortalité', paper presented at the Meeting on Sex Differentials in Mortality: Trends, Determinants and Consequences, Canberra, 1981.

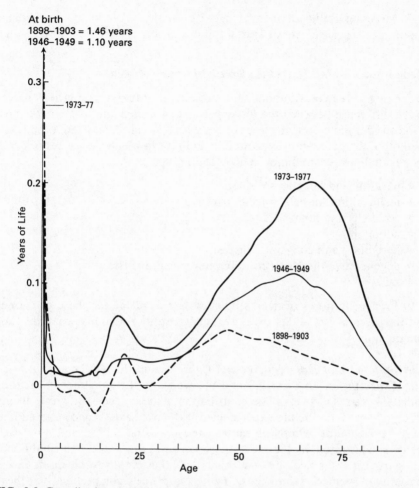

At birth
1898–1903 = 1.46 years
1946–1949 = 1.10 years

0.3

—— 1973–77

0.2

Years of Life

1973–1977

0.1

1946–1949

1898–1903

0

0   25   50   75

Age

FIG. 9.2 Contribution made by each age group to differences in life expectancy at birth between the sexes, 1898–1903, 1946–49, and 1973–77

to mortality during the first year of life. In 1973–77 the analogous figure was 0.26 years for an excess of 7.9 years—only about 3 per cent. This radical change has been brought about by the fall in infant mortality.

However, even at this level the contribution made by infant mortality to the difference between life expectancies exceeds that of any other single age group. But infant mortality stands on its own, and it is the cumulative contribution of successive age groups that henceforth is likely to be the most important factor in explaining differences between the life expectancies at birth. The dominant age ranges are those between 50 and 75 years. The very high excess mortality of men at age 20, on the other hand, is of minor importance, because overall mortality rates at this age are very low.

Medical Causes of the Increased Excess Mortality of Men

In looking at the contributions that mortality in different age groups makes to the difference between the life expectancies of men and women, we must also consider the principal causes of death.[35] Our calculations are based on a method of disaggregation suggested by Pollard, in which the causes of death are divided into seven major aetiological groups:[36]

- parasitic and infectious diseases
- malnutrition, diseases of the digestive system
- accidents and homicides
- neoplasms
- hereditary and congenital diseases
- degenerative diseases (including functional diseases)
- suicide.

In France, statistics of deaths by cause are available for these categories for the period 1925–78,[37] and we shall consider the first and the last quinquennia of this period.

The Importance of Different Age and Cause Groups for Differences between Life Expectancies. In Figs. 9.3 and 9.4 we show the situation in 1925–29 and 1974–78 respectively. The contribution made by each age group to the difference between the life expectancies of the two sexes is decomposed into these seven major groups of causes, and the contribution made by each group is illustrated in Fig. 9.3. In some age groups the contribution of particular causes is negative—in themselves they would result in an excess mortality of women. To make the figure more easily comprehensible, these negative contributions have been cumulated separately from the positive ones, and are shown below the horizontal axis, whereas the positive contributions are shown above it. In other words, where all the contributions are positive, their total yields the contribution of the age group concerned; where some are negative, the total contribution is the difference between the areas above and below the horizontal axis.

Some excess mortality of women persisted among young girls until just before the Second World War. Between 1925 and 1929 this was caused by deaths from infectious diseases and, to a lesser extent, by deaths from

---

[35] J. Pollard, 'Causes de décès et espérance de vie: Quelques comparaisons internationales', in J. Vallin, S. D'Souza, and A. Palloni (eds.), *Mesure et analyse de la mortalité: Nouvelles approches* (Paris, 1988), pp. 291–313.

[36] J. Vallin and F. Meslé, *Les Causes de décès en France de 1925 à 1978* (Paris, 1988).

[37] Vallin and Meslé, op. cit. in n. 35.

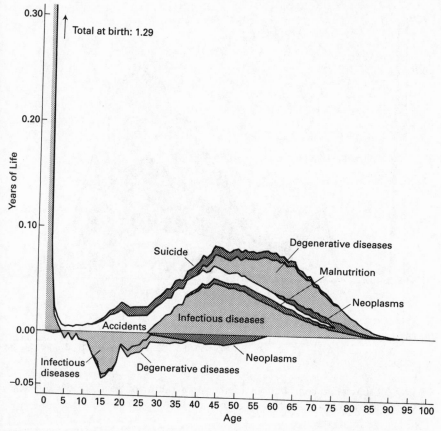

FIG. 9.3 Cumulative contributions of the main groups of causes of death to the difference between life expectancy at birth of the two sexes, by age, 1925–29

degenerative diseases and neoplasms. This excess was quite pronounced around the age of 15 years for deaths from infectious diseases; excess mortality of women from the other two groups of causes persisted to the age of 55, and perhaps shows the last traces of a non-negligible maternal mortality. The reduction in the excess mortality of women between the two wars was caused by a trade-off between their excess mortality from infectious diseases, neoplasms, and degenerative diseases, and men's excess mortality from accidents and suicide. The clear distinction between the contributions of deaths from infectious diseases and accidental deaths around the period of adolescence reinforces the hypothesis that young women received less care, but that this was compensated by the greater risks of violent death experienced by men. It should be borne in mind, however,

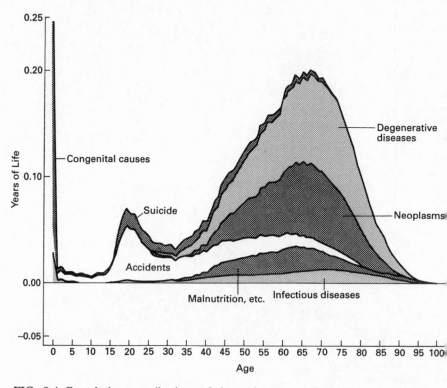

FIG. 9.4 Cumulative contributions of the main causes of death to the difference between life expectancy at birth of the two sexes, by age, 1974–78

that this contrast is found at ages where the overall mortality rate is now lowest.

Between 1925 and 1929, deaths from infectious diseases seemed to be the determining feature that caused differences between the life expectancies of the two sexes during the first year of life. However, in this instance the level of mortality is more important than the excess mortality of boys, which is generally quite low. High infant mortality rates are generally due to infectious disease. This conceals the importance of hereditary and congenital factors, which were to become much more apparent towards the end of the period.

As regards adult ages, we need to distinguish between two different situations in 1925–29. At ages above 55 years, all cause groups contributed to the excess mortality of men, but the main contribution to the difference between life expectancies came from deaths from infectious and degenerative diseases. At lower ages, deaths from infectious diseases accounted for more than half the difference, but deaths from other cause groups (especially deaths from neoplasms) actually tended to reduce it, as mortality from these causes is higher among women.

By 1974–78 the position had changed (see Fig. 9.4). There is no longer an excess mortality of women in any age–cause group. The contributions made by different causes of death to the difference between the life expectancies of the sexes have also changed radically. Deaths from infectious diseases have become marginal in determining the level of overall mortality, and, even though during the intervening period there was an excess mortality of men in all age groups from this cause, its contribution to the difference between life expectancies has become negligible. In the case of infant mortality, the contribution made by deaths from hereditary and congenital diseases has become predominant and confirms that, during the first year of life, the excess mortality of boys is due almost entirely to genetic causes. At around the age of 20, violent deaths account for almost the whole of the excess mortality of men. The contribution of this cause is not negligible at higher ages either, but is soon overtaken by deaths from malnutrition, neoplasms, and degenerative diseases, all of which make a massive contribution to the gap between the life expectancies of men and women.

The Contribution of Different Causes to Increases in Men's Excess Mortality. A comparison of the situation depicted in Figs. 9.3 and 9.4 makes it possible to estimate the contribution made by each group of causes to the increase in the difference between life expectancies from 4.33 years in 1925–29 to 7.99 years in 1974–78 (see Fig. 9.5). This increase has been brought about by changes in the importance of different causes of death in overall mortality, as well as by changes in the excess of men's mortality from these causes.

The part played by mortality from infectious diseases has been influenced above all by the much reduced importance of this cause of death. Originally, women's mortality from this cause exceeded that of men between the ages of 10 and 30 years. Its almost complete disappearance as a cause of death has resulted in an increased excess mortality of men.

The proportion of deaths from degenerative diseases in overall mortality has not changed greatly, but men's excess mortality from this cause has increased, and this has contributed to an increase in the difference between life expectancies. Excess mortality of men from accidental deaths has remained relatively stable, but the weight of this cause in overall mortality has increased. In the case of deaths from malnutrition and neoplasms, the two effects are combined: both the excess mortality of men and the weight of deaths from these causes has gone up. A more detailed analysis shows that this phenomenon was particularly pronounced for deaths from neoplasms of the respiratory system, and from alcoholism and cirrhosis of the liver.

The Increased Predominance of Environmental and Behavioural Factors. An examination of causes of death is insufficient on its own to prove the importance of social or genetic factors. For any cause of death, a difference

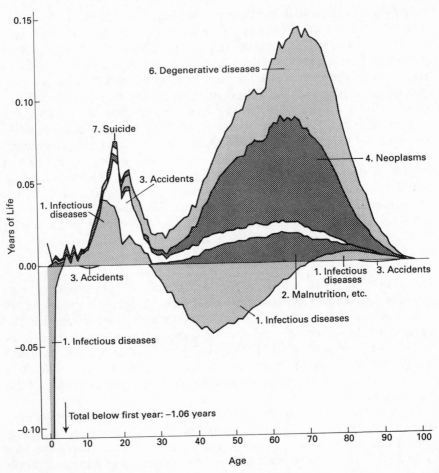

FIG. 9.5 Cumulative contribution to the increase in the differences between life expectancy at birth of the two sexes between 1925–29 and 1974–78

between the mortality of men and women can be interpreted as being biological (differential resistance to infection, for instance), or social (differential access to food or health care). However, Figs. 9.3 and 9.5 suggest interpretations which confirm some of the hypotheses that have been put forward.

The fact that an important part of the excess mortality of infants is linked to hereditary and congenital factors reinforces the view that this difference is biologically determined. The greater susceptibility of boy babies to infectious diseases does not contradict this assertion. Excess mortality has remained relatively stable during our period, and it is only the reduced importance of infectious diseases as a cause of death that has resulted in the mortality of infants from this cause appearing as a moderating factor in the difference between life expectancies, which is shown in Fig. 9.5. At these ages the struggle against infectious disease has, at least since 1920, not depended on the sex of the infant, and the slight handicap to which boys are subject has not changed.

The same is not true at other ages. For a long time, infectious diseases have taken a heavy toll among young women. The biological advantage that they enjoyed was cancelled by their lower social status and by particular susceptibility to certain diseases. Now that the status of women has improved at all ages (as has been the case for older women for some time) mortality from infectious disease has become heavier among men than among women. This excess is larger than in infancy, and a more detailed analysis shows that it is particularly pronounced for respiratory infections which are closely linked to smoking and industrial pollution, two exogenous factors which impinge on men more than they do on women.

Degenerative diseases which are linked to the attrition of the human organism tend to affect men more than women, because men are less resistant to them. But a higher incidence among men could also be connected with less healthy conditions of life. This second interpretation is supported by the fact that the excess mortality of men from these causes has increased considerably during the last half century.

The most important cause of death which has resulted in increasing the excess mortality of men is neoplasms, particularly neoplasms of the respiratory system which are directly linked to smoking and industrial pollution, and neoplasms of the oesophagus which are linked to alcoholism. Environment and behaviour both play an important and prominent role in this area.

Lastly, deaths from accidents and violence are considerably more frequent among men, as are deaths from alcoholism and cirrhosis of the liver. Though they do not form a very high proportion of all deaths, they make a contribution to the overall excess mortality of men and to its recent increase.

Convergence of Behaviour and Persistence of Men's Excess Mortality

If environmental or behavioural differences were the main causes of men's excess mortality, how can its persistence be explained at a time when these differences have become progressively less important?

Smoking, Drinking, Driving, and Excess Mortality

It has become commonplace in recent years to state that men's and women's behaviour has become more alike. Whereas tobacco consumption is declining among men, it has increased considerably among women. Women now commonly drive motor cars, and their labour-force participation rate has risen to a level near to that of men at a time when men's labour-force participation rates have been somewhat reduced. These developments were already apparent towards the end of the 1960s, and the authors of model life tables predicted that, as life expectancy increased, the difference between the sexes would diminish, so that the previous trend would be reversed.[38] However, their forecasts turned out to be wrong, in spite of the fact that they seemed well founded at the time. Not only have differences between the mortality of the two sexes continued to increase as life expectancy has reached higher levels, but the pace of increase has accelerated in some cases.[39]

Of course, even though there has been some convergence between the behaviour of men and women, differences persist. Men tend to smoke considerably more than women, they drive motor vehicles much more frequently, and their labour-force participation rates are still slightly higher. Moreover, in some areas, such as the incidence of alcoholism, the difference between men and women has changed only slightly. This might explain the persistence of an excess mortality of men, but it does not account for its increase.

In a discussion of the excess mortality of men, it is tempting to concentrate on those causes of death which lead to an increase in the overall death rate, and to suggest that these result from behaviour that is more characteristic of men than of women. However, this explanation does not take account of the fact that changes in the excess mortality of men have coincided with an extraordinary progress in health. Is it not possible that, in addition to negative factors which affect men more than women, there may be aspects of the life-style of the two sexes which enable women to derive greater benefits from progress in health and medical care than men?

Women's Life-Styles

The Legacy of the Past. Women's inferior social status in the past was not entirely disadvantageous. Though they were slaves to both production and reproduction, they were also regarded as weak and fragile, and were, therefore, afforded some degree of protection. Machismo and gallantry often went together. In patriarchal societies, women were protected from some dangerous activities, such as war and hunting. In moments of danger,

---

[38] A. J. Coale and P. Demeny, *Regional Model Life Tables and Stable Populations* (Princeton, NJ, 1966).

[39] J. Vallin, 'Sex Patterns of Mortality: A Comparative Study of Model Life Tables and Actual Populations with Special Reference to the Cases of Algeria and France', in A. Lopez and L. Ruzicka (eds.), *Sex Differentials in Mortality: Trends, Determinants, and Consequences* (Canberra, 1983), pp. 443–76.

the cry 'Women and children first' was heard. During the period of industrialization, the law prohibited the employment of women in some dangerous occupations, such as mining, or in night work, regulated their working hours, and later even protected their fertility by such measures as antenatal care and maternity leave. Towards the end of the nineteenth century a situation was reached in which women were prohibited from engaging in some forms of work in factories, and their participation in the labour force tended to be limited to occupations which were regarded as 'more fitted to their natures', such as home employment. They were thus spared not only the dangers of war and military service, but also a large part of the brutal conditions in heavy industry. Similarly, women smoked and drank less than men did, were subject to lower risks of death on the roads, and, because their sexual activities were more restricted, their health risks from venereal diseases (syphilis and gonorrhoea in the past, AIDS today) were lower.

Though it has been eroded to a large extent, some aspects of this protection have remained. Whilst women have gained an improved status in society, and have been able to reduce their reproductive burdens, they have also tended to retain some of the privileges that were attached to their former status, not only in the form of legal protection, but perhaps even more because they were thought to hold different attitudes to life and society.

The Move towards a Feminine Life-Style. The achievement of equal status by women does not mean that their behaviour will necessarily become more like that of men. Fundamental differences have persisted, and this goes some way to explaining why women have benefited more from modern progress in medicine than men.

Modern women smoke, drink, and drive, and it is not, therefore, surprising that men's excess mortality from these causes has tended to diminish. Some of the consequences of this convergence of behaviour are only likely to become apparent in the future; the effects of smoking, in particular, only manifest themselves with some delay. However, it would appear that, in spite of this convergence, women's behaviour in this respect is less risky than that of men. Although in recent generations the proportion of young girls who smoke cigarettes has become equal or sometimes even slightly higher than that of boys, the number of cigarettes smoked by regular smokers each day is much lower among women than among men.[40] Women's driving behaviour, too, is more prudent; on average they drive more slowly and take fewer risks than men. But these differences are less important than others which we now proceed to discuss.

[40] M. Blanc, 'Les Effets à long terme des programmes d'intervention contre le tabagisme: Application à la France', in J. Vallin and A. Lopez, *La Lutte contre la mort* (Paris, 1985), pp. 238–56.

TABLE 9.2. *Employed active population by major occupational groups and sex, France, 1982* (000s)

Occupational group	Men	Women	Women (%)
Farmers, artisans, shopkeepers	2,024	1,134	36
Managers, professionals, civil servants, engineers	1,853	336	15
Teachers, scientific workers, journalists, artists, clergy, clerical workers in public and private sector	994	720	42
Foremen, skilled and unskilled manual workers, agricultural workers, policemen, drivers	6,516	1,415	18
Primary schoolteachers, workers in the health and social services, lower ranks of the public service, clerical workers	1,619	4,855	75
TOTAL	13,005	8,460	39

Although the increase in women's labour-force participation rates has been spectacular during the last few decades, their distribution between occupations has remained fundamentally different from that of men (see Table 9.2).[41] It has often been noted that women reach positions of responsibility less frequently than men. Less stress has been put on the fact that women are, in general, more skilled than men, and are less often employed in low-grade occupations which demand hard physical work. In the French Census of 1982, 40 per cent of all employed persons recorded were female. Their participation in employment was, therefore, almost the same as that of men, but their distribution between different occupations was very different.[42] They were underrepresented in decision-making

[41] M. Levy and A. Labourie Racape, 'Le Salariat féminin en perspective', *Population et Sociétés*, 165 (1983), pp. 1–3.
[42] D. Dandoy-Marchant, *Tableaux de l'économie française* (Paris, 1986).

occupations (heads of enterprises, liberal professions), where they amounted to only 15 per cent of all those enumerated. In the more technical occupations, their proportions were even lower (6 per cent among engineers, and 9 per cent among technicians). They were equally underrepresented in industrial employment, handicrafts, and agriculture, both in skilled and unskilled work (18 per cent), and were particularly rare among supervisory personnel (only 6 per cent of foremen or equivalent grades were females). By contrast, the intermediate professions (teachers, ancillary health workers, the social services, the lower civil service, and clerical occupations) were largely staffed by women, who accounted for 75 per cent of all workers in this group. These occupations contained 57 per cent of the entire female labour force, and characterized the nature of women's employment. By contrast, well over half of all employed men worked in industry.

It is difficult not to link differences between the occupational profile of the male and female labour force with sex differentials in mortality. Men's death rates tend to be influenced considerably by their occupation. Men employed in professional and managerial occupations enjoy a life expectancy on their thirty-fifth birthday which is nine years longer than that of manual workers.[43] However, no such difference is found for women.[44] Women's employment tends to be concentrated in occupations that carry a low health risk (teaching, clerical work), but, even when they are employed in occupations in which the health risks for men are significant, women seem to be better protected. It would be necessary to study occupational mortality in much greater detail in order fully to understand this phenomenon; here we shall content ourselves with mentioning that, in the two occupations which appear to be the most dangerous in our society (policemen, and road transport drivers), the proportion of women is lowest (5 per cent and 2 per cent respectively). Although women work as hard as men do, and even harder when their domestic responsibilities are taken into account, their employment is concentrated in occupations in which the risk to health is lower. It is also possible that women arrange their work differently, and employ a working rhythm which is less dangerous for their health.

Finally, in general, women's attitudes to their bodies, their health, and life in general are very different from those of men. This is probably an aspect of evolution which is connected with their reproductive function. During a period when control of fertility has reduced the burden of maternity, medical services for the protection of mothers and infants, and obstetric and gynaecological services, have become increasingly important in medicine and have taken a larger share of medical resources. These developments have more than compensated for the higher risks that women run as reproducers. They have contributed to a general improvement in

[43] G. Desplanques, *La Mortalité des adultes suivant le milieu social, 1955–1971* (Paris, 1976); L'Inégalité devant la mort', *Économie et statistique* (1980), pp. 29–50.
[44] Desplanques (1980), op. cit. in n. 43.

women's health, and women nowadays use medical services more and take better care of their health than men do. To give just one example: the early detection of cervical cancer as a result of routine screening has been one of the main reasons for the reduction of mortality from uterine cancers in general.[45]

But the greater care that women give to their health is not confined to reproduction. The feminine life-style and culture have quite different effects on the human body than men's exaltation of virility. We might put this into an extreme form by saying that the quest for beauty is opposed to that for force and power. The former requires the body to be kept young and healthy for as long as possible; the latter subjects it to stresses and risks. Women pay greater attention to their bodily and health needs than men; they use medical services more frequently and are in closer contact with their medical practitioners.

More temperate in their use of tobacco and alcohol, women engage in fewer risky activities, take greater care of their health and their bodies, and have thus derived greater benefits than men from medical and social progress. Their advantage has been increased by recent developments in a different field: education. During the 1960s the proportion of girls who passed their *baccalauréat* examination came to exceed that of boys.[46] Even though women may reach the very highest educational levels less frequently than men, the average level of their education is higher, and this has given them another, and by no means less valuable, additional advantage in respect of their mortality.

---

[45] F. Hatton, R. Flammand, M. H. Bouvier-Colle, and L. Maujol, 'La Lutte contre la mortalité cancéreuse', in Vallin and Lopez, op. cit. in n. 40.

[46] M. Lévy, 'Garçons et filles à l'école', *Population et Sociétes*, 151 (1981), pp. 1–3.

10 Sex Inequalities in Morbidity and Mortality

VIVIANA EGIDI AND ARDUINO VERDECCHIA

When we move from a descriptive to an analytical approach to mortality in order to identify possible determinants of mortality and the differences between them, one of the first problems to crop up is that, in normal circumstances, death is simply one of a number of possible terminal events in a morbid process which began during previous stages of an individual's life. In the developed countries, in which the principal causes of death are now chronic and degenerative diseases which are often prolonged, the risk exists that, by continuing to analyse trends and differentials solely in terms of the negative outcome (death), we shall lose sight of the true mechanisms that underlie the process of morbidity. An analysis of the difference between the mortality of the two sexes will show this, as well as the far-reaching cognitive and methodological consequences of analysing the whole of the morbid process from onset to final outcome. A reconstruction of the whole chain of events, which may or may not end in death, will make it possible to account for the varying sizes, and often direction, of differentials which characterize each phase of the illness, and will show that these may be influenced—positively or negatively—by different variables. Some biological, behavioural, or environmental variables may operate during the phase of onset, and influence the type of illness and the part of the system that is affected. For instance, differences between the smoking and drinking habits of men and women, which continue to be widespread though declining, or the occupational hazards faced by the two sexes, will need to be considered. Other biological, behavioural, or environmental variables may be more active during an illness, and influence both its duration and its outcome. Women are generally more concerned about their health and use health facilities more frequently than men,[1] and consequently their illnesses may be diagnosed earlier and be more effectively treated.

The theoretical advantages that can be obtained by introducing morbidity into the analysis also render the phenomenon much more complex and raise

---

[1] See, e.g., L. M. Verbrugge, 'Longer Life but Worsening Health? Trends in Health and Mortality of Middle-Aged and Older Persons', *Milbank Memorial Fund Quarterly*, 62 (1984), pp. 475–519; Istituto Centrale di Statistica (ISTAT), *Indagine sulle condizioni di salute della popolazione e sul ricorso ai servizi sanitari*, Supplement to *Bollettino Mensile di Statistica*, 12 (Nov. 1980).

many methodological and practical problems. There is the difficulty of clearly defining what is meant by 'health' and 'illness'; the time-lag between the onset of illness, its perception by the patient, and diagnosis will all be different for different illnesses. There are problems related to time, and the possible reversibility of the morbid process. In more practical terms, there are problems resulting from the lack of and unreliability of morbidity statistics in many cases. We shall not examine all these aspects, each of which would deserve a study of its own, but, by using different definitions of health, we shall attempt to provide a concise overview of the possible implications of this approach on the study of sex differentials in mortality and the search for their causes.

Differential Morbidity or Differential Perception?

The definitions of health and illness range from very broad definitions in which the individual's perception of his own state of well-being (or sickness) is emphasized, to much narrower ones, in which health (or sickness) is identified with the absence (or presence) of a particular morbid process. Between these extremes there are a wide variety of definitions, each of which is focused on specific aspects.

The 'subjective' or 'perceptive' definition of health makes use of the 'quality of life', a concept which often defies analysis. Individuals will have their own personal opinions about their state of health, irrespective of whether a real threat to their health exists, and they will adjust their conduct accordingly. There is also a scale of degrees of 'illness', which may range from imperfect mental or physical well-being (to which the World Health Organization (WHO) has added 'social')[2] to a state of total inability to provide for one's most elementary needs, and to hospitalization.

Information on these aspects of health is collected directly by interviews, and generally shows that women are at a disadvantage which gradually decreases as one moves from purely subjective definitions to those based on degrees of declared disabilities.

In Table 10.1, we provide an example of summary data on the consequences of self-declared morbidity levels on the health status of the population, and offer a preliminary specification of the difference between the two sexes in this respect. The data have been taken from the results of a survey conducted in Italy in 1980,[3] when a representative sample of individuals of both sexes were asked to appraise their own health status. By using the life table for that calendar year, and estimating the number of years during which a fictitious cohort, subject to the mortality, morbidity, and disability levels of

[2] WHO, *Manual of Mortality Analysis of National Mortality Statistics for Public Health Purposes* (Geneva, 1977).
[3] ISTAT, op. cit. in n. 1.

the moment, lived in different health conditions,[4] it may be estimated that an Italian male with a life expectancy at birth of 71 years, will live for only 67 in a state of autonomy, and 61 in a state perceived as being in good health (i.e. 86 per cent of his mean life span). The difference is larger for women, whose life expectancy was 77 years, of which 72 were spent without disabilities, but only 64 (or 83 per cent) in good health. Thus, the difference between men's and women's survival in good health is smaller than the difference in their overall survival, three instead of nearly seven years, and only five of the extra seven years were lived in conditions in which the women were able to look after themselves.

One initial possible explanation of the reversal in the difference when the morbidity, and particularly the perceived morbidity, of the two sexes is compared, instead of their mortality, is that the pathologies that affect women may be less fatal than those which affect men. This hypothesis is confirmed from data on hospital admissions, which do not show any substantial difference between the two sexes (see Table 10.1). In fact, when the difference between the age structure of the two sexes is controlled, a higher proportion of women than of men mentioned diseases of the osteo-muscular system as causes of their poor health (in the Italian survey 25 per cent, compared with 18 per cent of men), circulatory problems (18 against 15 per cent), and endocrine illnesses (5 per cent compared with 3 per cent).[5] However, it is also true that, in Italy, at any rate, women's disadvantages are not restricted to the less lethal diseases. When asked to indicate present illnesses (after eliminating the effects of age structure), more women than men reported themselves as suffering from heart disease (the ratio of men to women being 0.84), and cancer (ratio 0.58). However, it should be noted that men and women both have different perceptions and show a different willingness to answer these questions, and that these differences are magnified when a 'subjective' definition of health is used, which is not based either on clinical examination or on objective parameters.[6] This drawback could have considerable effect as far as the more serious illnesses are concerned and make it impossible to use this kind of information to interpret the levels and differential features of mortality. To do this, it would be necessary to adopt more objective definitions based on the actual presence

[4] D. F. Sullivan, 'Conceptual Problems in Developing an Index of Health', *Vital and Health Statistics*, ser. 2, No. 17 (1966); D. F. Sullivan, 'A Single Index of Mortality and Morbidity', *Health Reports*, 86 (1971), pp. 347–54; R. Wilkins, 'La distribution de l'espérance de vie parmi les différents états de santé; composantes, méthode de calculs, et résultats pour le Québec, 1978', *Cahiers Québecois de Démographie*, 11 (1982), pp. 255–74.

[5] Similar results have been found in the health survey carried out in the United States; see L. M. Verbrugge, 'Sex Differences in Health Behavior, Morbidity, and Mortality', paper presented at the National Institutes of Health (NIH) Conference on Gender and Longevity, 17–18 Sept. 1987.

[6] For a detailed analysis of the psycho-social aspects of behavioural differences between the sexes in relation to the perception and evaluation of their symptoms, willingness to accept therapy, and also to answer questions on their health, see Verbrugge, op. cit. in n. 1.

TABLE 10.1. *Life expectancy, by health conditions and sex, Italy, 1980* (years)

Age	All conditions	Non-hospitalized life	Without disability	In good health
		Males		
0	70.6	70.3	66.8	60.6
30	42.9	42.6	39.6	33.7
50	24.5	24.3	21.5	16.9
60	16.8	16.6	14.1	10.6
71	9.8	9.6	7.6	5.6
		Females		
0	77.4	77.1	72.2	63.9
30	49.0	48.8	44.4	36.4
50	30.0	29.8	25.8	19.4
60	21.2	21.0	17.4	12.7
71	12.5	12.4	9.5	6.8
		Difference (F − M)		
0	6.8	6.8	5.4	3.3
30	6.1	6.2	4.8	2.7
50	5.5	5.5	4.3	2.5
60	4.4	4.4	3.3	2.1
71	2.7	2.8	1.9	1.2

Source: Authors' computations on ISTAT survey data.

of specific morbid processes, whose possible negative outcome (i.e. death) can easily be traced in the statistics on causes of death.

Disease registers which are being set up in an increasing number of countries provide much more relevant information for our purposes. Although they are generally restricted to some of the more important diseases (mainly cancers, and some diseases of the circulatory system) and often refer only to specific sub-populations, the information they contain is beginning to provide an organic picture that deserves further analysis. In this study we shall draw on this source to analyse the differences between cancer mortality of the sexes in the light of morbidity differences.

Cancer Morbidity in Adult Life

The explanation of sex differences in cancer mortality is one of the most important objectives of mortality analysis. Although men's excess mortality

TABLE 10.2. *Cancer mortality (observed) and incidence (estimated), of men. Italy, 1960 and 1983* (rates *10,000)

Age group	1960		1983		% annual change	
	Mortality	Incidence	Mortality	Incidence	Mortality	Incidence
			Males			
30–34	2.2	4.6	1.7	5.9	−1.1	1.1
40–44	6.8	12.9	7.6	17.4	0.5	1.3
50–54	23.6	36.9	30.9	53.4	1.2	1.6
60–64	61.1	90.6	78.2	142.4	1.1	2.0
30–69	22.3	34.5	30.7	55.7	1.3	2.1
Stand 1*			28.2	51.5	1.0	1.7
			Females			
30–34	2.7	7.6	1.9	9.0	−1.5	0.7
40–44	8.5	18.1	6.8	21.1	−1.0	0.7
50–54	19.1	38.8	17.0	46.0	−0.5	0.7
60–64	36.9	70.1	35.7	85.0	−0.1	0.8
30–69	17.4	33.9	17.0	42.3	−0.1	0.9
Stand 1*	16.5	32.3	14.9	38.0	−0.4	0.7
Stand 2†			15.9	39.9	−0.4	0.7

Ratio of incidence for males to that for females

Age group	1960		1983		Increase	
	Mortality	Incidence	Mortality	Incidence	Mortality	Incidence
30–34	81	61	89	66	8	5
40–44	80	71	112	82	32	11
50–54	124	95	182	116	58	21
60–64	166	129	219	168	53	38
30–69	128	102	181	132	53	30
Stand 1*	135	107	189	136	54	29

* Standardized against men's age structure for 1960.
† Standardized against women's age structure of 1960.

from these causes overall is lower than that from other diseases, their increasing importance as a cause of death gives them a decisive role in the increasing mortality gap between the two sexes in adult life.[7]

[7] V. Egidi, 'Trent'anni di evoluzione della mortalità in Italia', *Genus*, 50 (1984), pp. 71–106; J. Vallin and F. Meslé, *Les causes de décès en France de 1925 à 1978* (Paris, 1988).

To illustrate the differences that exist between the sexes at various stages of cancer, we shall mainly refer to Italian data that have been estimated in a research project on cancer mortality and morbidity. This will also make it possible to relate the incidence and survival rates in the population directly to mortality, by using data collected from various registers in Italy and other countries.[8]

In 1983 the incidence of cancer among men aged 30–69 was 5.6 per 1,000, and 4.2 among women (see Table 10.2). During the early 1960s the chances of surviving from cancer were lower, and for every cancer death about 1.5 new cases were diagnosed in men and 1.9 in women, with an incidence of 3.5 and 3.4 per 1,000 respectively.

There was a marked increase of incidence in all age groups, and reductions in the mortality from cancer, especially among women, seem to have been the result of improved survival rates, which offset the sharp rise in the risk of contracting cancer. This seems to resolve the paradox that is always noted when the trend in women's cancer mortality is analysed in relation to changes in their life-styles and behaviour during the past few years: a persistent decline in cancer mortality, even though more women are adopting life-styles that involve health risks. Morbidity data show that two quite distinct phenomena account for this apparent contradiction. First, there is a pronounced increase in the risk of contracting cancer, which confirms the unhealthy nature of the new life-styles, but this is matched by increased cancer survival rates, a phenomenon more marked among women than among men, even though their survival rates were higher initially (see also Fig. 10.2). This suggests that the greater care that women take of their health, and the increase in systematic screening for the early detection of mainly gynaecological cancers (cancer of the uterus and cancer of the breast), are now paying dividends.

The difference between the sexes changes considerably when incidence, rather than mortality, is considered. The disadvantage of men is much smaller (after controlling for difference between the age structures of the sexes, the ratio of incidence levels among the age group 30–69 is 1.36, compared with 1.89 for mortality). Moreover, whereas men's excess mortality from cancer appears at a relatively early age (40–44 in 1983, and 50–54 in 1960), women's excess morbidity rates continue to an advanced age (until 45–49 in 1983, 50–54 in 1960) (see Fig. 10.1). It is clear that the excess mortality of men from cancer, despite the excess morbidity of women, is due to the fact that the latter's survival rate is higher.

[8] For a description of the methods used, see R. Capocaccia, V. Egidi, A. Golini, and A. Verdecchia, 'From Mortality to Morbidity', paper presented at the 20th General Conference of the IUSSP (Florence, 1985); A. Verdecchia, R. Capocaccia, V. Egidi, and A. Golini, 'A Method for the Estimation of Levels and Trends of Chronic Disease Morbidity from Mortality Data', *Statistics in Medicine*, 8 (1989), pp. 201–16; V. Egidi, A. Golini, R. Capocaccia, and A. Verdecchia, 'Un modèle d'évaluation de mortalité: Le Cas du cancer', in J. Vallin and A. Palloni, *Mesure et analyse de la mortalité* (Paris, 1988), pp. 423–42.

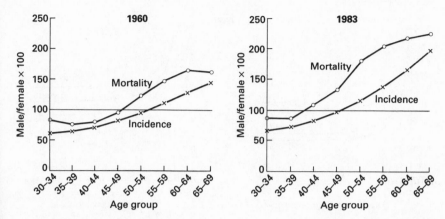

FIG. 10.1 Excess mortality of men (observed) and excess morbidity of men (estimated incidence) for cancer. Italy, 1960 and 1983

In Fig. 10.2 some of the features and synthetic indicators of the survival curves from cancers of different sites, which have been selected from international curves considered to describe best the capacity to treat cancer in Italy, are illustrated, after the proportions have been adjusted to reflect the structure of cancer by site in Italy.[9] The curves used are mainly site-specific survival curves produced in the United States Program for Cancer Surveillance and Epidemiology and End Results, which cover the periods 1950–54 and 1973–79.[10] As the American curves seemed to be too favourable for the Italian situation in relation to the main cancer sites among women (breast and uterus), survival curves produced by the Cancer Registry of Norway were used.[11]

Fatality rates increase with age, and range from a minimum of 34 per cent among men aged 30 at diagnosis to a maximum of 64 per cent when the diagnosis is made later in life, compared with analogous figures of 25 and 52 per cent among women. These survival curves suggest that the fatality rate for men was higher than that for women, the ratio being 1.3. However, this can be explained as being the effect of a different distribution of cancer sites in the two sexes, rather than as a difference between the rates for cancers of

[9] Regione Lombardia, 'Incidenza dei tumori e cause di morte in Lombardia', *Notizie sanità*, 10 (1986), pp. 10–85.

[10] L. M. Axtell, S. J. Cutler, and M. H. Myers, *End Result in Cancer* (Bethesda, Md., 1972); L. M. Axtell, A. J. Asire, and M. H. Myers, *Cancer Patient Survival* (Bethesda, Md., 1976); L. G. Ries, E. S. Pollack, and J. L. Young jnr., 'Cancer Patient Survival: Surveillance, Epidemiology and End Results Program, 1973–79', *Journal of the National Cancer Institute*, 70 (1983), pp. 693–707.

[11] Cancer Registry of Norway, *Survival of Cancer Patients Diagnosed in Norway 1968–1975* (Oslo, 1980).

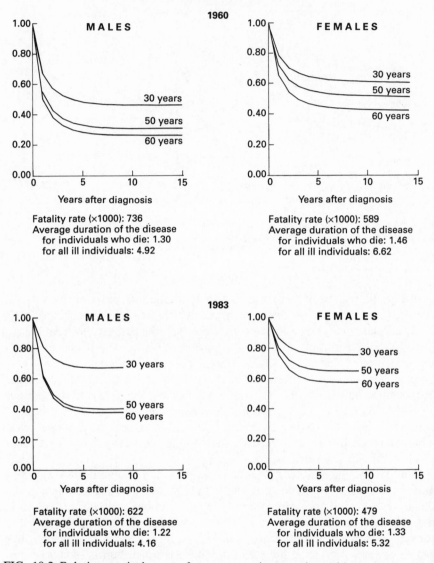

FIG. 10.2 Relative survival curves for cancer patients, estimated by sex and age at diagnosis. Italy, 1960 and 1983

the same site. If fatality rates from different sources are examined (see Table 10.3) for some of the main types of cancer, the differences between the sexes are generally very small (the difference is very large only for melanomas, but these form only a small proportion of new cancer cases),

TABLE 10.3. Fatality rates within five years of diagnosis, for selected cancer sites and percentage of total new cancer cases (values *100)

ICD* no.	Site	United States (SEER Programme, 1973–79)					Norway (1968–75)[†]					Switzerland (1973–77)[†]					Italy (1976–77)[‡]	
		Fatality			Percentage		Fatality			Percentage[a]		Fatality			Percentage		Percentage	
		M	F	M/F	M	F	M	F	M/F	M	F	M	F	M/F	M	F	M	F
151	Stomach	88	86	102	3	2	86	88	98	10	7	86	83	103	7	5	12	11
153	Colon	53	51	104	9	11	62	60	103	7	9	65	64	101	7	9	6	9
157	Pancreas	97	98	99	3	3	98§	98§	100§	4	3	97	99	98	3	3	2	2
162	Lung	90	86	105	21	7	92	89	103	12	3	91	86	105	21	4	22	3
172	Melanoma	29	20	145	2	2	41	22	186	3	3	56§	31§	180§	2	2	1	2
188	Bladder	28	31	90	7	2	59	65	91	7	2	61	63§	96§	9	2	8	2
189	Kidney	51	52	99	2	1	64	58	110	3	2	64	61§	104§	3	1	2	1
191	Brain	81	78	104	2	2	75	64	117	3	3	87	83	104	2	1	2	2
	TOTAL				49	30				49	32				54	27	55	32
174	Breast		28			27		26			23		33			32		26
180	Cervix Uteri		34			4		29			7		39			5		5
182	Corpus Uteri		13			10		25			5		28			7		7

* International Classification of Causes of Death.
† Registry of Geneva.
‡ Lombardy Cancer Registry.
§ Based on a relative survival with standard error ≥10%.
a Years 1973–77.

and the rates for women often seem higher than those for men. But because of the marked prevalence of cancer of the uterus (both the cervix uteri and the corpus uteri), which accounts for between 12 and 14 per cent of new cancer cases among women, and of cancer of the breast, which accounts for between 20 and 30 per cent), and with a fatality rate of between 25 and 30 per cent, the overall average risk of death among women is considerably lower.

Another component of the morbid process which may be different for the two sexes is the duration of the illness. In order to quantify this component, we have assumed that a sick individual can be considered 'cured' when the risk of his or her dying approximates that of others of the same sex and age (an excess mortality below one per thousand). Using this assumption, two measurements of duration have been calculated: the duration of illness for patients who die during the illness, and the overall duration, i.e. the duration for both those who die, and those who survive. The first of these measurements seems to have remained practically stationary over the years studied, with a slight fall for both sexes (from 1.3 to 1.2 years on average for men, and from 1.5 to 1.3 years for women), with a very small difference between the sexes. The average duration of the disease for all sufferers from cancer seems to have been more dynamic (mainly in the case of women), and the difference between the sexes is more marked. Over the years considered, the average duration fell from 4.9 to 4.2 years for men, and from 6.6 to 5.3 years for women.

The length of the illness, especially for men, is negatively related to age at diagnosis: it declines from an average of 5.8 years for men aged around 30 at diagnosis, to about 4.4 years for men aged 60 at diagnosis. The relationship is not as clear for women; the minimum duration occurs in cases diagnosed at the age of 40 (5.3 years), which is only approached again when age at diagnosis exceeds 60. As these survival curves refer to all cancers, it is evident that most of these variations in duration, age at diagnosis, and sex relate to changes in, and differential features of, cancers of different sites, as is the case with mortality.

After examining the various components of the morbidity process individually, and the different characteristics of each of them, it is not surprising to find that cancer in adults is more common among women than among men, and that women outnumber men among cancer patients (see Table 10.4). Up to the age of 45, more women develop cancer than men and more of them survive, and for longer periods than men.

Conclusion

The variability of the population in relation to morbidity is one of the main keys to understanding mortality, and differences in mortality. Because of

TABLE 10.4. *Prevalence rates* (×10,000) *estimated for Italy in 1983 and male/female ratio* (×100) *among cancer patients*

Age group	Prevalence rates Males	Females	Male/Female ratio among cancer patients
30–34	25.0	43.6	57.1
40–44	59.5	97.5	59.7
50–54	144.2	205.2	66.4
60–64	349.5	354.8	82.1
30–69	152.8	188.1	76.0
Standardized*		179.5	85.2

* Standardized against men's age structure.

the difficulties involved in an approach to this topic based on aggregate data, demographers have been discouraged from studying its implications, even though the amount of information available has increased during the past few years and deserves much more attention.

These general considerations are particularly important when it comes to a study of the differences between the mortality of the two sexes, as most of the indices of the health of the population that have been constructed in different countries suggest that for many pathologies, particularly in adult life, a higher mortality of men may be matched by a higher morbidity of women. The data relating to cancer, which we have briefly examined above, indicate that this apparent paradox needs to be interpreted in terms of the different siting and hence the different lethality of the morbid process. This would confirm an interpretation of the different mortality of the sexes, mainly in terms of differential risks to which men and women are exposed, and in terms of individual behaviour and life-styles, as well as risks encountered in the occupational environment.

There are also some sex differences within the morbidity process in terms of the same sites and ages at diagnosis, even though they are much smaller and do not always favour women. Is it possible that their level may be explained only by the biological difference between the sexes? Or is it, once again, the effect of social factors which makes it more likely that cancer is detected earlier in one sex than the other, thereby making it easier to treat?

The case of melanoma suggests that the second interpretation may be quite significant. This cancer is characterized by a very high excess mortality of men (see Table 10.3), and a large excess morbidity of women. For example, the ratio of the incidence between men and women is 0.74 in Denmark, 0.80 in Spain, 0.82 in Norway, and between 0.52 and 0.72 in the different registries of the United Kingdom. According to the data in the Norwegian registry, which have been used to analyse survival rates in terms of different stages of the disease (localized, regional metastases, distant metastases), it appears that the main reason for the higher survival rate of females is early diagnosis. Between the ages of 45 and 64 years, when the fatality rate of localized melanoma is about one-third of that from the same disease diagnosed at a more advanced stage, 78 per cent of the new cases of the disease diagnosed in women were localized, compared with only 60 per cent in men.[12] It seems that this may be a positive consequence of the fact that women traditionally take greater care of their bodies, including their appearance, which makes it possible for them to notice the early symptoms of the disease sooner, and therefore to deal with it more promptly.

Once we have eliminated the effect of the different structure of stage of the disease for melanoma, and also for cancers of many other sites (such as colon, rectum, liver, and pancreas for those aged below 55, respiratory tract, and the central nervous system),[13] there remain differences in lethality that are difficult to explain, except as a result of biological or genetic differences between the sexes. This field is as yet largely unexplored. The fact that women are protected from, for example, cardiovascular diseases at ages up to the menopause as a result of the action of their sex hormones is now widely accepted, even though the mechanism is not completely clear.[14] It is probable that there may be biological or genetic protection against other diseases, either through prevention of the onset of the disease, or by providing the female organism with greater resistance and a stronger reactive capacity to the disease once established, as the data on survival from cancer seem to suggest.

[12] Ibid.　　[13] Ibid.　　[14] Verbrugge, op. cit. in n. 1.

11 Effects of Women's Position on their Migration

LIN LEAN LIM

With the growing recognition that women feature prominently not only in associational migration with their families or spouses but also in autonomous migration, various attempts have been made to explain women's migration.[1] They refer to marriage-related reasons, culturally determined sex-role constraints, gender-related differentials in 'push-and-pull' factors, the vulnerable and insecure income position of women, and household structure and adaptation strategies as determinants of women's mobility. But there has been little systematic treatment of how women's position relative to that of men and of other women at different life-cycle stages, and in particular socio-economic and cultural contexts, affect women's motivations or incentives to

---

[1] E. Boserup, *Women's Role in Economic Development* (New York, 1970); J. Connell, B. Dasgupta, R. Laishley, and M. Lipton, *Migration from Rural Areas: The Evidence from Village Studies* (New Delhi, 1976); J. Connell, 'Status or Subjugation? Women, Migration and Development in the South Pacific', *International Migration Review*, 18 (1984), pp. 964–83; A. Singh, 'Rural–Urban Migration of Women among the Urban Poor in India', *Social Action*, 28 (1978), pp. 326–56; V. Thadani and M. P. Todaro, *Female Migration in Developing Countries: A Framework for Analysis* (New York, 1979); International Center for Research on Women, *Women in Migration: A Third World Focus* (Washington, 1979); K. Young, 'The Creation of Relative Surplus Population: A Case Study from Mexico', in L. Beneria (ed.), *Women and Development: The Sexual Division of Labor in Rural Societies* (New York, 1982); J. Balan, 'Selectivity of Migration in International and Internal Flows', paper presented at the UNESCO Symposium on Issues and Trends in Migration: Population Movements within and across International Boundaries, Paris, 1983; M. Morokvasic, 'Why do Women Migrate? Towards an Understanding of the Sex Selectivity in the Migratory Movements of Labor', *Studi emigrazione/Études migrations*, 20 (1983), p. 70; M. Morokvasic, 'Birds of Passage are also Women', *International Migration Review*, 18 (1984), pp. 137–66. J. T. Fawcett, S. Y. Khoo, and P. C. Smith (eds.), *Women in the Cities of Asia: Migration and Urban Adaptation* (Boulder, Colo., 1984); A. Phizackley (ed.), *One Way Ticket: Migration and Female Labour* (London, 1983); G. W. Jones, *Women in the Urban and Industrial Workforce Southeast and East Asia* (Canberra, 1984); J. R. Behrman and B. L. Wolfe, 'Micro Determinants of Female Migration in a Developing Country: Labor Market, Demographic Marriage Market and Economic Marriage Incentives', *Research in Population Economics*, 5 (1984), 137–66; B. Sassen-Koob, 'Notes on the Incorporation of Third World Women into Wage Labour through Immigration and Off-shore Production', *International Migration Review*, 18 (1984); S. E. Findley and L. Williams, 'Women who Go and Women who Stay: Reflections on Family Migration Processes in a Changing World', paper submitted to the Population and Employment Branch, ILD, Geneva, 1988.

move, their ability to move, their role in migration decision-making, and the types and patterns of migration they are involved in.

The difficulty is that there are, on the one hand, various dimensions of the position of women in the gender, class, or ethnic hierarchies that may be relevant to mobility behaviour, and, on the other, various types of both internal and international migration that may be differentially affected by these dimensions. Furthermore, the forces that determine a women's status also set the context for her mobility. Gender interactions take place and women's status is determined in different contexts or 'social fields'—the family, the community or kin-group, and the broader society or political system. These are also the contexts relevant for explaining migration. Both women's status and the effects on migration, therefore, need to be analysed as individual-level phenomena within the contexts of the family and community, and of the social, economic, and political settings in areas of both origin and destination. Women's migration can be seen as autonomous decision-making on the part of individual women, or as part of, or determined by, family decision-making, mainly as a household adaptation or survival strategy.

In this chapter I develop the meaning of women's relative position as a determinant of women's migration. The concern is with those aspects of gender relations or situations which lead to women being disadvantaged relative to men, and with their rights and obligations compared with those of men (and in some cases, other women) that have a bearing on their migration behaviour. Special attention is given to the structural and functional contexts in which both women's relative positions and their migration behaviour are determined. The chapter does not purport to offer a comprehensive theory of women's migration, but it suggests that a focus on women's relative position in the family and society throws useful light on the manner in which migration decisions are arrived at, and on sex differences in the motives and determinants of migration patterns. Although most of the relationships discussed apply to both internal and international migration of women, the chapter does not do justice to the policy-context which is so crucial in migration across national boundaries and which tends to affect men and women differently. The policies of receiving countries in particular can, by design or in actual operation, treat male and female migrants differently in terms of rights of entry and stay, and exercise of economic activity.

Frameworks for the Determinants of Women's Migration

In this section, the frameworks that have been proposed in the literature are briefly reviewed to note how women's relative position has been dealt with in explaining their migration. In view of the limitations in specific attempts to explain women's migration, the review is also extended to those general approaches that can be drawn upon to develop a more systematic treatment of women's status and the components of the migration process among women.

Until recently, it was conveniently assumed that women moved in association with either their parents or their husbands and that, therefore, no separate study of their motives for migration was needed. The assumption that women's migration reflects family or men's migration can be traced to patriarchal authority structures and the subordinate position of women in many societies which deter their autonomous migration. The implicit idea in associational migration is that women have little or no say in the decision to move and that the possibility that a woman may choose to accompany her husband or family, move on her own, or stay behind, does not arise.

Even in autonomous women's migration, marriage was the main factor singled out as an explanation. Women who migrated alone were assumed to be following, or looking for, husbands. The emphasis on the marriage explanation has been attributed in part to

the invisibility of (or lack of data on) women as economic producers and an over-emphasis on their roles as reproducers and homemakers (which) naturally led scholars and development experts to overlook any socio-economic significance of female migration and, thus, to dismiss the importance of analyzing sex difference in motives and determinants of migratory patterns.[2]

With increasing evidence from all over the world, the fact that women move for economic reasons could no longer be glossed over. But it was generally considered that men-oriented economic models of migration would cover women's migration equally well. The best-known exception is Thadani's and Todaro's attempt to modify the men-based model to explain women's migration by taking into account employment probabilities and income differences in the formal and informal sectors;[3] the chances of a woman achieving financial betterment and/or status mobility through marriage to a man of higher social status; marital migration, where women move in order to secure suitable husbands; associational migration, where a wife moves because her husband does; and culturally defined sex-role constraints upon the movement of women.

A variant of this model was used in an empirical study of micro-determinants of women's migration by Behrman and Wolfe, who focused on the usual labour market factors, 'demographic marriage market' considerations (namely the probability of finding a male companion/spouse), and 'economic marriage market' considerations or the expected earnings from the husband, given regional labour market factors and assortative mating.[4] Behrman and Wolfe

---

[2] International Center for Research on Women, op. cit. in n. 1, pp. 82–83.
[3] Thadani and Todaro, op. cit. in n. 1. See also V. Thadani and M. P. Todaro, 'Female Migration: A Conceptual Framework', in Fawcett, Khoo, and Smith, op. cit. in n. 1.
[4] Behrman and Wolfe, op. cit. in n. 1.

examined the relative impacts of these three sets of migration incentives conditional upon the individual woman's characteristics, in particular her level of education, and regional differences in labour and marriage markets.

While these models are admittedly useful in drawing attention to the distinctive marriage-related character of women's migration, there are a number of important weaknesses. Thadani's and Todaro's model has been criticized for appearing to be 'obsessed with marriage', so much so that it obscures our understanding of the economic and social factors that affect women's and men's migration differently.[5] These explanations are also based on the assumption that it is the woman herself who makes the decision to migrate. No account is taken of situations where the decision to move is not arrived at individually, nor of factors, such as socio-cultural pressures, that may force women to leave home. The focus on women in the marriageable and working ages also leaves unexplained the migration of young women in pursuit of education or employment, or of older women who move following changes in their life-course, such as widowhood or divorce.

There have been objections to treating women as a separate analytical category. Writers such as Leeds, Amin, and Morokvasic have argued against the introduction of sex into analytical frameworks on the grounds that separate analysis of women or men involves an 'individualistic, reductionist and motivational' emphasis that is sociologically inappropriate, and that reduces all 'structural elements to epiphenomena'.[6] Harbison has also argued that sex is not the only characteristic associated with differential migration, and that these differences do not require different structural models; all that is needed is that the relative components of the motivation to migrate be weighed differently for various individuals within a given society.[7]

What is proposed in this chapter is to consider women not as 'gender entities', but in relation to men within the context of their families and the social, political, and economic conditions that represent both opportunities and constraints for their mobility. The approach involves both macro and micro elements. This is, in fact, the commonly held view—that both macro- and micro-levels of interactions are important, that both the 'underlying determinants' that predispose towards migration, and the particular motives or 'triggers' that result in the individual decision to migrate should be considered, or that 'individual decisions always occur in the context of larger

[5] H. Ware, *Women, Demography and Development* (Canberra, 1981).

[6] A. Leeds, 'Women in the Migratory Process: A Reductionist Outlook', *Anthropological Quarterly*, 49 (1976), p. 73. See also S. Amin (ed.), *Modern Migrations in Western Africa* (Oxford, 1974); M. Morokvasic, 'Women in Migration: Beyond the Reductionist Outlook', in Phizackley, op. cit. in n. 1.

[7] S. F. Harbison, 'Family Structure and Family Strategy in Migration Decision Making', in G. F. de Jong and R. W. Gardner (eds.), *Migration Decision Making: Multidisciplinary Approaches to Microlevel Studies in Developed and Developing Countries* (New York, 1981).

systems, and thus must ultimately be explained or interpreted in the light of these systems.[8]

The larger systems or macro-structures have, of course, been variously described, ranging from the dominant forms of economy and polity and their major institutions, to development strategies and regulations or rules of entry and exit imposed by national governments. But clearly an integral aspect of the macro-structure would be the socio-cultural context, which, although commonly cited as an important determinant of migration,[9] has unfortunately been only vaguely defined. A crucial manifestation of socio-cultural orientations in any society, or an index or proxy of 'culture', would be the status of women relative to that of men. A focus on women's relative position could help to operationalize the socio-cultural context variables in an analysis of the determinants of migration. What is required is to explore how the cultural context and the forces of change that operate at the societal level affect both women's relative status and migration, and also the inter-actions among them.

At the macro-level, the factors associated with places of origin and desti-nation are also likely to be characterized by gender-related differences in push-and-pull variables.[10] 'Opportunity structure differentials' between areas[11] are often sex-selective. Some of these gender-related differences could reflect women's position relative to that of men. For example, cultural restrictions on the roles and 'freedoms' of women have been cited as a powerful negative factor in the place of origin, a push factor unique to women.[12] From an economic perspective, women's migration would be influenced by relative labour market opportunities for men and women, or by the degree of discrimination against women in employment and wages.

The relationship between women's relative position and migration could also be examined within a macro-framework in which the family or household is emphasized. It is in the familial setting that women's subordination to men's authority is most obvious and crucial in terms of influence on women's lives. The family or household is 'a primary arena for the expression of age and sex roles, kinship, socialization, and economic co-operation where the very stuff of culture is mediated and transformed into action'.[13] The family

[8] R. W. Gardner, 'Macrolevel Influences on the Migration Decision Making Process', in de Jong and Gardner, op. cit. in n. 7, p. 61.

[9] L. Mabogunje, 'Systems Approach to a Theory of Rural–Urban Migration', *Geographical Analysis*, 2 (1970); R. Pryor, *The Motivation of Migration* (Canberra, 1975); G. Hugo, 'Village Community Ties, Village Norms and Ethnic and Social Networks: A Review of Evidence from the Third World', in de Jong and Gardner, op. cit. in n. 7.

[10] E. S. Lee, 'A Theory of Migration', *Demography*, 3 (1968); J. R. Harris and M. P. Todaro, 'Migration, Unemployment and Development: A Two-Sector Analysis', *American Economic Review*, 70 (1970), pp. 126–42.

[11] G. F. de Jong and J. T. Fawcett, 'Motivations for Migration: An Assessment and a Value Expectancy Research Model', in de Jong and Gardner, op. cit. in n. 7, p. 55.

[12] Thadani and Todaro, op. cit. in n. 1.

[13] R. M. Netting, R. R. Wilk, and E. J. Arnold (eds.), *Households, Comparative and Historical Studies of a Domestic Group* (Berkeley, Calif., 1984), p. xxii.

also represents the structural and functional context within which migration motivations and values are shaped, human capital is accrued, information is received and interpreted, and decisions are put into operation. Harbison has argued persuasively that what is needed is a more coherent treatment of the family as the immediate context of the migration decision and that a useful approach is to consider the functions served by various aspects of family structure, and then to analyse how these functions affect the motivation to migrate.[14] The social and demographic structure of the family is identified by Harbison as influencing the costs and benefits of migration through its effects on an individual's status, well-being, and rights and obligations within the family. Harbison has also suggested that, in functioning as a subsistence unit, socialization and training unit, and communication and support network, the family will influence the migration of individual members. The family-structure and strategy approach offers a useful starting-point for explicit consideration of the position and roles of women within the family as determinants of women's migration.

Harbison's framework allows for situations where it is the family, rather than the individual woman, that makes the decision to move. A family strategy of migration may be the appropriate consideration where female members are so subordinate that they have little or no say in decision-making, and the family functions as the decision-making unit and the unit of economic maximization. The analysis of migration as a family- or household-adaptation or survival strategy has gained prominence as a consequence of the growing theoretical attention devoted to household processes and the household economy.[15] The household-strategy approach is associated with 'income pooling' as a household-adaptive strategy.

The household-strategy approach has been carried one step further to incorporate a life-course approach. Life-cycle changes have long been acknowledged as a crucial determinant of mobility.[16] The life-course approach is useful for taking the view that the family is not a static unit, but an entity that changes over the life-courses of its members, and for examining transitions and the woman's movements through different family configurations, and the determinants of the timing of such events as leaving home, entering the labour force, marriage, widowhood, etc. Gender-related differentials in migration propensities are closely linked to the life cycle. 'Sex selectivity is often linked to age selectivity due to their concurrence in the domestic

---

[14] Harbison, op. cit. in n. 7.

[15] See, e.g., N. T. Redclift and E. Mingione (eds.), *Beyond Employment: Household, Gender, and Subsistence* (Oxford, 1985); Netting, Wilk, and Arnold, op. cit. in n. 13.

[16] P. H. Rossi, *Why Families Move: A Study in the Social Psychology of Urban Residential Mobility* (New York, 1955); A. J. Speare and F. E. Kobrin, *A Dynamic Analysis of Household Change and Residential Mobility* (Providence, RI, 1984); S. E. Findley, *Planning for Internal Migration: A Review of Issues and Policies in Developing Countries* (Washington, 1977).

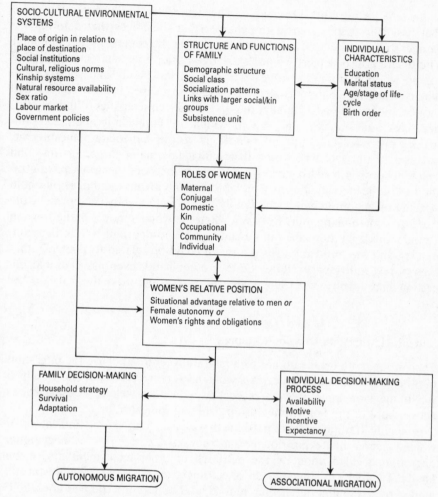

FIG. 11.1 The macro-structure: Women's relative position and migration

division of labour. It is crucial to consider their joint effects since both together affect and are affected by family institutions.'[17]

The Effects of Women's Relative Position on their Migration

Fig. 11.1 shows that three sets of influences operate on a woman's status and on her motives, potential, and process of migration: the macro-structural context, the structure and functions of her family, and her own individual

[17] Balan, op. cit. in n. 1, p. 5.

characteristics over her life course. The figure clearly illustrates the point that has been emphasized in the chapter that the forces that determine a woman's position relative to that of men also set the context for her mobility. The diagram also depicts women's relative position as being closely linked to, or accruing from, the roles they play in the family and society. The macro-structural context is depicted as having four paths of direct and indirect influence: on the family, the individual characteristics of the woman, her roles and statuses, and the individual or family migration decision-making process. The family refers not only to the immediate domestic unit, but also to the social networks that individuals maintain across time and space. The diagram also makes a distinction between decision-making on the part of the individual woman and the woman's involvement in a household strategy of migration where the family, or its male members, represent the basic decision-making unit. But even when the woman moves on her own in autonomous migration, the family could play an important role in decision-making and the motivation for the move could be related to family, rather than purely individual welfare. On the other hand, even associational migration may involve a certain degree of choice and an active role on her part.

Individual Migration Decision-Making Process

The autonomy to decide on her own migration, or to influence the migration of others, is itself an indicator of a woman's relative position. The extent to which the woman is able to place her individual welfare considerations above those of the family may also be another indicator.

In highly traditional and patrilineal societies, one of the indicators of women's subordinate position is that they take part only in associational migration decided upon by the patriarch or other male members of the family. Taeuber explained that Japanese migration decisions and adjustments tended to be familial rather than individual, because 'the codified household law prohibited a change of residence without the consent of the head of the household'.[18] In certain parts of India, Connell and others found that women's migration reflected family migration where the society was patrilineal with men controlling subordinate women.[19] But in the Philippines, where the tradition of autonomy for women has survived Catholicism and colonialism,[20] females predominate in many migration streams, even in international migration during recent years. Among the Zarma in Africa, where 'men and women are complementary with no relation of inferiority', it is often the

---

[18] I. B. Taeuber, 'Family Migration and Industrialization in Japan', in C. J. Jansen (ed.), *Readings in the Sociology of Migration* (London, 1970).

[19] Connell *et al.*, op. cit. in n. 1.

[20] A. Gonzalez and M. Hollsteiner, *Filipino Women as Partners of Men in Progress and Development* (Quezon City, 1976).

women who decide when men should leave the rural areas to earn a cash income.[21]

Where a woman has the autonomy to decide on a change in her behaviour pattern, or where her rights or obligations within the family or society include a personal mobility alternative, the influence of her roles and relative position on the motivation to migrate can be traced. The assumption is that various dimensions of the woman's roles and her relative position will affect her evaluation of the feasibility and attractiveness of the migration option. The higher her relative position within the family and society in the place of origin, the lower may be the incentive to migrate. The greater her subordination to the authority of men, the stronger her motivation to migrate, although her ability to move might be restricted.

The 'availability' of the migration option to an individual woman can be seen as a function of various constraints and facilitators related to her position relative to that of men within her family and society. Patriarchal authority structures may either proscribe or induce the migration of women. Where social norms demand attachment of women to the family structure, resulting family pressures may prevent any migration of unattached women. In Papua New Guinea, the range of social attitudes that constrain migration for women include

a preference for girls to retain their traditional roles as gardeners and homemakers, limited finance for education, the belief that it is a waste of time and money to educate girls, the view that boys are more dispensable in the village than their hardworking sisters, the fear that girls may 'play around' and become pregnant or marry outside their communities with a consequent loss of control over marriage exchanges and bride price payments and, finally, concern that girls will enter the westernized urban world and adopt unacceptable attitudes of behaviour.[22]

For young Hausa women in a society of seclusion and strict social control, migration tends to be considered tantamount to prostitution.[23] Where women are supposed to be protected by their menfolk, or where strong religious norms keep women in 'purdah', they are expected to remain in the care of their extended families while their menfolk migrate on their own.[24] Bourdieu, however, showed how different reference systems literally prepare girls in the villages of Béarn, France, to migrate to towns, but function as discouraging mechanisms for boys and men, and argued that the pursuit of the same motive through migration can be socially valued and stimulated for one sex and unrecognized and discouraged for the other.[25]

---

[21] F. Diarra, 'Les Relations entre les hommes et les femmes et les migrations de Zarma', in Amin, op. cit. in n. 6.

[22] Connell, op. cit. in n. 1, p. 966.

[23] R. Pittin, 'Migration of Women in Nigeria: The Hausa Case', *International Migration Review*, 18 (1984), pp. 1293–314.

[24] Ware, op. cit. in n. 5, p. 163.

[25] F. Bourdieu, 'Célibat et condition paysanne', *Études rurales*, 5–6 (1962), pp. 32–136.

Whether migration is a possible option would also depend on the weight of marriage customs governing women. Where culture decrees that a woman must marry into her husband's group as an outsider, marriage, by definition, entails migration for the woman. With marriage almost a *rite de passage* and socio-cultural norms dictating that parents will lose their daughters, who tend to marry out at an early age, a woman's status may be affected, in that her parents may have little incentive to invest in her education or training, while her in-laws may not approve of schooling for her. In Uttar Pradesh, women's options were greatly restricted by the 'fact that at marriage a daughter ceases to be a daughter and becomes nothing more than a daughter-in-law'.[26] In a matrilineal society, such as northern Thailand and among the Menangkabaus of Indonesia, it is commonly the husband who moves in with the woman's family. But the matrilineal society, in assigning women the responsibility of caring for the ancestral spirits, has tended to constrain their migration, even when they might have wanted to move with their husbands.[27]

In the case of married women, whether they move with their husbands in associational migration, stay behind in the place of origin, or move on their own would depend in part on the cultural acceptability of the separation of husband and wife. Prolonged separation of spouses appears more acceptable in developing countries than in European cultures, partly because the harsh realities of poverty necessitate the separation. Poor Filipino and, more recently, Sri Lankan women leave husbands and children to take on overseas contract work mainly as domestic servants, normally for at least two-year contracts. Whether women accompany their husbands may also depend on the relative importance of the woman's economic role in the area of origin, and the expectation and possibility of her continuing this role in the area of destination.

The impact of economic need can alter the constraints on women's freedom to move. Economic pressures often explain situations in which the social taboos on women's mobility are ignored, or where the 'niceties of proper female existence' are not applied to certain groups of migrant women.[28] In Sri Lanka, middle-class men claim that they would never consider sending their women to work as servants in another man's house, but poor Sri Lankan women may not be able to afford the luxury of conforming to social norms, since working as domestic servants in the Middle East may be the only way open to them to earn any income at all.[29] Of course, they may not even be the poorest of the poor, since information and resources (such as

---

[26] Ware, op. cit. in n. 5, p. 160.

[27] M. Muecke, 'Socio-cultural Correlates of Female Migration in North Thailand', paper presented at the 78th Annual Meeting of the American Anthropological Association, Cincinnati, 1979.

[28] M. E. Smith, 'The Portuguese Female Immigrant: The "Marginal Man"', *International Migration Review*, 14 (1980).

[29] G. Brochman, 'Escape Route to Dependency: Female Migration from Sri Lanka to the Middle East', *Asian and Pacific Population Forum*, 1 (1987), pp. 14–20.

passports and agency fees and commissions) are needed for the move overseas. Although Muslim women are notoriously restricted in their movements outside the home, economic necessity pushed many Turkish women to respond to opportunities in the labour markets of Western Europe since the 1960s, even though the movement of unaccompanied women to internal labour markets was still largely restricted.[30] As Morokvasic has noted, the socio-cultural constraints may not even apply to some categories of women already marginalized out of an acceptable (for women) and recognized status in a given society.[31] Those who have transgressed the limits of sometimes rigidly defined sex-role behaviour, such as having children out of wedlock, may even be under some social pressure to leave. Seller has quoted examples of maverick women who came to the United States because their political activities in their home countries angered their families.[32]

An important reason for migration that applies only to women and not to men is the desire to escape sex-role constraints or the limitations imposed by their subordinate position. Women 'came because they preferred the freedom and independence of even poorly paid work in the United States to the dependence of unpaid work in the home of parents or a future husband. For them, immigration was a rejection, conscious or unconscious, of traditional sex roles'.[33] In internal migration, too, women often state freedom from traditional norms and restrictions as a main reason for their migration, and this has been a major motivation of young, single Malay women who moved from the villages to urban areas in Malaysia.[34] For married Turkish women, too, migration is attractive as a means by which they can alter their previous inferior status in the household, where, as brides who have 'married in', they are essentially outsiders.[35]

Another motive for migration that is specific to women is marriage-related, as described in the models of Thadani and Todaro, and Behrman and Wolfe.[36] A large proportion of the sequential village migration in India is attributed to marriage reasons,[37] with the underlying explanations most often stated in terms of the emphasis placed on the conjugal and reproductive

[30] N. Abadan-Unat, 'Implications of Migration on Emancipation and Pseudo-Emancipation of Turkish Women', *International Migration Review*, 11 (1977).

[31] Morokvasic (1984), op. cit. in n. 1, p. 898.

[32] M. S. Seller (ed.), *Immigrant Women* (Philadelphia, 1981), p. 17.

[33] Ibid., p. 21.

[34] J. Ariffin, 'The Adaptation Process and Adaptive Strategies of Female Urban–Rural Migrants: The Case of Malay Factory Girls in Malaysia', paper presented at the Young Workers' Education Project Workshop on Social Development of Factory Workers, Universiti Sains Malaysia, Penang, 1981.

[35] A. Kudat, 'Structural Change in the Migrant Turkish Family', in R. E. Krane (ed.), *Manpower Mobility Across Cultural Boundaries* (Leiden, 1975); F. J. Davis and B. S. Heyl, 'Turkish Women and Guestworker Migration to West Germany', in R. J. Simon and C. B. Brettell (eds.), *International Migration: The Female Experience* (New Jersey, 1986).

[36] Thadani and Todaro, op. cit. in nn. 1, 3; Behrman and Wolfe, op. cit. in n. 1.

[37] International Center for Research on Women, op. cit. in n. 1, p. 97.

roles of women in such societies, and the unequal sex ratios not just within villages, but also within specific status and caste groups.[38] Marriage has also been a significant explanation of women's predominance in immigration to the United States since 1930.[39] Certainly, the phenomenon of Filipino 'mail order brides' who have been sought in increasing numbers by men in Britain, Sweden, Canada, Australia, and West Germany is closely related to the stereotype image of 'a quietly spoken, docile companion who combines sexual attraction with gratitude to her "master" for rescuing her from poverty'.[40] But there is also evidence of single women who emigrated to avoid an unwanted marriage, to evade family or Church pressures that customarily enforce stable marriage,[41] to formalize a separation,[42] or to get away from marital discord and physical violence by spouses.[43]

The International Center for Research on Women noted, however, that the motives of women migrants may differ from those of men only in expression; the reasons given need not correspond with the real reasons for migration. Women may cite marriage, because it is one of the few culturally accepted explanations or rationalizations for their autonomous migration, but the actual motivation may be economic.[44]

Although for women, as for men, economic factors are commonly the basic reason for migration, and there may be no sex-differential in the economic motive, the underlying trigger for women's migration may be related to their more insecure employment and income position compared with that of men. There have been indications that women's migration is more likely to occur in areas where men control agricultural ownership and production and where women have been displaced in rural areas by agricultural mechanization and the destruction of cottage industries.[45] Where women, because of their subordinate position, have little control over, or access to, resources, for instance through being disadvantaged in terms of property rights in patrilineal societies,[46] the incentive to migrate may be strong. For educated women in rural areas, the incentive to move may be even stronger, because there is often less for educated women to do in the villages than there is for educated men.[47] Of course, education itself is an important reason for migration. Where women were previously disadvantaged, the

---

[38] A. Bose, 'Migration Streams in India', *Population Review*, 2 (1967).

[39] M. Houston, R. Kramer, and J. H. Barrett, 'Female Predominance in Immigration to the United States since 1930: A First Look', *International Migration Review*, 18 (1984), pp. 908–63.

[40] *New Straits Times*, 7 Feb. 1988.

[41] Connell, op. cit. in n. 1, p. 966.

[42] N. Foner, 'Sex Roles and Sensibilities: Jamaican Women in New York and London', in Simon and Brettell, op. cit. in n. 35.

[43] M. Morokvasic, *Yugoslav Women in France, Germany, and Sweden* (Paris, 1980).

[44] International Center for Research on Women, op. cit. in n. 1, p. 87.

[45] Sassen-Koob, op. cit. in n. 1; Young, op. cit. in n. 1.

[46] Abadan-Unat, op. cit. in n. 30.

[47] Ware, op. cit. in n. 5, p. 147.

liberalization of educational opportunities may represent an important pull factor.

Women's relative position may also affect their perceptions of the chances of attaining their migration goals. The expectancy component of women's motivation to migrate would be influenced, for example, by opportunity-structure differentials that are gender-related. The bias of certain labour markets in favour of women workers, such as in the labour-intensive, export-oriented manufacturing sector or in overseas markets for domestic servants, would not only attract female workers but also strengthen their expectation that their migration goals would be achieved.

It has certainly been the phenomenal growth of female-intensive employment opportunities in the export-processing zones that has prompted unprecedented numbers of young single girls to migrate on their own to urban areas to take up wage employment for the first time, where previously they might have remained at home or on the farm waiting to marry and have children. Many urbanward migration streams are female-intensive in the Asian Pacific rim countries like Hong Kong, the Republic of Korea, Singapore, Malaysia, Philippines, and Thailand, because such an industrialization strategy has been applied in these countries since the 1960s. While the labour-intensive industrialization strategy has been the important pull-factor, this itself has been predicated on the exploitation of certain identified 'feminine' qualities and aspects of women's social position in these societies. The industrialization strategy has created a demand for women rather than for men, because women 'are generally tractable, being used to obedience to men within their traditional social structures, cheaper, and can be more easily laid off than men, due to their lower status, and tradition of economic dependence that leads them to view themselves as supplementary earners'. There is also a 'natural shedding' at marriage, when many choose to leave the labour force, and no maternity benefits need to be paid. Women are generally accustomed to painstaking work and have quite small and nimble fingers, and they seldom directly express anger, frustration, or resentment at work.[48] At the same time, several writers have pointed out that women in these Asian Pacific rim countries have been able to respond to the growth of employment opportunities through autonomous migration because there has been 'a lack of institutional barriers to entry . . . there are no socio-cultural barriers to female economic participation, and that demographic and education patterns ensure that there is a supply of qualified female labour'.[49]

---

[48] E. Eisold, *Young Women Workers in Export Industries: The Case of the Semiconductor Industry in Southeast Asia* (Geneva, 1984).

[49] S. E. Khoo, 'Development and Women's Participation in the Modern Economy: Asia and the Pacific', in UN, *Women's Economic Participation in Asia and the Pacific* (Bangkok, 1987), p. 33. See also Eisold, op. cit. in n. 48; L. L. Lim, *Economic Dynamism and Structural Transformation in the Asian Pacific Rim Countries: Contributions of the Second Sex* (Tokyo, 1988); Jones, op. cit. in n. 1.

It is also the subservient, insecure position of women, coupled with their abject poverty, that helps ensure a high demand for female labour in international labour markets. A significant feature of the world economy since the 1970s is temporary international labour migration with the sex-component turned upside down, where the women leave hearth and home in search of work, mainly as domestic servants, or in the entertainment industry. Again, the opportunities that are available overseas are related to women's traditional roles and lowly positions.[50] Countries like the Philippines, Sri Lanka, and Thailand have come to rely increasingly for their foreign-exchange earnings on the 'comparative advantage of women's disadvantages'.[51]

In terms of the influence of individual background characteristics on the relationship between a woman's status and migration, other than educational attainment and marital status which have already been discussed, the stage of her life cycle and birth order in the family could be significant. In so far as a woman's relative position is not static but changes over her life course, so, too, her propensity for autogenic migration would tend to alter. The timing of migration in relation to a woman's life cycle and that of her family often has consequences for women's strategies for dealing with changing roles in the migration process.[52]

Depending upon societal norms, changing marital status has been identified as a particularly salient motive for migration. At young, working, and marriageable ages, the motive for migration would tend to be stronger. As a young bride and new daughter-in-law, a woman may be in a singularly powerless position, even though her incentive to migrate may be strong to cut the links with her husband's family in patriarchal and patrilocal societies.[53] As a mother of young children with domestic responsibilities, her ability to migrate for income-generating purposes may be determined by her ability to manage multiple roles, or to find new solutions for 'old' roles. Where the emphasis in the society is on the reproductive and domestic roles of women, their migration at certain stages of their life cycle may be curtailed. Mexican women tend to be underrepresented among undocumented migrants to the United States primarily because of the presence and need to care for children.[54]

[50] *Asia Magazine*, 6 and 20 Sept. 1987; L. L. Lim, 'International Labour Migration in the ASEAN Region: The Main Perspectives', in National Union of Plantation Workers and Population Studies Unit, *Current Issues in Labour Migration in Malaysia* (Kuala Lumpur, 1988).
[51] S. E. Charlton, *Women in Third World Development* (Boulder, Colo., 1984).
[52] L. Lamphere, 'Working Mothers and Family Strategies: Portuguese and Colombian Women in a New England Community', in Simon and Brettell, op. cit. in n. 35.
[53] Ware, op. cit. in n. 5, p. 162.
[54] D. S. Massey, R. Alarcon, J. Durand, and H. Gonzalez, *Return to Aztlan: The Social Process of International Migration from Western Mexico* (Berkeley, Calif., 1987); M. P. Fernandez-Kelly, 'Mexican Border Industrialization, Female Labor Force Participation and Migration', in J. Nash and M. P. Fernandez-Kelly (eds.), *Women, Men, and the International Division of Labor* (Albany, NY, 1983).

As a widow or divorcee, a woman may also be marginalized in her own society and be pressured to leave.

A woman's birth order in her family may also affect her migration propensity. In traditional villages in Malaysia, it is usually easier for younger daughters to migrate than for the first daughter in the family. The eldest daughter is normally entrusted with the responsibilities for the household chores when the mother goes to work in the rice fields or rubber smallholdings. When the mother is old and unable to perform the household work, it is the eldest daughter who is expected to relieve her.[55] While birth order appears to be linked to women's migration through the household duties assigned to daughters; for men's migration, the link appears to be more through inheritance rights.[56]

The Influence of the Family and Family Decision-Making

The familial setting is crucial for understanding women's status and women's migration, because it is in the family that women's subordination to men's authority is the most obvious and crucial influence on women's lives. It is the family that assigns or defines roles for women which inevitably determine the relative motivation and incentive to migrate, and it is also the family that provides the resources and information that could support or discourage the move. Hugo has described the 'affinity, information and facilitating' influences of the family on individual migration.[57]

As indicated in the family block in Fig. 11.1, and as set out in Harbison's model, several aspects of the structure and functions of the family could affect women's roles and status, and, indirectly, the motivation to migrate. First, as a subsistence unit, the family assigns jobs in the family labour force, and whether the female member can move out would depend on whether her role can be filled by others in the family. As a subsistence unit, the family also governs the access of individual members to resources such as landholdings; where the female member has limited access to resources, the motivation for her to migrate may be strong. Secondly, as an economic maximization unit, the family may encourage the migration of female members, often as marriage migration or under the auspices of an extended kinship network. By providing access to its resources, the family reduces the sons' motives to migrate by encouraging marriage migration of daughters and providing financial and social support for the process, but increases both the availability and expectancy associated with migration for daughters.[58] Thirdly, as a socialization unit, the family could internalize social norms and

[55] Ariffin, op. cit. in n. 34.

[56] J. B. Wyon and J. E. Gordon, *The Khanna Study: Population Problems in the Rural Punjab* (Cambridge, Mass., 1971).

[57] Hugo, op. cit. in n. 9.

[58] Harbison, op. cit. in n. 7, p. 239.

values that encourage the independent behaviour of sons, and the sense of affinity and dependence of daughters. The related hypothesis is that, the stronger the feelings of attachment to the family, the lower the propensity to migrate. Perhaps most important for women's migration is the function of the family in terms of social connections and assistance, expressed through networks of rights and obligations. The availability and expectancy of women's motivation to migrate is greatly enhanced by kinship networks and the presence of kin in the place of destination. Women tend to make most use of the opportunities for transport, accommodation, and employment arranged primarily through social relationships.[59] Ariffin, in his Malaysian survey, stressed that almost all the young single migrant girls were allowed by their parents to migrate only because they were assured that their relatives in the city would look after their daughters.[60] In this context, too, 'chain migration' tends to be more important for women than for men.

Household strategies of migration can be viewed from two perspectives. One view is to assume that families make cost-benefit decisions that attempt to balance the earnings expected from migration against the expected costs of movement. The other is that families send members abroad not only to maximize earnings but also to minimize the risks associated with ties to the local economy.[61] In considering women's migration as part of household strategies, there are three possibilities: an individual family member will be 'selected out' for migration with the expectation that she/he will send back remittances to contribute to the family economic portfolio, an individual member will be sent out with the expectation that other family members will be sent for, or the family may migrate as a unit.

The role which women play as participants on these strategies—the amount of active participation in the decision-making process, whether they are passively selected out to migrate, or whether they are initiators of the idea even when they themselves do not move and it is only the men who move—would hinge on their position within the family and on power relations between family members. Even in associational migration, women could have a role in motivating the family to move or not to move. Among the Mossi of Upper Volta, attempts at resettling overcrowded rural populations originally failed because the Mossi wives refused to stay in the new areas where there were no markets or schools.[62]

Younger daughters tend to be the ones selected for migration because they are not needed to help in agricultural work or household chores, and

[59] G. Hugo, *Population Mobility in West Java* (Yogyakarta, 1978); K. Hart, 'Informal Income Opportunities and Urban Employment in Ghana', *Journal of Modern African Studies*, 11 (1971).

[60] Ariffin, op. cit. in n. 34, p. 14.

[61] D. S. Massey, 'Economic Development and International Migration', *Population and Development Review*, 14 (1988), pp. 383–413; E. Katz and O. Stark, 'Labour Migration and Risk Aversion in Less Developed Countries', *Journal of Labor Economics*, 4 (1986).

[62] Ware, op. cit. in n. 5, p. 162.

there are no viable alternatives for them in the rural areas. Daughters tend to be seen as particularly reliable sources of remittances as they are 'more willing and faithful than sons in sharing their savings with the family'.[63] By migrating, young single women are able to help other family members in ways that would not be possible if they stayed in the rural home. The migration of young women and the subsequent assistance is part of a strategy which, in the long run, helps to maintain the family as a unit.[64] Young and Salih found that

at times, the working daughter's income is even taken for granted by family members simply because of its regularity, as different from income from village work. In the same way, if any of the other members of the household needed extra money, for any out of the ordinary expenditure such as medical expenses, she is the one they turn to, simply because of her assured income.[65]

In other cases, it may be the women in the household who secure the first labour contract and who are 'strongly urged by their fathers, husbands, or other relatives to take up industrial jobs in foreign countries by which they could secure lucrative positions with higher income possibilities for their male relatives'.[66] In this way, where daughters were previously considered to be liabilities in the family, they have now become assets. Households may, in fact, decide to invest in the education of their daughters and attempt to follow a strategy that leads to upward mobility through sending their educated daughters into better-paid formal sector employment.[67]

Conclusion

In this chapter I have attempted to highlight the complex but important ways in which gender relations influence women's motives and potential for migration. Because of the complexity of the processes involved, it is not possible for policy purposes to predict that women's autonomy will automatically increase (or reduce) women's migration. What emerges from the chapter is that women's relative position will clearly determine the motives for their migration and the composition of migration streams (not just in terms of sex-selectivity, but also in terms of characteristics of the women who are able to move and whether they are involved only in associational and chain migration or in 'first-wave' autonomous migration). The com-

---

[63] Hart, op. cit. in n. 59, p. 133.

[64] L. Trager, 'Family Strategies and the Migration of Women: Migrants to Dagupan City, Philippines', *International Migration Review*, 18 (1984), pp. 1264–77, esp. p. 1274.

[65] M. L. Young and K. Salih, 'Industrialization, Retrenchment and Household Processes: Implications of the Recession', paper presented at the Himpunan Sains Social IV, Persatuan Sains Social, Malaysia, Kuala Lumpur, 1986.

[66] Abadan-Unat, op. cit. in n. 30.

[67] Trager, op. cit. in n. 64.

position of migration streams and the characteristics of the women who are motivated and able to move will have an impact on the labour-market dynamics in areas of both origin and destination.

The chapter has been focused only on women's relative position as a determinant of women's migration, but it has not dealt with the other very important side of the relationships. Fig. 11.1 did not indicate the interactive or feedback effects that even temporary migration could have in transforming the organization of sex roles in the society, the structure and functions of the family, or the roles and relative position of individual women. In so far as women migrate to escape subordination to men's authority, whether and how they achieve this goal, whether the emancipation of women is a cause or a consequence of autonomous women's migration, whether migration leads only to 'pseudo-emancipation' of women are all important questions. To show the impact of migration on women's status, however, would require not only clarification of the circumstances of migration and the socio-cultural environment, but also sorting out the changes in women's position that stem from the influence of migration on opportunities and social norms in the new environment, from those resulting from changes in women's roles or behavioural patterns. Of course, migrant status is itself a determinant of women's relative position.

Part II

Women's Position as an Outcome of Demographic Change

12 Historical Features of Women's Position in Society

SØLVI SOGNER

Historical Demography, History, and Women's History

When the battle-cry to make women more visible in history was raised during the 1960s and became louder during the 1970s, historical demographers and family historians felt more comfortable than most. Had they not meticulously registered women *and* men, actually even more women than men? Did they not work at the family-level, the very arena of women's actions? And did they not measure fertility per woman-year, make in-depth studies of breast-feeding practices, discuss post-partum amenorrhoea? Did they not in their researches discuss virtually all problems separately for each sex, and thus highlight living conditions for women as well as for men? Surely, the historical demographers were safe against any possible accusation of discriminating against women. They were appalled when such criticisms were directed against them.[1]

This self-righteous attitude is justified only up to a point. It tends to overlook women as historical actors in their own right—albeit passive actors—and fails to discuss what women's position in society may have meant for demographic development in general. This blindness to women is, of course, connected with what the researchers have been trying to achieve. Historical demography uses a statistical approach, and focuses on population conditions and population development at a level of abstraction where women as such seem hardly more interesting than men as such.

In a similar vein, general history has been concerned with the nation, the state, society at large, and, in the historical arena at this level, women have been conspicuously absent. A common explanation for women's absence from historiography has, therefore, been that they were not there to be

[1] M. Chaytor, 'Household and Kinship: Ryton in the Late Sixteenth and Early Seventeenth Centuries', *History Workshop*, 10 (1980), pp. 25–60; L. J. Jordanova, 'The History of the Family', in Cambridge Women's Studies Group, *Women in Society: Interdisciplinary Essays* (London, 1981), pp. 41–54; R. Rapp, E. Ross, and R. Bridenthal, 'Examining Family History', in J. Newton (ed.), *Sex and Class in Women's History* (1983), pp. 232–58; L. A. Tilly, 'Women's History and Family History: Fruitful Collaboration or Missed Connection?', *Journal of Family History*, 12 (1987), pp. 303–15.

studied! Protagonists of women's history have not been content with this explanation. They claim that, if looked for carefully, women will be found. They may be found in places that are unfamiliar to traditional research, but it is the historian's duty to look for them where they are. Women constitute more than half of *man*kind. Women's history, therefore, is central to our understanding of the past. If historians have defined the project of history so narrowly as to exclude women, they must reconsider what they are doing.

Women's historians are working to clarify women's roles in the past, and some considerable progress has been achieved since the 1970s.[2] A staggering amount of information on women's past has been published, belying the early sceptical attitude among historians that sources were not available to permit insights of this sort. The work has been characterized by ingenious use of source material, new and old, and a strong will to pursue the stated aim. We are still only in the initial phase of this work. Women's history is among the liveliest of research fields in history at present, and is pursued with great enthusiasm. The literature is much too comprehensive for exhaustive citation, and the references given here include only a few titles that I have found useful myself.

It is already becoming evident that the new insights that we have acquired into women's past are going to have a lasting impact on mainstream history. It will no longer be possible to claim that women's position in society can rightfully be subsumed under a general heading, as if it were no different from that of men. The concept of gender has been coined with this view in mind. The social and historical experiences of women differed from those of men, because of their sex. 'One is not born, but becomes a woman,' is a well-known quotation from Simone de Beauvoir. Male gender and female gender signify the respective social roles played by the sexes.[3] History as traditionally pursued has been focused mainly on men's experience and can be characterized as having been 'male-specific'. In order to make history genuinely general and all-comprising, women's experience must be recognized not as a special case, but as having as general an interest as men's history. The experiences of the two sexes are of equal importance to general history, and history must eventually be rewritten with this in mind.[4]

If this idea for history in general is accepted, it is natural to extend it to historical demography. Historical demographers and family historians

---

[2] N. Davis, 'Women's History in Transition: The European Case', *Feminist Studies* (1976), pp. 83–103; O. Hufton and J. Scott, 'Survey Articles: Women in History', *Past and Present*, 101 (1983), pp. 125–57; R. Bridenthal, C. Koonz, and S. Stuard (eds.), *Becoming Visible: Women in European History*, 2nd edn. (Boston, 1987); M. J. Boxer and J. H. Quataert (eds.), *Connecting Spheres: Women in the Western World, 1500 to the Present* (New York, 1987).

[3] J. Scott, 'Gender: A Useful Category of Historical Analysis', *American Historical Review*, 81 (1986), pp. 1053–75.

[4] G. Bock, *History, Women's History, Gender History* (Florence, 1987).

can and should profit from insights into women's history, in the same manner as demography proper may profit from women's studies. During the 1960s and 1970s, the heyday of historical demography, to have posed a problem in this manner would have seemed far-fetched, to say the least. A heavy theoretical determinism still saturated historical demographic thinking. 'Malthusian traps', 'self-regulating mechanisms of population homoeostasis', 'natural fertility' were honoured words from this period. It seemed almost preposterous to surmise that our ancient forefathers, not to mention our foremothers, had in any way been masters and mistresses of their own fate—the bourgeoisie of Geneva and the high nobility always excluded! Pierre Goubert discarded the idea that his peasants in Beauvais were capable of regulating their own fertility. But, slowly, a change in attitude among researchers has come about. While marriage and migration have been recognized all along as actions that are controlled individually or socially, even fertility has increasingly been seen as controlled by human will to a surprising extent. The same shift in attitude may be seen as beginning to take place in regard to mortality, where increasing importance is being attributed to life-styles, in historical societies as well as in society today.[5]

The more we accept the active influence exerted by our ancestors on demographic phenomena in the past, the greater is the need to differentiate between them. To do so socially, by class, is widely recognized and done. But to analyse by sex is a novelty, and the need to do so is not necessarily recognized as yet.

Certain aspects of this new approach by gender, as it is at present being conceptualized and researched in history, will be the theme of this chapter. The European experience since the Middle Ages will be taken as the case in point. Our concern here is not with the specifically demographic aspects of women's historical experience, but rather with the general features of women's position in society, as a background to our understanding of women's possible contribution to demographic change. Empirical results are slowly coming in, and show great regional and local, not to mention social, differences. We are not looking for a development from 'bad to good', or from 'good to bad'. Researchers do not seek value-judgements of this kind, but rather a fair evaluation of women's position in society as compared to men's, in different historical periods, and judged by the standards of the age. To turn such an undertaking into a study of oppression, harassment, and injustice must be avoided. The purpose is to understand how society functioned, and, in particular, the roles played by women. The provisional character of the points of view put forward should be borne in mind.

---

[5] G. Carlsson, 'Mortality: Trends, Fluctuations and their Socio-cultural Background', in A. Brändström and L.-G. Tedebrand (eds.), *Society, Health and Population during the Demographic Transition* (Umeå, 1988), pp. 395–411.

Women's Public Power

'I know I have the body of a weak and feeble woman, but I have the heart and stomach of a king,' said Queen Elizabeth I in her famous pep-talk to the English army at Tilbury in 1588, waiting for the Spanish Armada to attack the British coasts.[6]

Queen Elizabeth is exemplary in several ways. Women have certainly not been totally absent, either in the reality of the past, or in the history written about that past. Prominent women at least have been visible when on occasion they have held the main stage, wielding power.

The Queen's choice of words implies that one should have confidence in her because of her kingly, i.e. manly, qualities; pathetic, maybe, but realistic. Formal positions of power in society have traditionally been held by men, throughout history.

Changes of power in society will, however, depend on how society is organized, and are highly relevant not only for women's position, but also for men's. We must remember that political power was a privilege of élites right up to the rise of the modern democracies during the nineteenth and twentieth centuries. Queen Elizabeth I certainly held more power four hundred years ago than Queen Elizabeth II does today. But a most interesting phenomenon of recent years has been the position of power held by Margaret Thatcher.

Formal positions of power during the classical period of feudal medieval society reverted to women as well as to men, and this happened usually through inheritance, or marriage and subsequent widowhood. During the early Middle Ages this was certainly not so. Fiefs were, in principle, held in return for military service and counsel, and constituted the material part of the personal bondage between vassal and lord. When fiefs gradually became hereditary, problems arose. If a woman was the heir, the services due to be provided might be imperilled; because of 'the weakness of her sex', she could not furnish them herself. But solutions to the problem were found. Someone could be found to represent her, and assume the duty on her behalf. 'There can be no doubt that originally women were entirely excluded from any right of feudal succession, but here again the gradual "patrimonialization" of fiefs came to affect the issue . . . What had first been only an exceptional favour gradually became a general practice and finally a right.'[7]

As Jack Goody has pointed out, distinguishing features of the European inheritance system were women's right to inherit, and the possibility of transferring landed property to and through women, as inheritance or as dower.[8] Political office might also be linked to the inheritance of land, as in

---

[6] J. E. Neale, *Queen Elizabeth* (London, 1934), p. 298.
[7] F. L. Ganshof, *Feudalism* (New York, 1961), p. 143.
[8] J. Goody, J. Thirsk and E. P. Thompson (eds.), *Family and Inheritance: Rural Society in*

the case of feudalism, where civil, judicial, and military administration usually went with the fief. Hence, in this society familial considerations and marriage alliances might serve as means towards political ends. Women were, of course, important as pawns in these games, but it is reasonable to assume that they might also reap personal profits and increase their influence. We may claim that the state had not yet developed into so specialized an organization in its own right that familial ways of thinking had become obsolete for the upper echelons of society. For women and women's position this must have had some importance. But it would hardly be right—as some have done—to contend that medieval women in general occupied an altogether different and more dominating political position in society than later, although individual examples can be found.[9] What we can argue is that the social fabric of medieval and early modern society was still fluid, and hence women might exert formal political power in their own right in special circumstances.

The political consequences of the rise of the so-called nation state during early modern times, from the 1500s onwards, were in many ways detrimental to women. It can be argued that the formalization of the political institutions of the State, and the bureaucratization that went with it, increasingly petrified the division of society into a public and a private sector. With a steadily wider separation, it became increasingly difficult to move from one sector to the other. And women were increasingly confined within the private sector. The institutions of the new state were run by professional administrators who obtained access to these positions, not primarily through inheritance and family connections, but through proven abilities within a gradually growing educational system to which women were not admitted. Division of knowledge is an important concept for understanding the gender system; it has been argued very convincingly that superimposing a division of knowledge on top of an ancient division of labour between the sexes made the latter very durable, and strengthened inherent tendencies towards the creation of a hierarchy.[10]

The women's rights movement during the last century and the beginning of the present century developed from this state of affairs.[11] Women's public

Western Europe 1200–1800 (Cambridge, 1976); M. Kaplan (ed.), *The Marriage Bargain: Women and Dowries in European History* (New York, 1985).

[9] J. Kelly, 'Did Women have a Renaissance?', in Bridenthal, Koonz, and Stuard, op. cit. in n. 2; reprinted posthumously in J. Kelly, *Women, History and Theory: The Essays of Joan Kelly* (Chicago, 1984); reviewed by G. R. Elton, 'History according to St Joan', *American Scholar*, 54 (1985), pp. 549–55, and by M. C. Horowitz, 'The Woman Question in Renaissance Texts', *History of European Ideas*, 8 (1987), pp. 587–95.

[10] G. Kyle, 'Arbetsdelning, tidsfördelning och kunskapstilldelning: Om kvinnors och mäns samhällsvillkor', *Historisk tidskrift* (1987), pp. 481–504, with English summary.

[11] R. Evans, *The Feminists: Women's Emancipation Movements in Europe, America and Australasia, 1840–1920* (London, 1979); I. Blom, 'Women's Politics and Women in Politics in Norway since the End of the Nineteenth Century', *Scandinavian Journal of History*, 12 (1987), pp. 17–33.

role had weakened, as the public sector was growing in importance. The State was continually increasing its grip and influence on social matters, and passing laws and regulations on matters previously outside the public realm. The women's rights movement was focused on questions concerning political or public power such as the suffrage, age at legal majority, the right to a formal education, and the right to hold public office. It should be borne in mind that some of these rights were new for men as well during this period. They were gradually conceded to men in accordance with a general democratization of society. But this very democratization at first explicitly excluded women! Upper- and middle-class women regarded the extension of democratic rights to men of all classes, i.e. from lower classes than their own, as an affront to themselves. The women's rights movement was to a great extent an effort to put right what was in the process of being lost for women through the measures that formalized these rights and extended them to males in general! Neither should it be overlooked that when men of the upper and middle classes, who had monopolized political power for centuries, now acquiesced in conceding political rights to women, they were hoping for their support in return—a support badly needed at a time of increasing class consciousness and strife.

The political upheavals of the nineteenth century were hotly debated. John Stuart Mill was the first liberal feminist of some renown to break an age-old tradition according to which women were held to be of lesser quality than men, and naturally subordinate to them. The importance of religion and ideology combining forces and being superimposed on women's socio-economic reality had been decisive in conceptualizing this specific social role of women. All the major thinkers through the ages—from Plato and Aristotle in antiquity, by way of the Christian fathers like Augustine and Thomas Aquinas, to influential eighteenth-century philosophers like Rousseau—were agreed on women's natural inferiority. Women writers and women philosophers, however, had produced ample—but less well-known and less influential—written evidence of a feminist awareness of, and protest against, these ideas at least as far back as the late Middle Ages and the Renaissance. They may have argued their case very convincingly, but they were quite unsuccessful. Change came, for women of all classes as it did for men of the lower classes, only in the wake of the French Revolution and the new concepts of human rights—slowly, after setbacks and reactionary counter-movements.

Women, Family, Community, and Work

The women's rights movement was, characteristically, the first field of research that attracted those interested in women's history. It was an important theme. But history in confrontation with real life soon led to new research problems. Why was it, asked observers of women's actual position in society, that this position had changed so little even after women had obtained full legal equality? Why did not women in general make full use of their newly acquired rights as full citizens? Why were women still conspicuously absent from society's principal stage, in the power hierarchies? A fuller view was needed of the totality of women's situation. What did women actually do? What held them back? The dialectics of research and politics in this situation were striking.

Women have, in general, been greatly lacking in political power throughout history. Informal power is another matter.[12] By its very nature, this form of power is not easily measured. It is easier to assess women's position in this respect in an indirect way, by looking at how women were actually placed with respect to the possibility of exerting power and influence. We must then look for women in the home, at work, and in the local community.

The home, the family household, seemed the obvious place to look for women, as housework was women's very own domain, not shared by men. Women's reproductive role, as mothers of and carers for children and the family, seemed to bind them tightly to the home. And subsequent research has borne out all premonitions: bearing and raising children on the one hand, keeping house on the other, seem to have been the two main activities of the great majority of women throughout the ages. However, great fluctuations have been found to exist, by class, and by period. Fertility patterns varied, but we shall not deal with this subject here, as it will be familiar to demographers. Instead, we shall look more closely at the housework–housekeeping activity.

One does not have to go far back in time before the character of housework changed completely. The consumer household of today was the producer household of former days. The most extreme case would be the more-or-less self-sufficient farming household, which produced most of the commodities needed: clothes, food, implements, etc. But households in general were far more productive than we are used to, as an artisan's shop, etc., was closely connected with the living-quarters of the artisan's family, and women were intricately involved in its activities, as the arena of production and the arena of housework were more or less the same.

Women's work has attracted a lot of research attention during the last decade.[13] Women's double role as productive workers and as homemakers— triple role if their reproductive functions are included! —can be followed over the centuries along two lines of development. One leads to their role as professional housewife, the other to that of market-connected wage-worker.

---

[12] M. Stacey and M. Price, *Women, Power and Politics* (London, 1981).

[13] L. A. Tilly and J. W. Scott, *Women, Work and the Family* (New York, 1978); L. Charles and L. Duffin (eds.), *Women and Work in Preindustrial England* (Dover, 1985); B. A. Hanawalt (ed.), *Women and Work in Preindustrial Europe* (Bloomington, Ind., 1986).

Again, as in our discussion of women's political power, we are struck by the difficulty of comparing different historical periods. Just as the political organization of the State is different today from what it was hundreds of years ago, so the economic organization of production is different. Our way of looking at the problems is misguided. Even if 'women's place was in the home' for many centuries,[14] this does not mean that women did not contribute to the economic production of society, even by our current definitions which exclude housework as unproductive. Production in pre-industrial society was organized by household, for men as well as for women, and women participated in it fully.

But women's working space was more restricted than men's:

Working women were homebodies. Their participation in the economy rarely necessitated their leaving their quarter of a city, or their village. At most, they went to markets several miles from their household, or came from surrounding villages to find work as domestics or laborers in nearby towns . . . The merchant-class women . . . might control considerable capital as widows, but they never engaged in long-distance trade or went to the cloth fairs. Both the demands of family and household and the social attitudes that frowned on women traveling alone inhibited their personal participation in the larger market economy outside their cities and in the international markets.[15]

And women ordinarily performed tasks different from those of men. Basically, the sexual division of work—which seems to go back to times immemorial and the dawn of human society[16]—may be seen as the first step towards specialization, and as positive as regards possibilities of achievement, inasmuch as specialized insights and know-how are developed. Sexual division of work tended to lead to sexual division of knowledge, as well as separate areas of action, sexual division of space and time. It is not a question of rigid compartmentalization. There will be considerable overlap. What is considered men's or women's work has varied over time, by social class, by region, by age group, by marital status. Still, it seems fundamentally true that a division of activities by sex has been a near-to-basic characteristic of human society in history. Considering the biological differences between the two sexes, it is not difficult to accept this as having originally been a natural state of affairs in hunting and gathering societies millennia ago. What is more difficult to understand is the perpetuation of this state of affairs through history in societies based on different economic systems, such as the feudal agrarian economy of medieval times, the merchant capitalism of the early modern, or the industrial capitalism of the modern period.

---

[14] J. C. Brown, 'A Woman's Place was in the Home: Women's Work in Renaissance Tuscany', in M. W. Ferguson, M. Quilligan, and N. J. Vickers (eds.), *Rewriting the Renaissance: The Discourse of Sexual Differences in Early Modern Europe* (Chicago, 1986), pp. 206–24.

[15] Hanawalt, op. cit. in n. 13, p. viii.

[16] G. Lerner, *The Creation of Patriarchy* (Oxford, 1986); reviewed by M. S. Rosenhan, in *History of European Ideas*, 8 (1987), pp. 581–87.

In the countryside, the main divisions between men's and women's work would be between outdoor- and indoor-work, with flexible adjustments. In towns, women worked alongside men in the shop, but they usually performed different tasks. Women were active in the local market, but in general they did not take finished products to sell in distant markets and fairs, because their possibilities to move about freely were more restricted.

From the point of view of training for adult life and the acquisition of the necessary knowledge, women seem to have been trained by other women. If this could not be accomplished at home, by the mother or other females in the household, girls were sent to be trained elsewhere, mostly in other people's households. Girls were trained for homemaking and housework, but also for such production for the market as could be carried on at home. Training in a household production setting was also the boys' lot, but a wider spectrum of training possibilities was open to them. For instance, learning a trade within a guild-organized artisanry was not usually open to women. There were hardly any all-female guilds or guilds with equal membership. Even in these guilds, women did not hold magisterial office; the guilds were run by males.

However, women more often than men specialized in becoming generalists, to use a somewhat paradoxical expression. Women's work-pattern in the pre-industrial economy has been described as an economy of makeshift or expediency. It is very illuminating that, unless an artisan's daughter married a man in the trade that was carried on in her parental home, and of which she therefore had some knowledge, she would not be able to continue in this trade—but would be expected to adjust to her husband's trade, and thus change her work-pattern. To be flexible in this way—jills of all trades and mistresses of none—may have had negative consequences on women's work-performance. Having mostly received informal training and not being full guild members, women's work identity was weak, and their identity as family member strong.

A golden age of women's work and women's economic power in a pre-industrial economy has not so far been discovered. Women worked and worked hard, both within and outside their families. Women's role in the urban economy is of special interest, for here we find the dynamics of change that was to transform the agrarian economy. Women in towns were exceedingly active. They might run their own business and exert considerable influence in their own right, even if they were considered minors in the view of the law, and were not legally capable of entering into binding contracts, or of transacting business on an equal footing with men. However, in one study after another of the reality of women's activities it has been found that practice differed from theory. But, as a rule, women were excluded from leading positions within the formal organizations of work, in guilds, and from similar positions within municipal management. And, even if one finds women in a wide range of urban activities in the pre-industrial economy, these activities were not the most important. It seems invariably to have been the case that women's wages were lower, just as the law in general provided for a smaller share in inheritance for women: daughters often only inherited half the share of sons. In particular, severe restrictions were put upon the inheritance of land by women. This only changed gradually during the nineteenth century.

The traditionally dominant position of the family household within the social organization as we know it from historical research will, of necessity, have provided a practical arena of everyday life for women's influence and power. The ebb and flow of this form of influence, however, will have fluctuated with the changing importance of the household. A strong case can be made out for a sharp decrease during the last two centuries.[17] With the decreasing importance of the role of the household, combined with men's increasing importance on the public scene, women's traditional power-base in the family household was seriously eroded.

Women's craving for public power was not alarmingly loud, as long as they continued to retain considerable informal power in the family household, and the decisions made in the household carried considerable impact in the local community. Households did not exist in isolation: they will have co-operated within communities—in work, in borrowing and lending, in caring for the sick, for those giving birth, for the old, and for children. Women will have taken a prominent part in these mutual neighbourhood activities. Women's informal 'networks' have been focused as a means of local power for women, as, for example, through 'gossip': in a world without modern media of mass-communication gossip is news-transmission. Testifying in court, giving evidence about a person's reputation in the local community, was within women's realm. Women might even take political action: we find them taking part in bread-riots. It is interesting to note that this was not penalized by society—a kind of equivocal recognition of women's legal subordinate status, coupled with their household responsibilities.[18] In an extension of this line of reasoning, it is obvious that women may have exercised considerable influence on informal community control, and their interest in public affairs may have been limited to this. When, later on, community affairs were organized politically, as part of the general process of democratization, they became men's exclusive domain, dependent upon suffrage.

The growth of proto-industry enabled women increasingly to incorporate paid work within the setting of their household and local community tasks. Women constituted flexible and cheap labour, easily exploitable, as they were tied down by family responsibilities and the need for household sub-

---

[17] K. Hausen, 'Patriarchat', *Journal für Geschichte*, 5 (1986), pp. 12–21.

[18] O. Hufton, 'Women in the Family Economy in Eighteenth Century France', *French Historical Studies*, 9 (1975), pp. 1–22.

sistence. The household was no longer merely the unit of residence and the unit of production; it also became the unit of consumption: 'The new industries which produced household consumer goods fed on a new household consumption organized by a labour-intensive housewifery.'[19] The role of women in this transitional development towards a fully industrialized society, with its rigid segregation of household and workplace, is still deplorably underresearched.

It was the better-off middle classes that led the way, by creating 'separate spheres' and enviable models for the lower classes to emulate.[20] So successful was the economic growth caused by industrialism in Western societies that 'homemaking' became a common way of life, open to families of lower social and economic status. Where the wife had worked alongside her husband, albeit at different tasks, she was now able to develop into a 'professional' housewife, spending all her time in an all-female domain. Households were transformed into 'sanctums' and 'doll-houses'—warm, cosy, clean, even elegant. They were deprived of their economic functions, as production was transferred to the factories. The modern housewife acquired a new role as mistress of the house—no doubt in many ways a very satisfying role and of benefit to the whole family. She was helped in her chores by young unmarried servant girls. A small proportion of the female population never married. They might be 'maiden-aunts' who lived with the family, and helped out in a more-or-less genteel servant's role. Or they might be engaged in wage-work in the market. But the overall dominant career of women was to be a married housewife.

An important aim of the women's rights movement had been to secure access for women to different kinds of paid work outside the home. For, as production was increasingly transferred to the factories, so were job opportunities. Ordinary manual work of all kinds had always been open to everyone. The women's rights movement had been pioneered, naturally, by upper- and middle-class women who wanted working opportunities that befitted their social status, and which would not demean them. So they worked to give women access to employment that required some formal education or special privilege. To a considerable extent this was achieved—we must not underrate the provider-problem of middle- and upper-class fathers. However, even when women were admitted to education and jobs previously closed to them, they were paid less and received less education, so that they tended to occupy subordinate positions in the labour-market hierarchy. Their range of work opportunities was more restricted. Some of

---

[19] M. Berg, *The Age of Manufactures: Industry, Innovation and Work in Britain, 1700–1820* (Glasgow, 1985), p. 173.
[20] L. Davidoff and C. Hall, *Family Fortunes: Men and Women of the English Middle Class, 780–1850* (London, 1987).

these characteristics may have been the consequence of others, but they seem rather to have centred on the gender aspect.[21]

Working in the market, outside the household, was not considered suitable for married women at first. But this situation did not last for long. The women managed their households, at first with the help of servants. Gradually the servants disappeared, preferring better-paid jobs in the market, free of the authority of the mistress of the house. Being a housewife became a very solitary role. Where had all the people gone who used to work alongside her? The working companionship that traditional marriage had constituted no longer existed. Husbands went to offices and factories, the servants moved into wage employment, and the productive activities in the household vanished.

The most recent development has been the exodus of married women into the labour market, managing their households on the side. The timing differed somewhat, but the trend was unmistakeable. Married women in Western societies have fully entered into the labour market, and have become full-time producers-consumers. The security of the familial home has been exchanged for the social security of society. The husband's provider-function as wage-earner, to which the wife's complementary role as housewife fitted as hand in glove, has been superseded by the wife as co-earner. From her own wages she is able to buy the food, the clothes, the services which she formerly provided by the work of her own hands. They may be more expensive, but they are available, can be bought, and she is able to pay. The double-income household can afford the modern way of life. No longer are women confined to their homes, to housewifery. For better or worse, they are back in the mainstream of productive activity, as used to be the case in pre-industrial society.

During the last two centuries women have played their specific part in the transformation of the organization of the productive life of society. They have seen their households deprived of productive functions and of workers other than themselves. They became homemaking specialists in a way unknown in previous history. We may discern two different attitudes taken by women to this new situation. On the one hand, there are those who have claimed equal participation for women in the economic life of society; on the other, there are those who have stood up for professionalization of their domestic role, modelling their situation on career-structures in society at large. Gradually, the general economic development of society proved the latter point of view to lead to a dead end. Homemaking is increasingly seen as representing the residual of traditional society, unvalued in economic terms, in striking contrast to all other social activities that are remunerated and priced. Professional housewives feel increasingly ill at

[21] G. Hagemann, 'Feminism and the Sexual Division of Labour: Famale Labour in the Norwegian Telegraph Service around the Turn of the Century', *Scandinavian Journal of History*, 10 (1975), pp. 143–54.

ease. They are no longer formally subjected to the authority of their husbands, but what is the reality? In a society where cash is becoming increasingly important, the unpaid situation of a housewife dependent for housekeeping money on her husband's wages is difficult. It becomes no easier when the consumption pattern of the household is increasingly shifting towards demand for expensive articles produced in the market, and not in the household.

Conclusion

Family-organization in society, as we are apt to conceive it—wage-earning husband, homemaking wife—is a transitional historical situation, characteristic of industrialized Western society of the nineteenth and twentieth centuries. In the post-industrial society of today—on the eve of the twenty-first century—only the vestiges of this structure are perceived, and for an observer without preconceived ideas it could be hard to unravel the familial organization which we believe is still the fundamental structure of our society.

History does not repeat itself. It tends to move, not in circles but in spirals. And to the historical observer it seems that the wheel of change has come almost full circle. The public and the private, the workplace and the home, had traditionally not been separate worlds. But during the course of history two separate worlds seem to have developed. A man's world and a woman's world developed at the same time and were probably more completely separate than ever before. This is now changing, and involves, we may add, a return to a more sexually integrated society, more like pre-industrial society, but based on a different system of production, and with a changed ideology.

Women historians have argued that a different periodization of history may be called for, if we are to judge by what has been important for women. Great events and landmarks in the history of mankind, such as the Reformation or the French Revolution, have not meant the same great leaps forward for women as for men. In women's history, the adoption of female methods of birth control may have loomed larger than these more famous turning-points. The fertility decline of the demographic transition, we may add, is one of the few great events of history where women's interests and actions have been given serious consideration by historians of all persuasions. However, history is the common history of both sexes. Traditional periodization will, therefore, concern women just as well as men. Birth control by itself is hardly as important as the technological transformation of production in Western society.

But looking at historical change while bearing in mind women's particular role in its development may be a heuristic device to find new insights. Take, for example, the fall in mortality that began around 1800 and gathered momentum during the course of the nineteenth century. It coincided with the historical development of the upgrading of women's domestic role, and with it their partial withdrawal from productive life. What may have been the cumulative effect on health and mortality of improvements in domestic conditions, brought about little by little by hardly observable changes introduced in the household by women who nurtured new ideas about what homemaking should be like? Women have been notorious—and often made into a laughing-stock—for their hostility towards alcohol and tobacco, which are today commonly recognized as among the most important causes of behaviourally determined mortality. What did it mean for the health and well-being of the family when the mother who previously had two jobs could devote more time to housewifery—to cleaning and airing the clothes, the bedding, the living quarters; to preparing and preserving food? The dreary drudgery of housekeeping does not catch the imagination. We are wont to look for more flamboyant advances, and are apt to overlook the housewife as the primary health worker on the very scene of action, on every scene of action.

13 The Effects of Fertility, Family Organization, Sex Structure of the Labour Market, and Technology on the Position of Women

HELEN WARE

Much of the past confusion over findings relating to the status or position of women has stemmed from a failure clearly to define the concepts used. In the most wide-ranging study of the status of women in pre-industrial societies[1] no less than fifty-two measures of the status of women were used, which, with any plausibility, could only be combined into a minimum of nine coherent scales. These represented property control, power of women in kinship contexts, the value placed on the lives of women, the value placed on their labour, their domestic authority, the ritualized separation of the sexes, the control over women's sexual lives, the ritualized fear of women, and the level of joint participation of both sexes in basic activities.

In this chapter I shall only be concerned with three specific aspects of the position of women: their autonomy, their economic power, and their prestige. Whilst each of these attributes can be viewed in an absolute sense, wherever a comparison is made or implied it is with men, rather than with other women. It should be noted that this is contrary to the way in which the great majority of women around the world actually think; their normal practice is to compare themselves with other women with whose situation they are familiar. Thus, it is said that consciousness of the iniquitous traditional division of labour, and hence the women's liberation movement, only came to Wales with the breakdown of the extended family which left women in the new nuclear families to compare their lot, not, as before, with their mothers and grandmothers, but with their husbands.[2]

It has taken a long time to accept that there is no necessary correlation between different aspects of the position of women.

The treatment of woman is one thing, her legal status another, while the character and extent of her labours belong again to a distinct category. Whatever correlations

[1] M. K. Whyte, *The Status of Women in Preindustrial Society* (Princeton, NJ, 1978).
[2] C. Harris, 'Introduction', in *The Family and Social Change* (London, 1983).

exist between any two of these aspects are empirical; conceptually they are diverse, and only confusion can result from ignoring the fact.[3]

So, too, with our three variables. Whilst there are multiple and obvious links between women's autonomy and their economic power, these links are not as inevitable as many women reared in the Western liberal tradition would expect. In many traditional cultures women may, for example, have considerable control over the products of their own labour whilst, at the same time, being totally subject to control over their marital and sexual behaviour, even after widowhood.

The question of women's prestige relative to that of men is essentially dependent upon men's interpretation of tradition; it does not normally depend upon women themselves. As we move from generation to generation, it is an interesting question how far women's behaviour can ultimately influence their prestige as a sex. It has often been suggested, for example, that women's work in the United Kingdom during the First World War was a major factor in their being granted the vote by an all-male parliament *after* the war. Of course, the prestige of any individual woman is very much dependent upon her behaviour and personal characteristics. This is, after all, one of the major constraints upon women's autonomy—there are just so many more ways in which a woman, as opposed to a man, can lose prestige, especially by what is categorized as sexual misbehaviour.

Autonomy essentially means the right to make and stand by one's own decisions. For women this means

deciding whether and whom to marry; deciding to terminate a union, controlling one's sexual freedom pre- and extra-maritally, controlling one's freedom of movement; having access to educational opportunities; *de facto* share of household power . . . and controlling reproduction and completed family size to the extent that this is biologically possible.[4]

This list is a very feminine one, essentially because so many of the items concern the domestic rather than the public sphere. A broader listing, that would give due weight to the public domain, would include freedom of political expression, of work and mobility, of family formation, duration and size, of education, of health and sexual control, and of cultural and religious expression.[5] Traditionally, women have been culturally conditioned to value prestige above economic power and autonomy. Thus, they have been glad to observe purdah, and willing to accept poorly paid but 'respectable' work, and a position of total economic dependence upon their husbands, all because they have valued reputation above all else. Yet, women have also been prepared to let men have the appearance of prestige, to let them

---

[3] R. Lowie, *Primitive Society* (New York, 1920), p. 187.
[4] Blumberg, as quoted by J. Giele, 'Introduction', in *Women: Roles and Status in Eight Countries* (New York, 1977), p. 4.
[5] Cf. Giele's alternative list (ibid.).

appear to make the decisions, whilst their own input remains unseen and unacknowledged, especially when men are telling the story.[6] Commonly, men have the formal public power, whilst women have the informal domestic power.[7] Much of the modern debate concerning the position of women has come about as women in general have begun to move into the public domain (where some élite women have always participated).

There are vast cultural variations in the position of women around the world. The range of variation is very large, precisely because the pattern of interrelationships between different factors varies from society to society. Few generalizations about women are universally valid. One which is implicit and which should be treated with suspicion is the belief that the position of women in modern industrialized societies is superior to that of women in traditional agrarian societies. As the discussion below will show, this generalization is invalid. It is based on a misunderstanding of the situation of women in Third World countries, as well as a First World oriented view of the appropriate criteria by which to judge. It needs to be recognized that most indicators of the status of women are heavily dependent upon the context. Take the case of a society in which purdah is practised by those women who can afford it. To the women and men in that society, purdah is associated with high prestige; but, to outsiders, women from poor households, who are free to come and go as they please, will appear to have the preferred position. From a squatter settlement, a gilded cage appears to be a very attractive prospect. Twentieth-century Western women place a very high value on autonomy and independence, whereas previous generations and many Third World women today would place the emphasis upon family values and security. One indicator which is not covered here, but which transcends cultural biases, is the difference between men's and women's mortality rates.[8]

Fertility

Although reproduction is a biological function, the effects of fertility on the position of women are culturally determined, and vary greatly between cultures, and, within a culture, by the stage of the woman's life-cycle in which the birth occurs.

Involuntary childlessness represents an extreme case of the impact of fertility upon the position of women. In all cultures it is viewed extremely negatively. Even had the technical means been available, until the second half of this century voluntary childlessness would have been unthinkable.

[6] E. Friedl, 'The Position of Women: Appearance and Reality', *Anthropological Quarterly*, 40 (1967), pp. 97–108.
[7] P. Sanday, *Female Power and Male Dominance* (Cambridge, 1981).
[8] H. Ware, *Women, Demography and Development* (Canberra, 1981).

Traditionally, childlessness is a grave tragedy for both sexes, but has a greater impact on women than on men because there are far fewer, if any, non-reproductive roles available to women which confer prestige or give meaning to life. Childlessness may also severely damage women's autonomy and economic power, because in some societies childless women are believed to be jealous witches, and people are unwilling to associate with them for fear of being poisoned. In any case, most of these women's energies and economic resources will be spent in the search for a cure for their infertility. In some African cultures which award high status to women it is possible for them to buy their way out of childlessness by paying the bride-price for a wife who becomes the woman's wife (not the husband's) and whose children are treated just as her own biological children would have been.[9]

In contrast, in present-day Western industrialized cultures there has emerged the phenomenon of voluntarily childless or 'child-free' marriages as the life-style of a small but possibly trend-setting minority. As many of the functions formerly performed by children have been taken over by the State or other institutions (e.g. the provision of old-age security) or have become unnecessary (e.g. the provision of labour to the family farm), the economic motivation for having children has disappeared. Indeed, individual women are the richer for remaining childless, since there is no interruption to their careers to mortgage their earning capacity. What the childless woman loses is the ticket to a form of immortality which parenthood brings. Even in the emerging post-industrial societies, other factors being equal, childless women still experience lower prestige than their sisters who have children— if only because they have failed to demonstrate the 'superwoman' status so honoured by the media. However, for the woman with any non-domestic role, childlessness is of ever-decreasing importance as a factor in her prestige.

The birth of a woman's first child is a special event everywhere. Provided that the child is born within marriage, the impact upon the woman's prestige will be positive and strong. The impact upon the woman's autonomy and economic power is likely to be much more equivocal. In part, her autonomy is increased because she has given proof of having attained full adult status and become a mother as well as a wife. In cultures where a man's mother maintains considerable influence over his day-to-day behaviour even after marriage, it is often the birth of his first child which marks the beginning of the shift of domestic power in favour of his wife. Yet, because of the dependence of the child upon her, she may have lost a great deal of freedom of movement. Just how constraining motherhood of a young child is depends upon the cultural context, and especially on the availability of alternative facilities for child care. At the extreme, there are some cultures in northern Nigeria where the first child is considered to be both so valuable and so

---

[9] A. Molnos, *Cultural Source Materials for Population Planning in East Africa* (Nairobi, 1973).

highly at risk that she or he will be reared by a relative with previous child-rearing experience, such as the grandmother.[10] However, in general a new mother is likely to find herself relatively constrained, certainly with heightened prestige because of her new status, but also with reduced personal autonomy and very limited opportunities for income-generating activities. Yet in many traditional cultures the consequence of a woman remaining childless is that she is divorced for failure to reproduce, and left with considerable theoretical autonomy, but a very bleak economic outlook. The European Christian tradition is very unusual in having developed a form of marriage which left a husband whose wife did not produce children with no access to divorce or polygyny to secure a legitimate succession. It is also unusual in having provided, by way of the convent, a full role for women who never married, nor had children.

In some parts of west Africa the birth of the first child brings greater economic power to the mother, because the husband (or her mother) recognizes the event and the mother's new responsibilities by providing a small amount of capital for the establishment of a business, such as petty trading. The business will be compatible with the care of a very young child, because the child is tied in a wrapper on the mother's back, which leaves both hands and the head free for carrying loads whilst the child accompanies its mother everywhere.

In some cultures, the really significant event for the woman's prestige is the birth of the first son.[11] Indeed, it has even been possible to demonstrate the existence of selective infanticide of girl babies to ensure that surviving first-borns would be sons.[12] However, the sex of the child is unlikely to be a major influence on the mother's level of autonomy or economic status, except for the common belief that sons both need and deserve more attention than daughters, so that leaving a son to be cared for by someone else is likely to be less acceptable than leaving a daughter.

Extra-nuptial births are usually a special class of first births. In many traditional cultures such births are almost unthinkable. Young girls are married at puberty, precisely to avoid any such possibility. Any young woman faced with pregnancy before marriage would contemplate the bitter choice between abortion, infanticide, or suicide unless a rapid marriage could be arranged. In other cultures, children are welcome irrespective of the marital status of their mothers. Here the mother's family welcomes an additional member who would otherwise have become a part of the husband's family at a distance. Elsewhere, notably in the Caribbean and parts of Latin America, cohabitation is so commonplace that extra-nuptial births are treated

[10] M. F. Smith, *Baba of Karo: A Woman of the Muslim Hausa* (London, 1954).
[11] S. Gupta (ed.), *Women in Indian Folklore* (Calcutta, 1969).
[12] S. Scrimshaw, 'Infant Mortality and Fertility Behavior', *Population and Development Review*, 4 (1978), pp. 383–404.

little differently from nuptial births.[13] The disadvantage associated with the social acceptance of extra-nuptial births lies in the economic problems faced by single-parent female-headed households. Where men cannot control women's sexuality, they are likely to refuse to share the responsibility for the support of their children.

The impact of the number of children upon a woman's autonomy, economic power, and prestige depends upon the culture. In agrarian cultures where children bring positive economic returns to their parents, it is generally the case that the more children the better. This is true where children are needed for their labour, as old-age security, and to strengthen the family's power base. Thus, in some western African groups there are special chiefly titles for women who succeed in rearing a dozen living children, just as in Russia there are titles and medals. African women may also adopt considerable numbers of additional children to extend their personal influence. Traditionally, women often enter a new life-cycle stage when their older children become capable of caring for the younger ones. At this point, the woman can regain much of her freedom of personal movement and resume work which takes her away from home. She may well also begin to experience the rewards of motherhood as the children begin to bring money or other economic benefits into the household. Older sisters who learn to care for their younger siblings in this way are often educationally disadvantaged, in contrast to their brothers. Meanwhile, 'the relationship between a mother's child-rearing responsibilities and her labour-force participation, and hence her economic status, depends not on the number of her children, but on the age of the youngest child'.[14] Commonly, it is only the care of very young children which reduces the amount of time which women in developing countries can devote to market work: 'when a woman works outside the home the time required does not come out of housework or child care, but out of her leisure time.'[15]

A further life-cycle stage may be reached when the woman in a traditional culture is on the eve of becoming a grandmother for the first time. This is often deemed the signal for the woman to cease having sexual intercourse, or at least to refrain from public display of sexual activity through pregnancy.[16] Children born beyond this point certainly have an adverse impact on their mothers' status, since such women are held to be incapable of controlling their baser instincts.

---

[13] G. W. Roberts and S. Sinclair, *Women in Jamaica* (New York, 1978), ch. 1; S. de Vos, 'Latin American Households in Comparative Perspective', *Population Studies*, 41 (1987), pp. 501–17.

[14] J. Darian, 'Convenience of Work and the Job Constraint of Children', *Demography*, 12 (1975), pp. 245–58.

[15] T. Ho, 'The Cost of Child Rearing in the Philippines', *Population and Development Review*, 5 (1979), pp. 643–62.

[16] H. Ware, 'Social Influences on Late Fertility', *Journal of Biosocial Science*, 6 (1979), pp. 75–96.

In contexts where children have become an economic burden upon their parents, women have little to gain from births beyond the third or fourth (unless to secure a child of the desired sex). Indeed, except where there are obvious religious reasons for eschewing birth control, women who go on bearing children may well lose prestige, being regarded as either ignorant and improvident, or as pursuing a truly minority life-style.[17] One measure of the equality of the sexes is the extent to which parents with children of one sex only go on trying to produce a child of the opposite sex.[18]

It is relatively simple to examine the relationship between the fertility of individual women and their autonomy, economic power, and prestige. It is much more difficult to examine the relationship at a societal level. The problem lies in finding sufficient variation between fertility levels in traditional societies. In order to control for many probably confounding variables it would be ideal to be able to compare agrarian societies with different levels of fertility, as well as hunter–gatherer societies with high and low fertility. Unfortunately, however, there would appear to be no high-fertility hunter–gatherer groups. (Or, to be strictly accurate, no such societies in which mothers, on average, have large numbers of surviving children; in determining the position of women it is essentially the number of surviving children, not the number of pregnancies, which is relevant.) The fertility of women in hunter–gatherer societies has been relatively low due to extended birth spacing; these women also appear to enjoy relatively higher status than their more fertile sisters in settled agricultural societies. The reason why hunter–gatherer women are closer to equality with men would seem to be their obvious and strong contribution to the family economy, a contribution which is helped by their relatively low fertility. Traditional agrarian societies place a strong premium on high fertility, which is generally achieved. To find a natural experiment where levels of fertility in traditional societies with the same economic base are very different one has to look to the horticultural societies of the tropical African low-fertility belt and at their high-fertility neighbours.[19] Although the evidence is limited, it would not appear that such involuntary infertility, when it affects the society as a whole, has a marked effect on the position of women. In the case of industrialized societies, low fertility is almost the rule. In those few industrialized societies in which fertility has remained high, predominantly for religious reasons, the emphasis upon women's role as mothers has served to constrain their autonomy and limit their economic power, essentially because of their minimal participation in the paid labour force.

A vast deal of attention has been devoted to the question of the relationship between women's status and their fertility, but focusing on the causal

[17] H. Ware, 'The Limits of Acceptable Family Size', *Journal of Biosocial Science*, 5 (1973), pp. 309–28.

[18] N. Das, 'Sex Preference and Fertility Behaviour', *Demography*, 24 (1987), pp. 517–30.

[19] A. Retel Laurentin, *Infécondité en Afrique noire* (Paris, 1974).

link from status to fertility, not from fertility to status.[20] There are, of course, many theories to explain why women's status should be inferior to that of men, which posit women's reproductive role as the root cause of their inequality, but these theories do not deal with the impact of different levels of fertility on women's status.[21]

One aspect of the impact of declining fertility upon women's position is simply the extent to which it frees women's lives.[22] At the onset of adulthood, women who delay their first birth have the opportunity to extend their education and move into an occupation which needs formal qualifications, or an apprenticeship. Later on in married life, when all the children no longer need intensive care and have left home, there is a new stage—the so-called 'empty-nest' stage—which did not normally occur in earlier generations, when at least one parent was likely to die before the youngest child left home. The existence of this stage, together with the increasing tendency for couples to enjoy some years of married life before the arrival of children, has encouraged the growth of companionate and egalitarian marriages, and of higher divorce rates, as expectations of marriage fail to be met. It could also plausibly be argued that the generations of women who have limited their fertility have achieved higher status, because men can see them as something more than reproductive machines. It would appear that this relationship between lower fertility and higher status for women, by way of marriages where women and men plan the household economy together, could be seen as early as the late eighteenth century in France, where peasants practised birth control in order to avoid the further division of their lands.

One possible mechanism through which high fertility may have an impact upon the status of women at the societal level is where population growth results in a scarcity of basic resources.[23] Much of the available evidence would appear to suggest that, where the pressure of population on resources is acute, before the adoption of fertility regulation (whether by contraception or demographic measures, such as late marriage), the status of women is likely to be in decline.[24] In contrast, the adoption of contraceptive techniques, whose successful use is commonly associated with a considerable degree of co-operation between spouses, is generally matched by a rise in women's status.

[20] But see K. Piepmeier and T. Adkins, 'The Status of Women and Fertility', *Journal of Biosocial Science*, 5 (1983), pp. 507–20.

[21] K. Oppenheim Mason, *The Status of Women: A Review of its Relationship to Fertility and Mortality* (Population Studies Center; Ann Arbor, Mich., 1984).

[22] J. Ridley, 'The Effects of Population Change on the Role and Status of Women', in C. Safilios-Rothschild (ed.), *Companionate Marriages and Sexual Inequality: Are they compatible? Towards a Sociology of Women*, xerox (Lexington, Mass., 1972).

[23] Sanday, op. cit. in n. 7.

[24] T. Dyson and M. Moore, 'On Kinship Structure, Female Autonomy, and Demographic Behavior in India', *Population and Development Review*, 9 (1983), pp. 35–60.

In high-fertility societies, the biological aspects of reproduction often occupy a very large proportion of women's lives. Thus, in some high-fertility areas of Nigeria, the majority of women spend at least two-thirds of their adult lives either pregnant or breast-feeding.[25] Some have gone so far as to argue that declining fertility in itself is an index of the rise of the status of women: 'improvements in the domestic bargaining power of women in the interests of themselves and their children will be indexed by the reduction of completed family size.'[26] This raises the question whether women in high-fertility societies can achieve high status, or whether 'it's our very importance that degrades us. Whilst we were minding the children they stole our rights and liberties. The children made us slaves, and the men took advantage of it.'[27]

Family Organization

Family organization has a very important influence on the position of women. Two major sets of factors are involved: one is the extent to which women are restricted by being under the control of their relatives; the other the extent to which they are restricted by their responsibilities for the care of their children or other dependants. Broadly speaking, in traditional societies the first set of factors is the more important, whilst in industrial societies it is the latter which bears almost all the weight. The standard presentation of the situation of the Hindu woman, who passes from the control of her father to that of her husband, and eventually to that of her son, marks the extreme case of women under the control of their relatives.[28] Clearly, in a system which works like this there is very little scope for women's autonomy. A few individual women (like the widow in Kipling's *Kim* (1901)) may have the exceptional strength of character to break the rules. But the bulk of women will be in a life-long position of subordination. Whilst there are numerous accounts of the first two life-cycle stages of this pattern, the last stage in which the widowed mother becomes subject to the tutelage of her son presents some problems of plausibility, especially when combined with the tradition of wives who suffer under a domineering mother-in-law. The one woman whom any man is likely to regard with a certain degree of respect is his mother. Whilst he may be legally in control of her affairs, there is likely to be at least implicit consultation between the two. Such control is signifi-

---

[25] J. Harrington, 'Nutritional Stress and Economic Responsibility', in M. Buvinic, *Women and Poverty in the Third World* (Baltimore, 1983).

[26] R. Woods, 'Approaches to the Fertility Transition in Victorian England', *Population Studies*, 41 (1987), p. 297; see also O. Stark, 'Bargaining, Altruism and Economic Development', *Population and Development Review*, 10 (1984), pp. 679–92.

[27] H. G. Wells, *Ann Veronica* (London, 1909), ch. 11.

[28] Gupta, op. cit. in n. 11.

cant only where major property is involved. In the normal case of a family with limited resources, the son's 'control' of his mother effectively means that he is responsible for her upkeep and well-being. Indeed, such systems may break down under modern conditions of extreme poverty, as in Bangladesh, where there are now recorded cases of sons putting their mothers into the street.[29]

To understand how such family systems work it is important to look at biographical material. In all societies there are considerable differences between what is supposed to happen and what actually happens. Scattered evidence suggests that there are often ways in which individual women can manipulate apparently highly unyielding systems.[30] Also, in those extended family systems in which the older generation controls the younger, it is not only the women who have much of their autonomy circumscribed. Men, too, find that major decisions, such as when and whom to marry, are taken out of their control, and power does not come to them unless and until their fathers have died. Equally, the system only works because older women have control over young ones. The young daughter-in-law is put upon, but she may age into a redoubtable bullying mother-in-law in her turn.[31] The classical patriarch lords it over his sons and their wives whilst his wife controls her own domain, and very little is known about the extent to which his power is actually shared.

Where the extended family system is breaking down, it is the young women who experience the change as a form of liberation; many of the older women regret the loss of community and power. For poor women, the co-resident extended family may have much less reality than for the more affluent. When Indian husbands were found helping with the cooking in poor households, 'it was the economic importance of women which was critical in creating a more egalitarian relationship between the sexes'.[32] Poverty does not always result in the breakdown of extended family structures: in African and Latin American cities alike, women with children but no husbands survive by maintaining their extended family links.[33]

Marriage clearly plays a central role in any family system. There are many ways in which marriages can be structured so as to weight the odds against equal status for husband and wife. Examples are: the husband is at least half

---

[29] M. Cain, 'Class, Patriarchy and Women's Work in Bangladesh', *Population and Development Review*, 5 (1979), pp. 405–38.

[30] Smith, op. cit. in n. 10; A. Blank, 'The Role and Status of Maori Women', in P. Bunkle (ed.), *Women in New Zealand Society* (Sydney, 1980).

[31] M. Dobkin, 'Social Ranking in the Woman's World of Purdah: A Turkish example', *Anthropological Quarterly*, 40 (1967), pp. 65–72.

[32] S. Seymour, 'Some Determinants of Sex Roles in an Indian Town', *American Ethnologist*, 2 (1975), pp. 757–69.

[33] I. Schuster, 'Kinship, Life Cycle and Education in Lusaka', *Journal of Comparative Family Studies*, 18 (1987), pp. 363–87; M. Buvinic, *Women and Poverty in the Third World* (Baltimore, 1983).

a generation older than his wife; the husband is more highly trained and educated than his wife; the husband is bigger and taller than his wife; the husband is sexually experienced at marriage, the wife is not; after marriage the couple live with the husband's parents, or at least in his village away from her parents, so that she is a stranger. The fact that traditional societies exercise such care to ensure that marriages are not egalitarian is in itself revealing. Polygyny might appear to be another structural impediment to equality, but the picture is not quite so simple. The senior wife in a polygynous marriage is in a position of considerable power; because only part of her attention needs to be devoted to her husband, she has her free time and resources to devote to her own affairs.[34] Even for junior wives, polygyny offers a certain degree of freedom: in most polygynous systems wives roster sleeping with the husband, and only cook and clean for him when they are sleeping with him; at other times they have their own quarters. Apart from the spare time which this creates, where wives co-operate they can enjoy the efficiencies of the division of labour between economic roles, child care, and domestic chores.[35] Professional women in industrialized countries often joke that what they really need to achieve equality with men at work is to have wives too; in polygynous systems this is possible. Thus, in a Senegalese village, two-thirds of all households contain at least two married women, either because of polygyny or because of co-residence of mother-in-law and daughter-in-law. In either case, it is the senior, higher-status woman who engages in agricultural work, whilst the junior wife is relegated to housework and child care.[36] Whilst Westerners envisage the polygynous husband as choosing his own wives, the traditional pattern often involves the senior wife choosing her co-wives. Some marriages are prescribed by tradition—an example is the common obligation for a man to marry his brother's widow(s). Since neither partner has a choice, the degree of loss of autonomy is the same for both.

One clear indicator of the status of women is the position of those who never marry. In some societies such women are viewed with intense pity. Indeed, in some west African societies women who have no husband are 'married' to the chief to save them from dying unwed. Almost by definition, a society in which women can lead full and satisfying lives without marriage is a society in which women enjoy high status. In some cases, single women can stand alone only in a religious role, thereby in part denying their femininity. In other cases, women with sufficient economic resources can enjoy full lives, but this depends on there being a legal regime which allows them to hold property and make their own decisions.

---

[34] H. Ware, 'Polygyny: Women's Views in a Traditional Society', *Journal of Marriage and the Family*, 41 (1979), pp. 185–95.

[35] D. Rotimi, *Our Husband has Gone Mad Again* (Ibadan, 1977).

[36] D. Mackintosh, 'Domestic Labour and the Household', in S. Burma (ed.), *Fit Work for Women* (London, 1979).

It is now a commonplace to see the statement that one-third of the world's households are headed by women.[37] The available statistics would suggest that one-third is an exaggeration which remains uncorrected because of a lack of interest in the true situation by public authorities.[38] It is certainly true that the proportion of households headed by women in which the woman bears the economic responsibility for the household's welfare is growing. This is because of a wide range of factors, many of which are related to the breakdown of the extended family.[39] General factors include the migration of men in search of employment, men abandoning their family responsibilities, more widows surviving and living alone, and more women bearing children outside marriage. For the developing countries there is very little evidence on how far the increase of female headship reflects women's choices, rather than men's departures, but the increase in independent migration of women shows that choice plays some role.[40]

For individual women who are household heads, severe economic difficulties are the norm. These stem from the reality that women's incomes are lower than those of men on a day-to-day basis and even more so over a lifetime, since women spend less of their lives in the paid labour force. Even within poor populations, households headed by women suffer additional deprivations which reflect women's disadvantaged overall economic status. Yet, for women in general, the more women who are able to show their competence as household heads, the clearer it becomes that women have options and can survive without the support of men.[41] One of the greatest barriers to women learning to be self-sufficient is their failure to appreciate the reality of the likelihood of their becoming household heads. Even in industrialized societies such as Australia, where one in three marriages now ends in divorce, young women still fail to plan their working lives because they believe that they will leave the workforce at the birth of the first child.

As long as women marry men who are older than themselves and enjoy longer life expectancies than men, widowhood will remain a very common reason for women becoming household heads. In traditional societies, as women grow older they are often less defined by their biology. After the menopause, women may become honoured elders able to take on new political and religious roles. At a time when the culture may decree that men's status is in decline in parallel with their physical strength, women may be able to enter new worlds.[42] In contrast, in industrial societies women appear to lose status in middle age, as they lose their more obvious physical attractiveness and their children cease to need their intensive mothering

---

[37] R. Morgan, *Sisterhood is Global* (New York, 1984), pp. 1–2.
[38] Vos, op. cit. in n. 13.
[39] Buvinic, op. cit. in n. 33.
[40] J. Fawcett (ed.), *Women in the Cities of Asia* (Boulder, Colo., 1984).
[41] P. Peters, 'Women in Botswana', *Journal of Southern African Studies*, 11 (1984), pp. 150–54.
[42] E. Friedl, *Women and Men* (New York, 1975).

care.[43] Family structures which offer a rewarding role to grandmothers are clearly of benefit to middle-aged women who have focused their lives on domestic roles. For women with satisfying extra-domestic roles there is a need for a 'new' grandmother role, less time-intensive for the grandmother, and more instructive for the grandchild.

In the nuclear family of the industrialized societies, women make an all-or-nothing gamble; if the marriage is a failure, there is very little else to fall back on. Women whose expectations of their husbands are limited may be able to develop an alternative support network of female relatives from the extended family and of friends from their schooldays,[44] but their effort is often frustrated by the geographical mobility of the nuclear family in search of better employment possibilities for the male household head. More commonly, the wife's effort is devoted to the creation of a companionate marriage in which both partners maintain contact only with friends and relatives who are acceptable to husband and wife. This is only workable where there is equality between the partners, and especially where both have equivalent access to economic resources. Otherwise, a wife without resources of her own is completely dependent on the whim of the husband, for, in the case of divorce, especially when there are children, she is the one who will suffer a marked decline in position, whilst his economic position will usually improve.[45]

When researchers are looking for indicators of the status of women, fully half of those commonly used relate to kinship and the family.[46] Among factors believed to have a negative impact are purdah, levirate, polygyny, lineage emphasis, exogamy, dowry, arranged marriages, virginity at marriage, the sexual double stardard, and unilateral divorce by men. Positive factors are far less numerous and comprise conjugal families, women's property inheritance, cross-cousin marriages, and kin support for widows and divorcees. Some would add an egalitarian relationship between husband and wife, but this begs the question: which is cause and which is effect? Complex family structures appear to be associated with low status for women, whilst simpler structures seem to allow much more room for their autonomy, but complexity is also associated with greater possibilities for mutual assistance between women.

Surprisingly little attention has been given to the design of new family structures which could contribute to raising the status of women. Instead, much effort has been concentrated upon creating equality between partners in marriages within nuclear families to the neglect of possible alternatives. Some feminists have explored plans for women-only societies, but on

---

[43] P. Bart, 'The Sociology of the Middle Years', *Sociological Symposium*, 3 (1969); P. Weideger, *Menstruation and Menopause* (London, 1977).
[44] E. Bott, *Family and Social Network* (London, 1957).
[45] C. Safilios-Rothschild, op. cit. in n. 22.
[46] Mason, op. cit. in n. 21.

communal rather than family lines. Yet, many of the problems which women face in industrialized societies are exacerbated by the nature and restricted size of the nuclear family. A new, larger family structure based upon women could have a great deal to offer. Blood links between sisters seem to have been insufficiently explored. Similarly, women who work together share many problems, but rarely devote much effort to finding common solutions. When illiterate Nigerian women were asked what women could most effectively do to advance their own cause, the commonest response was that women could learn to band together to work for common goals.[47] One of the most negative features of the nuclear family is the way in which it cuts women off from each other. Men have their sports, clubs, and many other institutions of masculine solidarity outside the family, but women have shown much less initiative in creating feminine institutions to promote women's interests.

The Sex Structure of the Labour Market

Everywhere there are sex differences in labour-force participation, in the occupational distribution within the labour force, and in the performance of child-rearing and domestic chores. These differences are of vital importance because of their impact on access and control of income, of power, of prestige, and of technology. In modern industrial societies it is plausible to argue that, if women and men did actually play the same roles in the labour force with the same participation rates, the same occupational distribution, the same ranking within occupations, and the same wages and other rewards, then equality between the sexes would, indeed, have been achieved.

The central importance of these differences can be seen in the arguments of those who press for their retention.

The whole range of society, marriage and careers—and thus the social order—will best be served if most men have a position of economic superiority over the relevant women in the community and if in most jobs the sexes tend to be segregated by either level or function. These practices are seen as oppressive by some; but they make possible a society in which men can love and respect women and treat them humanely.[48]

In other words, men will only respect women on condition that women accept an inferior status.

It is only with a certain degree of affluence and sophistication that it becomes possible for families to afford the luxury of maintaining women who are full-time mothers and houseworkers and do not participate in

[47] Ware, op. cit. in n. 34.
[48] G. Gilder, *Sexual Suicide* (New York, 1975).

productive labour outside the home. In the rural areas of many developing countries there are no women who are solely engaged in home duties. However many children they have, women spend relatively little time on the domestic work of cooking, cleaning, and child care; the bulk of their time is spent in providing the types of services which are bought for money in industrialized countries. This fact is almost totally obscured by the available statistics, in which the classification of married women who engage in farm work depends upon the whim of national statisticians.[49] In a classic example, in the Algerian Census of 1966 enumerators were instructed that women who were housewives could not have any other occupation; as a consequence, the percentage of females recorded as economically active fell from 25 per cent in 1954 to 2 per cent in 1966.[50] The inadequacy of labour-force statistics is one reason why development programmes ignore women's key role in agricultural production. As a result, development plans, population plans, rural development, and agricultural output suffer; and the status of women remains unacceptably low.[51]

In rural areas in the Third World, almost all women are economically active, except those whose families can afford the luxury of allowing them to devote all their time to purely domestic tasks. As a consequence, in many cultures it becomes a matter of status for the woman and her family that she should not work (or be seen to work) outside the home, especially where there are religious constraints on the public appearance of women. Thus, in parts of Uttar Pradesh where high-caste Thakur women are forced by familial poverty to work on the land, they attempt to retain their honour by disguising themselves in men's clothes, or harvesting their crops at night.[52]

Especially in rural areas, most women in less developed countries are overworked rather than underemployed, and a more appropriate technology for the tasks they perform would be labour saving, in order to improve the quality of their employment, rather than employment-creative.[53] It is with migration to the towns that great distinctions appear: men find work in the formal sector, women in the informal sector, if at all. The difficulty of combining child care with fixed working hours outside the home also drives women to informal employment.[54] Meanwhile, mechanization of agriculture displaces women from paid agricultural employment. It is only when development is seen as failing to deliver that urgency to assist poor rural women has gained momentum.[55]

[49] Ware, op. cit. in n. 8, ch. 7.

[50] J. Blacker, 'A Critique of the International Definition of Economic Activity', *Population Bulletin of UNECWA*, 14 (1977).

[51] R. Dixon-Mueller, *Women's Work in Third World Agriculture* (Geneva, 1985).

[52] W. van der Velden, 'Honour at Work', *Manushi*, 7 (1986).

[53] ILO, *Director-General's Report to the World Employment Conference* (Geneva, 1978).

[54] R. Anker (ed.), *Sex Inequalities in Urban Employment in the Third World* (London, 1986).

[55] D. Kandiyoti, *Women in Rural Production Systems* (Paris, 1985).

Whilst women's participation in the paid labour force varies greatly around the world, women everywhere are burdened with the domestic tasks of housework and child care.[56] Even revolutions have not changed this.[57] Some have attempted to provide public services to replace domestic provisions, but attempts to make men take an equal share have been extremely rare.[58]

Around-the-world industrialization sees women heavily channelled into a limited range of occupations. In Swaziland and Australia alike, women in paid employment are very heavily concentrated in clerical occupations.[59] Similarly, in those uncommon instances where women do become apprentices, it is as hairdressers and dressmakers, not as motor mechanics or machine-tool makers. In developing countries a special effort needs to be made to ensure that women are not restricted to 'women's' occupations and industries, because it is much easier to prevent such traditions emerging than to dismantle them once established.[60]

Any analysis which looks at differentials in distributions begs the question whether, in order to be equal with men, women must behave in the same way as men. Theoretically, it would be possible to envisage a society in which women and men play different roles and yet receive the same economic and psychic rewards. Such a society does not appear to exist in reality,[61] and it is hard to envisage that it would be possible to move from existing societies, in which men have the predominant say in determining the rewards to various activities, to a new regime in which women's activities would be revalued to equivalence with those of men. Such a radical change could require the males first to take on the feminine role. One circumstance in which this might possibly happen would be in a general situation of below-replacement fertility. Where children are rare and highly valued, yet sufficient people cannot be found to care for them, the rewards for nurturing roles would rise sharply. Thus, only when women abandon 'child-nurturing' roles will such roles be revalued. What has tended to happen during this century, as women in industrialized societies have taken up non-domestic roles at a time when birth rates were falling, is that state hierarchies dominated by men have promoted back-to-the-hearth movements for women, restricting the range of non-domestic roles open to them. Women need to argue that children are too important to be left to them alone to care for. Mothers are inadequately

---

[56] L. Benaria (ed.), *Women and Development: The Sexual Division of Labor in Rural Societies* (Westport, Conn., 1985).

[57] S. Kruks and B. Wisner, 'The State, the Party and the Female Peasantry in Mozambique', *Journal of Southern African Studies*, 11 (1984), pp. 106–27.

[58] C. Adams and K. Winston, *Mothers at Work* (New York, 1980); L. Brown, 'Women in Post-Revolutionary Cuba', *Insurgent Sociologist*, 13 (1986), pp. 39–52.

[59] M. Russell, 'High Status, Low Pay', *Journal of Southern African Studies*, 12 (1986), pp. 293–307; D. Broom (ed.), *Unfinished Business: Social Justice for Women in Australia* (Sydney, 1984).

[60] M. d'Onofrio-Flores and S. Pfafflin (eds.), *Scientific-Technological Change and the Role of Women in Development* (Boulder, Colo., 1982).

[61] Whyte, op. cit. in n. 1.

rewarded, because they never go on strike, and because to date there has never been an acute shortage of persons willing to take on the role, nor acknowledgement that any special skills or qualities are needed. Lives are risked in childbirth and in warfare, but it is the latter occupation which people have to be invited to take up.

In all cultures the division of labour by sex is in reality a division of labour by status. 'In a culture where men weave and women fish, just as in a culture where men fish and women weave, it is axiomatic that whichever activity is assigned to the male is the activity with the greater prestige, power, status, and reward.'[62]

There is no shortage of reasons why there should be sex differences in labour-force participation. Women are socialized from earliest childhood to accept that they will be responsible for domestic matters and child-rearing, and to believe that some jobs are more appropriate for women than others. In line with this socialization, their education is limited in duration and circumscribed in content, especially in scientific and technical areas. Women are also socialized to plan for a shorter time frame, to think of getting a job, rather than of building a career. This is why women become nurses, and men doctors. In those societies, notably in socialist countries, where the starting salary of a physician is less than that of a factory worker, women are the doctors, except at the highest levels. Another exception is in those societies where, for reasons of modesty, male doctors should not handle female patients. Here, at least, some women get an opportunity to break the role barrier. Ways of ensuring that women who are in the labour force do not receive equal treatment with men are legion.

One highly controversial factor that affects the position of women in the labour force is the impact of protective legislation which regulates the conditions in which women can be employed. In Australia, early this century men reserved union protection for men, and argued for protective labour laws for women and children. Protective labour laws, though they have ameliorated some of the worst abuses of women's and child labour, have also limited the participation of adult women in many 'men's' jobs. Men sought to keep high-wage jobs for themselves and to raise men's wages generally.[63] This was at a time when the rate for women's wages was legally fixed at two-thirds of the men's rate. Some would argue that women should not receive any protection which is not also granted to men—that hazardous working conditions are to be outlawed irrespective of who is to be exposed to them. Others would maintain that women, and especially the foetuses which they may be carrying, should receive special protection in the interest of society as a whole. The Report of the Sixtieth Session of the International Labour Conference (1975) is a good example of trying to go both ways at

---

[62] K. Millet, cited in K. Weiss, 'Biological and Cultural Determinants of the Division of Labor by Sex', in D. McGuigan (ed.), *New Research on Women* (Ann Arbor, Mich., 1974).

[63] E. Ryan, *Two Thirds of a Man* (Sydney, 1984).

once. A discourse under the title 'Protective Legislation for Women Only: An Obstacle to Equality of Opportunity and Treatment' discusses the conflict between privilege under such laws and equality of treatment. However, it comes down in favour of protective legislation. Such an approach appears to suggest that women have to choose between equality and protection.[64] There is increasing recognition that substances which are deleterious to the female's reproductive system are also unlikely to be good for that of the male. Nor is it universally acceptable to assume that all women will be involved in reproduction.[65]

Apart from protective legislation related to women's reproductive roles, there is also legislation which restricts women's work at night, and the weights which they can lift. Here, too, where there are hazards, these are not restricted to women—men, too, are at risk. Australian evidence makes it very clear that the legal limit on weights to be lifted by women has been a major excuse for excluding them from 'masculine' industries, such as steel, with especially adverse impact in one-industry towns where women are excluded from almost all wage employment.[66]

In trade unions, too, participation of women, both as members and as officials, is very restricted, and unions can support discriminatory practices in the workplace.[67] Yet where unions support legislation it can reduce sex discrimination in employment and break down wage differentials.[68] There are two stages in securing equality for women: the first is to obtain equal pay for doing the same work; the second is to secure equal pay for work of equal value. In striving for recognition of work of equal value, women have to combat a long tradition in which their work is undervalued precisely because it is women's work; thus, when men move into a 'woman's' occupation, the status of that occupation rises, and conversely when women move into 'men's' occupations.

Technology

Since technology is thought of as being 'masculine', its impact upon women's lives has been seriously neglected.[69] A comprehensive account of its impact

---

[64] V. Hunt, 'Reproduction and Work', *Signs*, 1 (1975), pp. 543–52.

[65] L. Jones and M. Nunn, 'Reproductive Hazards in the Workplace', *Women and Environments*, 8 (1986), pp. 14–16; J. Stellman, 'Protective Legislation, Ionising Radiations and Health', *Women and Health*, 12 (1987), pp. 105–25.

[66] D. Covell and C. Refshauge, 'Women Sting the Giant: Compensation for Sex Discrimination in Employment', *Refractory Girl*, 30 (1987), pp. 44–46.

[67] E. Ryan and H. Prendergast, *Unions are for Women too! Power, Conflict, and Control in Australian Trade Unions* (Sydney, 1984).

[68] S. Dex and L. Shaw, *British and American Women at Work: Do Equal Opportunities Policies Matter?* (London, 1986); Broom, op. cit. in n. 59.

[69] K. Sorensen and A. Berg, 'Genderization of Technology among Norwegian Engineering Students', *Acta sociologica*, 30 (1987), pp. 151–71.

upon women would need to embrace the whole of humanity's development. Here it is only possible to skim over a limited range of issues: the claim that technology is, indeed, the essential determinant of the status of women; the impact of the introduction of new technologies on rural women in developing countries; the question of women's exclusion from technology; and, finally, three forms of modern technology that have a very special impact upon women: contraceptives; the new technologies related to the circumvention of infertility, and the choice of sex of children; and the multiplicity of new technologies that can be applied to housework.

Some anthropologists have argued that the level of technology is a powerful or even *the* most powerful determinant of the status of women in a society. Thus, it has been claimed that the subsistence technology of a society has crucial consequences for the sexual division of labour, the differential allocation of power and recognition to men and women, and the quality of the relationship between the sexes.[70] It has been suggested that relative equality between the sexes is more common amongst hunter–gatherers than amongst horticulturalists, because of the lesser scope for surpluses which can be used to bolster men's prestige. At both levels of technology, prestige goods only available to men (such as meat from hunting large animals, or men-only prestige crops) allow men to gain supremacy. Inputs by women into subsistence production are a necessary, but not a sufficient, condition for high status for women. At the two extremes, when women produce more than three-quarters or less than one-quarter of the goods of a society, their status is low because they are either severely exploited by the men, or severely dependent upon them. When women's contribution is in the middle range, they appear to be in the best situation through taking a reasonable share, which, to take account of their child-bearing responsibilities, should be somewhat less than half. A coverage of a worldwide range of cultures presents a curvilinear pattern with both hunter–gatherers and industrialized societies being more egalitarian than traditional plough-based agricultural societies.[71] Whilst generalizations are often misleading, it would appear to be accurate to point to an association between plough-agriculture and low status for women. It has been argued that women do not have sufficient strength to plough, a view which is reinforced by the traditional belief that, if a field is ploughed by a woman, the plants will wither and the animals die.[72]

In industrialized societies the widespread availability of machinery and mechanical aids removes one basic inequality between the sexes, since sheer physical strength is no longer a vital determinant of who can do certain jobs. (Of course, it has never been true that all men are stronger than all women, only that on average men have greater physical strength, especially for

---

[70] Friedl, op. cit. in n. 42.
[71] Whyte, op. cit. in n. 1.
[72] Adams and Winston, op. cit. in n. 58, p. 147.

short-term tasks, and when the difference is increased by reserving most protein for men's consumption.) Equally, with modern weapons, the female of the species is just as deadly as the male.

The culturally determined intricacies of the division of labour between the sexes are such that the introduction of new technologies cannot be sex-neutral in impact. Many rural women in developing countries identify their first priority as access to a means of earning cash incomes. Yet, when attempts are made to introduce improved techniques or technologies aimed at increasing productivity, the result can often be that men take over traditional women's industries. The introduction of mechanized agriculture to men often allows them to monopolize cash-crop production:

the introduction to men of many craft improvements has allowed them to monopolize activities which, in many countries, are traditionally women's work. The introduction of kick-wheels into pottery production, and its subsequent domination by men, is an example of this. The fact that women have been excluded has nothing to do with the technology itself, but rather with the assumptions and conditions under which it was introduced . . . There are no hard and fast rules about what men's activities are and what women's activities are. The only rule appears to be that when a new technology which brings upgraded skills and higher returns is introduced, the men take over.[73]

Women are cut off from access to credit and technology because of a lack of information, cultural constraints on their interaction with male bank officials and extension agents, and the lack of access to land or other property which could serve as collateral for loans. 'Closing the supply/demand circle, women's lack of control over economic resources and the importance given to their reproductive roles causes suppliers to perceive them as poor investment opportunities.'[74] Thus, even in what the World Bank proposes as a model resettlement scheme at Jengka Triangle in Malaysia, despite women's role in agricultural activities, especially rubber production, the extension services originally provided technical advice to men. Now extension officers do deal with women settlers and, in the event of divorce, half of all the loan repayments made by the household are remitted directly to the divorced wife in recognition of her contribution to the household economy.[75]

Often rural women find that the only types of innovation possible for them are those which involve the use of their own additional labour, rather than those which involve the reduction of labour by mechanization.[76] Depending on the traditional division of labour between the sexes, innovations introduced to help women may, in fact, benefit men. Thus, the introduction of solar-operated water pumps in the African Sahel was of much greater

[73] M. Carr, *Blacksmith, Baker, Roofing Sheet Maker: Employment for Rural Women* (London, 1984).
[74] ICRW, *Limits to Productivity: Improving Women's Access to Technology and Credit* (Washington, 1980).
[75] World Bank, *The Jengka Triangle Projects in Malaysia* (Washington, 1987).
[76] J. Wills, *A Study of Time Allocation by Rural Women* (Kampala, 1967).

benefit to the male cattle herders than to the women who had to carry the increased supply of water home.[77] For very many women in the rural areas of developing countries, women's priorities are for improved technologies for carrying water (preferrably pipes); for performing basic agricultural tasks; for reducing the massive burden of food-processing that is spent in hand-pounding and grinding; for carrying wood and other heavy loads which are traditionally assigned to women; and, finally, for cooking itself.[78] Often, when new technologies are introduced, women's tasks are taken over by men: mechanized agriculture is almost invariably a man's preserve—women are not allowed to drive tractors.[79] Technology can also exclude rural women where it changes the location of work—thus the introduction of rice mills in Bangladesh has excluded women who practise purdah.

Women are very rarely consulted about the introduction of new technologies—even in such women's areas as solar cooking.[80] Actually, solar cookers are a mixed blessing, since they involve cooking during the heat of the day in areas where cooking has traditionally been reserved for the relative cool of the evening. Similarly, enclosed stoves need less wood to be fetched, but they do not provide firelight to see by. Often women are resistant to what male designers may perceive as aesthetic changes, but which they see as vital defects.[81] Where women welcome new technologies, they may still be excluded from using them, because they are not trained to repair and maintain them. Around the world, it is men who are trained to repair water pumps, but it is women who use them and who have the greatest interest in ensuring that they are in working order.

Examples of new technologies which increase women's burdens relative to men's are legion. Often this is because water-carrying is a woman's responsibility: back-pack insecticide sprayers require mass water-carrying; so does keeping chickens in coops, rather than letting them roam free. The introduction of ploughing to clear the ground leaves much larger areas for women to weed; fertilizers also increase women's weeding burdens. When new technologies are introduced, it is vital that their direct and indirect impact upon the work and incomes of men and women be analysed separately, a requirement which has only begun to be met very recently, especially in agriculture.[82] In the industrialized countries, one of the areas in which technology is currently

[77] J. Dhamija, 'Handicrafts: A Source of Employment', *International Labour Review*, 112 (1976), pp. 459–65.

[78] R. Dauber and M. Cain, *Women and Technological Change in Developing Countries* (Boulder, Colo., 1980).

[79] A. Agarwal and S. Narain, 'Women and Natural Resources', *Social Action*, 35 (1985), pp. 301–25.

[80] M. Hoskins and F. Weber, *Household Level Appropriate Technology for Women* (Washington, 1981).

[81] M. Sarin, 'Some Insights into Rural Women's Lives', *Manushi*, 6 (1986), pp. 25–31.

[82] International Rice Research Institute, *Women in Rice Farming* (Aldershot, 1987); J. Jiggins, *Gender Related Impacts of the International Agricultural Research Centers* (Washington, 1987).

having the greatest impact on women's lives is that of 'women's' clerical work, where there is a rapid takeover by micro-electronics and the paperless office. This technological development makes much clerical work unnecessary, and much of the remainder little different from assembly-line work in the factory. It also makes it possible for women to do data-processing work at home, although in conditions which are far from liberating. In future, unpaid consumers, mostly women, will do much of the work which women used to be paid to do. In 1982, in the United States up to 60 per cent of all retail sales clerks, 85 per cent each of librarians, billing clerks and cashiers, 92 per cent of telephone operators, 94 per cent of bank tellers, and 98 per cent of telephone receptionists were women, all occupations which are very rapidly becoming obsolete owing to the computerization of daily life. In contrast, 90 per cent of electronic technicians and 95 per cent of television, computer, and home-appliance repair and installation technicians in the United States were men.[83] Yet, young women continue to crowd into clerical and other occupations which will become obsolete within a decade.[84]

Around the world, women are cut off from new technologies: from choosing them, from designing what they will do, from understanding and using them. Technology and the future have a distinctly masculine tone to them. In the industrialized countries, women are becoming increasingly concerned at their exclusion from the determination of the future path of technological innovation.[85] One example is the development of modern obstetrics and gynaecology to apply men's norms to the female system, so that the cyclic rhythms of women's bodies have come to be considered as being in some way in need of correction.[86] Similarly, there is concern at the increasing application of technology to childbirth itself—a process in which women were little consulted and which they are coming increasingly to reject— especially when births are induced so as to allow male obstetricians to meet their golf schedules. The new technologies for monitoring the condition of the foetus with a view to intervention also raise very difficult questions about whose welfare should receive first consideration: that of the mother or that of the foetus. The development of artificial infant foods has reduced the need for mothers to stay with their babies, at the cost of considerable risk to the health of the infant in developing countries. (The more satisfactory technique of storing the mother's own milk for bottle-feeding is also impracticable without refrigeration.) Thus, the technical fix has yet to meet the needs of women in developing countries. In general, women have even more to gain than men from an emphasis upon prevention in health services,

[83] J. Zimmerman, *Once upon the Future: A Woman's Guide to Tomorrow's Technology* (London, 1986); R. Gordon *et al.*, *Microelectronics in Transition* (Norwood, NJ, 1985).
[84] Economic Commission for South East Asia and the Pacific, *Women's Economic Participation in Asia and the Pacific* (Bangkok, 1987).
[85] Zimmerman, op. cit. in n. 83.
[86] K. McDonnell (ed.), *Adverse Effects: Women and the Pharmaceutical Industry* (Penang, 1986).

but their needs and preferences are not reflected in services planned by male administrators.

Yet women have also welcomed some reproductive technologies. During the early 1970s, when women in Melbourne, Australia, were asked to suggest the most important twentieth-century inventions for women, the contraceptive pill came first, followed by the electric washing machine, with the motor car as a poor third (author's unpublished pre-test).

Highly publicized feminist opposition to modern contraceptive methods on the grounds of their possible health risks and, often, of their 'unnaturalness' has served to obscure the major benefits which these technological innovations have brought to women. No woman can be truly autonomous without control over her own fertility, and this possibility was not easily attainable before the contraceptive pill became widely available, and before the IUD and sterilization operations. Before the 1960s, women could and did control their fertility, but failures were very common, and the risk of pregnancy was always a haunting one.[87] The new contraceptives have brought near-certainty to fertility control. They have also brought a new perspective to women who now start using contraception before the first birth and who, therefore, need to make a deliberate decision to become pregnant. The efficiency of the new contraceptives has also made carefully planned birth-spacing a practical possibility, further adding to women's autonomy. Acceptance of the new contraceptive technologies in industrialized societies has been so rapid and so widespread that it is easy to forget what a dramatic impact they have had on women's lives.

Currently, the most contentious forms of new technology for women are those reproductive technologies which increase fertility.[88] For some women, *in vitro* fertilization (IVF) is just another medical procedure which helps women who experience difficulty in becoming mothers. For other women the issue is much more complex, because they believe that this and other reproductive technologies have the potential to change the social relations between the sexes, to change concepts of maternity and paternity, and even to allow asexual reproduction through cloning. Among feminists there are major differences of opinion, with some seeing the possibility of creating for the first time a society without men. Others offer unqualified opposition on the grounds that the procedures are designed by men, and involve unknown risks and far-reaching consequences which cannot yet be evaluated. Yet other feminists are prepared to offer qualified support for the procedures, depending on the exact circumstances.[89] One concern of many feminists is

[87] J. Caldwell and H. Ware, 'The Evolution of Family Planning in Australia', *Population Studies*, 27 (1973), pp. 7–31.

[88] L. Koch and J. Morgall, 'Towards a Feminist Assessment of Reproductive Technology', *Acta sociologica*, 30 (1987), pp. 173–91.

[89] A. Donchin, 'The Future of Mothering: Reproductive Technology and Feminist Theory', *Hypatia*, 1 (1986), pp. 121–37.

that all the emphasis upon motherhood as woman's (only) destiny is to be deplored as a retrograde step, and involves the loss of many gains in having women accepted in a multiplicity of roles. Another concern is the amount of state and medical control over women's lives which is involved in the implementation and regulation of the new technology.[90]

Surrogacy is one new possibility which opens up vast questions about the relationships between women. As a gesture of love between sisters or friends it allows of a very special kind of selflessness. However, as a trade between women with money but no possibility of carrying a pregnancy to term, and women with very little to sell except the rent on their wombs, it opens up extreme potentialities for exploitation never possible before.

These technologies are so recent that it is very difficult to predict what kind of impact they will have. The end result may be much less dramatic than many of the predictions. A small number of women may continue to make use of these technologies without any dramatic impact on the position of women in general. It is now some years since the birth of the first *in vitro* baby, and, whilst it is still taking legislatures of the world some time to catch up with the new technologies, the social impact to date has been limited.

The reproductive technology which could have the most dramatic impact upon the position of women is that which allows the selection of the sex of children. At present this is only possible through selective abortion of foetuses of the 'wrong' sex. Where parents have a strong preference about the sex of their children, in nine cultures out of ten the preference is for sons.[91] However, this does not mean that, if parents could readily choose the sex of their children, nine boys would be born for every girl. The majority of parents would almost certainly still leave the choice to nature; a small proportion would only venture into sex selection after the birth of two or three daughters; an even smaller proportion would be likely to make the choice for themselves from the start, opting to have sons first, and then daughters. Beyond such a prediction we move into a field of total speculation. As women become scarcer, would they also become more highly valued? Or would a society faced with sex selection on a mass scale step in to prevent the practice, or use social engineering to give equal value to children of either sex (as the Chinese have endeavoured to do in support of their one-child programme)?

One constant objective of feminist movements in pressing for increased autonomy has been to open up new choices for individual women, always recognizing the possibility that only some women will wish to go through the newly unlocked doors, but making the choice available to all. If, in the case of the new reproductive technologies, feminists argue that women should

[90] P. Spallone, 'The Warnock Report: The Politics of Reproductive Technology', *Women's Studies International Forum*, 9 (1986), pp. 543–50.

[91] N. Williamson, *Sons or Daughters: A Cross-Cultural Survey of Parental Preferences* (Beverly Hills, Calif., 1976).

not have the opportunity to choose to use them, this is a new restrictive approach whose validity should be subject to especially intensive scrutiny. (A similar analysis should be applied to the argument of some feminists that as natural pacifists women should not be allowed to make careers in the armed forces—an exclusion which cuts women off from many apprenticeships in technical areas).

If there is one area in which women might have been expected to have a considerable impact upon technology, it would be housework. Yet, even here women have taken very little part, essentially because the major transformations (piped water, gas, and then electricity) have been highly capital-intensive, and women did not have access to the capital required.[92] From another angle, it is highly misleading to argue that technology has not reduced the burden of labour associated with housework. Hot water from a tap, light and clean washing at the flip of a switch, without any advance to the world of pre-cooked meals direct from the freezer to the microwave oven—there can be no question that the labour and time associated with housework have been reduced by technology. If women still spend very many hours each week at housework (as the surveys nearly all suggest), it is because the number and range of tasks which women at home choose to perform has increased dramatically. Many women who work 'double shift', caring for a home and family and holding down a paid job, would doubt the sanity of women reported as vacuum-cleaning daily and washing their curtains every two weeks.[93] The riddle is why women do not insist that men take their fair share of housework (which, in a household where both husband and wife are in full-time employment outside the home, is half). Child care is a task which may be delegated to other people, but which is unlikely to be acceptably reduced by technology in the foreseeable future.

Women have been less enthusiastic about new technologies than men, who see most problems in terms of a technical fix. In France, the one technical advance about which men and women are equally enthusiastic is solar energy. Women who espouse traditional family values are the most opposed to new technologies.[94]

Conclusion

Starting from the premiss that the position of women is multi-faceted and cannot be captured by any one index, I have, in this chapter, laid great emphasis upon complexities and interrelationships. Even within individual societies, women face very different issues depending upon their economic

[92] C. Davidson, *A Woman's Work is Never Done: A History of Housework* (London, 1986).
[93] A. Oakley, *The Sociology of Housework* (London, 1974).
[94] J. Fagnani, 'Women's Attitude towards New Technology', *Women and Environments*, 8 (1986), pp. 17–19.

and demographic circumstances. Across societies, there are vast cultural variations, so that knowledge of the level of technology and fertility in itself is of limited assistance in understanding the position of women. The one measure which is the most revealing, where the statistics accurately mirror reality, is the occupational and income distributions of the population by sex. Women need to fight on many fronts, but the really crucial battles are in the economic sphere. This does not mean that women have to accept a masculine definition of what are to be counted as important problems, nor of what are appropriate solutions. Child care is a good example of a question which women have yet to put on the political agenda. Even where women have economic power, they have yet to translate it into political power; hence their subordinate position.

14 'Birds in a Cage': Institutional Change and Women's Position in Bangladesh*

SHAPAN ADNAN

As one perceptive writer phrased it in her autobiography in 1876, for generations the existence of Bengali women has been akin to that of 'birds in a cage'.[1] Prescribed limits of permissible behaviour, laid down by an array of male-dominated institutions ranging from the family to the segmented labour market, have served as the invisible bars of this figurative cage. The complex dimensions of the subordination of women by men in Bangladesh are by now reasonably well documented, particularly given the spate of studies undertaken during the 1980s.[2]

However, as distinct from the portrayal of static differentials in the relationship between the two sexes, a critical question relates to the nature of changes over time in women's position, as well as to the social and economic institutions which serve to define and delimit their roles. In

[1] S. Ghosh, 'Birds in a Cage: Changes in Bengal Social Life as Recorded in Autobiographies by Women', *Economic and Political Weekly*, 21 (1986), pp. WS/88–WS/96.

[2] These will be cited in context below. Overviews of the existing literature at various points of time have been provided by T. Schaffer, *Profile of Women in Bangladesh* (Dhaka, 1986); UNICEF, *An Analysis of the Situation of Children in Bangladesh* (Dhaka, 1987), ch. 7; and S. Khan, *The Fifty Per Cent: Women in Development and Policy in Bangladesh* (Dhaka, 1988). More recently R. Jahan, *Women and Development and Policy in Bangladesh* (Dhaka, 1989) has cited indicators which show that women's status in Bangladesh is lowest among the countries of the world.

* Since presenting the original version of this paper, I have had the benefit of comments and criticisms from many more friends and colleagues than I could possibly name. However, special thanks are due to Carmen Mirò, Tim Dyson, Martin Greeley, Rounaq Jahan, Sarah White, Syed M. Hashemi, and Ahmed Kamal. I am particularly indebted to Bruce Currey, Susan Davis, and Naushaba Hyder for their generosity in providing me with access to their respective collections of source materials. For letting me have copies of relevant documents and publications, I am obliged to Neela Matin, Farida Akhter, Hussain Zillur Rahman, Elisabeth Eie, J. S. Parsons, Raka Rashid, Shamim Hamid, and Shireen Haq. Thanks are also due to Khawja S. Huda and Azfar Hossain of *ADAB News* for making the first draft of this paper widely available. While revising the paper, I greatly missed Shekar Bose and the invaluable research assistance which he had provided when I wrote the first draft. However, I am indebted to Saleh Akbar Khandaker and Abu M. Sufiyan for giving me support with data management, word processing, and text production for this revised version for publication. Needless to say, the responsibility for any remaining errors remains mine.

assessing this aspect of the matter, what assumes greater significance than the typical or average picture at any time are the emergent trends, as well as the causal factors that underlie and direct such change.

In this chapter it is argued that recent trends of change in the position of women in Bangladesh have been, in part, impelled by a number of critical 'parametric' shifts at the macro-level, which involve economic, demographic, and socio-political factors. These shifts constitute elements of an overall process of uneven capitalist development in which market forces, to some extent directed by the profit-oriented logic of capital accumulation, have attempted to make use of available female labour for their own ends. During the course of this process, structures of family and kinship, as well as social institutions and production relationships, have been subjected to specific kinds of economic compulsions, e.g., ensuring subsistence, or making normal profit. As a consequence, many of these structures have been constrained either to adapt to such changes, or to disintegrate, giving rise to alternative institutional forms which are more suited to the changed circumstances.

Equally, the changing position of women has been influenced by the State and its policy-makers, as well as by interested external agencies, such as 'donor' institutions. Indeed, such deliberate and conscious policy interventions have significantly affected women's lives, directly as well as indirectly.[3] Another crucial factor has been the choice and implanting of particular technologies, which have had a wide range of consequences for women's lives, including their economic and social security.

For the present, my principal objective is to assess the extent to which the pre-existing social and economic institutions of Bangladesh have proved to be resilient, or malleable, in the face of the varied pressures generated by the process of capitalist development. Since these very institutions have often served to delimit the role and position of women, modifications undergone by them can also be expected to have led to consequential changes. In particular, these might well have induced shifts in the macro-level social and economic environment within which individual women, differentiated by class position, have had to make adaptive choices. Furthermore, conscious and organized activism by groups of women themselves, with or without assistance from others, is also likely to have played a crucial part in the story.

I begin by summarizing the typical position of women within the traditional structures of family and kinship, as well as the broader social and political arenas. The treatment attempts to interrelate these aspects of the subject with the critical economic–demographic shifts that have taken place during recent decades, and which have differentially affected the position of women in distinct classes. This is followed by an assessment of trends in women's

---

[3] For further documentation, see Jahan, op. cit. in n. 2.

participation in production and market-based activities, as well as of the double-edged role of capital in making use of female labour for profit-maximizing purposes. Next, the consequential impact of these changes upon women's position in the familial, social, and political arenas, as well as related trends in their socio-demographic attributes, are taken up for discussion. The major findings and broader perspectives which emerge from the argument are restated in conclusion.

Constraints of time and space make it impossible in this chapter to deal at any great length with certain other aspects of women's position, including such vital issues as policy-making, technological innovation, and the rising trend of violence against women. However, such issues will be touched upon in context and, wherever available, relevant references will be cited for the interested reader.[4]

The Family and the Kin-Group

Even today, for the majority of women in Bangladesh, the world consists of their immediate family, and the households of near relatives and neighbours. Very few are involved in any social institution apart from the family, and this often applies even to middle-class women in urban areas. Indeed, the boundaries of the homestead, and its kin-based extensions, circumscribe the indoor arena within which women spend most of their lives.

At work, there is the cultural institution of *parda*, which requires that women, apart from minor girls, be isolated from contact with all men outside their immediate family and near relatives.[5] They remain confined to the interior of their homes and are expected not even to meet or to talk with male visitors who come to the house. Movements outside the home are allowed 'only at prescribed times and for prescribed purposes'—for example, to attend school or to visit relatives.[6] It follows that the orthodox practice of *parda* virtually prohibits women from going to public places, such as meetings and markets, as well as from taking part in public activities, such as elections.[7] In a manner of speaking, women are permitted to move to 'indoor' spaces of other (prescribed) households, but not to 'outdoor'

---

[4] Thanks are due to Ahmed Kamal for pointing out some of these aspects which could not be covered in this chapter.

[5] See M. Chen, 'Poverty, Gender and Work in Bangladesh', *Economic and Political Weekly*, 21 (1986), pp. 217–22; E. Sattar, 'Village Women's Work', in *Women for Women: Bangladesh 1975* (Dhaka, 1975), pp. 33–65; R. Jahan, 'Women in Bangladesh', in ibid., pp. 1–30; M. Cain, S. R. Khanam, and S. Nahar, 'Class, Patriarchy and Women's Work in Bangladesh', *Population and Development Review*, 5 (1979), pp. 405–38.

[6] Chen, op. cit. in n. 5.

[7] R. Rashid, *Women's Markets: Pilot Project Activity* (Dhaka, 1988). On the 'market taboo' against women's participation in the market, she points out that in Bangla *bajarer meye* or 'market woman' is a colloquial term with the derogatory connotation of a woman of loose morals, which is not, of course, necessarily true.

spaces, which constitute 'the public "male" sphere of economic, social and political life'.[8]

In practice, adherence to *parda* restrictions is often more symbolic than real. For example, poorer women who are in need of outside work cannot afford to remain indoors, and make token concessions to the practice by putting on a veil or covering their heads when going out. Urban middle-class women tend to dispense with the practice altogether. None the less, most women do not, or cannot, go to public places or take part in public events, thus reflecting the continued presence of *parda* in more attenuated forms.[9]

Another dimension of *parda* is the rigidly laid down sexual division of labour within households, which, broadly speaking, allocates indoor work to women, and outdoor work to men.[10] Thus, typically, women in rural Bangladesh tend not to do agricultural work in the fields, but are almost entirely responsible for post-harvest processing of crops, as well as for other productive activities carried out in the proximity of the homestead (e.g. kitchen-gardening, poultry-keeping, and craftwork). Further, women alone perform all the familiar chores of domestic work (e.g. cooking and cleaning), and thus often have a double working day, even though their work may remain invisible to men's eyes.[11] Indeed, when services provided by women take the form of unpaid family labour, with no market prices being required, their work is usually not regarded as 'income-earning' by men, despite the fact that such labour manifestly results in net value added. The result is to undervalue the position of women in economic terms by socially categorizing them as dependants, while their (unpaid) family labour is taken for granted.[12]

The institution of *parda* has its cultural roots in deeply embedded notions of the *izzat* or honour of women.[13] Girls are brought up by parents with the social imperative of marrying them off as soon as possible. A paramount consideration for a good marriage is that the girl remain chaste, and does not behave in ways which compromise her honour and reputation as a virtuous woman; the same also applies after marriage to keep *izzat* intact. Indeed, any woman venturing out on her own, outside prescribed *parda*

[8] Chen, op. cit. in n. 5.

[9] F. E. McCarthy, 'The Status and Condition of Rural Women in Bangladesh', in Government of Bangladesh, *Agrarian Structure and Change: Rural Development Experience and Policies in Bangladesh* (Dhaka, 1978).

[10] K. M. A. Aziz and C. Maloney, *Life Stages, Gender and Fertility in Bangladesh* (Dhaka, 1985), p. 76; Cain, Khanam, and Nahar, op. cit. in n. 5, pp. 413–18; Chen, op. cit. in n. 5, p. 218.

[11] M. Chen, 'Overview of Women's Program, 1980–86: India and Bangladesh', mimeo. (Oxfam, 1986), p. 2.

[12] Sattar, op. cit. in n. 5; S. Adnan and R. Islam, 'Social Change and Rural Women; Possibilities of Participation', in *Women and Development* (Dhaka, 1977); Cain, Khanam, and Nahar, op. cit. in n. 5; McCarthy, op. cit. in n. 9.

[13] Aziz and Moloney, op. cit. in n. 10, pp. 48–79; N. Kabeer, 'Subordination and Struggle: Women in Bangladesh', *New Left Review*, 168 (1988), pp. 100–1.

limits, is perceived to be risking violation of her *izzat* by forbidden men. Any such event could result in loss of honour not only for herself, but also for the rest of her family.[14]

Given their perceived status as economic dependants who require to be protected, women in Bangladesh are not expected to become independent persons in a social sense. Rather, they are required to remain under the protective guardianship of successive male kinsmen at different stages of their lives: father or brother, husband, and, eventually, son. This also implies that women are often incapable of making, or are not permitted to make, their own decisions.[15] In particular, major decisions by women which involve the world beyond the family have to be vetted by the head of the household[16]—a role which invariably goes to men, except in certain special circumstances (see below).

Women's dependence on men within the family and extended kin-group is further reinforced by their unequal legal status, as well as by asymmetrical rules of inheritance of property.[17] While Hindu law does not provide any inheritance for daughters from their parents, Muslim law does nominally give each daughter half of the share accruing to each son.[18] In practice, most Muslim women in Bangladesh do not claim such property, particularly land. This serves to maintain good relations with their brothers, on whom they might well have to fall back in the event of widowhood or divorce. Even if a married woman does claim her inherited property, it is usually worked by her husband, who may thus also control the income yielded. In either case, it is men (brothers or husbands) who actually take over *de facto* control of property inherited by women, even though the latter might still continue to remain as the nominal owners.

[14] It is a salutary reminder to note that such cultural practices are not limited to societies such as contemporary Bangladesh, as might easily be presumed otherwise. Consider the following extract about life in the docklands of East London during the 1930s, just a generation or two earlier.

> Morals were high on the list, and respectability was the cheapest luxury one could afford . . . it was very unwise or unfortunate if a girl managed to get herself into trouble. Not only did this affect her whole way of life, but the rest of the family were involved, and this was something to be avoided at all costs. Her chances of marrying were narrowed down as second hand [*sic*] made a man look shallow in the eyes of his fellow creatures. Brothers were given an unwritten authority to watch out for their sisters and reprimand them, if seen with a boy after dark or in a doorway. (M. Barritt,) *The Barritts of Wapping High Street* (London, 1977), pp. 23–24)

[15] K. Westergaard, *Pauperization and Rural Women in Bangladesh: A Case Study* (Comilla, 1983), pp. 69–94.

[16] H. Knudsen *et al.*, *The Awareness of the Rural Poor: A Study in Nizsenbag Village, Senbag Upazila* (Nokhali, 1986).

[17] S. Sobhan, *Legal Status of Women in Bangladesh* (Dhaka, 1978); UNICEF, op. cit. in n. 2, pp. 75–76; Khan, op. cit. in n. 2; R. Bhuyian, 'Legal Status of Women in Bangladesh', in Government of Bangladesh, *Situation of Women in Bangladesh* (Dhaka, 1985).

[18] P. J. Bertocci, 'Elusive Villages: Social Structure and Community Organization in Rural East Pakistan', unpublished Ph.D. dissertation (Michigan State University, 1970); Westergaard, op. cit. in n. 15, pp. 69–72.

The successive roles which a woman has to undertake during successive stages of her life cycle reflect this position of dependency on men, and the consequential insecurity arising from it.[19] Once married, the young bride moves from the benevolent discipline of her paternal household to her husband's family, as required by the patrilocal system of residence. Often, this means having to adapt to a large extended family, where the new wife has to 'prove her worth' to her mother-in-law and other female relatives.[20] Paramount to the consolidation of her identity and status amongst her in-laws is the socio-biological role of reproducing the patrilineage. This crucially requires her to give birth to one or more sons—since daughters will not eventually 'stay' with the family. Any reluctance or failing on her part as a child-bearing and child-rearing 'machine' may lead to abuse and physical assault from her husband and in-laws.[21] A woman who is sterile or has not been able to give birth to sons faces the prospect of being divorced or having to put up with additional marriages by her husband.[22] Even for the woman herself, birth of one or more sons provides some assurance of future security in the event of widowhood and lack of support from her paternal, or her husband's, family.

Thus, women's dependency upon, and subordination to, men is conditioned by a whole range of practices embedded in the institutions of the family and the kin-group. Indeed, these provide the constituent elements of the well-documented system of patriarchy in Bangladesh which institutionalizes the subordination of women, in the sense of their structured dependency on men.[23]

Macro-Level Shifts Affecting Family Composition

Between 1961 and 1981 the population of Bangladesh grew by 63 per cent to reach nearly 90 million in 1981.[24] Given a limited land area, this has meant

[19] Aziz and Moloney, op. cit. in n. 10, pp. 48–90.

[20] Jahan, op. cit. in n. 5; M. Chen, *A Quiet Revolution: Women in Transition in Rural Bangladesh* (Dhaka, 1986), p. 56.

[21] Acts of violence against women for reasons such as these, as well as others concerned with demand for dowry, etc., appear to have increased during recent times. Such violence constitutes the culminating stage of various deeply rooted socio-psychological pressures in Bangladesh society. For further discussion of these in the context of rural and urban areas, see J. Arens and J. van Beurden, *Jhagrapur: Poor Peasants and Women in a Village in Bangladesh* (Amsterdam and Birmingham, 1977); UBINIG, *Violence on Women: Definitions and Analysis* (Dhaka, 1986, in Bangla); Kabeer, op. cit. in n. 13. The corresponding picture for India is given by M. Kishwar, 'Nature of Women's Mobilization in Rural India: An Exploratory Essay', *Economic and Political Weekly*, 24–31 Dec. 1988, pp. 2756–57.

[22] Polygyny is practised by both Muslims and Hindus in Bangladesh, as well as in the wider south Asian region.

[23] Cain, Khanam, and Nahar, op. cit. in n. 5, pp. 406–8; Chen, op. cit. in n. 20, pp. 58–59; Chen, op. cit. in n. 5, p. 219.

[24] Bangladesh Bureau of Statistics (BBS), *Bangladesh Population Census 1981, National Series: Analytical Findings and National Tables* (Dhaka, 1984), p. 33.

an aggregate downward shift in distribution of owned landholdings because of two crucial factors. First, there has been the cumulative partitioning of landed property, through complex processes of inheritance, into increasingly smaller holdings. Secondly, market-based interaction between households of differing economic strengths has led to a process of differentiation of the peasantry, resulting in net polarization between landholding strata. The combined result of both these factors has been to increase massively the relative weight of landless and land-poor households within the total population.[25]

By 1983–4 the proportion of rural households which owned or operated[26] holdings of less than half an acre (0–0.20 hectare) amounted to 57 per cent, while those with holdings between half and one acre (0.21–0.40 hectare) accounted for another 12.3 per cent.[27] The overwhelming majority (nearly 70 per cent) of households were thus land-poor, if not altogether landless. There was also massive out-migration by land-poor families from the countryside to the towns and cities. While urban areas had contained about 5 per cent of the total population in 1961, the corresponding proportion had increased to nearly 15 per cent by 1981.[28]

These major economic–demographic shifts were associated with corresponding changes in family composition and its distribution by types. With decreasing amounts of landed property to bind them together, large extended families tended to break down into smaller units.[29] In fact, nuclear and supplemented nuclear families accounted for the majority (52.2 per cent) of all households in Bangladesh in 1982.[30] Furthermore, the incidence of

---

[25] S. Adnan and H. Z. Rahman, 'Peasant Classes and Land Mobility: Structural Reproduction and Change in Rural Bangladesh', *Bangladesh Historical Studies*, 3 (1978), pp. 161–215; W. van Schendel, *Peasant Mobility: The Odds of Life in Rural Bangladesh* (New Delhi, 1982). For further discussion of these economic, demographic, and social shifts which have affected the nature of family composition at village level, see the evidence from a wide range of sources, cited in S. Adnan, *Annotation of Village Studies in Bangladesh and West Bengal: A Review of Socio-economic Trends over 1942–1988* (Comilla, 1990), chs. 4, 5, 9. Longitudinal evidence on changes in family composition in a particular village of Chittagong (Shangkhomala) over the 12-year period 1974–86 is documented in S. Adnan, *Two Village Studies of Landlessness in Rural Bangladesh* (Dhaka, 1986).

[26] Operated holdings refer to the area actually cultivated by a given household. This does not necessarily equal the land owned by the household, since part may be leased out, whilst land belonging to others may be leased in for cultivation.

[27] BBS, *The Bangladesh Census of Agriculture and Livestock, 1983–84* (Dhaka, 1986), i. 70.

[28] BBS, op. cit. in n. 24, p. 36. This increase in the proportion of the urban population is partly due to 'census redefinition' by the BBS as explained in S. Adnan, *Socio-economic Trends in Greater Nokhali, 1975–87* (Nokhali, 1988). However, there is no doubt that the extent of urbanization has increased during these periods, despite some of the spurious exaggeration in the census data.

[29] S. Adnan, 'Class Structure and Fertility in Rural Bangladesh: Reflections on the Political Economy of Population Growth', in IUSSP, *Economic and Demographic Change, Issues for the 1980s: Proceedings of the Conference in Helsinki, 1978* (Liège, 1979), ii. 87–118; Adnan (1990), op. cit. in n. 25.

[30] BBS, *Statistical Yearbook of Bangladesh* (Dhaka, 1986), p. 183.

nuclear families was relatively greater among the landless than the more landed groups. Disaggregated data from a village in Chittagong in 1986 indicated that nuclear and sub-nuclear families accounted for 74 per cent of households which owned less than one acre of land, compared to 43 per cent of those households which owned holdings of more than one acre.[31]

Greater incidence of nuclear and sub-nuclear families amongst the landless and the land-poor has meant that wives in these households do not usually have to cope with the hierarchical authority and supervision of their mothers-in-law and other female relatives. While this has given them a certain autonomy in running their own households, it has also exposed them to greater risks of destitution in the event of divorce or widowhood.[32]

At the same time, lack of land and other means of production has meant that these households cannot always meet their subsistence requirements from the incomes earned by their male members alone.[33] Nor can the women deploy their spare working hours in self-employed productive activities within their own households, because they lack the necessary means—for example, the land or livestock required for post-harvest processing of crops or animal husbandry. In other words, the economic pressure on poorer women to deploy their labour in market-based activities and add to the men's incomes in order to ensure the minimal requirements for their families' survival has become compulsive in many cases. As a result, the traditional supply constraints on the participation of women in the labour market have been coming under increasing stress, with profound structural consequences (see below).

In fact, such drastic changes in women's position within the family and kinship structures are most strikingly evident in the 'limiting case' of households headed by women. These emerge when women have to take over the headship of the household because their husbands have died or migrated elsewhere, or when they have been divorced or deserted.[34] In 1982

---

[31] Adnan (1986), op. cit. in n. 25, pp. 28–29; Cain, Khanam, and Nahar, op. cit. in n. 5, p. 410.

[32] Such women can no longer expect to receive support from the extended family and the wider kin group, as would have been customary in the past. See W. B. Arthur and G. McNicoll, 'An Analytical Survey of Population and Development in Bangladesh', *Population and Development Review*, 4 (1978), pp. 23–80; Cain, Khanam, and Nahar, op. cit. in n. 5; Adnan, op. cit. in n. 29; Chen, op. cit. in n. 20, p. 70; Adnan (1990), op. cit. in n. 25, ch. 9 on Social Structure.

[33] M. Cain, 'The Economic Activities of Children in a Village in Bangladesh', *Population and Development Review*, 3 (1977), pp. 201–27; M. Greeley, 'Rural Technology, Rural Institutions and the Rural Poorest: The Case of Rice Processing in Bangladesh', in M. Greeley and M. Howes (eds.), *Rural Technology: Rural Institutions and the Rural Poorest* (Comilla, 1982), pp. 128–51; R. Jahan, 'Women Workers in the Garments Industry: Women's Work and Family Strategies in Bangladesh', mimeo., draft final report submitted to the Kathmandu Workshop on Women's Work and Family Strategies, sponsored by the UN University, 1987, p. 48; R. I. Rahman, *The Wage Employment Market for Rural Women in Bangladesh* (Bangladesh, 1986), pp. 22–23.

[34] Cain, Khanam, and Nahar, op. cit. in n. 5, pp. 410–11; Chen, op. cit. in n. 20, pp. 70–71. The discussion groups held by UBINIG have, however, regarded the very concept of a

15.4 per cent of households in Bangladesh were reported to be headed by women. Amongst such female heads of households in 1982, the overwhelming majority (58.8 per cent) were widowed or divorced. The proportion was greater in the rural (16.5 per cent) than in the urban areas (6.9 per cent)—possibly because of emigration to the cities of rural men who left their women and children behind.[35]

As noted earlier, the customary social conditioning of women in Bangladesh hardly prepares them for the role of household head, which requires the ability to take independent decisions. Where there are no income transfers arriving regularly (e.g. from migrant husbands), the predicament of female heads has the added dimension of a frightening financial independence'.[36] These women have little option but to fend for themselves and their families. Adherence to the strictures of *parda* becomes a luxury which they cannot possibly afford. Since such women have to begin to deal with 'men's spaces in the outside world', and earn incomes through participation in the market whenever necessary, a critical feature of patriarchal domination is also undermined in the process (see below).

The Social and Political Arenas

Beyond the family and the kin-group lie the social institutions of the community. These serve to co-ordinate activities of individual households which, in the general case, are unrelated by kinship ties. In rural Bangladesh, the pre-eminent social institution that mediates such activities and interactions is the community group, usually known as the *shamaj*.[37] Households that

female-headed household as questionable, if not altogether misconceived, given a pervasively patriarchal society. See UBINIG, *Life and Struggles of Women in Slums: A Neglected Sector of Development Programmes* (Dhaka, 1986, in Bangla), pp. 10–20. Farhad Mazhar, for example, has argued that such households should be regarded as 'male-less' families. In the urban slums of Dhaka, such families are found to be living together, organizing themselves into a certain kind of communal life-style. The numbers of such families are reported to be increasing. More significantly, however, such changes are symptomatic of new forms of familial organization, which appear to be replacing traditional ones. In this sense, they might well be the prototypes of qualitatively different 'family ties' of the future, if present trends were to persist.

[35] BBS, op. cit. in n. 30, p. 182; BBS, *Selected Statistics and Indicators on Demographic and Socio-economic Situation of Women in Bangladesh* (Dhaka, 1989), p. 24. In fact, these reported national figures for both urban and rural areas might well be underestimates. In a study of urban garment workers in Dhaka it was found that 18% of the women considered themselves heads of their respective families (Jahan, op. cit. in n. 33, pp. 45–46, table 11). However, in practice, a much larger proportion of women acted as *de facto* heads of their respective households, since they were the major breadwinners. In a national-level sample survey conducted in 1988 it was found that, while 15.1% of rural households were headed by women *de jure*, another 9.4% were so headed *de facto*, giving a total of 24.5% (C. Safilios-Rothschild and S. Mahmud, *Women's Roles in Agriculture. Present Trends and Potential for Growth* (Dhaka, 1989), table 7 in appendix II).

[36] Chen, op. cit. in n. 20, pp. 62–63.

[37] It is also known as the *mallot, reyai*, etc., in different parts of the country. For a detailed analysis of the characteristics of the *shamaj*, see Bertocci, op. cit. in n. 18; S. Adnan, 'Peasant

belong to a particular *shamaj* have reciprocal rights and obligations, and are expected to co-operate at times of critical life-cycle rituals such as birth, death, or marriage. The *shamaj* also has other overt and covert roles to perform, including the resolution of conflicts between its member households. In the latter case, a specific arbitrating mechanism known as the *shalish* operates, which is essentially a kind of indigenous court, presided over by leaders of the *shamaj* concerned (*shamajpradhans*). Additional members may also be called to sit on the *shalish* bench,[38] these are usually rich and influential men, who often hold offices in local government (e.g. as chairmen and members of the Union and *Upazila* councils). Those who sit on the *shalish* bench as judges are known as *shalishkars*.

Apart from their overt functions, the institutions of the *shamaj* and *shalish* also serve as covert instruments for exercising power and authority by the *shamajpradhans* and *shalishkars*, who tend to come from the dominant classes in terms of land and wealth. In particular, *shamajpradhans* and *shalishkars* can, and often do, manipulate these institutions to lay down prescriptive codes of 'approved' behaviour for members of all classes belonging to their *shamaj*, as well as to censure all those, including women, who are deemed to have displayed forms of deviant behaviour.[39]

Traditionally, women are excluded from participation in the institutions of the *shamaj* and the *shalish*, which remain public spaces in the forbidden sphere of 'men's' activities. There are hardly any documented instances of women being *shamajpradhans* or *shalishkars* (but see below). When a woman is a disputant in a case before the *shalish*, she is usually required to be represented by a male guardian, such as a kinsman (father, brother, husband, or son) or by her *shamajpradhan*. Even women who now move and work outside, and have thus freed themselves from *parda* restrictions at the level of the family, are unable to become *shamajpradhans* or *shalishkars*, or to represent themselves in person in *shalish* proceedings.[40]

Furthermore, such restrictions on the participation of women in the social arena are imposed by dominant men from amongst the community as a whole, rather than the particular male guardians or kinsmen of the women

Ideology and Societal Maintenance. Conflicting Patterns from Bangladesh', *ADAB News*, 15 (1988), pp. 1–19; S. Adnan, *The Roots of Power: A Study in the Political Economy of Rural Bangladesh* (Dhaka, forthcoming).

[38] S. Adnan and R. Islam, 'Social Structure and Implication for Resource Allocation in a Chittagong Village', in Institute of Engineers, *Integrated Rural Development: Proceedings of the Seminar* (Dhaka, 1977), i. 53–63; Adnan, op. cit. in n. 37.

[39] Detailed analysis of the overt, as well as the covert, functions of the *shalish*, based on case-study evidence is provided in Adnan, op. cit. in n. 37.

[40] Cain, Khanam, and Nahar, op. cit. in n. 5, p. 407; Chen, op. cit. in n. 20, pp. 175–84. However, some instances of direct participation by women do occur, depending upon the nature of the case. Furthermore, village women can and do participate in *shalish* activities behind the scenes, e.g. by investigating pregnancies which involve disputed paternity. I am indebted to Sarah White for criticisms which have led to some moderation of the position which I had taken in the original version of this chapter.

concerned. In other words, it is the male leadership of the dominant class in terms of power and wealth which manipulates the rules of social institutions to restrict and regulate the movement and activities of all women, including those who come from the poorest classes.[41]

Men's *shamaj* leadership is enthusiastically aided and abetted in this particular role by the clergy at village level. This is particularly true of Muslims, since the sacred texts of Islam are quite explicit about the inferiority of women to men, as well as the approved limits of women's participation outside their proper places in the domestic arena.[42] However, the vociferous condemnation of women's activities outside their homes by *mullahs* and *moulanas* (Muslim priests) goes well beyond what is laid down in the sacred scriptures. Significantly, many such *mullahs* and *moulanas* depend for their livelihood on the payments made by committees that administer the mosques and *madrashas* (religious schools) in which they are employed. These committees are invariably dominated by rich and influential men, and typically include the *shamajpradhans* and *shalishkars* of the local community.[43] Not surprisingly, the *moulanas* and *mullahs* are often known to serve as the mouthpieces of their employers. In this sense, the varied pronouncements on women and their 'proper places' by the religious establishment are not generally independent of the local-level relationships of power and influence.

In fact, the institutions of the *shamaj* and the *shalish* not only tend to exclude women from participation, but also intervene directly or indirectly in the internal affairs of their member households in issues related to women and their social status. Often, the women concerned are placed merely in the role of symbolic objects, so that the ostensible contentions about their position and honour simply serve to mask deeper conflicts about social, political, and economic interests between, or within, the male leaderships of the *shamaj* groups involved.

The classic instance of interventions of this kind relates to forbidden or improper marriages, as perceived by the male leaderships of *shamaj* groups. For example, in a Pabna village, a Muslim *shamaj* eventually disintegrated because one of its men had remarried his wife—having divorced her initially—in a ceremony which was regarded by some as having been improperly conducted.[44] In this case, the *shamaj* broke into two groups which consisted of immigrant households from outside, and indigenous families from the locality. In this case, long-standing tensions had been

[41] Chen, op. cit. in n. 20. Typically, the menfolk of such women are not even in a position to become *shamajpradhans* or *shalishkars*.

[42] Arens and van Beurden, op. cit. in n. 21, pp. 32–33; Cain, Khanam, and Nahar, op. cit. in n. 5, p. 407; Chen, op. cit. in n. 20, pp. 171–84; Adnan, op. cit. in n. 37; Adnan and Islam, op. cit. in n. 12.

[43] Adnan, op. cit. in n. 37; Chen, op. cit. in n. 20, p. 171; Bangladesh Rural Advancement Committee, *Group Evolution in Manikganj Project: Two Case Studies* (Dhaka, 1984), pp. 49–50.

[44] Adnan, op. cit. in n. 37.

simmering between these two groups. When this controversial remarriage occurred, the opportunity was seized by dominant men of both groups, who eventually forced the break-up of the *shamaj* concerned.

In another instance in the same village, an upper caste Hindu girl eloped with, and later married, a lower-caste Hindu boy.[45] This caused serious loss of face for the upper-caste households, members of which also monopolized the leadership of the Hindu *shamaj* concerned. Later, when this controversial couple invited all *shamaj* members to a life-cycle ritual for its young son, not only did leading households from the upper-caste refuse to accept the invitation, but they eventually expelled all the lower-caste households from the *shamaj* for having taken part in that ceremony. Here, too, the conflict about a woman and her 'improper' marriage served to ignite an already strained relationship between the two caste groups, which dated back to earlier conflicts about their respective contributions of money and resources for the annual *Kali-puja* ceremony at the local temple.[46]

These two instances illustrate the ways in which women in rural Bangladesh often have thrust upon them the role of symbolic objects about whom issues of honour are fought out by groups of related men, who might well have other interests at stake in precipitating such conflicts. Such an imposed role for women, who remain virtually passive otherwise, can arise precisely because of their traditional status as protected beings whose honour has perforce to be defended by their men.

The other side of the coin is that women who have lost their honour, in the sense of being no longer socially recognized as modest or chaste, are also perceived to have been deprived of their significance as symbolic objects of social and familial protection. No issues of honour are fought about them, whether in substantive or symbolic terms. Such loss of honour and its consequences can be quite unintended on the part of the women concerned. Thus, many victims of rape are no longer sheltered by their former families, even if they manage to survive the ordeal, since the act of violation stigmatizes the families as much as the women themselves.

In an incident of abduction and rape in a Chittagong village, the young girl concerned was neither able to return to her poor and helpless parents, nor was she taken in marriage by the man who had violated her, despite directives of the local *shalish*.[47] She ended up by having to move from the

---

[45] Ibid.

[46] Comparable instances have been documented for Bogra villages as early as 1942 by R. Mukherjee, *Six Villages of Bengal* (Bombay, 1971). It is to be noted, however, that issues of *izzat*, or honour, do not arise only in respect of women. In Bangladesh society, cultural applicability of notions of *izzat* extends to men as much as to women, though in different forms and contexts. For a more detailed discussion, see Adnan, op. cit. in n. 37. I am indebted to Syed M. Heshemi for comments on this point.

[47] Based on fieldwork evidence collected by S. M. Abu Zaker in my restudy of a Chittagong village in 1987. The instance of a comparable act of violence on women in the same village a decade earlier, as well as the conspicuous silence of the village *shalish* regarding any sanctions

house of one rich man to another, taking refuge wherever she could, and even having to serve as a mistress to some. Women in predicaments of this kind, uprooted from their familial moorings, become more-or-less undisguised objects of pleasure, in contrast to their normative status of being objects of honour. The same applies, though for somewhat different reasons, to those village women who, while continuing to remain a part of their nearly destitute families, are more or less driven to prostitution by their poverty.[48]

In the relative anonymity of urban settings, however, women are far less fettered by such social restrictions. Since institutions comparable to the *shamaj* and the *shalish* are far less active—if at all—there is less scope for interference in the private affairs of women in particular households by any male 'guardians' who claim to represent the 'voice of the community'.[49] Instead, women are faced by conflict between their roles within families and kin-groups on the one hand, and the labour market on the other (see below).

Politics

By and large, women in Bangladesh have little say in politics and desist from taking more than a subordinate role in this arena.[50] This is so, despite the fact that two of the foremost opposition leaders at national level are women. In fact, of the two, one is the daughter, and the other the widow, of an assassinated ex-president. Significantly, both have assumed somewhat symbolic leadership roles—less in their own right, than through a process which might be best categorized under the Weberian notion of the transfer of charisma.[51]

At the grass roots, however, the overwhelming majority of poorer women do not take an active part in either national or local politics, nor are they expected to do so by men. Even when they are mobilized to cast their votes, women tend to vote as they are told—either by their husbands or by male *shamajpradhans* and local notables.[52]

against the rich and powerful culprit concerned, is documented in an earlier paper (see Adnan and Islam, op. cit. in n. 12, p. 49).

[48] Arens and van Beurden, op. cit. in n. 21, p. 49.

[49] None the less, some influence is exerted by public opinion in the urban localities and slums in which women industrial workers live (see Jahan, op. cit. in n. 33).

[50] Jahan, op. cit. in n. 5; K. Jalal, 'Women in Politics', in *Women for Women, Bangladesh 1975* (Dhaka, 1975), pp. 204–14; N. Chowdhury, 'Women in Politics in Bangladesh', in Government of Bangladesh, op. cit. in n. 17; S. R. Qadir and M. Islam, *Women Representatives at the Union Level as Change Agent of Development* (Dhaka, 1987).

[51] M. Weber, *Economy and Society: An Outline of Interpretive Sociology*, ed. G. Roth and C. Wittich (Berkeley, Calif., 1978), pp. 1123–225.

[52] Most women did not even have the vote until 1956, when universal adult franchise was first introduced in what was then East Pakistan, and is now Bangladesh; see Qadir and Islam, op. cit. in n. 50, p. 3; Knudsen *et al.*, op. cit. in n. 16, p. 31; Westergaard, op. cit. in n. 15, pp. 91–93; Bangladesh Rural Advancement Committee, op. cit. in n. 43, p. 67.

This applies even to those women who are nominated to be members of local self-government bodies such as the Union *Parishad* (UP). As Qadir and Islam have noted in their study of such local-level women 'representatives', 'they carried their subordinate role from the family to the *Parishad*. For all practical purposes, it is seen that the Union *Parishad* is an all-male business'. As such, women's votes and voices are usually taken for granted by men—not only from their own families, but also from the dominant classes, who tend to be the leading actors in the electoral and broader political scenes.

Production and the Market

As noted earlier, the more-or-less rigid sexual division of labour within atomistic household units allocates all activities regarded as domestic work to women alone. In addition, for an increasing proportion of the women in Bangladesh, either their own labour power, or the products of such labour, are being integrated into the market. The critical questions here relate to the nature and extent of such market involvements and the consequences of these for women's position—not only in the economic spheres of production and exchange, but also in the familial and socio-political arenas.[53] Further-more, these questions have to be set firmly in the context of the general process of uneven development of the economy, as well as the profit-oriented imperatives of capitalist production in particular.[54]

For analytical clarity, however, it is useful to sketch out at the outset a typology of women's work in market and non-market terms.[55] Goods and services produced within the household, for familial consumption alone, clearly correspond to the production of use-values. On the other hand, goods produced at home, but sold in the market as commodities, constitute

---

[53] The findings of a study on women who worked in 'Food for Works' (FFW) programmes suggested that they were interested in 'markets specifically designed for women's use' (M. E. Marum and M. K. Hasna, *Women at Work in Bangladesh: A Study of Women's Food for Work Programs* (Dhaka, 1982), p. 121). In a later and related study R. Rashid (op. cit. in n. 7) found that women's participation in market-based enterprises could prove to be viable, provided certain conditions were met.

[54] Theoretical expositions of the 'paradigm of capitalist development' are given in S. Adnan, 'Peasant Production and Capitalist Development: A Model with Reference to Bangladesh', unpublished Ph.D. dissertation (University of Cambridge, 1984), and S. Adnan, 'Classical and Contemporary Approaches to Agrarian Capitalism', *Economic and Political Weekly*, 20 (1985), pp. PE/53–PE/64. The nature of uneven capitalist development in Bangladesh by sectors and types of activity will become evident from the examples cited in context below. I am indebted to Syed M. Heshemi for comments and discussion on this point.

[55] The theoretical distinction between market and non-market sectors of the economy is analysed in detail by Adnan (1984), op. cit. in n. 54, chs. 2, 3. See also discussion by S. Hamid, 'Women's Non-Market Work and its Impact on GDP: The Case of Bangladesh', mimeo. (Bangladesh Institute of Development Studies, Dhaka, 1989).

production of exchange-values.[56] In both cases, however, women perform as unpaid family labour, rather than as wage-workers. The labour process continues to remain under familial control and supervision, with no formal wage contract being either required or made.

Correlatively, women's wage work, too, can take different forms. Apart from outright employment in fields and factories, women also undertake indoor employment in the households of others, which is more attuned to *parda* considerations. Indeed, women do not even have to move out of their own homes to work on contract with merchant-manufacturers through a variety of 'putting-out' systems, such as in the making of *bidi* (country cigarettes).[57] In these cases, women receive wages for piecework. Thus, even in purely theoretical terms, working at home does not preclude wage work by any means, nor does the institution of *parda* constitute any insurmountable barrier to the penetration of the market forces of capitalism.

It is not surprising that women's involvements with the market have initially tended to follow those options which were more in keeping with *parda* considerations. This has essentially meant working in indoor situations, such as producing goods for sale at home, or being employed for domestic and post-harvest processing work in the interior of the homesteads of others. In recent years, however, a small but growing number of women have dispensed with *parda* considerations altogether and taken up 'outdoor' wage employment in fields, factories, and other public spaces. The macro-level dimensions of women's involvement in productive activities are briefly sketched below, followed by discussion of the forces that have been responsible for these trends.

Recent Trends in Women's Work

During the 1980s the economy of Bangladesh has been subject to pressure from varied quarters. These include recessions in the world market, domestic stagnation, and, not least, strident directives from the World Bank and associated multilateral agencies to shift towards policies of greater privatization and trade liberalization. Consequently, the national economy has been undergoing a wide range of macro-level structural adjustments. It is likely that, at the margin, it has been the poorest women of the country who have been hit hardest by these adjustment processes.[58] Such macro-level

---

[56] K. Marx, *Capital* (Harmondsworth, 1976), i. Unpaid family labour which produces exchange values or commodities for sale on the market accords with the theoretical construct of simple commodity production, as contrasted with capitalist commodity production. For a brief exposition of the conceptual distinctions involved, see Adnan (1985), op. cit. in n. 54, pp. PE/53–PE/55.

[57] Adnan, op. cit. in n. 28. See also Adnan (1984), op. cit. in n. 54 for theoretical elaboration.

[58] See S. Mahmud and W. Mahmud, 'Structural Adjustment and Women—The Case of Bangladesh', mimeo. (Bangladesh Institute for Development Studies, Dhaka, 1989), pp. 1–4, for discussion of these processes of structural adjustment and their impact on women's position in the economy.

factors, which have affected women's work-patterns in recent years, have to be borne in mind when we look at the national data and interpret recent trends.

If full-time housewives, who produce use-values, are *included* as part of the active labour force—contrary to conventional economic practice—then women in Bangladesh accounted for 47.7 per cent and 50.4 per cent of all persons in productive employment in the years 1974 and 1983–84 respectively.[59] In other words, the number of women more or less equalled that of men in the total employed labour force, when it was defined to include both market and non-market (household) work. Furthermore, the refined activity rate for women came to 79.9 per cent and 82.3 per cent in 1974 and 1983–84 respectively, which clearly shows that the overwhelming majority of women were economically productive.[60]

Even if we adopt conventional economic practice and exclude housewives and others involved in household work, it is still significant that the number of all employed (i.e. self-employed and wage-employed) women rose from 0.9 million in 1974 to 2.4 million in 1983–84—i.e. by 167 per cent.[61] Their proportion in the total employed population increased from 4.2 per cent in 1974 to 8.6 per cent in 1983–84. In other words, women's participation in the employed population increased both absolutely and relatively, compared with men, during this decade.[62]

The pattern of women's involvement in the various markets of the economy is revealed in greater detail if we look at the activities (sectors) in which they worked, as well as the capacities (job roles) in which they did so. In 1983–84 the majority of employed women (according to the conventional definition) were working in a variety of services in the tertiary sector (63 per cent), followed by different manufacturing activities in the secondary sector (28 per cent).[63] In contrast, only 9 per cent of the women were involved in

---

[59] Recalculated from BBS, op. cit. in n. 30, p. 192, table 3.2, by adding to the conventionally employed labour force all those who were listed as being involved in household work, including housewives. Using this altered definition, the total labour force in 1974 and 1983–84 came to 39.2 million and 51.8 million respectively, of whom women accounted for 18.7 million and 26.1 million. Cf. the discussion by Hamid, op. cit. in n. 55.

[60] The refined activity rate is defined as the size of the employed labour force expressed as a percentage of the total number of persons aged 10 years and over. The figures have been recalculated in accordance with the altered definition of the labour force given in n. 59 above. Comparable data are now available from the Labour Force Surveys of 1984–85 and 1985–86 (BBS, op. cit. in n. 35, pp. 98–100).

[61] BBS, op. cit. in n. 30, p. 192.

[62] As is evident, these conclusions have been drawn solely on the basis of stock data. Since comparable flow data on the duration and intensity of women's work on a national scale are not available, it is not possible to provide more precise estimates. Cf. discussion in Mahmud and Mahmud, op. cit. in n. 58.

[63] The data refer to 2.2 million of the 2.4 million women who were employed in 1983–84. This is because the sectors in which fewer than 25,000 women were employed have been excluded from this particular table in BBS, *Labour Force Survey, 1983–84: Final Report* (Dhaka, 1986), p. 40, table 3c. Fig. 14.1 has been recalculated after reorganizing the data on a sectoral basis.

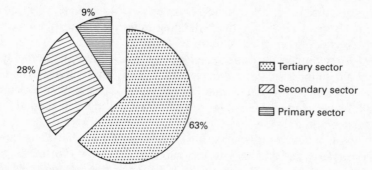

FIG. 14.1 Distribution of working women in Bangladesh, by sectors, 1983–84
Source: BBS, op. cit. in n. 63

the primary sector consisting of agriculture and related activities.[64] The relative weights of the three sectors is illustrated in Fig. 14.1.

Further disaggregation of the data indicates that, by and large, women were working in the interstices of the economy rather than the mainstream sectors of crop production and formal industry. Nearly half (49 per cent) were involved as maids and helpers in domestic work and in post-harvest processing. Another 6 per cent were accounted for by trading activities of various kinds, while primary and secondary schoolteachers constituted nearly 2 per cent. About 1.2 per cent of the women were clerical workers, while 3.6 per cent were labourers in various activities. The proportion of women in all other professional activities combined was found to be insignificant compared to the total for the tertiary sector. In the manufacturing sector, women figured as weavers (7 per cent), *bidi*-makers (6 per cent), grain-millers (5 per cent), basket and brush-makers (3 per cent), potters (2 per cent), and spinners (2 per cent). Most of these were informal sector activities, where the women worked either at home, or in small workshops. Finally, of the 9 per cent of women employed in agriculture, 7 per cent were labourers who worked in the fields.[65]

Of interest, too, were the roles in which these women related to production

[64] In the sample survey by Safilios-Rothschild and Mahmud (op. cit. in n. 35), figures for women's participation rates in agricultural activities are much larger. These results, whilst correcting for possible underestimates in the BBS data, probably overstate the true values. However, constraints of space and time do not permit a more detailed critique of the survey, including its method, in the present chapter.

[65] Smaller-scale studies have provided comparable evidence of women's participation in a wide range of occupations, both in agriculture and outside. See Q. K. Ahmad, *Female Employment in Bangladesh: A Review of Status and Policy* (Dhaka, 1985), pp. 19–64; Rahman, op. cit. in n. 33, pp. 39–41; Wallace *et al.*, *The Invisible Resource: Women and Work in Rural Bangladesh* (Boulder, Colo., 1987). However, in a field survey of two villages in April–June 1985, Rahman (op. cit. in n. 33, pp. 39–41) found that none of the working women had been engaged in agricultural field operations.

organization—that is, their places in the overall scheme of production relations. By and large, the overwhelming majority were wage employees, who worked either as casual labourers, or under more stable job contracts: nearly 69 per cent in rural areas and 84 per cent in urban.[66] Self-employed and unpaid family workers who produced goods and services for various markets accounted for 31 per cent in rural, and 15 per cent in urban areas. Overall, 72 per cent of the employed women earned their livelihood through the labour market.

As regards job conditions, data for 1983–84 indicated that women worked 44.7 hours per week on average, compared to 52.4 hours for men—that is, their workload amounted to about 85 per cent of that of men.[67] However, many of these women had to work additional varying hours on domestic tasks in their homes, so that their total workload almost certainly matched, if it did not exceed, that of men. On the other hand, women in wage employment were invariably paid lower rates than men. Taking all forms of hired employment together, the average wage level for women came to 60 per cent of that of men.[68] For casual daily labour only, women's wage rates were 50 per cent or even less of what was given to men.[69]

Interestingly, the difference between the 'average' wage rates for men and women who worked as daily labourers appears to have declined considerably between 1983–84 and 1985–86.[70] When disaggregated by sector, however, women's wage rates in non-agricultural work during the same period have stubbornly remained at around half those for men, whereas agricultural wage rates have shown a pronounced tendency towards convergence for the two sexes. This suggests the emergence of a trend towards the breakdown of sex-based segmentation in the agricultural labour market, counterpoised by the persistence of such pre-existing institutional barriers in the non-agricultural sectors. Unfortunately, the data currently available do not permit us to go beyond this somewhat tentative conjecture, particularly as regards national trends.

The national income accounts currently available for Bangladesh do not disaggregate data by sex. However, Hamid has recently attempted to estimate the relative contribution of women to the gross domestic product

---

[66] The figures have been recalculated from BBS, op. cit. in n. 63, p. 48, table 8. Basing himself on various studies which provided information on women, Ahmad (op. cit. in n. 65, p. 27) concluded that 'there can be no doubt that large numbers of rural and industrial workers are not counted in official statistics'. Note also Ahmad's discussion on p. 56, table 17. Cf. also Rahman, op. cit. in n. 33.

[67] BBS, op. cit. in n. 63, p. 52, table 1; Ahmad, op. cit. in n. 65, pp. 22–23.

[68] Ahmad, op. cit. in n. 65. In absolute terms, the average weekly earnings of all categories of hired workers came to Tk. 67.2 and Tk. 40.4 for men and women respectively (BBS, op. cit. in n. 63, p. 60, table 6). See also Ahmad, op. cit. in n. 65, p. 28; Jahan, op. cit. in n. 2, p. 6.

[69] In absolute terms, the average wage for daily labourers varied in the range of Tk. 14–18 for men, whilst it was around Tk. 7 for women (BBS, op. cit. in n. 63, p. 62, table 8).

[70] BBS, op. cit. in n. 35, p. 115, for the data and concepts used.

(GDP), including their non-market work within the household.[71] He found that, under certain assumptions, particularly when the work of both sexes is valued at equal wage rates (actual or imputed), women's share in the 'national average' of the household's daily subsistence income amounted to 64 per cent, compared to 35 per cent for men.

Capital and Female Labour

The overall picture of women's participation in market-based activities shows that some have been able to overcome traditional 'barriers to entry' and take part in typically 'non-female' sectors, such as agricultural crop production. None the less, the bulk of the women remain in the interstices of the economy, and either provide various household services or manufacture minor products. They remain a marginal segment of the labour force, and constitute a reservoir of cheap labour which is largely tapped by various informal sector activities—whether as poorly paid wage-workers, or as unpaid family labour.[72] Much of this informal sector employment is generated by small-scale capital, industrial or commercial (e.g. in the 'putting-out' systems).[73] In this sense, the process of incorporating women's labour power from peasant households, as well as the urban proletariat and semi-proletariat, in the circulation of small-scale capital is already well under way in Bangladesh—a symptom of particular stages in the process of capitalist development.[74]

[71] For details of concepts used and method of estimation, see Hamid, op. cit. in n. 55, pp. 161–9, table 8.

[72] In the report by UBINIG (op. cit. in n. 34, p. 10), these women are identified as members of the industrial reserve army, as postulated by Marx. Some of the theoretical issues involved here have been elaborated in S. Adnan, 'Conceptualizing Fertility Trends in Peripheral Formations', in C. Höhn and R. Mackensen (eds.), *Determinants of Fertility Trends: Theories Re-examined; Proceedings of the Seminar held in Bad Homburg* (IUSSP, Liège, 1982). See also the studies by Ahmad (op. cit. in n. 65), and Jahan (op. cit. in n. 33, pp. 26–27).

[73] Studies of the urban informal sector in Bangladesh are provided by F. Akhter, *Women in Slums: Living Conditions and Opportunities* (Dhaka, 1985); A. M. T. H. Amin, 'Urban Informal Sector: Employment Potential and Problems', in R. Islam and M. Muqtada (eds.), *Bangladesh: Selected Issues in Employment and Development* (Geneva, 1986). See also UBINIG, op. cit. in n. 34, pp. 28–29; Adnan, op. cit. in n. 28, p. 256.

[74] The argument that capitalist development in agriculture can take different forms in its initial stages and, moreover, often incorporates labour powers from the poorer peasant households in its circulation processes was originally put forward by both Kautsky and Lenin. See J. Najai (eds.), 'Summary of Selected Parts of Kautsky's "The Agrarian Question"', *Economy and Society*, 5 (1976), pp. 2–3; V. I. Lenin, 'The Development of Capitalism in Russia', *Collected Works*, (Moscow, 1960), iii. 95–96; V. I. Lenin, 'Capitalism in Agriculture: Kautsky's Book and Mr Bulgakov's Article', *Collected Works* (Moscow, 1960), iv. 112. A brief restatement of this classical argument is given in Adnan (1985), op. cit. in n. 54, pp. PE/58–PE/59. However, even in its later stages, international capitalism has demonstrated the propensity to search for, and make use of, remaining reservoirs of cheap labour, whether male or female, in industry or agriculture. See G. Standing, *Global Feminization through Flexible Labour: Labour Market Analysis and Employment Planning* (Geneva, 1989); N. Heyzer (ed.), *Daughters in Industry* (Kuala Lumpur, 1988); 'Asian Women Wage Earners:

However, the impact of capitalist development on wage employment for women has cut both ways, particularly when it involves the adoption of new technology.[75] The pre-eminent example here is that of post-harvest processing of paddy. This activity has customarily accounted for the bulk of the wage employment obtained by poorer women in rural areas. Usually, such women were hired by richer houeholds to do the work indoors, using traditional (non-mechanized) means. However, the growth of mechanized rice-mills (particularly following rural electrification), which requires much lower labour inputs, has resulted in large numbers of women being deprived of this precarious livelihood. Here, the profit-oriented imperative of capitalist production has worked with its characteristic logic to generate unemployment, despite the fact that most of the women workers who were made redundant belonged to the poorest classes, and desperately needed the work from which they were displaced.

On the other hand, the recent boom in the garment industry of Bangladesh, fuelled by export demands from the world market, has provided an unprecedented source of growing employment for women in the mainstream sector of formal industry.[76] Apart from the traditional aptitude of women in this field, the critical considerations for the employers have been the relative 'docility' of female workers, as well as their acceptance of abnormally long working hours, abysmal working conditions, and wage rates considerably lower than those of men.[77] Significantly, women in this industry are

Their Situation and Possibilities for Donor Intervention', revised version of paper presented at the WPF Nairobi Symposium.

[75] Cf. Jahan, op. cit. in n. 2, p. 5, for an overview of the mixed impact of technological innovation on women's position in Bangladesh. Earlier studies which provide documentation include: Arens and van Beurden, op. cit. in n. 21, pp. 43–45; B. Harriss, 'Post-Harvest Rice Processing Systems in Rural Bangladesh: Technology, Economics and Employment', *Bangladesh Journal of Development Economics*, 2 (1979), pp. 23–50; Greeley, op. cit. in n. 33; K. U. Ahmed, 'The Impact of New Paddy Post Harvest Technology on the Rural Poor in Bangladesh', in M. Greeley and M. Howes, op. cit. in n. 33; Adnan, op. cit. in n. 28; Chen, op. cit. in n. 20, pp. 114–19.

[76] Within the industrial and other non-agricultural sectors, women in Bangladesh have traditionally been employed in handloom-weaving, food-processing, tea plantations, etc. See Schaffer, op. cit. in n. 2, p. 29; Mahmud and Mahmud, op. cit. in n. 58, p. 11. The export-oriented garment industry came into existence only after 1976, and grew rapidly to consist of 700–750 production units by Feb. 1987. See Ahmad, op. cit. in n. 65, pp. 30–31; UBINIG, *Export-Related Development Review of Labour and Industrial Policies in the Context of Women's Work* (Dhaka, 1985, in Bangla), p. 17; N. Hyder, 'Ready-made Garments Industry in Bangladesh, mimeo. (Bangladesh Institute of Development Studies, Dhaka, 1988). Women accounted for 90 per cent of the industry's labour force, which, at its peak, numbered around 200,000 (UNICEF, op. cit. in n. 2, p. 77; Khan, op. cit. in n. 2, table 24, pp. 63–64). Of those, between 60,000 and 80,000 workers were estimated to be relatively permanent employees, while the rest were employed periodically, as and when required by export demand (Mahmud and Mahmud, op. cit. in n. 58, p. 22). On this basis, women garment workers accounted for about 5% of the female population of working age.

[77] Jahan, op. cit. in n. 33, pp. 49–60, and H. Hossain, R. Jahan, and S. Sobhan, 'Industrialization and Women Workers in Bangladesh: From Home-Based Work to the Factories', in N. Heyzer (1988), op. cit. in n. 74. These studies provide details about the deplorable working conditions of women garment workers, including the practice of *ad hoc* appointments, with only

invariably found to be concentrated among shop-floor workers, whereas men dominate in management and executive positions.[78]

Most of these garment manufacturers operate on contracts and sub-contracts from middlemen in the world market.[79] Their prime consideration in getting the work done in Bangladesh (as in other poor countries) has been the availability of a virtually unlimited supply of extraordinarily cheap female labour. However, a number of other significant considerations, relating to the geopolitics of the world market have also been reported to operate behind some of the relocation of the garment industry in Bangladesh from other countries.[80]

Not surprisingly, employment generated by linkages with the capitalist world market has also entailed characteristic risks and uncertainties for the women so employed. Periodic fluctuations in the import quota allocated to ready-made garments from Bangladesh by the United States, the EC, and other major capitalist economies (i.e. export demand) have led to corresponding cycles of lay-offs and re-employment among the women workers concerned.[81] For the women made redundant by this process, a return to their former places of residence, particularly villages, is virtually impossible. Used to freer urban life-styles as industrial wage-earners, they are unable, or unwilling, either to revert to domestic service in the towns, or to go back to their villages and put up with the restrictions of the *shamaj* and the *shalish*.

Many of these unemployed women, who have become, as it were, locked into the city, have been compelled to choose between very difficult avenues of survival. The extraordinary rise in the volume of organized urban prostitution during the last decade indicates one kind of forced choice which has been made by at least some of these women. They have, indeed, broken out

---

time cards rather than letters of appointment, long shifts, unpaid overtime work, neglect of industrial safety regulations, inadequate medical facilities, and absence of crèches for children, in violation of existing labour laws. In addition, forms of extra-economic coercion and intimidation were, in some cases, practised by the management to control female workers, including hired hoodlums and bribed policemen.

[78] UBINIG, *Income, Employment Generation and Credit Facilities for Women in the Context of Bangladesh* (Dhaka, 1986, in Bangla), pp. 24–25; Jahan, op. cit. in n. 33, pp. 31–33, tables 1, 2.

[79] UBINIG, op. cit. in n. 76, p. 19; Jahan, op. cit. in n. 33, pp. 30–31; Standing, op. cit. in n. 74; Heyzer, op. cit. in n. 74.

[80] Hossain, Jahan, and Sobhan, op. cit. in n. 77.

[81] UNICEF, op. cit. in n. 2, p. 77; Heyzer (1988), op. cit. in n. 74. After the imposition of quotas on garments from Bangladesh by the United States and the EC countries in the summer of 1985, the number of factories rapidly declined from around 750 (Hossain, Jahan, and Sobhan, op. cit. in n. 77, pp. 115–16); Hyder, op. cit. in n. 76; Jahan, op. cit. in n. 33, p. 9; UBINIG, op. cit. in n. 76, p. 176; Schaffer, op. cit. in n. 2, p. 29. By mid-September of that year, 60 factories had been closed and another 500 smaller units were facing the possibility of imminent closure. Over 7,000 workers, mostly women from the poorest sections of society, were immediately thrown out of their jobs. The industry as a whole was plagued by unused excess capacity. See Hyder, op. cit. in n. 76.

of *parda* and patriarchy, and become relatively independent, but only to enter the highly uncertain existence offered by the urban and industrial labour markets.[82] The accelerated pace of the merchandizing of women's bodies, as well as the concomitant disenchantment of the traditional ideal of female *izzat* or honour, has constituted a complementary facet of the growing incorporation of women's work into the circulation of national and international capital.

Overall, the increasing role of capital in the economy of Bangladesh has had the double-edged consequence of generating employment for women, or throwing them out of work, depending upon market-based considerations of relative profitability. In the process, pre-existing forms of production organization (e.g. household-based paddy processing) have been decomposed, while some of the labour power made redundant has been recomposed into newer forms of production and labour processes carried out under the direct supervision of capitalist employers.[83] The net effect has been to restructure segments of the female labour of the country in accordance with the interests of national and international capital.

Supply and Demand Constraints Compared

Where have all the wage-workers and other income-earners amongst the women come from? Micro-level studies leave little doubt that the majority of women who enter the labour and product markets are precisely those who have no other ways of meeting the subsistence needs of their families.[84] This applies, in the limiting case, to widowed and divorced women without any external support, who have to fend for themselves, as well as for their children. But, even more significantly, this has also been true of many married women, who were living with their husbands and other kinsmen. Such women, compelled to take wage employment, have come particularly from households which owned little land, and where the incomes of male earners have not been sufficient to provide for the family's total subsistence needs.[85] Given such predicaments, married women have been positively

---

[82] UBINIG, op. cit. in n. 34; Z. R. Khan and H. K. Arefeen, *Socio-economic Study on Training and Rehabilitation of Destitute Women (Prostitutes)* (Dhaka, 1988).

[83] Some of these processes correspond to forms of the formal and the real subsumption of labour under capital in the specific analytical sense used by Marx. For further clarification of these concepts in the context of the south Asian debate, see Adnan (1985), op. cit. in n. 54.

[84] Adnan and Islam, op. cit. in n. 12; Arens and van Beurden, op. cit. in n. 21, pp. 43–46; Westergaard, op. cit. in n. 15, pp. 52–61; Chen, op. cit. in n. 20, pp. 60–68; Rahman, op. cit. in n. 33, pp. 29–32; Jahan, op. cit. in n. 33, pp. 40–44, tables 7, 8; Arthur and McNicoll, op. cit. in n. 32, p. 63; Cain, Khanam, and Nahar, op. cit. in n. 5, pp. 408–12.

[85] Greeley, op. cit. in n. 33, pp. 137–41; Westergaard, op. cit. in n. 15, p. 55; Rahman, op. cit. in n. 33, pp. 31–32; Ahmad, op. cit. in n. 65, p. 31; Chen, op. cit. in n. 20, pp. 167–70; McCarthy, op. cit. in n. 9, p. 154; Marum and Hasna, op. cit. in n. 53, pp. 19–23.

encouraged by their husbands and families to earn market-based incomes, rather than discouraged, as would traditionally have been the case.

The institutions of *parda* and patriarchy, with their traditional restrictions on the income-earning employment of women outside the household, have thus not proved to be such rigid and inflexible barriers when confronted with the exigency of survival itself. The primacy of the economic imperative in affecting women's position could not have been more vividly demonstrated.[86] In fact, the evidence so far would suggest that, given an opportunity to earn market incomes, women in Bangladesh have not been at all averse to taking it up. If anything, women have not found as much work as they need to meet the subsistence requirements of their families, particularly amongst the vast numbers of landless and asset-less households which constitute the rural and urban proletariat.[87]

The picture is succinctly summarized in a UNICEF report:

agencies involved in public works projects in the rural areas have found that poor women will take advantage of job opportunities in road maintenance and similar work, provided that some effort is made to reserve a segment of the work for female labour. This reflects to some extent a change in attitudes as this type of work—physical labour carried out in full view of the public—has traditionally been considered inappropriate for women. It also reflects the growing landlessness and desperation in the Bangladeshi countryside. Women who are left without the resources to feed themselves or their children, especially those without a male breadwinner, will take whatever opportunities are available, and can apparently do so with little family or public criticism.[88]

It would thus appear that there is no insurmountable supply constraint, resulting from the institutions of *parda* and patriarchy, which is holding up the flow of women into the labour market. On the contrary, the real constraints are those of inadequate effective demand for women's labour, as well as institutional barriers within the labour market which segment it, so that women are barred from entry to certain sectors. Recent trends suggest that such institutional barriers have begun to give way, and that women workers have now established footholds in the principal sectors of the economy—agricultural crop production and formal industry.[89]

[86] This is not to say that other factors have not had any part to play in the story. For example, the availability of labour-saving technology or of improved methods of contraception has released women's actual or potential time from more traditional chores and duties. This has enabled at least some women to devote more time to direct income-earning options (see Jahan, op. cit. in n. 2, p. 5).

[87] Rashid, op. cit. in n. 7; Chen, op. cit. in n. 20, pp. 70–75; McCarthy, op. cit. in n. 9, pp. 153–57; Rahman, op. cit. in n. 33.

[88] UNICEF, op. cit. in n. 2, p. 77.

[89] Tentative supporting evidence at macro-level for such a trend includes the declining differential between men's and women's money wage rates in agriculture between 1983–84 and 1985–86, as noted earlier (BBS, op. cit. in n. 35, p. 115). See also Safilios-Rothschild and Mahmud, op. cit. in n. 35, for the more strident view that such institutional barriers against women's participation in agricultural work and decision-making have virtually disappeared in

However, the problem of insufficient demand for women's labour persists and forms part of the more general problem of the unemployment (and underemployment) of both male and female members of the labour force. Indeed, this reflects the macro-level problems of uneven capitalist development and inadequate rates of accumulation and investment of productive capital in the Bangladesh economy. Further treatment of these issues, however, lies outside the scope of this chapter.[90]

Effects on Women's Position

The Family and the Kin-Group

In the preceding sections we have already noted some of the changes that have occurred in women's position in Bangladesh during the last decade or so. Here, we look at some of these aspects in greater depth. Earning incomes through the labour and product markets has, to some extent, affected women's position in relation to men belonging to their families, the extended kin-group, as well as the broader community. For the women themselves, the act of breaking out of *parda* and having an independent earning capacity has undermined some of the basic premises of patriarchal control over them. While the proportion of such women still remains relatively small, they provide an example to the rest about what can potentially be achieved. Indeed, it is now possible, at least in principle, for the average woman to question her inferior status, as well as the social restrictions imposed upon her, in ways that were inconceivable even a generation ago.[91]

Not surprisingly, the capacity to earn market incomes has also tended to lead to the re-evaluation of the status of women by their immediate families, and particularly by the men—their fathers, husbands, and brothers.[92] The impact has been all the more striking because these women have been

contemporary Bangladesh. This view, once again, appears to overstate the case, given the weight of the rest of the available evidence.

[90] Constraints on the capitalist development of agriculture in Bangladesh, as well as more generally in developing countries, are discussed in Adnan, op. cit. in n. 72; S. Adnan, 'Reflections on the POPOLCOM Studies on the Determinants of Fertility', paper presented at the Seminar on Studies on Determinants of Fertility Behaviour for Population Policies aimed at Reducing Fertility in Developing Countries, IUSSP, Colombo, 1980; S. Adnan, 'The Conditions of the Peasantry in Bangladesh', in J. M. Mencher (ed.), *Social Anthropology of Peasantry: Proceedings of the Post-Plenary Session of the World Congress of Ethnography, Lucknow, December 1978* (Bombay, 1983); Adnan (1984), op. cit. in n. 54, ch. 5.

[91] Chen, op. cit. in n. 20, pp. 165–93. For a historical overview of women's struggles for their rights in Bangladesh, see Kabeer, op. cit. in n. 13. A longitudinal study of some poor village women in Comilla for the period 1966–78 documents the ways in which these women were able to help their families and children by income-earning activities, which led to a qualitative enhancement of their status and position within the household, as well as in the village community (McCarthy, op. cit. in n. 9, pp. 154–55).

[92] Ahmad, op. cit. in n. 65, p. 61, table 27; Rahman, op. cit. in n. 33, pp. 77–78, table 35; Jahan, op, cit. in n. 33, pp. 78–79.

earning incomes in situations where large numbers of men remain unemployed or, in many cases, are unable to earn the total income required to maintain their families. Some women industrial workers reported that they were the sole earning members of their families, and that their dependants included parents, as well as brothers and sisters.[93] Comparable findings have also been reported for wage-workers amongst rural women.[94]

Interviews with female garment workers showed that their value in the 'marriage market' had risen recently, because potential grooms now expressed a preference for brides who were capable of earning an income. Such a rise in the value of women, whether as earning wives, daughters, or sisters, can, in its turn, be expected to generate a rise in the valuation of female children in the future.[95] The birth of a girl no longer necessarily implies that she will represent a certain burden for her parents, encouraging them to marry her off as early as possible. On the contrary, parents dependent upon unmarried, but earning, daughters are likely to want to 'retain' them in the family for as long as is culturally permissible.

These considerations would lead us to expect a rise in the age at marriage of girls, and greater familial interest in their education and training, rather than simply on their child-bearing and child-rearing capacities. In fact, the mean age at marriage of women has risen significantly during the recent past, from 15.9 in 1974 to 18.0 in 1985.[96] The proportion of currently married women in the age group 10–14 declined from 32 per cent in 1961 to only 7 per cent in 1981; the corresponding figures for the age group 15–19 were 89 per cent in 1961 and 65 per cent in 1981.[97] The data for 1981 also reflect the influence of urbanization: while 28.7 per cent of rural women in the age group 15–19 had never been married, the corresponding figure for urban women was 45.1 per cent.

Total fertility (TF) (the sum of age-specific fertility rates) declined more

---

[93] Based on interviews with female workers in garment factories in Chittagong by S. Khanam in 1987. See also UBINIG, op. cit. in n. 76; Jahan, op. cit. in n. 33; Hossain, Jahan, and Sobhan, op. cit. in n. 77.

[94] Marum and Hasna, op. cit. in n. 53, p. 120; Rahman, op. cit. in n. 33, pp. 76–78. In fact, Rushidan I. Rahman found that 25% of the village women in her sample of respondents were the sole earners in their respective households. Others were joint or part-time earners. Taking together all the women in the sample, it was found that they contributed 35% of the aggregate family incomes.

[95] Continued persistence of this trend could serve to reverse the rise of the dowry system among Muslims. This phenomenon dates back only to the last few decades, contrary to the traditional practice of providing bridewealth amongst the Muslims of Bengal (Mukherjee, op. cit. in n. 46). Cf. R. Ahmed, 'Changing Marriage Transactions and Rise of Demand System in Bangladesh', Economic and Political Weekly, 22 (1987).

[96] BBS, op. cit. in n. 30, p. 105. However, the corresponding figures for 1986 and 1987 were 17.5 and 17.9 years respectively. These would suggest that the rising trend in women's mean age at marriage might have flattened out during the recent past. Data on the long-term trends which go back to 1931 are available in BBS, op. cit. in n. 35. For a recent review of the evidence, cf. Jahan, op. cit. in n. 2.

[97] BBS, op. cit. in n. 24, pp. 58–63.

or less regularly from 6.34 in 1975 to 4.42 in 1987.[98] Disaggregated data show that, between 1980 and 1987, total fertility was consistently lower in urban than in rural areas. However, both declined absolutely over this period to reach 3.05 in urban and 4.65 in rural areas in 1987. Age-specific fertility rates fell in all age groups (with minor exceptions) in urban areas. Up to 1984, age-specific fertility rates in rural areas increased for the age group 20–29, but declined amongst the younger age group 15–19, as well as among older women.

Micro-level evidence also suggests a higher prevalence of contraceptive use by women labourers in the Food for Works (FFW) programmes. In a review of the available evidence, Schaffer found some support for the view that current use of contraceptives became more prevalent with employment.[99] These findings, if generally valid, would have self-evident implications for policy-making, as well as for future trends in fertility rates in Bangladesh.

Recent data indicate that the literacy rate of women has been rising, while men's literacy rate has stagnated or even declined. Between 1961 and 1981, in the population aged 5 years and older, the men's literacy rate fell from 31.4 to 31.0, while that for women rose from 10.7 to 16.0.[100] School-attendance rates of girls have consistently risen in all age groups between 5 and 24 during the period 1974–81, while those of boys have declined in some age groups during the same period.[101] Between 1972 and 1985 the number of girls attending primary school nearly doubled, and their proportion amongst all students increased from 34.6 per cent to 40.5 per cent. During the same period, the number of girls attending secondary school almost doubled as well, and their proportion amongst all students rose from 24.2 per cent to 29.3 per cent. Comparable trends in the absolute and relative growth of female students can be seen in institutions of higher education, including the 'general'[102] universities, where women accounted for 20.0 per cent of all students in 1984–85, compared to 17.9 per cent in 1980–81.[103]

There are undoubtedly other factors at work, apart from the need to earn market incomes, to explain these socio-demographic trends relating to

---

[98] BBS, op. cit. in n. 30, pp. 125–27; BBS, op. cit. in n. 35, p. 35.

[99] Schaffer, op. cit. in n. 2, p. 31. See also Marum and Hasna; op. cit. in n. 53, p. 124.

[100] BBS, op. cit. in n. 24, p. 84. Provisional figures for 1984 indicate that the literacy rate of females aged 5 and over rose to 20.3 (BBS, op. cit. in n. 35, p. 123). However, the corresponding literacy rate for men in 1987 also showed an upswing with a value of 34.6. In urban areas alone, the difference between the literacy rates of men and women narrowed somewhat during the 26 years from 1961 to 1987, from 1.7 to 1.3 (recalculated from the raw BBS data, cited above).

[101] BBS, op. cit. in n. 24, p. 88; BBS, op. cit. in n. 30, pp. 801–15.

[102] There are four 'general' universities presently operating in Bangladesh; the others are concerned with technical subjects, such as engineering or agriculture.

[103] BBS, *Bangladesh Education in Statistics* (Dhaka, 1985), p. 84; BBS, op. cit. in n. 30, p. 787. Trends in women's employment in teaching and other sectors are summarized in UNICEF, op. cit. in n. 2, p. 77. More detailed data on trends in women's education and employment are available in BBS, op. cit. in n. 35, pp. 85–158.

women. For example, education for girls has been invested with matrimonial significance because of shifts in the preferred demand for the type of brides in the marriage market. Studies report that educated men now prefer to have wives who are themselves educated.[104] Even conservative parents have been receptive to stimuli such as these, since the changing requirements of the marriageability of their daughters drew precisely upon traditional sentiments. Overall, however, trends in these socio-demographic indicators are consistent with critical shifts in the actual and potential economic activities of women noted earlier.

The availability of wage employment and petty self-employment in manufacturing and various service sector activities has also resulted in a significant decline in the number of women prepared to work as domestic servants. While this has made life somewhat uncomfortable for better-off women accustomed to having maids, the trend is perhaps symptomatic of the growing range of alternative options which are becoming available to poorer women in Bangladesh.[105]

Finally, for women working in urban industry, as well as their families, systematic changes in life-styles have been dictated by their working conditions and the imperatives of industrial discipline, including the requirements of shift-work. It is now a common sight to see groups of women workers, particularly from the garment industry, returning home from work late in the evening, all by themselves. Even a decade earlier it would have been virtually inconceivable for young women to move around in the city at such hours without a male escort.[106]

The Social and Political Arenas

The capability to earn an income does not, 'by itself' necessarily lead to any improvement in the status and rights of women in the broader social and political arenas (e.g. the *shamaj* and the *shalish*), as distinct from the family and the kin-group. In one assessment of women wage-workers in villages of Comilla it was stated that 'the type of work available to poor women is real drudgery for very low pay . . . As far as the women are concerned, there is certainly nothing liberating about this.'[107] In another village-level study,

[104] T. A. Abdullah (*Village Women as I saw them* (Dhaka, 1974), pp. 21–22) interviewed women workers in the garment industry and reported that they would like their daughters to be educated and employed, providing working conditions improved. See also Jahan, op. cit. in n. 33, pp. 87–88; Schaffer, op. cit. in n. 2, p. 31.
[105] Some aspects of this matter are dealt with in UBINIG, op. cit. in n. 34; UBINIG, *Women's Role in Agriculture and Livestock Raising* (Dhaka, 1986, in Bangla); UBINIG, op. cit. in n. 76, pp. 7–8.
[106] UBINIG, op. cit. in n. 76, p. 7. However, Jahan (op. cit. in n. 33, pp. 62–63) has noted that women who worked until very late still ran the risk of being molested, or even raped, on their way home.
[107] Westergaard, op. cit. in n. 15, p. 62; Rahman, op. cit. in n. 33, pp. 77–78, table 36.

R. I. Rahman found that, while 65 per cent of the women respondents reported that income-earning had helped to improve their status within their own families, this had not necessarily been true in other contexts. In fact, most other villagers did not treat women who undertook wage labour with respect. Even for working women in the city, Roushan Jahan noted that,

> while neighbours in urban areas do not have the control potential of a village *shamaj*, their attitudes bear some weight, especially in the case of young unmarried women . . . We note a curious mixture of disapproval and envy aroused by young unmarried girls working in a 'garment' factory, which despite crass exploitation, compared to other work-places in the informal sector, generally pays well.

Evidence from case studies in rural areas suggests that the position of women in the social arena has tended to improve only where they have been organized in groups by external agencies. Some of these groups were subsequently able to campaign actively for their own rights and entitlements.[108] Virtually all such attempts in rural areas have faced varying levels of resistance from the male *shamajpradhans* and other notables in the locality, not to speak of the religious establishment. Furthermore, not all women have joined together in this effort, since the interests of women from different economic classes have often been conflicting.[109] For example, women in richer families have tended to oppose the development of women's groups amongst the poorest classes and, along with their menfolk, have been in a position to deny the latter employment in post-harvest processing activities.

In fact, attempts by poorer rural women to find paid employment have achieved some success, despite frequent opposition from personalized employers (male and female), largely because of the availability of employment and support from more impersonal[110] institutional sources. Amongst these, the FFW programme, run by the *Upazila* (sub-district) and the Union administrations, has played an important part.[111] Other sources of support have been various agencies such as non-governmental organizations (NGOs) and semi-autonomous government-funded institutions such as the Grameen

[108] P. Streefland *et al.*, *Different Ways to Support the Rural Poor: Effects of Two Development Approaches in Bangladesh* (Dhaka, 1986); Chen, op. cit. in n. 20, pp. 139–93; Bangladesh Rural Advancement Committee, op. cit. in n. 43, pp. 48–68.

[109] Adnan and Islam, op. cit. in n. 12; Kabeer, op. cit. in n. 3, p. 114.

[110] Such impersonal institutional employers include various government agencies, NGOs, as well as external donor agencies. See T. M. Thein, 'Factors Contributing to Success of Women in Development Projects in Bangladesh', mimeo. (United Nations Fund for Population Activities, Dhaka). A survey and review of 100 such projects aimed at women has been provided by T. C. Schaffer, *Survey of Development Projects and Activities for Women in Bangladesh* (Dhaka, 1986), who also pointed to their inherent limitations and problems of implementation. Measures of positive discrimination towards women by the Bangladesh government appear to have led to an increase in the number of women employees in the public health sector between 1981 and 1986 (BBS, op. cit. in n. 35, p. 65; see also Chen, op. cit. in n. 11).

[111] Greeley, op. cit. in n. 33, p. 138; Marum and Hasna, op. cit. in n. 53, pp. 120–22; Mahmud and Mahmud, op. cit. in n. 58, p. 20.

Bank.[112] In certain cases such institutions have operated as catalysts in organizing rural women into groups and have attempted to 'conscientize'[113] them through forms of 'functional' education and other motivational programmes.[114] While claims of success have been uneven rather than universal, the more active of these women's groups are reported to have been able to bargain successfully with local employers and *shamajpradhans*, as well as the Union and *Upazila* officials concerned, in attempts to improve their wages, shares of development resources, etc.

These efforts appear to have led to qualitative improvements in women's position in certain cases.[115] One women's group, which had grown on the basis of self-employment programmes aided by an NGO, was able not only to defy the local *shalish* which had given rulings directed against its activities, but also to call for a separate *shalish* of its own, in defiance of the pre-existing male-dominated power structure of the area.[116] Though their votes had been taken for granted in the past, another women's group in Manikganj reported that, at present, all the candidates in the forthcoming UP elections were concerned to placate them, in order to get their votes.[117] This had enabled the group to bargain with the candidates about the resources and assistance which they could expect to get in return. In other areas, women from a number of groups reportedly took militant action against local officials who had denied them their due share of public resources such as rationed goods and government medical facilities.[118] More generally, women in organized groups reported that their social status in the local community had improved since the formation of the group; even the rich and powerful now

[112] Streefland *et al.*, op. cit. in n. 108. The impact on women of credit supplied by the bank and certain other institutional sources is documented in M. Hossain and R. Afsar, *Credit for Women's Involvement in Economic Activities in Rural Bangladesh* (Dhaka, 1988), and M. Haque, 'Case Study, Grameen Bank', in Government of Bangladesh, *Situation of Women in Bangladesh* (Dhaka, 1985). An overview of various types of NGO programmes aimed at women is provided by J. A. Rahman, 'Role of NGOs in the Field of Women's Development in Bangladesh', ibid.
[113] The term 'conscientization' is used in the specific analytical sense defined by P. Freire, *Pedagogy of the Oppressed* (Harmondsworth, 1972), and as applied by his followers.
[114] Bangladesh Rural Advancement Committee, op. cit. in n. 43, pp. 50–52. Most of these initiatives by NGOs and government agencies are funded by external donors. Typically, donor preferences and predilections have put more stress on women's reproductive roles in the context of controlling their fertility, rather than giving due attention to women's rights, health, education, and productive capabilities (Schaffer, op. cit. in n. 110; Jahan, op. cit. in n. 2, pp. 13–14; Adnan, op. cit. in n. 29). In contrast, programmes of conscientization, or even consciousness raising, have been much less favourably regarded by donors.
[115] Jahan, op. cit. in n. 2, p. 11.
[116] Chen, op. cit. in n. 20, p. 184.
[117] Bangladesh Rural Advancement Committee, op. cit. in n. 43, pp. 65–67.
[118] Chen, op. cit. in n. 20, pp. 186–88; Streefland *et al.*, op. cit. in n. 108, p. 62. In fact, a fair number of NGOs have reported comparable actions and successes in their programmes which involved poor women, such as Gano Shastya Kendra Proshika (Dakha), Proshika (Comilla), Nijera Kori, and Gano Shahajya Sangstha. Constraints of space do not permit citation of further details from all these cases in this chapter. I am, however, planning to write a more comprehensive study which will take account of instances such as those listed above.

behaved in a relatively civil manner, compared with the disdain displayed towards them in earlier times.[119]

In fact, overarching organizational structures to unite poor women may be beginning to crystallize in the rural areas. One author reports that 'individual groups of earth-digging women have begun to contact each other to form an informal union'.[120] Their aim is to ensure that the groups do not undercut each other in the labour market. This would enable them to maintain a common front against their employers, in order to ensure a minimum wage rate for all. Collective stands of this kind on economic issues could potentially provide the basis for politically-oriented group or class actions by women in the course of future developments.

However, in urban areas, the limits, as much as the potentialities, of such collective action are already beginning to become evident. This applies particularly to industrial employment which brings large numbers of women together on the factory floor.[121] The extent of unionization of women workers still remains surprisingly low, despite strikingly bad working conditions and lack of amenities (such as separate and adequate toilet facilities for women, crèches for children, as well as medical aid available on the spot), as required by the law.

In fact, the government agencies concerned often fail to enforce existing labour laws.[122] Women workers who attempt to set up unions are frequently victimized by dismissal, or intimidation by hired hoodlums. Even the unions to which women belong are often dominated by men, so that the specific demands and interests of women workers are sacrificed in favour of more male-oriented demands.

Despite the existence of such constraints, women industrial workers have, in some instances, succeeded in realizing their demands, given support from like-minded political parties and trade unions. Interestingly, Schaffer has noted that the women themselves put greater priority on raising their wages rather than, say, improving their working conditions.[123]

---

[119] To some extent, such improvements could also have been the result of project design in which co-option of the local power structure had been 'built-in'. See Thein, op. cit. in n. 110, for illustrations of relatively 'successful' projects for women which have been operated on this basis. However, since these 'success stories' did not involve any challenge to the pre-existing authority of male gate keepers, their actual contribution to freeing women from men's domination continues to remain a matter for debate.

[120] Chen, op. cit. in n. 20, p. 183.

[121] UBINIG, op. cit. in n. 76, pp. 10–13; Jahan, op. cit. in n. 33, pp. 60–80; N. Hossain and J. S. Brar, 'The Garments Workers of Bangladesh: Earnings and Perceptions towards Unionism', *Journal of Business Administration*, 14 (1988); Schaffer, op. cit. in n. 2, p. 29.

[122] UBINIG, op. cit. in n. 76, pp. 10–40; Jahan, op. cit. in n. 33; Hossain, Jahan, and Sobhan, op. cit. in n. 77, pp. 126–27.

[123] Schaffer, op. cit. in n. 2, p. 29. Cf. UBINIG, op. cit. in n. 76, pp. 36–40. It has been reported that women workers would rather face the disadvantages of working in garment factories, because they still consider this preferable to any of the other options presently available to them, including 'domestic servitude' (UBINIG, op. cit. in n. 105, p. 10). Even when perfectly aware of the excessive exploitation and profit-making practised by their employers,

During the last two decades, women's participation in politics and institutions of government has also increased, though hardly at a dramatic pace. In the Union *Parishad* elections of 1973, a woman was elected chairman in only one UP, out of a potential total exceeding four thousand.[124] In the subsequent UP elections of 1977 and 1984 four and six women respectively were elected to the chair. During the 1979 parliamentary election, only seventeen women candidates contested the three-hundred-odd seats in the whole country.[125] While four of them came second in their respective constituencies, none was elected a member of parliament. However, arrangements for nominating women MPs were made at later stages by the ruling party. None the less, as noted earlier, such nominated women members acted in a compliant manner, in accordance with the directives of the male leadership which had been instrumental in selecting them for such positions. In effect, they served as 'token' figures ostensibly representing women's interests, rather than being *bona fide* representatives of their sex, on an equal footing with men.

During the last UP elections, held in February 1988, a fair number of women in the countryside contested the offices of chairman and members, and some even managed to win. While their absolute numbers are still small despite recent increases, political endeavours of this kind by women would have been inconceivable even a generation earlier. Another promising trend in the politicization of women has been the substantial growth of grass-root organizations amongst them in recent times.[126]

While such instances are still few and far between, they are, none the less, symptomatic of emergent trends in women's growing assertiveness in Bangladesh. To the extent that organized, and even militant, actions by women's groups are a function of the intensity of their desperation, the macro-level economic–demographic trends of polarization and landlessness noted earlier, coupled with the double-edged consequences of capitalist development, are likely to accelerate the pace of women's emancipation even further in the coming decades.

Perspectives

Women in Bangladesh have been in subordinate positions to men in familial, social, political, and economic arenas for generations, as symbolized in the

women workers often do not risk forming unions, because this could result in their dismissal, or even the closure of the factory concerned, which would, of course, lead to the loss of their precarious employment.

[124] Qadir and Islam, op. cit. in n. 50, p. 3. The UP is the lowest tier in the structure of self-government institutions. No term comparable to 'chairperson' is yet in use in rural Bangladesh, even when the incumbent is a woman.

[125] Schaffer, op. cit. in n. 2, pp. 30–31.

[126] Jahan, op. cit. in n. 2, pp. 10–11.

institution of *parda*. Apart from the various social–biological roles allocated to them in the sexual division of labour, women have also had to perform in passive roles of symbolic significance to men and their social contentions— ranging from objects of honour and protection to objects of pleasure. Furthermore, this state of affairs continues to hold true for the majority of women, particularly in the rural interior, even today.

However, during the 1980s symptomatic changes have been taking place in women's position within the family and kin-group, as well as in the sociopolitical arenas beyond. The major supply-side impetus for such change has come from economic–demographic shifts generated by the differentiation of the peasantry. The pressures on survival engendered by these have left little option for the majority of households amongst the landless and asset-less classes other than to permit their women to take part in market-based income-earning activities. The avenues of work initially taken up by women were those which were more attuned to *parda* considerations. However, with increasing competition for scarce work, women have begun to break out of *parda* restrictions altogether and to take part in 'outdoor' activities in full view of the public. Indeed, the overwhelming majority of such income-earning women have entered the labour market as wage-earners.

On the demand side, apart from household-based wage employment in domestic services, most of the income-earning options for women have been generated by the circulation of small-scale industrial and mercantile capital in the informal sector, operating through the labour and product markets. In other cases, such as the new but rapidly growing garment industry, the volume of women's employment has fluctuated with the vagaries of the world market, controlled more by international, than by national, capital.[127] The profit-oriented pursuit of capitalist production has also resulted in the systematic displacement of previously employed women in certain activities such as household-based post-harvest processing of crops.

Overall, this process of uneven capitalist development has served to decompose traditional labour processes more attuned to *parda* considerations, and reintegrate the elements of such production, including women's labour, into production processes under the direct supervision of capital. A growing proportion of available female labour power has thus been subsumed under capital, i.e., restructured to meet the job conditions and requirements of capitalist production, in avenues which are relatively more profitable. Confronted with the exigencies of survival, apparently robust institutions and enduring practices such as *parda* and patriarchy have begun to give way, adapting themselves to the changing imperatives of capital, mediated by the transactional relationships of the market.

In fact, the real limit to further economic participation by women in the

---

[127] See UBINIG, op. cit. in n. 78, pp. 15–23, on female labour in Bangladesh and its linkages with the world capitalist system.

labour and product markets is no longer a supply constraint arising from social–institutional restrictions on their (i.e. women's) mobility and participation in 'outdoor' work. Rather, the essential constraint is that of insufficient effective demand for women's labour and the kind of products and services they are currently involved in producing in the informal sector.[128] This consideration applies more generally to the underemployment of both the male and the female labour force, and results from the existence of structural limits to the capitalist development of the national economy as a whole.

None the less, improvements in women's income-earning capabilities, to the extent that these have taken place, have led to a certain re-evaluation of their roles and positions by the respective families and kin-groups, as well as by the community at large. Greater investment in women's education, rising ages at marriage, as well as declining fertility rates observed during the last decade, are consistent with the hypothesis of changing social perceptions regarding the increasing value of women. The other side of the coin is the greater merchandizing of women's roles as objects of pleasure and the concomitant disenchantment of traditional notions of female *izzat* or honour.

While income-earning capabilities have enabled women to enhance their status and independence at the level of the family and the kin-group, they have not necessarily enabled them automatically to gain entry into or hold leadership positions in social and political institutions. This consideration applies particularly to the *shamaj* and the *shalish*, as well as the institutions of local self-government such as the UP. These still tend to be largely monopolized by male leaders, particularly from the dominant classes. In the few instances where women have made inroads into these institutions in the broader social and political arena, such changes have resulted from the organized activism of women's groups, mostly from the poorest classes, with or without support from 'external' institutions such as NGOs and governmental agencies.

To conclude: if the analysis in this chapter is correct, then continuing differentiation of the peasantry during coming decades can be expected to lead to further intensification of economic pressure on poorer households for meeting subsistence needs. This is likely to result in even greater numbers of women being compelled to break out of the bonds of *parda* and patriarchy, and possibly to work actively, to improve their lot. It is probable that these emergent trends will be associated with greater unionization, if not politicization, of women, under new forms of leadership which are more capable of representing the common interests of both men and women from the poorest classes.[129]

---

[128] Hossain and Afsar, op. cit. in n. 112.

[129] However, there are other complexities involved in attempting to pool the forces of men and women workers. As Jahan (op. cit. in n. 33, p. 75) has noted for the garment industry: 'In-depth interviews reveal that relationships sour when a female worker challenges the socially accepted norms of male superiority or proves to be more efficient than her male colleagues.'

On the other hand, whether the growing numbers of women who will be thrown into the labour market during the coming years will all be able to find viable avenues of survival remains a matter for conjecture. Much will depend on the extent to which the prevalent demand constraints on women's employment are removed, together with the activation of more dynamic trends of growth. This will require not only that the present structural constraints to further capitalist development of the economy be eased, but also that the remaining institutional barriers to women's entry into the mainstream sectors of the labour market be removed.[130] While the figurative cage circumscribing women's existence has begun to show signs of breaking up, it is yet to be prised wide open.

[130] Jahan, op. cit. in n. 2, pp. 18–22, provides a critical appraisal of the government's policies and performance in respect of removal of such institutional barriers.

15 Labour Migration and Female-Headed Households

PAULINA MAKINWA-ADEBUSOYE

Information on households headed by females in different countries is fragmentary and may not always be comparable, because of variations in definition. The criterion used to define whether a woman is head of a household varies from region to region. The general assumption is that the household is a basic unit of society for joint decision-making, reproduction, production, consumption, and accumulation of capital and other resources, to which husband and wife, or wives, contribute, and in which the husband or the oldest male predominates, irrespective of the amount that he contributes to resources. This sexist and culture-bound concept of the household imposes a level of dependence and invisibility on women that distorts and prevents a clear understanding of social reality. This cultural bias is reflected in published data which indicate unrealistically low proportions of households headed by females, particularly in Africa, where each wife or unmarried mother is the centre or head of a unit of production, consumption, and reproduction which depends on her for its survival. But the culturally accepted definition of household head is so internalized that in response to survey questions most enumerators, and even female respondents, routinely assign the headship to any available male, because a female head of household is considered to be unusual. In a situation in which the supremacy of men is a normative ideal, a respondent's 12-year-old son can be regarded as head of the household.[1] Furthermore, age-specific headship rates for women include both married and unmarried women, although the latter are not generally considered to be household heads.

Despite these shortcomings, the data provide important information. First, households headed by females represent a significant proportion of the total, and their number is increasing. Secondly, the proportion of such households is, on average, higher in countries classified by the United Nations as low-income countries in 1960 than in high-income countries, except for very young and very old women (aged 15–24 and 65+ years).[2] Thirdly, in spite

[1] J. S. Newman, *Women of the World: Sub-Saharan Africa* (Washington, 1984), p. 114.
[2] UN, *Estimates and Projections of the Number of Households by Country, 1975–2000* (New York, 1981).

of differences between levels, there is in most countries a specific pattern to women's household headship; headship rates increase with age, and reflect an increase in widowhood and in disrupted marriages at older ages.[3]

Households headed by women account for over 40 per cent of all households in Botswana and Lesotho; in the latter country the figure was 45.2 per cent in 1980. The available data for selected countries in 1970 and 1980 show that such households amounted to more than 30 per cent of all households in some Caribbean countries, where there is a tradition of women's out-migration, and where a woman may be reported as being head of household, even when there is a male partner present.[4] Similarly, figures for Latin America show that women are heads of about 20 per cent of households in the region. Households headed by women account for between 14 and 21 per cent of all households in the six Latin American countries sampled by de Vos (Colombia, Costa Rica, Dominican Republic, Mexico, Panama, and Peru).[5] Other factors such as widowhood (the life expectancy of females exceeds that of males), and the tradition of woman marriages in parts of Africa, contribute to the establishment and increase in the number of households headed by women. But there can be no doubt that sex-specific labour migration is one major factor which leads to the continuous withdrawal of men from rural areas and results in households in which women are heads either *de facto* whilst men are temporarily absent, or *de jure* when they are permanently so.

A substantial volume and variety of labour migration, both internal and international, is a prominent feature of development processes in many countries of the Third World. Several 'push' factors have been identified in the vast body of literature on the subject: low agricultural incomes, unemployment and underemployment, landlessness, and lack of productive assets. In addition there are 'pull' factors in receiving areas, particularly wage employment in the towns, which are major reasons for the continuing exodus from rural areas of many countries in the Third World. The extent of women's participation in rural out-migration varies greatly in different geographical regions, and depends on the normal availability of urban jobs, as well as on non-economic constraints on women, particularly in areas where women are primarily responsible for subsistence food production. At present, men predominate among migrants in Africa. The situation is different in Latin America and the Caribbean, where during the last two decades women have predominated in the movement to towns.

---

[3] UN, op. cit. in n. 2; Susan, de Vos, 'Latin American Households in Comparative Perspective', *Population Studies*, 41 (1987), pp. 501–17.

[4] C. Safilios-Rothschild, *Socio-economic Indicators of Women's Status in Developing Countries, 1970–1980* (New York, 1986).

[5] de Vos, op. cit. in n. 3.

A full understanding of the consequences of labour migration requires an examination on two levels: micro and macro. At the macro-level, migration results in changes in the supply of labour, and the structure of employment, technology, and incomes in rural and urban areas. The macro-level consequences will be largely ignored in this chapter, which is concerned mainly with a discussion of the impact of migration on households and their members, especially women.

At the micro-level, labour migration has far-reaching consequences for individual migrants and households, which are, however, generally positive. Evidence from case studies and regional analyses has repeatedly shown that individual migrants and members of their households are better off than would have been the case in the absence of migration. But these gains are achieved at substantial cost, especially when extensive out-migration leads to the breakdown of familial authority and creates profound changes in the roles played by male and female members of the household before migration.

Men's and women's labour migrations have critical effects on household formation, structure, and division of labour between the sexes. However, given the magnitude and visibility of problems associated with rapidly growing cities in poor countries, much of the research has been devoted to the impact of migration on towns and on individual migrants. One result has been a relative neglect of studies that deal with the impact of migration on family structure, particularly its effects on the changing role and status of women in urban and rural areas. Where migration consists predominantly of men, significant and growing proportions of women who are left behind in rural areas have had to assume new decision-making roles as effective household heads, with full responsibility for their own and their children's survival. Autonomous women migrants to urban areas also establish their own households.

In this chapter we shall focus attention on households headed by women who have been left behind in rural areas, when men have migrated to wage employment in the towns. Discussion of female-headed households in urban areas that are created when women themselves are urban immigrants should be adequately covered in Chapter 11, in which women's position in the migration process is examined. Furthermore, many country case studies in Africa, the Middle East, and Asia have shown that female-headed households in these areas are mainly the result of men's out-migration. Special attention will be given to the African continent, where, as a result of the forceful imposition of an alien culture and a capitalist mode of production based (as in South Africa) on legal sanctions, a highly socially and economically disruptive situation has been created in certain rural areas from which men migrate to urban jobs for periods of years, and return for periodic vacations before finally retiring to their rural homes.

The Proletarianization of the African Peasantry

As a result of low levels of industrialization and an overwhelming dependence on agriculture, labour migration has increasingly replaced subsistence farming as the chief occupation in many African countries. The situation is particularly acute in some capitalist countries that have aptly been labelled as 'labour reserves', in which deliberate colonial policies have created underdeveloped rural areas and led to a situation in which adult males have been forced to participate in capitalist wage employment to supplement rural incomes which were insufficient for subsistence. It is a well known fact of African history that, apart from the inadequacies of subsistence agriculture, the establishment, perpetuation, and present directions of labour migration are rooted in past colonial policies which were designed to enrich the metropolitan countries at the expense of African colonies. Following the Balkanization of Africa, many colonial regimes systematically redirected economic activity from agriculture and trade to export-oriented mining and the production of cash crops. Undeveloped neglected countryside became areas of labour surplus from which workers were provided—sometimes by coercive measures—for some favoured mining areas and agriculturally prosperous pockets that specialized in cash crops for export. In the meantime, the need for cash earnings increased in direct response to other aspects of colonial administration, notably the monetization of the economy, the introduction of taxation (head, hut, and cattle taxes), and the introduction of imported consumer goods.[6]

The degree of proletarianization of the African peasantry and the ravages of the migrant labour system differ in different areas. Their impact is more pronounced in east and south Africa, where the process was legalized through special laws which enabled the minority white settlers to obtain control of most of the arable land. In Kenya, for example, the fertile highlands became the 'white highlands', leaving the large population of indigenous Kenyans as landless natives. At the time of Swaziland's independence in 1968, 45 per cent of the land was cultivated in large plantations that were owned by whites. At present, under the policy of separate development, native Africans in the Republic of South Africa, who represent 70 per cent of the total population, are restricted to special enclaves, which consist of the poorest 13 per cent of the available land. In these countries, the low agricultural productivity in the tribal reserves, and the need to earn money to pay tax and supplement their incomes, has literally forced men to become mobile and seek wage employment in mines and agricultural plantations, and lately in urban industries. Whilst the attainment of political indepen-

---

[6] A. L. Magobunje, *Urbanization in Nigeria* (London, 1968); S. Amin (ed.), *Modern Migrations in Western Africa* (Oxford, 1974); S. Stichter, *Migrant Labourers* (Cambridge, 1985).

dence has reduced some of the glaring imbalances in countries in east and south-central Africa, others, notably Lesotho, Botswana, and Swaziland, whose economies are inextricably meshed with, and dependent on, that of the Republic of South Africa, have remained its labour reservoir.

The climate in west Africa is sufficiently inhospitable to have precluded the establishment of sizeable settler communities. However, colonial policies such as monetization of the economy, the introduction of a variety of taxes, and accelerated economic development of some mining enclaves and areas of plantation agriculture, more or less compelled adult men to sell their labour for wages. However, when cash crops, such as cocoa and coffee, were introduced, west African peasant farmers on small plots took advantage of the lucrative opportunities, and provided a new stimulus for commerce. Thus, in spite of the large number of adult men who migrated in west Africa, they seemed to be able successfully to combine seasonal migration with wage employment in the towns, or with periods of self-employment (generally as traders) in towns, and with subsistence or cash-crop agriculture. To a large extent, rural areas in west Africa have managed to sustain a growing population, and some areas of cash-crop cultivation have succeeded in attracting additional migrant labour.

Seasonal migration of agricultural labour from the north to the southern farms and plantations for limited periods has remained a major form of migration in west Africa. The seasonal nature of the migration is reflected in the local description of migrants as *mai cin rani*, literally translated as 'people who ate away the dry season elsewhere'. The tradition of living in large urban agglomerations, which predates the colonial regime, accounts for yet another feature of migration in west Africa. Particularly among the Yoruba of south-west Nigeria, migrants have dual residence, and divide their time between two homes, one urban and the other rural. Farmers spend, on average, three days of each week in the city and four days on the farms.[7] This feature reflects the almost perfect harmonization of rural–urban migration with temporary wage or self-employment.

Out-migration of men which results from the disruption of the imposed peripheral capitalist economy does not guarantee security for the migrants. The insecurity of urban wage employment and the uncertainties of old age and retirement ensure that migrants maintain close links with households and female kin in the rural sending areas, to which they will return on retirement from wage employment. In this way, the rural-based economy, though mainly dependent on women's labour, continues to subsidize the urban economy in two major ways: through the reproduction and socialization of future generations of urban workers, and through the production of food for the ever-growing reserves of non-agricultural workers in urban jobs on

---

[7] Magobunje, op. cit. in n. 6; G. J. A. Ojo, 'The Journey to Agricultural Work in Yorubaland', *Annals of the Association of American Geographers* (1972).

low wages. In other words, the migrant labour system was a method of 'artificially' expanding the industrial reserve army for urban jobs. Its artificiality derives from its continuing link with rural areas—the means of production and sustenance of the labour force—from which the reserve is drawn.

As will be shown below, out-migration of men from rural areas has led to the disintegration of family ties, and changes in the decision-making roles of family members. It has increased the number of households headed by women both *de jure* and *de facto*, as many women are compelled to make decisions, in the absence of adult males, about the allocation of family resources between livestock raising and arable farming, about what types of crops to grow, and where and when to procure additional labour.

Changing Household Structures and Women's Response

Once established, labour migration, though no longer forced, and undertaken mainly for economic reasons, has retained its colonial stamp. At present, internal and international migrations within Africa continue to pull a considerable number of adult men from rural areas to urban wage employment. The disruptions occasioned by a rural–urban migration that consists predominantly of men are better understood, if they are placed in the context of the norms which were common to pre-colonial and pre-migration rural households and the rural economy.

The traditional African economic system was based on subsistence agriculture. It revolved round the household, which functioned as a well-ordered unit of production, consumption, and reproduction. Each household produced mainly for its own sustenance, and whatever surplus remained was traded or exchanged within the confines of the village, or between neighbouring villages. Ownership of land, the main source of wealth, was vested in the community, whose authorized elders apportioned land to male heads of households to meet residential and farming needs. Individuals usually only had rights to the usufruct of the land. Polygyny was the predominant form of marriage, and each wife as head of a matricentred sub-unit of the household was apportioned land by the male head to ensure that unit's self-sufficiency. Thus, in pre-colonial Africa, women played a strategic role in rural food systems as producers, processors, preservers, and marketers. Under the prevailing sexual division of labour, men did the heavy, but periodic farming jobs, such as tree-felling, clearing, bush-burning, and the general preparation of virgin land for farming. Women undertook the less taxing forms of work, such as hoeing, processing, and marketing, which were labelled 'women's jobs', and were usually spread throughout the year. As heads of matrifocal sub-units of a household or households, women had the primary responsibility for producing the family's food.

The imposition of a capitalist mode of production during the colonial period greatly disrupted this traditional household-centred economic system. In particular, the need for cash earnings to pay taxes and buy imported consumer goods, and the colonial emphasis on cash crops, which were dominated by men, led to the gradual withdrawal of male labour from subsistence farming in rural areas to plantations and urban wage labour. The temporary or permanent absence of male members of the household meant that the number of households or sub-units headed by women increased, as women made decisions about daily household tasks, and became effective managers of farms that had been abandoned by men.

As men moved from rural areas to towns for wage employment, women who were left behind devised complex ways of coping. In addition to the recurrent theme in the literature on 'migration and women who wait'—a marked increase in the workload of women caused by persistent migration of men—there came a breakdown in familial authority, as is shown by instances of the failure of young men to meet their obligations to children left with unmarried mothers, and a weakening of the familial and group support system on which women traditionally relied to provide extra agricultural labour, whenever necessary.[8]

In a positive response, women changed into major providers and sole sources of sustenance for family members. They either had to do the work left by urban-based husbands and male relatives, or arrange for hired help or other means to accomplish the task. Even though women may have been spared the heavy tasks such as tree-felling and preparing land for ploughing, they have remained responsible for specific jobs such as weeding, hoeing, and food processing, including pounding, threshing, and winnowing of grain.[9] In many countries, as in Senegal, women have sole responsibility for providing the family's food.[10] In addition to these agricultural tasks, when men migrate, women take on extra responsibility for obtaining additional male labour that is essential for agricultural production, notably the preparation of land for ploughing. Husbands in town may sometimes provide money for hiring such labour.

Thus, women's positive response to persistent migration of men by taking on added responsibility as *de facto* farm managers in sole charge of subsistence farming is causing fundamental changes in the hierarchical structure of

---

[8] B. B. Brown, *Women, Migrant Labour, and Social Change in Botswana* (Boston, 1980); S. Kossoudji and E. Mueller, 'The Economic and Demographic Studies of Female-headed Households in Rural Botswana', *Economic Development and Cultural Change*, 31 (1983), pp. 831–59; M. Mueller, 'Women and Men: Power and Powerlessness in Lesotho', *Signs*, 3 (1977), pp. 154–66; Stichter, op. cit. in n. 6.

[9] P. K. Makinwa-Adebusoye, 'The Socio-economic Contribution of Nigerian Women to National Development', commissioned paper read at the Seminar on Nigerian Women and National Development, Institute of African Studies, University of Ibadan, mimeo. (1985); J. Bukh, *The Village Woman in Ghana* (Uppsala, 1979).

[10] E. Boserup, *Women's Role in Economic Development* (New York, 1970).

households. The out-migration of men is affecting relations between husbands and wives and patterns of authority in the home, as residential boundaries no longer coincide with the functional boundaries which existed between husbands and wives in the period before migration. Because labour migration increasingly precludes jóint decision-making by conjugal partners, and joint performance or management of capital and other resources, a significant number of women who, in the absence of male relatives, must manage alone are amongst the poorest of the rural poor. An increasing number of female heads of households with no access to employment opportunities and who lack capital necessary for agricultural production are heavily dependent on irregular and often inadequate remittances from migrant male relatives.[11] Drastic changes in household organization have uncovered an equally great reservoir of resourcefulness and resilience among many women in their attempts to fight poverty and cope effectively with the enforced migratory labour of their male relatives.

In these trying situations, some women have gained in status and added importance, as they have taken a leading part in local politics in order to fill the vacuum created by the absence of migrant men. They have participated in village co-operatives and actively as members of land-allocating and other committees that are responsible for overseeing village affairs.[12] However, a significant number of other women cannot cope so positively and exhibit varying degrees of depression and anxiety.[13]

Poverty of Female-Headed Households

Regardless of survival strategies in the absence of men, households headed by women are among the poorest in the world. Recent fieldwork in Botswana, Lesotho, Chile, Brazil, and some Commonwealth Caribbean countries has shown consistently that households headed by women are poorer than those headed by men.[14]

Several factors contribute to the poverty of households headed by women. The most notable are the subordinate position of women in patriarchal societies; the notion which has now become firmly entrenched as a result of colonial rule that women are dependent housewives to be supported by male wage-earners; and, lastly, the deliberate restriction, often backed by legal sanctions, of employment opportunities open to women in urban centres.

[11] Kossoudji and Mueller, op. cit. in n. 8; Brown, op. cit. in n. 8; W. Elkan, 'Labour Migration from Botswana, Lesotho and Swaziland', *Economic Development and Cultural Change*, 28 (1980), pp. 583–96.
[12] Mueller, op. cit. in n. 8; Stichter, op. cit. in n. 6.
[13] H. Sibisi, 'How African Women Cope with Migrant Labour in South Africa', *Signs*, 3 (1977), pp. 167–77.
[14] Brown, op. cit. in n. 8; Kossoudji and Mueller, op. cit. in n. 8; N. Youssef, *et al.*, *Women in Migration: A Third World Focus* (Washington, 1979).

The hierarchical structure of patriarchal societies vested control of resources, land, cattle, and other capital including bridewealth in village elders and chiefs who were superior to junior male members. Women were, and still are, considered subordinate to all men. In this socio-cultural milieu, women's mobility, their social and economic lives, and their sexuality were all subject to the control of chiefs, village elders, and heads of lineages. Women achieve access to important agricultural inputs, such as land, male labour, and draught animals, through their male relations—husbands and sons. Change in a woman's status brought about by loss of male kin through death or out-migration is usually accompanied by several grievous losses: the loss of usufructuary rights to land, the loss of male labour to clear new farmlands, and expensive delay in ploughing or sowing, resulting from their inability to procure labour or draught animals. As has been shown in several country case studies which are quoted in the next section, these losses contribute a great deal to the impoverishment of women who depend on subsistence agriculture, when the male members of their household have migrated.

Another pervasive feature of traditional societies is a rigidly enforced gender-based division of labour which assigns the greater share of subsistence agriculture and provision of family sustenance to women. This ensures that women are virtually tied to the countryside, where they are indispensable as food-producers, child-bearers, and child-minders. Men, who are unimpeded by such burdens, are left free to migrate and participate in wage employment in the towns.

Colonial governments superimposed the Western model of administration and economic development with its sexual bias on this traditional structure. The Christian colonial perception of women as dependent housewives, confined to their homes and engaged in 'women's activities', such as laundry, embroidery, and cookery, coincided with and reinforced restriction and control of women by male elders. At the same time, the preference for male wage-earners, who under colonial rule were metamorphosed into family 'breadwinners', and the systematic exclusion of women from urban wage employment ensured the continuation of women's dependency. In countries such as Botswana, Lesotho, and Swaziland, only male contract workers were permitted into dormitories restricted to men in urban centres. There were other legal sanctions and regulations, such as the need for passes and licences for petty trading, which effectively restricted women's participation in the urban economy.

Internalization of new roles—female housewives and male breadwinners—was at the basis of the pervasive inequality in education, which worked to the detriment of girls, for whom education was thought to be unprofitable. In many African countries, provision for the education of girls, particularly at secondary and tertiary levels, which is necessary for urban wage employment, lags far behind that for the education of boys. Educationally unprepared, and constrained by their role as housewives and child-rearers, women in urban centres are predominant in low-paid employment, or in the informal sector, where remuneration is low and uncertain.

Female-Headed Households in Contrasting Labour-Exporting Areas

The effects of the out-migration of men on the economy which was based on the household and the sexual division of labour within households vary, depending on the prevailing mix of migration and farming and the extent of cash-crop production as an alternative source of income. Although there is some overlap, a classification based on variations in the extent of cash-crop production and the degree and frequency of out-migration of men yields three broad categories of labour-exporting areas in Africa. At one end are cash-cropping regions where out-migration has not affected subsistence farming adversely. In this category are the coffee- and cocoa-producing areas of coastal west Africa. At the opposite end are impoverished rural areas—the classic 'labour reserves'—which form the main source of labour supply for agricultural plantations, and urban mines and industries. Two countries in South Africa, Lesotho and Botswana, are typical examples of countries where excessive and continuous out-migration of men has greatly undermined subsistence farming. The remainder of the African countryside falls into an intermediate category, which has variously been described as 'auxiliary reserves' and which represents the 'classic migration condition', in which the migration process and farming have been synchronized so that there is a functioning subsistence economy. In these areas migration has not undermined subsistence farming.[15]

The impact of migration on the status of women has varied greatly in each of the three types of area. The factors perceived as responsible for these differences are the volume and persistence of men's migration, the extent to which the migration of men can be synchronized with work on the farm, and the extent of cash-crop cultivation. Thus, areas of extensive cash-crop plantations and farms in the southern Ivory Coast and Ghana do not only sustain large populations, but are also regions of net out-migration. Similarly, in spite of significant out-migration, food-growing areas in the Ibo heartland of south-eastern Nigeria and in other parts of both west and east Africa have remained self-sufficient in food production, because the migration of men is seasonal and thus ensures the availability of male labour, which is restricted seasonally to the arduous tasks of forest clearing and general preparation of the land for farming. At the other extreme of labour reserves, where men are persistently absent for lengthy periods without adequate compensatory hired male labour, the result has been a decline in agricultural productivity,

---

[15] Amin, op. cit. in n. 6; Stichter, op. cit. in n. 6.

rural poverty, and substantial increases in the workload of abandoned rural women who become *de facto* managers of families and farms.

Cash-Crop Areas

The advantages enjoyed by peasant agriculture in the production of both food and cash crops in the humid coastal belt of west Africa have been well documented.[16] The growing and sale of cash crops have remained an almost exclusive preserve of men, whilst women have specialized in food-crop production and provided help in the preparation of cash crops for marketing. Since the prevalence of smallholders resulted in a situation in which large populations who provide the necessary labour could be absorbed, large families were and remain the norm, and most marriages were polygynous. Where extra labour was required to produce cash crops, this was supplied by migrant workers. The prevailing climatic conditions and the resulting areas of cash-crop production directed the north–south direction of migration in west Africa. Migrants moved from the drier north with its marked seasonal pattern of rainfall and limited agricultural opportunities to the south, a coastal belt in which migrants were offered greater opportunities to work as farm labourers or share croppers. Climate has affected migration in east Africa in a similar way—that is from the interior towards the agricultural plantations of the more humid coastal areas.

Cash-crop exporting areas are generally areas of net-immigration, even though many owner-farmers are absent for lengthy periods as they feel the need to subsidize farm earnings with income from other types of employment, mainly independent trading (with capital originally derived from farming), or wage employment. This is the general pattern among cocoa-farming communities in western Nigeria.[17] In western Nigeria, as in other west African cash-crop areas, the relative ease with which the labour of absentee farmers can be replaced by hired workers has meant that women have not had to take on additional farmwork which did not traditionally fall to them.

The peculiar characteristics of polygynous households that are prevalent in these areas need to be emphasized. Polygynous households consist of a male head, usually the husband, and several wives/mothers and their off-spring, which are divided into functional sub-units headed by each wife/mother. One writer has called such households 'hearthholds'.[18] A hearthhold

---

[16] C. K. Eicher and C. Liedholm (eds.), *Growth and Development of the Nigerian Economy* (East Lansing, Mich., 1970).

[17] P. O. Olusanya, 'In-Migration and the Development of Absentee Farming in the Forest Zone of Southwest Nigeria', A. Adepoju (ed.), *Internal Migration in Nigeria: Proceedings of a Seminar on Internal Migration in Nigeria,* mimeo. (Ile-Ife University, 1975).

[18] F. I. Ekejubia, 'Contemporary Households and Major Socio-economic Transitions in Eastern Nigeria: Towards a Reconceptualization of the Household', paper presented at the Workshop on Conceptualizing the Household: Issues and Theory, Method, and Application, Cambridge, Mass., 1984.

is often a unit of reproduction/production to which the male head contributes, usually by providing the female head with sufficient land to form a viable self-supporting unit. As males are extracted, even though only temporarily, from the rural settings, women's traditional roles as heads of hearthholds have become more prominent. Women continue to assume major responsibility for themselves and their own children. The need to cater for their own and their husbands' relatives is an additional incentive to earn an independent income for those women who have always had appreciable decision-making powers in the domestic sphere. In this milieu, women's economic status has been and remains high. But culturally ascribed modes of behaviour ensure that women remain subordinate to men. There is evidence that, where women traders have become 'commercial' migrants, their status has changed subtly, as they have assumed equal decision-making roles with their migrant husbands.[19] None the less, female heads of hearthholds which are significant units of production, child care, and decision-making remain essentially subordinate to men.

Not all cash-crop producing areas are areas of net-immigration, and concealed within the composite picture are pockets of rural poverty which are more like the classic 'labour reserves', and with similar consequences for women's autonomy and economic power. As has been reported by Stichter in a study of four Kikuyu villages located in cash-crop producing areas,[20] Kershaw found that the impact of cash-crop cultivation on women's status varied with family income.[21] In very poor families, some of which did not own land, both husband and wife had to work for wages in towns whenever possible. Since the men were absent for longer, women gained in status as they took on most of the daily decisions about farms and home management. However, their extreme poverty cancelled out the apparent improvement in their status.

In fairly well-to-do households with seven or more acres of land, husbands migrated to urban employment. Women's workloads increased, as they sometimes had to work on their husbands' cash-crop farms as well as undertake subsistence farming, which was regarded almost exclusively as women's work. In such situations, the wife had the right to make decisions about whatever income she earned, but the husband retained his traditional decision-making role in family affairs and retained control over the high income from cash crops.

Kershaw found that women were worst off in areas in which men had abandoned subsistence farming to cultivate cash crops, which they later abandoned for wage employment in towns. This situation is similar to that

[19] N. Sudarkasa, 'Women and Migration in Contemporary West Africa', *Signs*, 3 (1977), pp. 178–89.
[20] Stichter, op. cit. in n. 6.
[21] G. Kershaw, 'The Changing Roles of Men and Women in the Kikuyu Family by Socio-Economic Status', *Rural Africana*, 29 (1975).

found among the Seti of the southern Cameroons, where women supplied 84 per cent of all the work in producing food crops. As men chose to concentrate on cocoa production, women were faced with substantial increases in their share of farmwork and gradually replaced the traditional staple crop, yam, with cassava and plantain, which require less labour. However, despite the bigger workload on women, men have retained their predominant role in making decisions about household income, including income generated by women.[22]

At the time when the Ewe of southern Ghana adopted cocoa production, migration of men was not extensive. As in the case of the southern Cameroons, men's preference for the more lucrative production of cash crops resulted in an increase in women's workloads, as they were left to supply all the labour needed to produce food crops. In this setting, however, women were free to diversify their activities into trading in foodstuffs, and thus became economically less dependent on men. The Ewe women have also substituted cultivation of cassava or maize for the more labour-intensive cultivation of yam, the traditional staple food crop. Since the 1950s, out-migration of men has increased, and this has resulted in high divorce rates and the establishment of female-headed households. As men spent long periods in wage labour away from farms, more wives gained decision-making powers as farm managers and heads of households. Bukh has reported that 42 per cent of all households in her study area were *de facto* or *de jure* headed by women.[23] The relative poverty of these households, however, greatly undermines any gain that may have accrued to women.

Labour Reserves

Typical labour reserves are rural economies in which men's earnings from out-migration are necessary to sustain rural life, subsistence farming has been greatly undermined; and poverty is widespread. This description best applies to impoverished rural economies such as Botswana, Lesotho, and the native reserves in South Africa. Yet, some scholars who wrote during the 1960s argued that the impact of labour migration in countries of central and southern Africa has had beneficial effects and caused no disruption to family life, either because population pressure and the rising number of livestock had not exacted its full toll on farmlands, or because of a misguided attempt to rationalize the obnoxious apartheid policy of the government of South Africa. Mitchell noted that 'the tribal system tends to accommodate itself to the new circumstances in which it may find itself'.[24] Southall expatiated on the benefits of labour migration to the African family when he wrote that

[22] Stichter, op. cit. in n. 6, pp. 76–77.
[23] Ibid., p. 43.
[24] J. C. Mitchell, 'Wage Labour and African Population Movements in Central Africa', in K. M. Barbour and R. M. Prothero (eds.), *Essays on African Population* (London, 1961), p. 237.

African family systems ensure for most a net economic advantage from the maintenance of two production units, one based on his tribal home and operated by his wives and relations for much of the time, and the other based on his own cash-earning facilities away from home. The net advantage remains, however highly paid the absentee may be.[25]

Yudelman rationalized the separation of families and consequent hardships and insisted that circulatory migration was necessary to maximize family income. According to him,

the prevailing circumstances provide an economic inducement for men to work for short periods in the wage economy while leaving their families in the subsistence sector. Cash incomes earned in traditional agriculture are low, but the combination of free land and security provided through kin groups enable families to maintain themselves at low cost by producing subsistence crops. On the other hand, average returns to African workers in the wage sector are low in relation to the cost of maintaining a family at places of employment. Under these conditions, a family's real income is low, if the family as a whole farms, or if they all move into the wage sector. But if the family splits, and the male works for wages while the other members of the family maintain themselves in rent-free housing by producing subsistence crops, total family incomes are higher than if the family remained together.[26]

Present realities, amply documented in several case studies, have debunked the myth that families in rural labour reserves are better off as a result of the out-migration of men. On the contrary, there is ample evidence that persistent migration has resulted in the disintegration of rural households. The absence of adult males causes a breakdown in familial authority and a weakening or total lack of the support system needed for agricultural production.[27] In Lesotho, Botswana, and Swaziland—classic labour reserves— the data show that people now marry later, that there are large numbers of children born to unmarried mothers, and that the percentage of widows is extremely high.[28]

Botswana, Lesotho, and Swaziland, though politically independent, are economically a peripheral part of the dominant South African economy. Past colonial domination, reinforced by the obnoxious ideology of apartheid, has crippled the economies of these three countries in order to establish and perpetuate a system of enforced migration of adult males, who, together with blacks resident in South Africa, provide cheap labour for the coal and

[25] A. W. Southall, 'Population Movement in East Africa', in Barbour and Prothero, op. cit. in n. 24, pp. 191–92.

[26] Yudelman, *Africans on the Land*, cited in G. Coleman, *International Labour Migration from Malawi* (1979).

[27] Brown, op. cit. in n. 8; Kossoudji and Mueller, op. cit. in n. 8; Mueller, op. cit. in n. 8; Stichter, op. cit. in n. 6.

[28] S. Marks and E. Unterhalter, 'Women and the Migrant Labour System in Southern Africa', in UN, *Migratory Labour in South Africa*, papers presented to the Conference on Migratory Labour in Southern Africa, Lusaka, 4–8 April 1978.

gold mines, and to some extent for agriculture and urban industries as well.[29] It is the official policy of the South African government to promote large-scale migration of Africans from within and without the Republic, as is shown by an address given by the Deputy Chairman of the Bantu Affairs Commission, who said in the House of Assembly in February 1968 that 'we are trying to introduce the migratory labour pattern as far as possible in every sphere, that is in fact the entire basis of our policy, as far as the White economy is concerned'.[30] Other laws, such as the Bantu Laws Amendment Act of 1964, prohibited women from leaving rural areas, unless they had a job to go to in town.[31]

The most distinctive feature of labour migration from these reserves to South Africa is that it is circular, because the South African government does not permit migrants to stay for longer than two years at a time. Male migrants are also compelled to leave their wives behind, because of a deliberate policy to house the worker on his own. During the early 1970s, 99 per cent of the 380,000 migrant workers in the gold mines of the Witwatersrand and the Orange Free State were accommodated as single men in hostels or compounds, each of which contained between one thousand and eight thousand persons.[32] Because these three poor countries cannot survive solely by subsistence farming, male migrants must return continuously to the mines until they reach retirement age.

Thus, in order to meet South Africa's labour needs, the male population of Botswana, Lesotho, and Swaziland, as well as the blacks on the South African native reserves, are unavoidably tied to wage labour in South Africa, whilst simultaneously remaining dependent on the rural areas for security and for a place to retire to, when they become too old to migrate. Rural ties are also necessary to sustain migrants' families and to ensure the reproduction of future generations of cheap labour. As it has been succinctly stated:

South Africa needed a large labour reserve not just so that the reserve could bear part of the cost of subsistence, but also so that the reserve could bear part of the cost of reproduction of the labour force; a place where women go into confinement, give birth, and then raise the children at no cost to apartheid, while the men return to the mines and factories of South Africa to work, leaving the women behind. Though migrant men are victims of this system, the women bear a greater burden, being dependent on men who themselves have little control over the conditions under which their sell their labour.[33]

[29] Brown, op. cit. in n. 8; Elkan, op. cit. in n. 11.
[30] J. W. B. Perry, 'Sources for the Study of Migration in Southern Africa', in L. A. Kosinski and R. M. Prothero (eds.), *People on the Move* (London, 1975), p. 121.
[31] Marks and Unterhalter, op. cit. in n. 28.
[32] F. Wilson, 'International Migration in Southern Africa', *International Migration Review*, 10 (1976), pp. 451–88.
[33] Brown, op. cit. in n. 8, p. 9.

For political and other reasons, the numbers of migrants from other traditional sending countries have decreased in recent years. The government of Malawi stopped further migration to South Africa, following a plane crash which claimed the lives of miners who were returning home from South Africa. Independence for Mozambique similarly led to the termination of agreements between the Portuguese and South African governments to supply workers for the latter country. However, the numbers of migrant workers from Botswana and Lesotho have continued to increase.

According to the Botswana National Development Plan of 1976–81, at any given period an estimated 40 per cent of rural households were temporarily or permanently without adult male members.[34] A recent census in Lesotho was more specific: between 42 and 44 per cent of the males aged 20–59 years, and more than half of the adult men aged 20–39 years (between 51 and 52 per cent), were absent from Lesotho at any given time.[35] On average, Basotho men (from Lesotho) spend between thirteen and sixteen years of their adult lives working outside the country.

When adult men are absent permanently or temporarily, women assume decision-making roles in family matters and over subsistence agriculture. They become more autonomous, as is shown by the rising numbers of households headed by women that result from the lengthy absences of their husbands, and by the high proportion of single, divorced, and widowed women. According to a study in a district of Zululand in 1973, in a total of 150 families there were thirty-eight men aged between 14 and 55 years, compared with 233 women in the same age range.[36]

It was reported in the Rural Income Distribution Survey conducted by the Botswana Central Statistical Office in 1974–75 that 28 per cent of the 957 households included in the survey were headed *de jure* by women, and an additional 6 per cent were headed *de facto* by women. In the districts of Botswana studied by Brown, households headed by women *de jure* came to 35 per cent of the total. Of these, 20 per cent were headed by widows, and 15 per cent by single women. The proportion of households headed by women would have been higher if *de facto* female heads, with absent husbands, had been added.[37]

In the Lesotho village studied by Murray in 1974, 70 per cent of the households were effectively managed by women: 44 per cent *de jure*, managed by widowed, separated, or unmarried women, the rest being households from which the adult men were temporarily absent.[38] In South Africa, 67 per cent of all households in the Transkei were headed by women *de jure* or *de facto*.[39]

---

[34] Kossoudji and Mueller, op. cit. in n. 8.
[35] Stichter, op. cit. in n. 6, p. 55.
[36] Marks and Unterhalter, op. cit. in n. 28.   [37] Brown, op. cit. in n. 8.
[38] Reported in Stichter, op. cit. in n. 6, p. 78.   [39] Ibid., p. 78.

Besides effectively coping and supporting themselves and their dependants, women who head households in the absence of adult males gained in status, as it is they who make most of the decisions concerning crop production, and organize co-operative activities in the village centred around agricultural production.[40]

The gains, if they may be regarded as such, of women in decision-making power are overshadowed by lack of access to capital and inputs for agricultural production. All available case studies and regional analyses show that households headed by women in labour-exporting areas are generally very poor.[41] In the Rural Income Distribution Survey in Botswana it was shown that 44 per cent of the households headed by women were in the three lowest deciles of the income distribution, compared with only 25 per cent of the households headed by men, and that on a per adult equivalent basis the welfare attained by members of households headed by women still appears to be nearly 25 per cent lower than that attained in households headed by men.[42]

The reasons for this poverty are rooted in the low level of women's assets. Women on their own have little opportunity for accumulating capital in cash or kind, or in the form of livestock, particularly cattle. Another important reason is the heavy burden of child dependency, as women in female-headed households have about as many children as women in households headed by men.[43] Because of the scarcity of help on the farm or of adult male relatives, women must depend on co-operative labour or organized work parties to produce enough, or they might resort to sharecropping to hoe or plough for planting. Even then, many households headed by women may be unable to cultivate the available land, because of the lack of some vital means necessary for agricultural production. Families are increasingly dependent on the cash earnings of migrants, as subsistence output may need to be supplemented by purchased food.

In 1970, over 50 per cent of the households in Lesotho owned no cattle, and only 35 per cent owned a plough. Two years later, the situation appears to have deteriorated. Although 1972 was climatically a good year, 22 per cent of the fields in Lesotho remained uncultivated.[44] Similarly, in the area of Botswana studied by Brown, most households headed by females did not plough in that year. The reason most frequently cited was 'nothing to plough with', meaning that there was no money to hire a tractor, no children who would do the ploughing, or no seeds to plant.[45] It was shown in the Rural Income Distribution Survey of 1974–75 that the amounts received per house-

[40] Mueller, op. cit. in n. 8.
[41] Brown, op. cit. in n. 8; Kossoudji and Mueller, op. cit. in n. 8; Mueller, op. cit. in n. 8.
[42] Kossoudji and Mueller, op. cit. in n. 8.
[43] Ibid.; Brown, op. cit. in n. 8; Mueller, op. cit. in n. 8.
[44] Stichter, op. cit. in n. 6, p. 57.
[45] Brown, op. cit. in n. 8.

hold for certain economic activities favoured households headed by men. In particular, such households received at least two-and-a-half times as much income from animal husbandry and trading as did households headed by women. Only when transfer payments (migrants' remittances) were considered did households headed by women receive more income than those headed by men. However, since a significant proportion of migrants' remittances went to fathers, so that wives who were *de facto* heads of households had no control over their disbursement, remittances represented an unreliable source of income.[46]

Thus, pervading poverty denies women access to valuable resources, and forces greater reliance on incomes earned by migrants who themselves have little control over their wages or other working conditions. Consequently, though women's power as heads of household, farm managers, organizers of co-operative structures of rural life, and active participants in local politics grows in the absence of men, it is, as Mueller has aptly summed it up, 'power within a context of increasing powerlessness'.[47] It is not surprising that the almost superhuman effort required to cope with such situations of abject poverty, coupled with lack of power to effect any change for the better, has led to great stress, depression, anxiety, and complete mental breakdown in some women.[48]

Outside Africa

Absence of husbands and other adult male members of rural households is also widespread in countries outside Africa. Recent international labour migration in the Arab Near East and in other Middle Eastern and Asian countries has had a negative impact on agriculture. After adult males have departed, most of the agricultural work is left to women and older relatives, so that agricultural production declines. Women are consistently called upon to take on a heavier agricultural workload, often with reduced capital. Evidence from the Middle East and India has not justified the expectation that migrants' remittances suffice to offset the loss of agricultural labour, as such remittances are often controlled by the extended family, rather than by migrants' wives.[49]

The percentage of women workers increased in Indian villages from which migration was high, as more women joined the labour force to replace men who had migrated. Turkish women have been reported as driving their own tractors and cultivating the family's land during their husbands' absence. In the same circumstances, Yemeni women have assumed control of family farms, and participated in farming activities traditionally considered to have been reserved to men, such as ploughing, planting, and harvesting. These

---

[46] Kossoudji and Mueller, op. cit. in n. 8.   [47] Mueller, op. cit. in n. 8.
[48] Sibisi, op. cit. in n. 13.   [49] Youssef *et al.*, op. cit. in n. 14.

women have, in some instances, made investment decisions outside the agricultural sector, as they participated in home electrification, group well-drilling, and cattle investment.[50]

The disadvantageous position of such women has been noted. The increase in their agricultural workload has not significantly improved their economic situation. In parts of India, men who have migrated to seek wage employment usually return to their rural homes at harvest time to help and maintain control over the farm income. In Yemen, women agricultural workers receive much lower incomes than their male counterparts.[51]

Conclusion

It would be simplistic to regard labour migration *per se* as the cause of all social disruption and of the growth of households headed by women, but there is abundant evidence that labour migration has had a critical effect on many rural areas, and on the women who live and work there. Out-migration of husbands and other adult male relatives puts enormous burdens on the women who are left behind and who become heads of temporarily or permanently abandoned households. Women who are left alone have difficulty in coping with both household responsibilities and farm management. Because they do not always get the help they need—they experience problems in hiring labour and find it difficult to organize kin or communal networks as reciprocal work groups which consist mainly of men—and because they have less access to capital and technological knowledge, the productivity of agriculture declines. Women are discouraged, and their productivity falls; in some instances they abandon the cultivation of the more nutritious and labour-intensive crops, such as yams, which require constant weeding and care, in favour of less labour-intensive crops, such as cassava, with a lower nutritive value, but which require less attention. Case studies have shown that cash remittances from members of the family who have migrated may be irregular, cease altogether, or be controlled by older male relatives, who often fail to dispense them in accordance with the needs of their female relations.

Important consequences of labour migration are the loss of male labour to rural areas and the weakening of the traditional family structure. Women who are left behind are wives, unmarried mothers, widows, children, and old people. Regardless of the type of rural economy—cash crops or bare subsistence farming—labour migration has brought considerable distortions to rural society by creating a preponderance of women and an abnormally high proportion of children and old people, thus resulting in a high rural dependency rate and increasing poverty.

[50] Ibid.   [51] Ibid.

Capitalist economic systems in Third World countries which result in male migrant labour have affected women's decision-making roles for better and for worse. Some gains have resulted for women who have emerged as household heads and farm managers responsible for day-to-day decisions at home and on the farm. There are examples of women who have increased family investment outside agriculture, and others who have played an active part as community leaders. In general, it may be true, as Lipton has commented, that, in the absence of working men, women gain by becoming more important in the workforce and becoming heads of their households.[52] But the real issue is that few or no resources are placed at women's disposal to back up their newly acquired decision-making powers. In most of Africa, women are not allowed to own land, the most important form of capital for rural dwellers, and they can only gain access to land through male relatives. This is the reason for the extreme poverty experienced by the majority of households headed by women. Financial dependency, the force and weight of a culture that ascribes family leadership to the male, while treating wives and daughters as legal minors, and the psychological trauma resulting from the loss of emotional security when male relatives, especially spouses, are removed are factors that render the women's gain more illusory than real.

[52] M. Lipton, 'Migration from Rural Areas of Poor Countries: The Impact of Rural Productivity on Income Distribution', *World Development*, 8 (1980), pp. 1–24.

16 Occupational and Conjugal Inequalities and Insecurity: Effects on Family Organization and Size

CHRISTINE OPPONG

Given the current climate of world economic crisis and the impacts upon individuals and families of high levels of unemployment, decreasing value of earnings, and financial uncertainty, I have chosen in this chapter to concentrate on the relatively deprived—on the one hand, women in the region with the gravest economic problems: Africa; and, on the other, that segment of the population in the richest countries which is most poverty stricken: mothers. This approach gives two vastly different types of context in which to examine briefly women's positions in relation to fertility, family organization, and labour markets, at three stages of their life cycles. The contexts selected are volatile and changing situations, in which dramatic and unfortunate trends with serious repercussions at both the household and national levels have occurred and which have been documented with tragic clarity. Issues of major concern for both national policy formulation and planning of several kinds are highlighted—issues that are basic to the physical and social survival, not only of individual women and their dependent children, but also of societies themselves. To provide a sharp contrast for the discussion, emphasis is given, on the one hand, to situations in which low or below-replacement fertility and longevity are the norm and, on the other, to situations in which very high fertility and high mortality are pervasive. In both cases, the capacity of societies to reproduce both physically and socially is at risk.

The major crises of motherhood, conjugal relations, and old age are highlighted. First, in the crisis of motherhood, how can millions of women maintain, physically and socially, children who are born in circumstances of dwindling resources and social support? Secondly, in the crisis of conjugal relations, how can complementary, supportive, heterosexual relations be maintained in the face of the widespread breakdown of institutional supports

The kind encouragement and interest of my colleague Liba Paukert is gratefully acknowledged. Responsibility for the content of this paper rests solely with the author.

TABLE 16.1. *Persons below the poverty line, less developed countries (excluding China), 1980–1995 (millions)*

Region	1980	1985	1995 (trend growth in GDP; no change in income distribution)	1995 (improved GDP growth; no change in income distribution)	1995 (trend growth in GDP; improved income distribution)	1995 (improved GDP growth; improved income distribution)
Africa (479)*	210	278	405	316	317	213
Asia (1,407)	562	538	450	360	319	239
Developing America (360)	47	65	58	46	5	3
TOTAL (2,246)	819	881	913	722	641	455

* 1980 population in parentheses.

Source: ILO, Working Document (WEP 2-46-04-03 Doc. 1), op. cit. in n. 2.

for procreation and shared socialization—as a result of general economic insecurity and the desperate search for income in one region, and of spreading retreats into self-centred individualism and attempted self-sufficiency in the other? Thirdly, there is the crisis of social and economic security in old age. These crises are viewed within the contexts of increasing impoverishment, continuing sexual segregation and discrimination in marriage and labour markets, and highly skewed patterns of divisions of domestic labour and responsibilities for child maintenance and child care.

Recent economic recession has involved underemployment, increases in unemployment, and part-time and insecure employment contracts, and women's unemployment rates have been growing faster than those of males. The singular vulnerability of women has recently been re-emphasized.[1] In several regions, poverty has been increasing in both rural and urban areas, and projections for the future, in the light of current economic performance and fertility levels, dependency burdens, and employment prospects, show that numbers in poverty will grow rapidly in the future. The main conclusions of a range of international analyses of the global economic situation have been that, for the next few years, world-output growth will remain low in both industrialized and developing countries; for this reason unemployment and poverty will not decrease, and in many countries could even increase.[2] Indeed, the International Labour Organization (ILO) has estimated that during the first half of the 1980s the numbers in extreme poverty increased from 819 to 881 million, with substantial increases in Africa and Latin America. Table 16.1 shows the various scenarios to be expected, with different levels of growth of GDP, and either change or no change in income distribution. The picture is grimmest for Africa, where incomes per head are estimated to have been 7 per cent lower in 1987 than in 1978, and where real wages in non-agricultural sectors have dropped considerably in many countries (see Table 16.2). Meanwhile, in sub-Saharan Africa the proportions of young dependants are expected to increase sharply in the future (see Table 16.3).

Adolescence and Teenage Mothers

Globally there are an estimated quarter of a billion (245 million) women aged 15–19, of whom over 80 per cent live in the developing world. By

---

[1] G. Standing, *Global Feminization through Flexible Labour: Labour Market Analysis and Employment Planning* (Geneva, 1989).

[2] See the following studies made by the ILO: Working Document, High-Level Meeting on Employment and Structural Adjustment, Geneva, 23–25 Nov. 1987 (WEP 2-46-04-03 Doc. 1); Background Document, High-Level Meeting on Employment and Structural Adjustment (WEP 2-46-04-03 Doc. 2); *Overview of the Employment Situation in the World* (GB 238/CE/1/1 238th Session; Geneva, Nov. 1987).

TABLE 16.2. Development of non-agricultural real wages, by country, between 1980 and the most recent year available (1980 = 100)

Country*	Latest available year	Index
Burundi	1985	113
Kenya	1985	78
Malawi	1984	76
Mauritius	1985	90
Swaziland	1983	95
United Republic of Tanzania	1983	60
Zambia	1984	67
Zimbabwe	1984	89

* Countries for which a data series covering at least three years was available.

Source: As for Table 16.1.

2020, the figure for the world is likely to be 320 million.[3] In developed countries, the absolute numbers are likely to drop by 2020. In the developing countries they will increase by 75 million, including in Africa a tripling of the number of girls aged 15–19. The population age pyramids show the stark contrast between the situation of the developing and developed countries in this respect. The data on the percentages in this age group who report sexual activity vary considerably from country to country. In some cultures, a high proportion of girls in this age group are married.

In sub-Saharan Africa, the latest available figures show proportions of women aged 15–19 who have ever been married or lived in consensual unions as ranging from 33 per cent to levels as high as 61 per cent in Ethiopia and Mauritania. In eleven countries records show that more than 30 per cent of teenage girls are married. Figures on fertility rates for teenagers for the African region are the highest in the world with very few exceptions, being around 200 in thirty-three countries of the region. Teenage mothers thus contribute generally more than 15 per cent to the index of total fertility. Several governments in the region have recently expressed grave concern (notably during the plenary sessions of the World Conference 'Equality, Development, and Peace' which was held in Nairobi in 1985 to end the United Nations Decade for Women) about the effects of early

[3] J. Senderowitz and J. M. Paxman, 'Adolescent Fertility. Worldwide Concern', Population Bulletin, 40 (Apr. 1985).

TABLE 16.3. *Dependants aged 25 years or less and 60 years or over as percentage of total economically active population, all ages, 1950–2025*

Region/country	Dependants under 25 years				Dependants 60 years or over			
	1950	1985*	2000*	2025*	1950	1985*	2000*	2025*
World	79	88	82	71	10	15	17	26
Less developed countries	84	98	90	75	7	10	13	22
Africa	101	130	140	110	6	7	8	11
North Africa	160	195	159	96	11	16	17	26
Sub-Saharan Africa[†]	90	119	137	112	4	5	6	8
Asia and the Pacific	76	88	76	62	7	10	13	25
South Asia	96	128	111	78	7	11	13	24
SE Asia and Pacific	94	106	87	62	6	8	11	22
China	56	52	42	41	8	10	14	30
West Asia	112	151	140	94	6	11	13	19
Latin America and the Caribbean	134	137	117	87	9	14	16	26
South America	131	130	115	87	9	16	18	29
Central America	153	161	127	87	8	10	12	21
Caribbean	111	116	98	85	8	16	17	26
More developed countries	69	59	55	55	16	27	33	46
Market-economy countries	73	59	53	54	19	30	34	49
Europe	64	59	53	54	22	37	42	58
North America	79	57	54	55	19	26	27	43
Japan	94	60	50	54	10	19	30	44
Australia and New Zealand	75	64	55	50	23	26	28	43
Centrally planned economy countries	63	60	59	57	10	24	32	40
USSR	65	60	61	59	9	24	33	41
Eastern Europe	59	57	52	50	12	25	29	39
Yugoslavia	71	71	60	57	12	21	32	46
Albania	82	94	80	62	9	11	14	24

* Projections.
† Excluding the Republic of South Africa.

Source: ILO, Background Document (WEP 2-46-04-03 Doc. 2), op. cit. in n. 2.

motherhood on girls' health, education, and training opportunities. Of particular concern are cases where schoolgirls become pregnant, and as a consequence are compelled to curtail their education and often to bear children out of wedlock or become involved in illegal and dangerous abortion procedures.[4] In most countries, unmarried women constitute a majority of those who resort to illegal abortion, and many of them are teenage girls. However, data are scarce.[5] Some common factors appear in a wide spectrum of cultures: the loosening of community and familial constraints and sanctions following migration and urbanization; the increased freedom of the young to meet and mix with their peers; the growing gap between the onset of puberty and marriage; widespread ignorance about human reproduction; the frequent lack of access to methods of birth control. Many factors inhibit the systematic use of contraceptives by sexually active teenagers, even when they are theoretically available, including those associated with the attitudes and practices of the service delivery agencies. The size of the problem is in many cases apparent from the evidence of failed abortion cases that reach maternity wards, as well as the incidence of girls who drop out of school. Indeed, the impacts of teenage child-bearing are serious and affect health, social and economic status, and demographic outcomes. Globally, pregnancy-related deaths are the main cause of death among girls between the ages of 15 and 19. Their babies also suffer high health risks, including low birth-weight, prematurity, stillbirth, and death, not to mention neglect and abandonment. Moreover, early pregnancies increase the growing numbers of single mothers who have to cope alone with their own and their children's needs, as traditional familial supports dwindle, following the migration of kin, and as young men become fathers but not husbands, an event impossible to imagine a generation ago. Those who have support from grandmothers are fortunate.[6] Many such young mothers, as well as their children born out of wedlock, are in extreme poverty, and suffer from the effects of illiteracy, malnutrition, and disease. An early start to child-bearing in the teenage years is also linked to larger completed family size and shorter time span between generations, and thus contributes to rapid population growth, as well as to poverty. Given the current proportions and numbers of teenage women, their fertility will continue to have a major impact upon future world population growth.[7]

Some declines in adolescent fertility have been documented, but an unfortunate trend, that is poorly documented, is the increasing proportion of births to teenagers outside marriage, in both developing and developed countries. The United States provides a startling and well-recorded example. Between 1970 and 1982 the proportion of births out of wedlock to women

[4] B. Gyepe Gabrah, *Adolescent Fertility in sub-Saharan Africa: An Overview* (Boston, 1985); F. Akuffo, 'Teenage Pregnancies and School Dropouts', in C. Oppong (ed.), *Sex Roles, Population and Development in West Africa* (London, 1987).

[5] F. M. Coeytaux, 'Induced Abortion in sub-Saharan Africa: What we do and do not know', *Studies in Family Planning*, 19 (1988).

[6] B. Ingstad and A. Saugestad, 'Unmarried Mothers in Changing Tswana Society: Implications for Household Form and Viability', *Forum for Urviklingstrudier*, 4 (Oslo, 1984).

[7] See Senderowitz and Paxman, op. cit. in n. 3. See also the recommendation of the International Population Conference, Mexico City, Aug. 1984.

aged 15–19 rose from 17 per cent to 37 per cent among white women and from 62 per cent to 87 per cent among black women. In 1982 the proportion of extramarital births to women aged below 20 was 51 per cent. In the same year, it was 51 per cent in England and Wales; it was 38 per cent in France in 1980. Teenage child-bearing outside marriage is already a common occurrence in the Caribbean. It is apparently escalating in other developing areas with increasing urbanization and lack of customary marriages at younger ages. Given the common social and economic deprivations and vulnerability of such teenage mothers and their infants, this trend is particularly disturbing.

Various laws affect sex education and fertility regulation. However, in many countries there is no specific legislation on this subject, and in these there is often no sex education either. Another issue is the age at which young people are considered competent to take decisions about their own health. A high percentage of teenage wives in developing countries are unable to make their own decisions about family planning. Their husbands or kin not infrequently control the decision-making process, either by law or by social custom. Significantly, in developing countries restrictions on access to modern contraceptives are associated with high infant mortality rates.[8]

In some countries, in which contraception is acceptable for teenagers, it is not available for the unmarried. In fact, the provision of birth-control information and services to the public is a relatively recent event, and the usual target populations are married women with children.[9] Only recently have programmes been extended to unmarried persons, including adolescent women.[10] In no country, developed or developing, are these programmes fully adequate to meet existing needs, and in no country are they viewed without some conflict or concern.[11]

Yet the world resolved that to have adequate information and services for all individuals and couples so they can determine 'freely and responsibly the number and spacing' of their children was a fundamental human right.[12] The responsibility for carrying out this resolution rests with individual government, and their health and educational institutions.

Working Mothers: Industrialized Market Economies

In industrialized market economies, at least during the first half of the 1980s, more women than men entered the labour force, and during the ten-

[8] I. Wasserman and D. Usui, 'Indicators of Contraceptive Policy for Nations at Three Levels of Development', *Social Indicators Research*, 12 (1983), pp. 153–68.

[9] W. Bleek, 'Family and Family Planning in Southern Ghana', in Oppong, op. cit. in n. 4.

[10] Senderowitz and Paxman, op. cit. in n. 3.

[11] Ibid.

[12] See the resolutions of the UN Conference on Human Rights, Teheran, 1968, the World Population Conference in Bucharest, 1974, and the International Population Conference in Mexico City, 1984.

year period the increase in women's labour-force participation amounted to 63.2 per cent of the total increase. During the coming decades, women's activity rates in these countries are expected to continue to increase for the age group 20–64, and to decrease for those aged less than 20 and over 64. This increase has happened in spite of massive economic recession. However, women remain concentrated to a large extent in jobs that require lower levels of skill, are of lower status, and pay lower wages. Much of their employment is part-time. And many part-time workers fall outside the scope of labour legislation and are not entitled to maternity or retirement benefits which are available to most full-time workers. Thus, in ten European countries women constitute only 31 per cent of full-time workers and over 84 per cent of part-time workers.

These increases in recorded labour-force participation among women in the United States and Western Europe have occurred during a period when marriage as an institution has been declining. Since 1960, there has been an increasing tendency to postpone marriage, or to avoid it altogether. The probability that marriage will end in divorce has risen, and the rise has quickened in pace during the 1970s. Rates of remarriage have levelled off or declined, and the proportion of women's adult lives spent in the married state is declining.[13] Suggested causes for these trends include increased incomes available to women, the relatively low pay prospects of young adults in relation to their material aspirations, the shortage of eligible men in the marriage market, giving men increased bargaining power, and the elimination of the functions of marriage and the family.[14] Other causes which might be added include increased availability of sexual gratification outside a legally formalized marriage relationship, the declining interest in procreation, and the unwillingness to enter what is, for men, an increasingly costly relationship, in terms of expectations of shared domestic responsibilities and child care—in other words, increasingly prevalent norms of gender equality. For potential husbands there are fewer desired or unique advantages to be gained and increasingly higher costs; hence the rapid rise in the numbers of unmarried women and single mothers living in poverty. Ironically, more research has focused on the changing roles of women in respect of motherhood than on those of men in relation to fatherhood.

In Europe, among the changing elements linked to the declining marriage rate, rising divorce trends, and declines in remarriage are the growing numbers of childless women, changing conjugal and sex roles, and more alternatives to legal marriage—in other words, easy access to sexual and domestic services without the obligations and long-term commitments of the

[13] T. J. Espenshade, 'Marriage Trends in America: Estimates, Implications and Underlying Causes', *Population and Development Review*, 11 (1985), pp. 193–246.
[14] Ibid., pp. 238–39.

marriage bond.[15] Stress is increasingly placed upon individualist and self-centred values and decisions throughout the life course. Personal happiness and individual fulfilment are increasingly seen to be the major goals of both young and old.

Whereas, during an earlier era, shifts to smaller families and adoption of contraception resulted from increased devotion to the lavishing of resources on fewer 'higher-quality' children, the present strict control of births and resort to abortion is more likely to be a result of the rejection of children and of the altruistic self-sacrifice required on the part of parents.[16] However, these individualist trends involve serious social costs, and, as we have been warned, 'the greater the number of individuals choosing to maximise freedom of discretionary time and resources by forgoing the traditional parental roles, the greater is the threat to societal viability'.[17] Moreover, it is important to realize that the retreat from parental responsibilities has been faster among men than among women, so that women have been left with a larger share of child maintenance and child care to cope with, with consequential effects on their levels of living, relative to those of their male coevals.

Pauperization of Mothers

In the United States during the 1970s it became increasingly clear that, although women's participation in the labour market had increased noticeably, and affirmative action programmes had been set up and more women had entered the professions, women as a group were becoming poorer and poorer. The cause was not difficult to find. More and more women were being left alone to support the dependent children that they had borne, and the male partners who had fathered the children were not sharing the costs fairly, either in time or in money. The 'divorce revolution', and legal reforms supposedly designed to create more equitable settlements, ended up by impoverishing divorced women and their children.[18] Thus the 'feminization of poverty' was attributed not only to women's low pay, but to the unequal burdens of child dependency which women were shouldering. In contrast,

---

[15] J. Schmidt and C. Höhn, 'Socio-cultural Change with Reference to Female Employment, Educational Characteristics and Housing Conditions in Western Countries where Fertility is Around or Below Replacement', in IUSSP, *International Population Conference, Manila* (Liège, 1981), i. 159–80.

[16] P. Ariès, 'Two Successive Motivations for the Declining Birth Rate in the West: Notes and Commentary', *Population and Development Review*, 6 (1980), pp. 645–50.

[17] W. C. Mackey, *Fathering Behaviors: The Dynamics of the Man–Child Bond* (New York, 1985), p. 154.

[18] L. J. Weitzman, 'The Divorce Revolution in the United States: The Unexpected Consequences for Women and Children', in M. T. Meuders-Klein and J. Eekelaar (eds.), *Family, State and Individual Economic Sercurity*, i. *Family* (Brussels, 1988).

men were in poverty because they were unemployed.[19] Feminization of poverty is in fact pauperization of motherhood. Single women living alone are not poor. It is women with dependent children who are poor.[20] Between 1960 and 1981 the number of poor persons in families headed by women *increased* by 48 per cent, while the number of poor persons in all other families *decreased* by 48 per cent; at the same time the percentage of families below the poverty line headed by a woman increased from 20 to 40 per cent.[21] The effects upon children are enormous. About 90 per cent of children in single-parent households live with their mothers, and over half of these households were in poverty in 1981. In fact, the proportion of children living in poverty in the United States has increased steadily since 1975, and dramatically since 1981, at which time the health status of children appeared to be adversely affected, presumably because of recession, increased poverty rates for households with children, and lower health benefits and social services. At the same time, large numbers of small children are left alone after school and even look after younger brothers and sisters, as mothers out at work try to earn sufficient income to maintain them.[22] The proportion of children who lived with one parent (the mother) increased from 9 per cent in 1960, to 13 per cent in 1970, to 21 per cent in 1981, and is expected to continue to increase. One-quarter of all children were expected to live with their lone mother by 1990.

As a result of these dramatic developments, the growth in female-headed households in the United States over the past two decades has been described as explosive, and their economic position as precarious.[23] Moreover, a longitudinal analysis of data on the economic impacts of divorce and marital separation for the United States has shown that the economic costs of divorce and separation are greater for women than for men.[24] The main component of women's post-divorce income is income derived from their own labour. By the fifth year after divorce, it accounts for 70 per cent. Even during the first year after divorce, alimony and child support account for only one-tenth of total average family income. While the average man who divorces is actually subsequently better-off, poverty rates for divorced women increase substantially, as children normally remain with the mother, whose

---

[19] D. Pearce, 'The Feminization of Poverty: Women, Work and Welfare': *Urban and Social Change Review*, 2 (1978), pp. 28–36. W. Sarvasy and J. van Allen, 'Fighting the Feminization of Poverty: Socialist–Feminist Analysis and Strategy', *Review of Radical Political Economy*, 16 (1984), pp. 89–110.

[20] N. Folbre, 'The Pauperization of Motherhood: Patriarchy and Public Policy in the United States', *Review of Radical Political Economy*, 16 (1984), pp. 72–88; see also anon., 'Off to Work', *Economist*, 24 Oct. 1987.

[21] Folbre, op. cit. in n. 20.

[22] C. A. Miller and J. E. Coulter, 'The World Economic Crisis and the Children: A United States Case Study', *World Development*, 12 (1984), pp. 339–64.

[23] G. J. Duncan and S. D. Hoffman, 'A Reconsideration of the Economic Consequences of Marital Dissolution', *Demography*, 22 (1985).

[24] Ibid.

potential earnings in the labour market are usually lower than their father's, or who has to work longer hours to earn the same amount of pay.[25] Moreover, her child-care responsibilities limit her economic activities.

Interestingly a change has been shown to have occurred from paternal right to maternal obligations in the custody of children after divorce, as children have changed from being an ultimate source of labour assistance and earnings for parents to a cause of heavy expenditure, providing little if any material return, in this part of the world.[26] Children no longer provide significant economic benefits to parents, but do provide significant economic benefits to the older generation as a whole, through their contributions to the social security system. Mothers, and single mothers in particular, pay a disproportionate share of the costs of rearing the next generation, and public policies exacerbate this inequality. 'Patriarchy has gone public' in the sense that employers and the state have proved reluctant, if not more reluctant than individual fathers, to help out with child support.[27]

Living Alone or with Dependent Children

The growth in solitary living and single parenthood is mirrored in the growth in numbers of one-person households, and in particular of adults who live alone. Thus, for example, in the United States between 1970 and 1980, the number of households increased from under 63 million to 79 million, with a marked decrease in average size of household. Among the changes were a rapid increase in the number of men living alone and of two unrelated adults living together. In family households, there was a 15 per cent increase in mother–child households. In fact, the data provided evidence of 'a continued trend of increased propensities for persons of all ages and marital statuses to form their own households, rather than to share households with others'.[28] So marked is this trend, that it has been forecast in the United States that, by the end of the century, the traditional married-couple family may account for fewer than half of all households, because numbers of single-parent families and non-family households (mainly people living alone) are growing faster. The last two categories are poorer and use welfare more often than couple-based households. Thus, by the year 2000 the conjugal family households are expected to add only 800,000 households to welfare recipients, while households composed of a mother and dependent children are expected to add 1.4 million, and non-family (or single-person households) the same

[25] Ibid., p. 495.
[26] Folbre, op. cit. in n. 20.
[27] Ibid., p. 85.
[28] J. A. Sweet, 'Components of Change in the Number of Households', *Demography*, 21 (1984).

TABLE 16.4. *Living arrangements of children under 18 years old, United States, 1970 and 1982 (000s)**

Living arrangement of children and marital status of parent	1970 All races		White (%)	Black (%)	1982 All races		White (%)	Black (%)	Per cent change, 1970–82, all races
	Number	%			Number	%			
Children under 18	70,510		59,588	9,973	62,407		51,086	9,377	−11.5
Per cent	—	100.0	100.0	100.0	—	100.0	100.0	100.0	—
Living with									
Two parents	59,694	84.7	89.1	58.2	46,797	75.0	80.8	42.4	−21.6
One parent	8,438	12.0	8.7	31.5	13,701	22.0	17.2	49.2	62.4
Mother only	7,678	10.9	7.8	29.3	12,512	20.0	15.3	47.2	63.0
Divorced	2,338	3.3	3.1	4.4	5,103	8.2	8.0	9.6	118.3
Married	3,351	4.8	2.8	16.2	3,518	5.6	4.3	13.6	5.0
Separated	2,413	3.4	1.7	13.5	3,099	5.0	3.6	12.7	28.4
Widowed	1,421	2.0	1.7	4.1	1,123	1.8	1.5	3.3	−21.0
Never-married	565	0.8	0.2	4.5	2,768	4.4	1.6	20.8	389.9
Father only	760	1.1	0.9	2.2	1,189	1.9	1.9	2.0	56.4
Other, including living with relatives	2,378	3.4	2.2	10.3	1,908	3.1	2.0	8.4	−19.8

* Excludes persons under 18 years old who were maintaining households or family groups.

Sources: US Bureau of the Census, 'Marital Status and Family Status, March 1970', *Current Population Reports*, Series P-20, no. 212 (1971); and 'Marital Status and Living Arrangements, March 1982', *Current Population Reports*, Series P-20, no. 380 (1983) (from Epenshade, op. cit. in n. 13).

number. (See Table 16.4 for evidence of changes in living arrangements of children in the United States between 1970 and 1982.)

This trend in residential and family patterns has been marked in most industrialized nations since 1945. Those living alone are young single adults, and single and formerly married older women. Among the explanations brought forward for this trend have been factors such as rising real incomes, lack of availability of kin, and changing tastes, norms, and values regarding privacy and autonomy. Burch raised the important issue of the rights of household members and growing pressures to equality of access to household goods, such as privacy and autonomy.[29] He concluded that the increasing homogeneity of age/sex roles and the freedom to indulge in ephemeral sexual activities favour household dissolution and separate living through two separate mechanisms. One is that they increase perceptions of household crowding and competition. The other is that at the same time they make individuals less dependent upon one another.[30]

Labour Force Discrimination and Segregation: Unpaid Domestic Labour and Underpaid Wage Labour

Women's poverty in comparatively rich industrialized countries is frequently related to the breakdown of marital contracts, under which women had been responsible for household work and child care, and to their unequal share of parental responsibility; but it is also attributable to the persistent sex segregation in the labour markets. Women are adversely affected by the gender biases of both the marriage and the labour markets.[31] Women combine unpaid domestic labour with underpaid wage labour. The combination of these two aspects of women's lives makes them markedly more vulnerable to poverty than their male counterparts.

During the early 1970s it was found in the United States that, while women were participating more in the labour force, they were in fact suffering increasing occupational and income discrimination.[32] Later analysis of sixty-one countries indicated that the percentage of women in the labour force appears to be strongly related to occupational discrimination.[33] Their very availability helps to keep wages low, and conditions of work poor.

---

[29] T. K. Burch, 'Changing Age–Sex Roles and Household Crowding: A Theoretical Note', in IUSSP, *Proceedings of the International Population Conference, Florence, 1985* (Liège, 1985), iii.

[30] Ibid., p. 259. See also E. Durkheim, *The Division of Labor in Society* (Glencoe, Ill., 1933), 60–61.

[31] Sarvasy and van Allen, op. cit. in n. 19.

[32] R. Tsuchigane and N. Dodge, *Economic Discrimination against Women in the United States* (Lexington, Mass., 1974).

[33] M. Semyonov, 'The Social Context of Women's Labor Force Participation', *American Journal of Sociology*, 86 (1980).

Moreover, part-time work, often forced upon them by competing domestic demands for their time, reinforces women's low status in the labour market and does not provide the kinds of benefits they need to become economically autonomous, or, indeed, to provide adequately for their dependants.[34]

During the early 1980s the majority of working mothers were concentrated in part-time jobs that were typically low-paid and occupationally segregated. Recent analysts in the United States have argued that separate and distinct occupational labour markets exist for men and women, instead of the single, gender-neutral, isomorphic occupational structure, assumed in previous literature.[35] There is growing evidence of the increase of part-time, insecure, unpensioned employment for women, many of whom are struggling alone with domestic and parental responsibilities.

Thus, two disturbing trends are noted for women in comparatively wealthy industrialized countries—decreasing long-term status, and security from both conjugal and occupational roles. On the one hand, increasing numbers and proportions of women are bearing, rearing, and maintaining children without benefit of support from the begetters of their children, and are left alone coping, as teenagers or middle-aged women, with a multiplicity of demands made upon them by their dependent offspring. On the other hand, the numbers of women in insecure, part-time, daily-rated employment are increasing. Indications are that prostitution may also be increasing. Short-term sexual contracts are partial substitutes for long-term commitments of shared responsibilities, procreation, and legal and economic bonds. Women's labour and sexual access are found in markets in which prices tend to be kept low by oversupply. Those with the long-term social status and economic security of legally protected, sexual, procreative, and labour contracts are fortunate. The diminution of access to these is occurring, ironically enough, at a time when political and legal pressure is strong for more equal contracts for women and men, both in the home and in the market place.

Mothers in African Countries: Overwork, Unemployment, and Dependency

The intense and widespread activity of women in agricultural production is characteristic of African economies. Statistics for the region show that in nineteen countries, in spite of the underrecording of women's work, over 40 per cent of the labour in agriculture is recorded as female. Yet the extent to which women have been excluded from agricultural statistics and development

---

[34] V. Smith, 'The Circular Trap: Women and Part-time Work', *Berkeley Journal of Sociology*, 28 (1983), pp. 1–17.

[35] J. Lorence, 'Gender Differences in Occupational Labour Market Structure', *Work and Occupations*, 14 (1987).

plans is increasingly well documented,[36] as is the extent to which agricultural development assistance has been unevenly divided, benefiting male farmers, who often concentrate on cash crops, and neglecting small-scale food production for subsistence and sale, which is often in the hands of women. Thus there is a tendency in some cases for subsistence agriculture to remain primitive and feminized, and for cash-cropping and large plantations to be increasingly under the control of men.[37]

Women often have to work as casual labourers, as well as grow and process food for their families, and, even though they may contribute to labour for cash-crop cultivation, they may have no access to the income earned.[38] Land resettlement programmes are noted to discriminate against women, whose demand for land is often ignored.[39] Recent micro-level farm analyses of the different productive activities and responsibilities of women and men have clearly shown how inadequate data on women's work, and insufficient concern for the part they play in agriculture, may prevent the successful design of agricultural development projects.[40]

Women work in sectors and engage in occupations where working conditions are labour-intensive and arduous and tools are primitive, and in low-skilled, industrial, and service jobs. For the most part they belong to occupational categories, such as unpaid family workers and own-account workers, which are outside the scope of labour legislation. In the modern sector they are segregated in a few jobs and occupations. Industrial working conditions are often hazardous, fatiguing, and insecure. It has been observed that, although urbanization and economic development have opened up possibilities for mobility and access to better work opportunities, most women in the urban labour market find themselves confined to the informal sector.

In industry, women find jobs such as food-processing and packaging, tobacco manufacturing, and garment-making, partly because of their alleged agility and manual dexterity. However, employment is often on a precarious basis (work by day, or temporary or seasonal work); hence the tendency to prefer women workers, who are mainly illiterate, unskilled, and non-unionized. These industries in most cases provide low-paid, insecure jobs, which many women are forced to accept, in view of their need for cash income to maintain themselves and their dependants.

[36] See, e.g., B. Rogers, *The Domestication of Women* (London, 1980); D. Hirschmann, 'Bureaucracy and Rural Women: Illustrations from Malawi', *Rural Africana*, 21 (1985).

[37] For Zambia, see K. Crehan, 'Women in Development in North-west Zambia: From Producer to Housewife', *Review of African Political Economy*, 27–28 (1983), pp. 51–66. For Zimbabwe, see S. Jacobs, 'Women and Land Resettlement in Zimbabwe', *Review of African Political Economy*, 27–28 (1983), pp. 33–49.

[38] For Kenya, see R. Feldman, 'Women's Groups and Women's Subordination: An Analysis of Policies towards Rural Women in Kenya', *Review of African Political Economy*, 27–28 (1983), pp. 67–85.

[39] For Zimbabwe, see Jacobs, op. cit. in n. 37.

[40] M. R. Burfisher and N. R. Horenstein, 'Sex Roles and Development Effects on the Nigerian Tiv Farm Household', *Rural Africana*, 21 (1985), pp. 31–49.

TABLE 16.5. *Unemployment by sex and age group, selected African countries, latest year available* (%)

Country	Age group			
	All	Under 20	20–24	Over 25
Botswana (1984)				
All	25.3	32.8	37.8	20.7
Males	19.3	23.5	28.8	16.3
Females	30.6	44.1	44.1	24.6
Malawi (1983)				
All	5.4	9.8	7.8	3.3
Males	4.9	9.7	6.1	2.9
Females	5.9	9.8	9.2	3.7
Nigeria (1983)				
All	5.7	27.6	16.1	1.8
Males	5.1	22.2	15.2	1.6
Females	6.9	42.0	18.2	2.1

Source: ILO, Background Document, op. cit. in n. 2.

The proportions of women employers and women working on their own account vary very much from country to country, from a negligible percentage to a majority. In some countries, the majority of self-employed women work in the agricultural sector, as do the men. Unpaid family workers mainly labour on farms.

In some cases, formal-sector employment has not increased, which means increasing unemployment for school-leavers, especially girls (see Table 16.5). At a time when the demand for jobs is increasing, as the numbers of school-leavers rise and rural–urban migration continues apace, the urban employment market is actually shrinking. Furthermore, there is widespread evidence of imbalance between the sexes in the modern sector or in urban employment, in which higher levels of schooling and training are required,[41] for girls continue to have less access than boys to schooling at every level, especially the higher grades. Moreover, obtaining wage employment does not necessarily 'liberate women', but may rather reproduce and reinforce their subordination to men.[42] Women experience discrimination from male co-workers, and their lack of participation and power in trade unions and labour organizations weakens their positions, and inhibits their promotion

[41] C. Oppong, 'La Femme africaine: Mère, épouse et travailleuse: Inégalités et Ségrégation', in D. Tabutin (ed.), *Population et sociétés en Afrique du Sud du Sahara* (Paris, 1988).
[42] C. Dennis, 'Capitalist Development and Women's Work: A Nigerian Case Study', *Review of African Political Economy*, 27–28 (1983), pp. 100–19.

and advancement.[43] The low proportion of women found in managerial, administrative, and higher professional positions, in addition to the small numbers in political offices, demonstrates that women play a limited part in institutional decision-making processes. In the modern non-agricultural sector, earnings, promotion, and recruitment are frequently biased towards men, even when legally equality is assured. Among the contributing factors are the lower levels of education and training of women, as well as the manifold effects of family and domestic responsibilities and the biases of employers.[44]

Since marriage for the most part occurs early, as was noted above, and child-bearing normally continues throughout the reproductive years, whatever the woman's occupation, women's work is typically carried out simultaneously with the bearing and rearing of an average of six or more children, who commonly begin to help their mothers and other older relatives as soon as they are old enough.

The burdens of work, household-based duties, and subsistence borne by women, including carrying water and gathering fuel, severely limit their chances of earning, though many women make money in home-based cottage industries.[45] West African time-budget studies in Ghana and Nigeria have shown that women may spend six or more hours a day preparing food for consumption.[46] The more women become involved in income-earning activities, the more they may seek to delegate household tasks, which do not produce an income, to children and others. Indeed, the subsistence and survival of many families is only ensured by the labour inputs of children in fetching fuel and water, and assisting mothers in other home-based tasks, making the need for, and availability of, child-labour a critical disincentive for changing traditional, pro-natalist family goals. An array of factors—unequal access to education and wage employment, especially in the few secure, pensioned positions; early marriage and subsequent frequent polygyny, divorce, separation, and early widowhood; heavy continuous manual labour in domestic and agricultural tasks and lack of women's individual rights to land or other productive assets—all of these either put a premium upon, or do not hinder, repeated child-bearing and large family size, and thus result in the high levels of fertility found in the African region.[47] Children are their mothers' most precious assets. They provide desperately needed labour to assist in farm, home, and market. They provide the links

[43] R. Pittin, 'Women Work and Ideology in Nigeria: Problems and Solutions', in *Review of African Political Economy*, No. 52 (1991), pp. 38–52.

[44] L. Adeokun, A. Adepoju, F. A. Ilori, and A. A. Adewuyi, *The Ife Labour Market: A Nigerian Case Study* (Geneva, 1984).

[45] On Nigeria, see Pittin, op. cit. in n. 43.

[46] See E. Ardayfio, *The Rural Energy Crisis in Ghana: Its Implications on Women's Work and Household Survival* (Geneva, 1986).

[47] C. Oppong, 'Employment and Development', in M. T. Meulders-Klein and J. Eekelaar (eds.), *Family, State and Individual Economic Security*, ii. *State* (Brussels, 1988).

of kinship, without which wives would have no enduring rights to their marital homes or husbands' assets, including land, and thus security, as well as economic status in old age. Without them, conjugal links are tenuous and fragile. Without them, daily laborious tasks cannot be completed. Without them, a woman in virilocal marriage remains a marginal outsider. Without them, a woman can never achieve full social or spiritual status.

Often precipitated into motherhood before they realise it; often bearing children for more than one husband, or in the competitive situation of polygynous marriage; often lacking the necessary means even when the desire exists, to cease child-bearing, and knowing that their greatest source of assistance, support, loyalty, comfort, and security will be their sons and daughters—African women typically continue to bear infants throughout their reproductive lives, making them the most fertile women in the world.[48]

Signs of change in child-bearing aspirations, or the adoption of a small family size norm or modern contraceptive regimes, are only apparent among the few women in occupations that provide relatively high benefits of social and economic status in formal employment contexts—whose children are not a source of labour but an object of expenditure of individual money and time, and a focus of high parental ambitions for success in education and employment. Characteristic associated changes in individual conjugal and kin roles, as well as modes of child care, have been described in several studies in Ghana.[49]

As Boserup has indicated,[50] the structural changes which have elsewhere led increasing proportions of populations to engage in occupations conducive to lower fertility have not occurred widely in Africa. Few women have gained access to high-level, well-paid, secure jobs in formal-sector employment. In addition, the inducements to have large families continue. The use of child-labour has not radically declined. Land reform has not provided security through land ownership. Sources of non-familial support in old age and emergencies have not developed. In most of Africa, these changes have yet to take place. Until they do, women are likely to continue obtaining their assistance, support, and security from many children.

Mothers Alone in the Less Developed World

There is increasing evidence to show the extent to which lone mothers in Africa and the rest of the developing world—abandoned wives, widows,

[48] Ibid. and op. cit. n. 41.

[49] C. Oppong (ed.), *Female and Male in West Africa* (London, 1983); C. Oppong, 'Some Aspects of Anthropological Contributions to the Study of Fertility', in G. Farooq and G. Simmons (eds.), *Research and Policy Issues in the Analysis of Fertility Behaviour in Developing Countries* (London, 1985); C. Oppong and K. Abu, *Seven Roles of Women: Impact of Education, Migration and Employment on Ghanaian Mothers* (Geneva, 1987).

[50] E. Boserup, 'Economic and Demographic Interrelationships in Sub-Saharan Africa', *Population and Development Review*, 11 (1985).

divorcees, and single women—are battling alone to raise their children, without or with only little support from the fathers who begat their children. In many developing countries, and especially in Africa, as many as three in ten households are maintained by women alone. Indeed, it has been estimated that between one-quarter and one-third of all households are maintained and headed by women. Moreover, because women usually have less of the resources required in the modern world (education, secure employment, land, credit, equipment, etc.), such households are more likely than others to suffer severe poverty, and put the children who grow up in them at severe risk. Some of the women are abandoned wives, others are single mothers who bore their children without benefit of social fathers. Being a mother, though unmarried and without conjugal support, is widespread in a number of countries, and a matter of concern to national governments.

Migration, lack of marriage, conjugal separation, and marital instability have in a number of countries led to increasing marginalization of fathers. A dissociation of the roles of wife and mother has been observed in some cultures, with large proportions of single women, if not the majority, expected to produce children, and fathers doing little or nothing to support their offspring. This leads numbers of young mothers to seek support from their own mothers, leaving children with grandmothers in rural areas and depending upon them to provide long-term social security. The consequent burdens upon older women are being increasingly recognized and documented.[51]

The Position of the Elderly

In traditional social systems the aged ideally remain secure in the care of their offspring, siblings' offspring, or grandchildren. But the position of the aged is changing radically in all regions, as kin disperse and single-person households become the norm in some areas. Concern is increasing in many countries for the welfare of the rising numbers of elderly, who often include a majority of women.[52] In countries with lower fertility, as well as increased life expectancy, the elderly have fewer descendants to whom they can turn, and, unless employment and population policies fully take these demographic trends into account, conditions for the aged may become increasingly worse. At the World Assembly on Ageing in 1982 representatives from many countries spoke of the need to plan for the elderly, and of the shortage of resources for planning. The conclusion was that, given the shortage of other resources, most of the aged will continue to have to rely upon their children for social and economic security, providing a persistent pro-natalist

[51] B. Ingstad, *The Grandmother and Household Viability in Botswana: Family Planning, Child Care and Survival in Changing Tswana Society* (Geneva, 1989).

[52] Oppong, op. cit. in n. 47.

pressure.[53] Many of the elderly in need of assistance are widows in rural areas, from which the young, healthy, and strong have migrated to earn urban incomes.

A collection of descriptive studies of the situations of African widows and mothers from several ethnic groups, with different forms of kinship reckoning and domestic organization, has demonstrated clearly the significance of children for a woman's social and economic security in old age and widowhood. In some African societies, widows form one-quarter of the adult female population. It is motherhood, not marriage, which supports their later life.[54]

Marriage may indeed often be a source of maintenance and security for women in middle age, when maternal responsibilities are likely to be heaviest. But elderly women can seldom rely on husbands or in-laws to support and care for them: comparatively large age differences are usual between husbands and wives, and women have longer life expectancy; polygyny, but not polyandry, is prevalent; widow inheritance is dying out; customs of terminal separation of spouses in old age continue and women frequently lack economic or social rights as widows in their marital homes. Sons and daughters, rather than husbands, typically provide maintenance, security, and social status for elderly women, a factor which provides a continuing incentive for high fertility. In older age groups, larger proportions of women than men have no spouse, as a result of divorce, separation, and widowhood, which result in increasing numbers of lone women having to maintain homes and dependants.

As Western women writers are increasingly beginning to realize, a bias in favour of the importance of marriage in women's lives has prevailed, which prevents them from realizing the significance in other cultures of *parenthood* over marriage ties and status. Little communal support is available to widows. Corporate group responsibility is often merely an idealization of a reality, which mainly consists of self-reliance and dependence upon children—hence the deprivation, to be avoided at all costs, of the childless widow. More recently, scattered reports from a number of African societies have suggested that, in some societies, widows are becoming vulnerable to economic pressures and becoming landless and homeless, if they lack adult children.[55]

The countries of the industrialized sector of the world are inhabited by rapidly ageing populations, in which old women frequently form the majority, and there is growing concern regarding the potentially heavy burdens of old age which will have to be borne, and different policies have been adopted in

---

[53] M. Cain, *Women's Status and Fertility in Developing Countries: Son Preference and Economic Security* (New York, 1984).

[54] B. Potash (ed.), *Widows in African Societies: Choices and Constraints* (Stanford, Calif., 1986).

[55] Ibid.

different countries.[56] Many older women in the United States for example, live in cities, often in great difficulty and in isolation. 'The old suffer not only from low incomes and poor health in comparison to younger people but from a more pernicious deprivation—loss of function and status.'[57] Their deprivations are many and have been enumerated. They include their relative powerlessness to decide their children's occupational and marital fates; at the same time their control of material resources is low. Again, their skills are mainly outdated and useless. Nor are they valued as links with the past, or for their nearness to the spiritual world. Few are in extended-family households. Only one in ten elderly men and two in ten elderly women reside with descendants. Most elderly widows live alone, or with non-relatives. Elderly widows are among the most poverty-stricken of all people, with the smallest resources for housing and other services.

Conclusion

Our purpose in this chapter has been to relate 'the position of women' to fertility, family organization, and economic activity, and to deal with a range of issues within this broad field, using data from selected socio-historical settings. The object has not been systematically to test a set of hypotheses, nor to demonstrate global correlations between two or more well-documented variables across a range of contrasting cultures. Much work of this kind has already been done and provides the bedrock of data upon which the Oslo Conference's discussions were based. The object has been, rather, to explore several dimensions of a set of crisis issues, which currently affect the lives of millions of women, both in the richest and in the poorest countries of the world. The focus has been some aspects of the roles of women—occupational, maternal, conjugal, and kin at different stages of their lives, in very diverse cultural and socio-economic settings, their widespread vulnerability at each life-cycle stage, and their heavy burdens of responsibility. These affect and are affected by fertility levels, and are exacerbated by the pervasive inequalities and mutually reinforcing gender biases that persist in family organization and labour markets.

[56] K. Davis and P. van den Oever, 'Age Relations and Public Policy in Industrial Societies', *Population and Development Review*, 7 (1981).
[57] Ibid., p. 128.

Index